BEYOND
the
HORIZON

For Marjorie
and to the memory
of my good friend
and shipmate. - Bill

Best - w

Jou

GW00746660

JACK CLOSE
Memoirs

RIVERHEAD
RIVERHEAD

Copyright © 2010 Jack Close & family

First published in Great Britain in 2010 by Riverhead

A CIP catalogue record for this book is
available from the British Library

ISBN 0-9550237-8-5

Design and Production by Riverhead, Hull
44-46 High Street, Hull, East Yorkshire. HU1 1PS
Telephone: 01482 318218
email: mike@riverheadbooks.karoo.co.uk

Printed by: Fisk Printers, Hull

Dedication

To my children,
Deborah and Andrew,

to reassure them that I did have a life, once.

Also to the memory of
Dan, Geoff and George,

without whom
my life wouldn't have been half as much fun.

Acknowledgements

My thanks go to:

Marion Toffolo,
who encouraged me to get it all together,

Dorothea Desforges,
who helped me start writing,

Simon Fisk,
who regularly retrieved it from the depths
of the computer,

Richard Fry,
for his patience and computer expertise,

and especially
Eileen,
for her unfailing support, proof-readings
and 24-hour coffee.

CONTENTS

PART 1
GROWING UP IN THE THIRTIES

PART 2
THE WAR YEARS

PART 3
BEYOND THE HORIZON

PART 1

GROWING UP IN THE THIRTIES

1: THOSE RESPONSIBLE

In the hours before dawn, I lay in bed listening to the clogs of the workmen making their way to the fish dock. St. Andrews Dock was the most important dock in the world; hundreds of trawlers were based there, thousands of people depended on it for a living and it supported a whole community with its own way of life. Trawlers came and went through the lock gates and the fish quays bustled with urgent activity, whilst engines with long lines of wagons waited impatiently to transport their contents to the nation's fish shops.

The men who worked on the dock on Hessle Road either cycled there, walked or caught a tram. The trams went into their sheds around midnight and there were a few hours of darkness before they came out again and went clanking along the main roads to pick up the new day's workmen. We lived in Hawthorne Avenue, which ran from Anlaby Road to Hessle Road, so if you lived on Anlaby Road and needed to reach the fish dock in the early hours what did you do? You clomped past all the houses in your metal tipped clogs and woke the babies up, that's what you did. Not content with wondering about the clumping noises, there were roaring noises to think about as lorries made their way to the dock. Lying in bed between my parents I watched the lights and shadows criss-crossing the ceiling and wondered why the noise approaching from the right brought light and shadows to the left of the window, then moved round the other way, throwing shadows to the right of the window as the noise faded away to the left? These were deep mysteries indeed. Another mystery was why they called it Hawthorne Avenue at one end and Hawthorn Avenue at the other, but I never did solve that one.

Our house was in the middle of a terrace, everyone else had front rooms but ours was given over to the Post Office and shop, the room behind the shop serving as our front room. At the end of a narrow passage was the living room; next came the scullery with a stone sink and copper boiler under which a fire was lit every

Monday for wash-day. A coalhouse and a WC were outside, enclosed in a covered veranda which led to a cramped back garden that the cat scratched up and which smelt of sour earth throughout the summer. A low wooden gate opened onto a narrow passage leading to the street, and a lilac tree in next-door's garden drooped over our fence, an oasis amongst the brick walls and dustbins. Upstairs, there was a bedroom over the shop, a smaller bedroom behind, and a bathroom and bedroom at the back, the latter being my room until leaving home, its window overlooking our back garden and those of houses in adjoining Stirling Street.

Being an only child, there were no escapades with brothers or sisters, so for excitement I put my fingers in the mangle. The veranda housed a metal dolly tub with its four-legged wooden dolly-stick and there was a large mangle with two wooden rollers, turned by a handle attached to a wheel. Mother was busy turning the handle one washday, the water being squeezed out of my pyjamas as they disappeared from sight between the rollers. Obviously something was not right here so I reached up and tried to retrieve the pyjamas before they were lost forever, receiving a couple of split finger-ends as life-long souvenirs. A lady came to the house regularly to cut and perm mother's hair, using tongs which she heated over a meths flame burning in the lid of the metal container that housed all her bits and pieces. She gave me a trim from time to time and one day snipped a piece out of my ear whilst talking to mother and not looking what she was doing. To deal with tantrums, mother would drag me outside and put my head under the cold water tap, on other occasions she locked me in my bedroom, but this ceased to be a viable option after a handy chair helped me to splinter the door panels. For my next trick I knelt on a tin lid; these were thin, sharp and the tin-openers of the day left them with jagged edges; if you made two holes in the middle of the lid, slotted string through and twirled it around, a humming sound was produced, the general effect being that of a miniature circular saw and about as lethal.

My parents were not religious, nevertheless they followed tradition and took me to be christened at St. Matthews's church at the top of the Boulevard. Before she was married, mam had a much loved dog called Jack; I often wondered about that. Dad's paternal family included a schoolteacher from Northumberland who met with what must have been a fairly unusual fate in 1921, an automobile accident. Also there was a great uncle who became the unlucky victim of a bomb in Sweden in 1908, a cause celebre which resulted in changes to the civil laws of that country. Dad's maternal side came mainly from Holderness: the Barnfathers of Thorngumbald, the Tutons of Owthorne and the Deightons of Bridlington, the latter being Churchwardens at the Priory Church in the town. Other relatives came from Hollym, Elstronwick, Humbleton and the delightfully named Skeckling-with-Burstwick. My grandparents, Granville Close and Elizabeth Jane Barnfarther, were married at Paul in 1894 and my father, Stanley, was born in Hull in 1898.

Mother's ancestors were more flamboyant. Her maiden name was d'Andilly and her father was born in America, though the family seems to trace back to France in the Middle Ages. In the village of Herment in the Auvergne lived a family of the lesser nobility called Arnauld, who served the Bourbon family and attended the King as Constable of France. The family enjoyed the protection of the Queen Mother, Catherine de Medici, and for many years lived quietly enough, serving the Crown and accumulating Brownie points. In 1585, Antoine Arnauld, then Procureur Generale of France and a Councillor of State to Henry IV, married Catherine Marion de Druy, who brought as her dowry the estate of Andilly, north of Paris, some of the children henceforth taking the name d'Andilly. One of the children was called to the Vatican and two were appointed by the Pope as Abbesses to Port Royal des Champs, a monastery near Paris. Port Royal was to become the home of Jansenism, a break-away low-church within the Church of Rome, the d'Andilly family being strongly supportive of the movement. They held to the doctrine of justification by grace through faith rather than by works and these precepts brought the family into conflict with Louis XIV, his Bishops and the Jesuits, and when Cardinal Richlieu also joined in, it heralded the end of Port Royal in the early 18th Century. Despite being King's Counsellors and under the patronage of Anne of Austria, the Queen Mother, the forces arraigned against the Jansenists proved too strong and the family fled France to escape persecution, dispersing throughout Europe.

My great grandparents, George Auguste Roubier d'Andilly, (son of Joseph Auguste Roubier d'Andilly, an Army Captain), and Elizabeth Harnew of, 'Red House', Thorne Levels in East Yorkshire, sailed to the New World in 1863. Great-grandfather doubtless intended pursuing his career as a professor of languages; with impeccable timing they arrived in the middle of the American Civil War. Their first child, my great-aunt Hetty, was born in New York in 1865; great-uncle George William Roubier d'Andilly was born in Chicago in 1867, and in 1871 my grandfather, Lucien Ludovic Camille Roubier d'Andilly, was born in Napoleonville, Louisiana. Great-grandfather died in America in 1872, cause unknown, and Elizabeth brought the three small children, Hetty, George and Lucien, back to England. In 1900 Lucien married Ella Constance Lamb, daughter of a mariner, and my mother, Phyllis Constance d'Andilly, was born in Villa Place, Hessle Road, Kingston-upon-Hull in 1902. Grandfather Lucien, a seaman, died in 1921. My mother married Stanley Close in 1924 at St. Stephens Church in Hull and I arrived on the 14th of September 1925 at 43 Hawthorn Avenue.

We took a holiday cottage at Flamborough and there is a photo of me on the beach at Thornwick Bay, gazing out to sea, bemused. So would you be, sitting on a lump of chalk in a wet nappy. Dad smoked like a chimney on a 24-hour basis, but apart from that both my parents followed healthy pursuits, playing tennis, walking or cycling everywhere. Popular recreations in the twenties and thirties were hiking and cycling, the latter also being the most practical form of getting around for most people, and the roads were thronged with cyclists. We owned a tandem and I was secured on the back of it, sitting on a cushion. At weekends we explored the East Riding, particularly the seaside at Hilston, Grimston and Tunstall where it was quiet and we had the beach almost to ourselves for games, sandcastles and the sandwiches we'd brought along. But there were snags, the clay cliffs were notorious for crumbling away and more often than not the roughly-hewn steps that led down to the beach would have been washed away since our last visit, so instead of climbing down to the sands in an orderly fashion, we often arrived there in a good-humoured, disorderly heap.

Walking along Anlaby Road, past the Wheeler Street tram-sheds, over the railway crossing, Triangle garage on the left and Gordon Armstrong's garage opposite, there was a tennis court hidden away behind the advertising hoardings at the junction with Boothferry Road, where mam and dad played tennis on summer evenings. The road underneath the railway bridge on Boothferry Road regularly flooded in heavy rain, the land on the far side had once been the home of the Hull Golf Club and later became Boothferry Park, the home of Hull City, the world's greatest football team. The road led over open countryside towards Hessle and the area where the Gipsyville estate would be built. Anlaby

Road curved to the right and led past the White City, the remains of a fine house behind a long brick wall with an imposing stone column entrance and a derelict lodge situated across the western corner of Calvert Lane. As you passed between the pillars at the entrance, there opened up a wide expanse of grassland extending to the railway sidings on the north side. The Yorkshire Show was held there, and in the early 1930s a mad Frenchman demonstrated the latest aviation novelty, the 'Flying Flea'. Galas and many other events, including a circus, also took place and for a while there was a roller skating rink, a craze of the time. A mile or so further along Anlaby Road lay Anlaby Common, a scattering of houses gathered around the pub.

Boothferry Road led to Hessle Common, which began opposite Peter Pan Park and continued over flat grassy scrubland to Hessle, a favourite family walk on Sunday afternoons. The Peter Pan boating lake was popular, with a number of paddle boats for hire and room to sail model yachts. When still quite small I was taken to the Wenlock Barracks on Anlaby Road to watch a circus troupe performing in a traditional sawdust ring. Some clowns drove into the middle of the ring in a ramshackle motor car which began to fall apart bit by bit, causing gales of laughter which lasted long after we got home; also there were white horses with riders and, next to us, a metal tunnel which shepherded a group of lions into the ring.

Josie Kearney was a friend, about my age, who lived a couple of doors away, and one day we decided it would be a good idea to clean the walls of the passage that led to the street, taking a bucket of water and borrowing two of mother's best handkerchiefs to work with. Contrary to expectations, this community effort on our part was not received with enthusiasm. Other neighbours were the Brown family, Mr Headspith a fish merchant, Mrs Turner who ran the toy shop opposite, Mrs Tredgett the greengrocer, Mr Attle of the fish and chip shop, Mr Leake the plumber and Mr de-Boer the butcher.

2: SCHOOL DAYS

The big day arrived when mother took me to start school. This was Wheeler Street School in the next street, only a few minutes walk from home, and was an Elementary Board School with Infant, Junior and Senior departments. Built in 1902, it had an infants' playground and a girls' playground, the latter separated from the boys' playground by a brick wall; all the play areas were concrete. A domestic science block was enclosed in the girls' playground and a square tower with a bell completed the group of buildings. Across the road from the school was Ostler's Bakery where you could get a bag of stale buns for 1d and the smell of baking bread wafting through the morning classrooms was a distraction to those of us with hollow legs. A sweet shop stood on the corner of Ringrose Street and Wheeler Street, run by two elderly sisters named Sheard, and all manner of temptations were on display in boxes and jars on the wooden counter. A few yards past the shop were the school swings and then came Crawley's field which stretched to the railway lines and had a pond in it which could be used for skating in winter, if you didn't get chased off first. There was usually a Penna's ice cream cart outside the school gates at school-leaving time, but few of us had any spare money to buy cornets or sandwiches. If you hung around until there was no further trade coming out of the school, the lad in charge of the handcart sometimes dispensed free 'sliders', a very thin ice cream sandwich produced from the hand-held metal dispenser.

When mother took me to school on that first morning in September 1930 I was just coming up to five years old. There had been no pre-schools, nurseries or playgroups, this was it, straight from home to school. Also starting on that first day was William Daniel Garnett, son of a trawler skipper, who lived further down the avenue in Newington Street. We were to become best friends, remaining so until Dan died in America many years later. Wheeler Street School provided a sound basic education including the repetitive times tables which, once learnt you don't forget, and the school had a good reputation under its headmaster, George Chipperfield, all pupils were able to read and write before moving from the Infants to the Junior School.

The Junior School was a little more serious than the Infants and also issued School Reports. Dad had to see these and write, 'A very pleasing report', on the back whilst I stood looking over his shoulder threatening to let his tyres down. Progression through the Juniors was from September 1932 to July 1935, aged seven to ten. The number of pupils in the class varied between 45 and 50 and my position fluctuated between 4th and 19th, with comments like, 'intelligent and keen', giving way to, 'Jack is easily led into mischief'. English, Writing and Composition marks were good but there was room for improvement in Arithmetic; and there was no homework.

We always seemed to have an animal of some sort, dogs, cats, rabbits and a canary, which was let out of its cage every evening and flew around the kitchen leaving its messages everywhere. One day on my way to school a stray dog that was accompanying me was attacked by another dog. Whilst trying to separate them I was bitten deeply on the wrist and had to be patched up with iodine and bandages, there was no talk of a tetanus shot or seeing a doctor. Goodwill towards animals extended to Mr Lonsdale's horse, which brought milk every day in a large churn on a two-wheel farm cart. Mother plied the horse with an apple, sugar lumps and half a loaf of bread, so it surely couldn't have needed feeding when it got home. The milk was ladled out of the churn into our jug, which was hurriedly carried indoors before the horse got its head into it.

Hitler was playing his game of dares with Europe's politicians in the thirties, only Churchill having a clue as to what he was really up to, though few were listening to him. All the boys around my age were being drawn inexorably into an unimaginably dark future that we could neither comprehend nor avoid. My life at home was not, to me, anything special, but the first glimmerings of social awareness had begun to appear. The south of the country appeared warm and sunny, a Betjeman Metroland, while the north watched the dole queues lengthen and the hunger marches form.

Britain was in the grip of the depression and it showed in school as elsewhere. There were children who came to school without shoes, who smelt, who had nits and who went off at dinnertime with pieces of paper entitling them to free dinners at a nearby school that had kitchens. Many of my school friends came from families where the father was in work one week and out of work the next; other families had no one working in the household at all. Even when jobs were steady they were mostly poorly paid, and almost every family struggled to make ends meet.

Dad's shop was primarily a sub post-office but also sold sweets, tobacco, magazines and evening papers; there was also a small lending-library in which Edgar Wallace detective stories and cowboy tales seemed most in demand. We employed paperboys and if they didn't turn up muggins filled in at short notice. One of our paperboys was coloured and being harassed during his deliveries, so dad sent me on the paper-round with him for a few nights. There was little social unrest that directly affected us, but some strands were obviously simmering beneath the surface, because one night in the late thirties the plate glass window of a glazier's shop on Anlaby Road was smashed with a brick, the proprietors being Jewish, and I remember dad, a friend of the family, going round there to offer support.

My bedroom sported a single light bulb above the bed but the switch was unfortunately near the door, so, fed up with getting out of a warm bed to switch the light off at night after I had finished reading, I ran a length of string from the knob on the switch over a series of grooved Meccano wheels along the walls and ceiling until it reached a convenient point above my head. On winter mornings I would lie in bed contemplating the ice patterns on the inside of the window and the ice in the glass of water at my bedside, listening to the factory buzzers across the city calling the faithful to toil. The hooters went off at various times from six o'clock to eight o'clock, usually five minutes to the hour and then on the hour. As they all had different tones we could identify them by name, 'Shipham's buzzer, it must be five to seven', and so on. About ten minutes to nine I was usually eating the last of the bacon sandwiches on my way to school just as the shop was getting ready to open. The house and shop were cold in the early mornings and the solitary paraffin stove that we possessed hardly made an impression, being moved around to warm the kitchen, bathroom or even the shop as the occasion required.

Some days the shop was busier than others and mother helped behind the counter during the morning, leaving her with no time to prepare a meal at mid-day. On these days I was turned round at the door when I got home from school, given some money and despatched to Anderson's fish and chip shop for '2 and 1 cut 3 times', (a two-penny cut-fish and a pennyworth of chips 3 times), and this was eaten in the living room between serving customers in the shop. In the summer, banana sandwiches were on the menu at teatime, otherwise it was tomato sandwiches with sugar on them. Mother put sugar on most things, including lettuce. Sunday dinner was roast meat and potatoes with two veg., the favourite meal during the week was rabbit pie with a crust straight out of the oven, mashed potatoes and gravy. At teatime there was always a plate of buttered bread on the table, sometimes sliced meat, otherwise it was bread and jam and cups of tea. Christmas meant a goose and all the trimmings for Xmas dinner. In the run up to the big day, home-made paper chains were strung from corner to corner across the living room, and prized family ornaments handed down over the years were hung on the newly purchased tree. Bought decorations were few, mostly concertinered paper chains and paper lanterns. Mother's birthdays were marked by a small bottle of 'California Poppy' perfume and some Scent Cards, which were sold at the school for a penny each in aid of school funds. The cards were for placing in drawers and wardrobes to provide the aroma of roses or violets to offset the smell of mothballs.

Ours was a working class neighbourhood in which we were one of the fortunate families because of dad's steady job. However he was not all that well paid for the hours he worked, which extended before and after the official opening hours of 0900-1900 and he often worked late, particularly if the day's transactions didn't balance in the evening cash-up, or at the big cash-up each weekend. It was a six-day week, only many years later did 'half day closing' arrive, at first on Thursday afternoon then on Saturday. The latter was hugely pleasing to dad as it meant he could follow his beloved Hull City every week, including Reserve matches in the Midland League. A full day's clerical work was also needed on the last Sunday of every month; but it was all better than many families around us because it was secure and permanent.

My first class in senior school was a minor disaster, I was coming up eleven, and there were fifty or more pupils in the crowded classroom. Kenneth Simpson and I shared a double desk, we were both at that daft age where we talked incessantly and found everything hilarious. The wooden floor of the classroom was tiered in seven or eight stages so that all the desks had a good view of the teacher and the blackboard, but this worked both ways as the teacher also had a good view of us. Our desk was on the top row with our backs to the brown and green glazed wall tiles and we talked our heads off most of the time. 'Fanny', as the class called the teacher, was an embittered old dear who took every stifled laugh and suppressed giggle as being directed towards her. What we laughed at didn't involve her at all, nevertheless I was called out to the front of the class and caned every day without fail, six strokes on the left hand and six strokes on the right, sometimes twice a day. It really hurt, and if she was particularly annoyed she used the curved end of the cane, so that was really twelve plus twelve. My term position was 21st, the report observing, 'Talks too much'.

Having got the silliness out of my system that year, the following terms saw me remaining in the top three till the bitter end. But there were more important things to concern me than exam results. There were girls! Wonderful gorgeous creatures, why had I not noticed them before? Where had they been hiding? Why had I not been told about all this? Sunlit vistas opened up, and no further time was to be wasted on swopping cigarette cards, collecting conkers and the like. My first romantic encounter was with a blue-eyed blonde called Barbara whom all the boys wanted to court. She wore blue cotton polka-dot dresses, except when she wore red cotton polka-dot dresses; either way she wore matching knickers. She lived some distance away and I walked her home after school, along Anlaby Road, down Calvert Lane, along the ten-foot by the railway embankment, past the bushes and the wild flowers of summer, arriving back home late for tea to raised eyebrows and ready with a pack of thinly veiled lies. It was wonderful, and lasted until she moved schools and we lost touch. But the memory, the beautiful and totally innocent memory, lingered on. And not only with me; over fifty years later, meeting a friend not seen since leaving school, almost the first thing he said to me was, 'You used to go out with Barbara didn't you?' So she must have been special, and I wasn't the only one to treasure her memory.

A regular Saturday job was to buy hay for the rabbit from a corn and feed merchant called Clayton, down the archway in the part of Hawthorn Avenue that jutted out near Greek Street. To carry the hay I took one of the canvas bags used for delivering the evening papers; we didn't do morning papers as dad said he wasn't built to get up early in the morning. The hay cost tuppence a bundle and was bulky to carry. If no hay was available at Clayton's it was necessary to go further afield to a pet supply shop in Woodcock Street which was run in the early 1930s by a Mr Frith.

If there were any ailments in the house, mother took down the medicine tin, with its bandages, cotton wool and lotions, from the top shelf of the cupboard next to the fireplace. TCP was the standard antiseptic for cuts and grazes, and a dressing and wodge of cotton wool was bandaged onto the wound. Sweet Nitre was given by the spoonful for any internal complaints. Goose-fat soaked bandages wound round the chest were good for coughs and colds, though you paid the price for this as nobody wanted to sit next to you at school. Bran poultices were like small bean bags but softer, and when warmed in the oven next to the coal fire they gave off a pleasant aroma and felt comforting when applied to the skin. Robolene tasted like sticky malt toffee and was welcomed, but Scott's Emulsion tasted awful; both were popular off-the-shelf tonics. At school there were occasional visits from the 'nit nurse' who rummaged through your hair, and the School Inspector, who seemed mainly interested in truancy. Ken and I played truant once, only getting as far as the farm field adjoining Ringrose Street and didn't find the experience very exciting, so we didn't bother again.

Mother did all her own baking and, on visits to the town, we called at the Balloon Stores for twopenny-worth of yeast which came neatly wrapped in a small greaseproof package with a blue pattern of an airship or a balloon on it. Other local grocery shops were Meadow Dairy, Gallons, Home and Colonial and Cussons. Bread was baked in the oven next to the fire, which had first to be stoked up to the required temperature. Bran poultices could be warmed at the same time. Gloves and clothing were warmed by being hung over the string which went from one side of the kitchen range to the other, just below the mantelpiece. Shoes were propped up against the fender in front of the fire; luxury on a cold winter's morning.

Anything in the way of more serious illness required a visit to the chemist for advice, or something appropriate made up in a bottle. The last resort was a visit to the doctor, this cost serious money and many were the families who should have had proper medical attention but didn't get it because they couldn't afford to pay the doctor, or buy the medicines they needed. There were no healthy-living promotions, it was simply a question of survival, you ate what you could afford to buy and got whatever medicines from the chemist or doctor that your purse allowed and if you didn't have any money you went without. We paid 3d a week into the National Deposit Friendly Society to help with any medical bills and it was my job to take the money round to the agent's house in Parkfield Drive on Thursday evenings. All adult males seemed to smoke like chimneys, a habit probably exacerbated by the 1914 war. 'Passive smoking' lay far into the future, but it certainly existed in our house, where dad smoked Park Drive, Capstan, Black Cat or Gold Flake cigarettes throughout his waking hours. Cinema screens of the time were usually only visible through a thick blue haze of cigarette and pipe smoke.

There was a blue-painted wooden police box at the corner of Seymour Street, into which policemen disappeared at regular intervals to phone HQ or make cups of tea. Law and Order on the streets was not much of a problem. Bobbies on the beat were respected symbols of authority, there was discipline in the homes and in the schools, so it seldom reached the stage where the law needed to step in as far as children were concerned. A misplaced volley sent a football through a window in the shop at the top of Wheeler Street and I went inside to own up. The shopkeeper came to see dad, congratulated him on my honesty and refused payment for the damage. People lived very close to each other, especially down the terraces, respected each other, and whole neighbourhoods were virtually self-policing. With little money in the house, any disruption to a basic living routine was potentially another worry that families could well do without.

3: THE GREAT CHURCH ORGAN TRAFFIC JAM

As the '30s rolled on, sport came to the fore in all directions and most summer evenings were spent on the school playing fields at the bottom of Northfield Road, playing scratch games of cricket or kicking a ball about until it became too dark to see. The field was enclosed by triangular wooden palings but there were always one or two of these that were loose, providing a place to clamber through. A man on a cycle was employed by the Corporation to police the various playing fields, scaring off the gangs of youngsters playing games thereon. He was on a hiding to nothing, being easily outwitted, and as long as we weren't actually digging up the cordoned-off cricket pitch to plant potatoes he didn't bother us. Cork balls could be bought for 3d or 6d whereas a leather ball cost 5/-, the 'corkies' chipped easily and had a short life.

Mr Thomas, the school sports master, brought me into the soccer team early and I was captain of the 1st X1 during the last two years of school. Wheeler Street was in the Central Division of the Schools League and one year topped the table, Played 18, Won 17, Lost 0, Drawn 1, points 35; Paisley Street came second with 29 points. The Hull Daily Mail printed reports of school matches sent in by the schools' sports masters, so we sometimes saw our names in the green Sports Mail on Saturday nights, which was encouraging. I played at right back, with a friend, Ted Collinson, at right half, between us bottling up that side of the field, and in the autumn of 1939 just as everything shut down for the war, I was booked for a trial with Hull City Boys. The trial, along with all other sporting activities was cancelled, as the country prepared to face the threat of war. Perhaps more satisfying to me than captaining the soccer 1st XI, was captaining the cricket 1st X1; but I would have liked that football trial all the same.

Important football matches like the Cup Final were broadcast by the BBC, and to help listeners follow the game a diagram of a soccer pitch was printed in the Radio Times. The diagram was overlaid with numbered squares, and when the commentator was in full flow saying, 'And now it's Bastin going down the wing for Arsenal', a voice over his shoulder would pipe up, 'Square one'. As Cliff progressed further down the wing the voice squeaked out 'Square two' hurriedly followed by 'Square three'. Soccer commentaries have seldom been as much fun since.

Geography lessons intrigued me. The world map was red from one side to the other, showing the British Empire, its possessions territories and colonies, and it all appeared grand and noble to us; we were the children of Empire and the Empire ruled fairly and benignly over much of the globe.

Balancing my love life with sport presented problems, because there were Saturday morning matinees at some cinemas at the same time as Wheeler Street FC, in its blue and white quartered shirts, was engaged in battles to the death on the football field. It was just possible to get home from the morning's exertions on the pitch, scrape the mud off my boots, rub in some dubbing, have a wash, shell 2d worth of peanuts from the green-grocers and collect Joyce from her house in Parkfield Drive in time for the 3d afternoon matinee at the Carlton at the top of the street. Saturdays could be very busy, especially if we had an away match to Southcoates Avenue or Craven Street in the Cup; then there would be a combined rush of young bodies at the end of the match as the muddied team clomped aboard trams or buses in East Hull to get back across the city as quickly as possible in time for the afternoon matinee.

Besides the Carlton there were other picture palaces within easy reach, the West Park, Regis, Eureka, Langham and the Priory. I would have been about four or five when the talkies arrived on the scene, and some of the early children's serials like The Hand of Zorro or The Clutching Hand were jumpy in more ways than one. Tom Mix was the popular cowboy of the day but my own favourites were Ken Maynard and Hopalong Cassidy. Charlie Chaplin, Harold Lloyd and Laurel and Hardy, all seemed clever rather than funny; it was the Three Stooges, Buster Keaton, Chester Conklin, Ben Blue and the Keystone Kops who raised smiles and brought real laughter to the aisles, Abbot and Costello later taking up their mantle.

Simone Simon, the French actress, raised more than a smile, and I fell seriously in love with her after seeing the film Girls Dormitory, and was never quite the same after being captivated by that little button nose and adorable cheeky face. At least not until meeting Hilda, who was hot stuff down the passage at the side of her house and swiftly took my lascivious thoughts away from Simone. This liaison could have ended in disaster but for the fact that her father was in the army and the family kept uprooting to go off and join him at a new camp, often splitting us up just in time. Life was hard for youngsters, nobody told you anything and you learnt about life behind the bike shed, when you'd learnt about it and were about to put it into practice everybody hinted strongly that you ought to stop it, even before you'd started. Nobody loves a lover, despite what Emerson says. There were few children's parties in the '30s because parents couldn't afford them. Of those I recall, the most popular bit was not the potted beef sandwiches, jelly and custard, or the Vimto, but Postman's Knock, where you could isolate a likely girl in a cupboard or a walk-in pantry long enough to exchange a few kisses before being located. There was no exchanging of presents and only small gifts were given if it was a birthday party.

Following dad's example I took up smoking, only cinnamon sticks at first, but you have to start somewhere. Dan and I joined the Scout group at the Church of the Transfiguration in Albert Avenue, where we had a great time under the enthusiastic scoutmaster the Reverend Noel Duckworth, inevitably known as 'Duckie'. His basic approach was to knacker everybody right from the start, so that all the hormones and testosterone that were swilling about were swiftly dissipated, and the unruly pack of young males made more manageable. To this end, the first game was usually British Bulldog where one boy stood with his hands braced against the wall, legs apart, back slightly bent and everyone lined up to take a running jump and land on top of him, clinging on until eventually the whole mass collapsed on the floor. The flattened boy would be retrieved from beneath the pile of bodies and propped against the wall to recover; the game continuing until everyone had been duly squashed in turn. The supposed aim was for one boy to support the rest without collapsing, but nobody ever got that far. This and similar games worked off a lot of surplus energy.

Duckie was our hero; all 5ft of him had coxed the Cambridge

boat to victory in the University Boat Races of 1934, 1935 and 1936 and he was also an Olympic oarsman. One year he took our Scout troop camping in a farmer's field halfway up Oliver's Mount, near Scarborough. We were there for a week, playing cricket and football in the field and on the sands, exploring the countryside, bathing in the sea, boxing with the only two pairs of careworn gloves we possessed, (one size fits all), sleeping under canvas in large bell-tents with our feet towards the centre pole, singing round the campfire and generally doing all the things Scouts are supposed to do. I still recall the breakfasts; crisp, sizzling bacon, with eggs and milk fresh from the farm, eaten in the cold mornings with the dew still on the grass, all your friends around you and another day on the beach to look forward to. The simplest things in life are often the best.

The church hall was also used for Dances, Whist Drives and wild Beetle Drives. Occasionally groups of Scouts were co-opted to help for the communal good and one summer evening Dan and I were sent off with a handcart to the Church of the Ascension on Calvert Road to bring back a small church organ. All went well on the return journey until the wheels of the handcart became stuck in some metal tracks in the road, the weight of the organ forcing us further into trouble. We couldn't shift it and were holding up traffic; people came to help and they couldn't shift it either. Eventually, somebody arrived with a metal bar and willing hands helped to ease the wheels out of the tracks and back onto the road. We moved off to loud cheers from what, by then, seemed to be hundreds of involved on-lookers and lines of backed-up traffic.

There was an increase in road traffic as the '30s wore on, and Belisha Crossings and 30 mph speed limits were introduced in built-up areas. Neither of these measures was enough to save a school friend, Cecil Pine, who was killed by a car at the top of the Avenue. His father had a butchers' shop at the corner of Northfield Road and Cecil was trying out his new roller skates on the concrete shop front when he ran straight onto the main road. Everyone at school went off roller skates for some time afterwards.

Dental problems appeared and mother took me to the School Clinic, a large double-fronted house in Coltman Street. The dentist gave me an injection and five seconds later yanked the tooth out. Screams and mayhem all round. Mother's maternal instincts, plus a generous helping of French temperament, came to the fore and she pulled me out of the chair, gave the dentist an earful and took me, still yelling, out into the street and off home. So much for children's dental care in the '30s. For the next year visits were made twice a week after school to a private dentist, Mr Parker, near Park Street on Anlaby Road. Memories are still vivid of the gas cylinder being wheeled out of a cupboard and the sickly smell of the gas as the mask closed over my face. Mother came with me on the first occasion, but after that it was the regular routine of taking the 1/2d tram ride along Anlaby Road after school and returning home by myself. The treatment must have cost a packet in those days.

During the school year everyone saved 1d a week towards the annual school trip, a great event which took place just before school broke up for the summer holidays. Charabancs, single-decker and double-decker open-topped buses, were still on the roads and popular in the summertime, but for our school trips we travelled in single-deck saloon buses, which usually came from the Grey-de-Luxe garage in Albert Avenue. There would be three or four of these gleaming chariots ready at the school gates at eight o'clock on the morning of the big day. Anywhere up to 200 excited youngsters, clutching their packing-up, would board in semi-orderly fashion and the battle commenced for the seats at the back or next to the windows. Last minute shouted instructions from parents were ignored as a forest of waving arms spilled out of the windows. The convoy set off for Scarborough, the Peak District, the Blue John Mines, wherever, the destination wasn't important, it was the getting away that mattered.

Stops were made on the way to eat our sandwiches and buy tea or bottles of Ruddock's Dandelion and Burdock or Sarsaparilla, with their intriguing glass stoppers and metal clips, (1d back on the empties). An hour or two would be spent at the destination and another stop made on the way back at a 'surprise' location, somewhere like Knaresborough Castle or Mother Shipton's Well. These stops were looked upon as places to get up to some communal mischief, or even some romantic action should the opportunity arise. Tea was taken at a pre-arranged roadside café on the return journey and was often the high spot of the day for hungry youngsters, with potted beef, York ham, ox-tongue sandwiches, salad, cakes, jam, jelly and custard and cups of tea. By nine o'clock we were back at the school gates, where our parents were waiting for us. There were children for whom this would probably be the only outing they had in the whole year; there were yet others who didn't come on the trip because their parents couldn't afford the penny a week that it cost.

4: SUMMER HOLIDAYS

Summer holidays meant two weeks in the country and two weeks at the seaside. Mother was a friend of the Stephenson family who lived at the Mill Farm at Burton Pidsea, and as soon as school shut down for the month of August I was all ready, packed and eagerly awaiting the East Yorkshire bus that would take me into the heart of the East Riding countryside. The farm and the mill were on the outskirts of the village, down a winding lane that drew you into the gently rolling farmlands beyond. In the yard attached to the farmhouse there were old steam engines and tractors, long disused, and now growing old gracefully in a coating of grime and rust. Hens were nesting in the boiler where the door was rusted open and it was not hard to find fresh eggs for breakfast, either there or in the nearby hedgerows.

The silent steam giants were a natural playground; the steering wheels turned, the occasional lever moved and even the gauges, stuck at some long evaporated water pressure, looked the part; imagination had full play when climbing onto the footplate and grasping the controls. After scouring the hedges for eggs there were walks down the lane away from the village, with the sweeping skies of Holderness, the smell of hay and warm earth, wild flowers in profusion along the verges, the buzz of honey bees and flocks of birds.

Inside, the old farmhouse was cool in the summer heat; the walls were thick, my bedroom a haven of peace and quiet with the smell and sounds of the countryside drifting in through the open casement window. It was a long way from the smell of kipper houses and the fish-meal factory. Scarcely any traffic found its way down the lane and it was very tranquil. On very warm nights my small tent was erected in the front garden and I slept under the stars, listening to the owls, the rustling in the hedgerows and other unfamiliar country sounds. The five storey brick mill had been built in 1830 but had last ground flour during the Great War and its sails were long gone. Climbing the steps to the wooden platform and opening the rickety door, inside it was dark, full of long-disused machinery bedecked with cobwebs and smelling of rust and old wood, giving off a spooky atmosphere. There were orders not to go in there because of the rotting wood and the gaps in the floor, but many visits were made when no one was about.

The shops were at the other end of the village, some distance from the mill, and were seldom visited, but a house at the top of the lane displayed sweets in its front window and received most of my pocket money. There was another escapee from the city staying in the village, a schoolboy named Jimmy Cutting, and we joined forces in searching for eggs, walking in the fields or looking in the hedgerows for birds' nests which, to our credit, we didn't plunder or disturb. The only part of the holiday that didn't appeal was the earth closet. This small building was next to the hedge that ran by the lane and was some little way from the house. In approved country style there was no privacy, three holes being cut from one large piece of wood. Wild horses wouldn't drag me out there in the dark, crossing my legs instead; all night if necessary. Neatly torn squares of newspaper hung on a nail, otherwise you tore off part of the newspaper left lying around.

When boarding the bus to go home at the end of the holiday I was likely to be chewing straw and talking with a strong East Riding accent, however this was soon eradicated when, a day or two later, I joined the train at a bustling smoky Paragon Station to spend a seaside holiday with my grandparents in Bridlington. In younger days I helped the train speed on its journey by operating the metal handles that were set into the carriage woodwork, above the padded seats. Finding out later that all this did was to open and close the mushroom vents on the roof of the carriage, took some of the magic away. But now grown up, having put childish things behind me, I counted the number of telegraph poles that whizzed past in sixty seconds. Dividing one by the other, in accordance with a secret formula learnt from a boys' magazine, gave me the speed of the train, but I never got it right, sometimes our local seaside excursion was travelling faster than the 'Flying Scotsman'.

The thirties saw rivalry on the railways between the LNER and pretenders like the LMS, GWR and the Southern Railway. In 1934 the 'Flying Scotsman', no. 4472, in its apple green livery, became the first steam locomotive to reach 100mph, and all the boys at school re-affirmed their allegiance to the LNER as well as Yorkshire cricket. Nigel Gresley was the chief engineer for the LNER and his stable of A4 Pacific locomotives included the 'Silver Link', the first of the streamliners that ran from London to Edinburgh for most of the decade. When challenged by the LMS 'Coronation Scot', the LNER fielded another A4, 'Mallard', reaching 126mph and taking the world's speed record for a steam locomotive. Being pro-LNER at school extended to model railways, a boy owning any other railway company was considered slightly suspect.

My grandparents had taken rooms in a house at the corner of Tennyson Avenue and Blackburn Avenue in Bridlington. Letty, one of the ladies who ran the boarding house, served our meals at a long shiny wooden table, in a dining room cluttered with aspidistras. She talked in a near-incomprehensible West Riding accent about being 'mafted' and 'fair wemelled' and every Sunday, dressed in a long black skirt and bonnet, walked to the Seamen's Bethel down by the harbour. In the hallway was the seaside smell of rubber beach shoes, squeezed-out swimming costumes, a scattering of sand, buckets and spades and the jar with seaweed, tiny crabs and wriggly things in it. A notice on the wall told you what the mealtimes were and what time the front door would be locked at night.

Later in the thirties my grandparents left Tennyson Avenue for a bungalow in St. Chad Road, living there for a number of years after grandpa retired from being a Supervisor at the G.P.O. in Hull. When he met me off the train at Bridlington he always bought me a 2d red and gold wrapped bar of Nestle's chocolate from the sentry-like machine that stood on the platform. We walked the mile or so from the station, down a passage and over the railway lines, through Duke's Park recreation ground to the bungalow, me chattering away and asking him, once more, about the Royal Mail Train, and the T.P.O. he occasionally supervised that received the bags of mail slung onto the 'catch and drop' sorting coach as it sped through the night between Edinburgh and London.

The bungalow was only yards from the main railway line that took the Hull train up the incline to Sewerby, then on to Filey and Scarborough. My bedroom faced this stretch of line and provided a splendid view of the passing trains. Being the summertime there were lots of passenger trains, each with many coaches in tow, struggling up the slope, all of them full of holidaymakers on their way to the seaside. There were goods trains too, and numerous small note-books were filled with engine numbers, dates and time of day, directions up or down the line and the number of passenger coaches or goods wagons. Also entered were mysterious figures like 0-4-0, 4-6-2, a secret code known only to train-spotting cognoscenti like myself and a handful of others. The best part was the night-time, the train whistles echoing through the darkness as they approached the walkover at Dukes' crossing. This was followed by the hissing of steam and the sound of an overworked tank engine being asked to do the work of a Stanier Black 5, laboriously hauling scores of heavy coal wagons up the gradient. Most of the heavy goods traffic went through at night, but sometimes trains came whistling down the hill at speed, easing up as they approached the station. That was quite a different sound to conjure with and there would be the added excitement of lighted coaches flashing past; all of this whilst lying in bed, supposedly asleep.

But this was the seaside, and the beach was the main attraction. Occasionally grandpa hired a green canvas square-shaped tent for the day from the Corporation, complete with groundsheet and deckchairs. On those days we were down on the beach early to secure a favoured spot in front of the stately Alexandra Hotel, for soon there would be lots of holidaymakers leaving their lodgings, the sands quickly filling up with people sunbathing, paddling, playing cricket, and sandcastles would spring up everywhere. We took swimming costumes, bought a tray of tea from a nearby café for 1/- (6d back on return of crockery in good order), and stayed on the sands all day. Men wended their way between the groups on the beach, carrying canvas satchels over their shoulders selling daily papers, the News Chronicle, Daily Sketch, Daily Herald and magazines like Tit-Bits, Answers, John Bull, Everybody's and Daltons Weekly. They also sold coloured celluloid windmills, dark celluloid sun-shades and Union Jack flags to grace the tops of sandcastles. An ice-cream stall sometimes set up on the sands, very attractive with its Union Jacks flying and gaily striped canvas awning, whilst above us, on the wood-bolstered promenade, were the 'Stop Me and Buy One' Eldorado, and Walls tricycles selling their own brands of ice-cream.

Nearby was the White City amusements; I favoured the 1d circular pinball machine that paid out 2d for red, 2d for black and 5d for white. I had worked out a profitable system for this machine and got lots of pay-outs, but always left with less than I started with. Offshore, flying parallel with the beach, biplanes towed advertising banners which stood out clearly against the blue sky, whilst other planes wrote messages in smoke by forming letters with their manoeuvres. A little way out to sea, cobles were taking holiday-makers around the bay, speedboats catering for the more adventurous. Whilst this was going on, children would be watching the Punch and Judy show or looking for crabs and other small creatures in the pools by the side of the wooden breakwaters, collecting them in a jam-jar with string round the

30

rim to carry home. If the sea was calm, my wind-up clockwork motorboat had its rudder set at an angle that would take it in a wide circle, before being launched into the waves. The rudder had to be set at an angle if you were on your own, otherwise the last you saw of the boat it was heading for Holland. My small wooden yacht also had its outings in the sea but was happier in the yacht pool on the Spa, where the calm water ensured safer sailing.

The few shillings taken on holiday had been saved out of pocket money and was supplemented by parents and grandparents. My pocket money didn't amount to very much but was augmented by my Auntie Agnes, who came most Wednesday evenings after finishing work as a clerk at the Waterloo Mills in Wincolmlee. She once took me into her world of long wooden desks, high stools and the smell of grain and harvest fields. She paid for one or more of my weekly boys' magazines which included the Adventure, Champion, Wizard, Rover, Skipper and Hotspur, ('Six-Gun' Solomon was the greatest cowboy ever), Film Fun and Chips. Slightly up-market magazines were the Boys Own Paper, the Magnet and the Gem, where Frank Richards brought Tom Merry, Harry Wharton and Billy Bunter to life. There was also the Meccano Magazine, which had articles about ships and trains. The Fretwork Weekly was bought during a period of enthusiasm for guiding fretsaws around bits of plywood, making egg-racks, useless bookshelves or superfluous tea-pot stands and smelling the house out with small pots of cow-heel glue in the process. Reading any magazines that came my way, I occasionally sent away for itching powder, periscopes that looked over walls, fingerprint packs and detective kits with moustache disguises and invisible ink. A well-known advert of the period showed a muscular male running along the beach kicking up sand over innocent sunbathers as he raced along. Underneath the drawing were the words 'Are you tired of having sand kicked in your face?', or something similar. Saving yourself from this fate worse than death cost little, the price of a Charles Atlas bodybuilding course, so I sent away for the literature, did some exercises for a week and laid on the beach to see what happened. Nothing much did. If exercise didn't appeal there was always Pelmanism, which exercised the mind and gave you inner confidence.

Any serious money, like a shilling, went to buy aviation magazines, Flight or The Aeroplane. Flying captured everyone's imagination in the twenties and thirties. Daredevils, women along with men, took off from any old strip of grass in planes held together with string and tried to beat each other to the ends of the earth. Newspapers offered large sums of money to those able to conquer new routes or to fly upside down from Croyden to Capetown and back on 6 gallons of petrol. Well maybe not; but it was the golden age of flying and everyone wanted to be a winner. In 1938 an Irishman, later nicknamed 'Wrong Way' Corrigan, set off to fly from Britain to the continent but ended up in America, claiming his compass had failed or a strong head wind had sprung up, or whatever. He received the fame and publicity that he doubtless sought, plus the money that went along with his story.

My parents joined in the fun before those exciting days of flying faded away forever. In the late thirties, during a holiday in London, the three of us went up in a de-Haviland Dragon 'Rapide', a twin-engine biplane, from Croydon Airport. Croydon was the airport for London, very busy, and the starting point for many of the record-breaking flights of the period, including those of Amy Johnson. The plane carried seven or eight passengers and we each had our own window seat. The smell of leather and petrol pervaded the cabin but was soon superseded by the smell of fear from some of us as we bumped along the grass runway. Then it was all wonderful, smooth and noisy and we were airborne. It was a ten-minute sightseeing flight over London and well worth 7/6d.

Meantime, back on the beach at Bridlington the days were passing, and I had yet to pursue my fascination with show business as represented by concert parties. There was a premier troupe that performed in the evenings in the Floral Hall on the sea front, and on sunny afternoons on the outdoor stage across the road from the Greyhound Inn. This was Fred Rayne's concert party, the North Regionals, which sometimes rose to the dizzy heights of broadcasting on the wireless. Deck chairs could be hired for 3d, or 6d if you wanted the front row. If it was wet, the show was transferred to the Floral Hall, a pavilion on the Princess Parade, next to the floral clock. This was an ideal setting, arboreal, with shrubs, hanging baskets, colourful floral displays and in the hot summers the pavilion smelt like a tropical forest. On the other side of the town was the Spa, where Herman Darewski and Ceres Harper and their orchestras played for concerts and dancing. Popular songs of the day were Alone, Blue Moon and The Lady in Red.

The Bing Boys were at the other end of the market and performed on the north sands, fitting their shows in between the tides which waited for no man. They erected a wooden stage, fairly stable, which sagged in the middle and must have made things difficult for the dancers. At either side of the stage, at the back, was a curtained opening giving access to a tiny area which served as a changing room, from where the performers made their entrance. A piano was positioned on wooden boards laid on the sand, as there was no room for it on the stage. The stage was set up about a hundred feet from the promenade as the tide was receding, in order to gain the maximum performance time before the tide came in again. This provided an area in which to set up a few deck chairs, near enough to attract the attention of passing holiday-makers on the promenade above. Those performers who were not currently involved on the stage, passed among the transient crowd on the sands and on the promenade, bearing with them small cloth bags with wooden handles, encouraging contributions. The show ran continuously until the tide came in, at which time there was a scramble to save the piano, the props and the stage from the encroaching sea. This was often voted by the onlookers as the most entertaining part of the show.

Groups of donkeys also assembled on the sands, coming down Trinity Cut and under the promenade, standing in a group ready to take children for rides along the beach. Nearby were two bowling greens, one flat and one crown, where Grandpa sometimes took time off from sandcastle duty to play the occasional game. Also using the beach was a one-armed man who, tides permitting, arrived early in the morning to smooth out an area of sand on which he drew caricatures, topical scenes, flags and emblems, colouring them in with powdered chalk. These pictures and designs were very attractive and people threw pennies down to him from the promenade. There were quite a few men in the '30s with only one arm or leg and using crutches, a legacy of the Great War, and they were now trying to earn a living in diverse ways. Other free entertainment included a man who, bound in chains and padlocked, jumped into the sea near the North Pier steps at high tide. He would emerge, eventually, safe and sound, with the chains hanging loose, to receive the bag of money that his assistant had collected from the assembled onlookers. On the beach, games of cricket and football took over any vacant patch of sand; kites were popular, there were two types, the box kites which flew with little wind or effort, and the shield-shaped racing kites which needed a run along the sands to get them airborne.

The Yorkshireman was a river tug belonging to the United

Towing Company of Hull, which came to Bridlington for the summer season and took pleasure trippers to local beauty spots like Flamborough Head. She left the quayside with an accordionist on board playing loudly to impress the onlookers, but he ran out of enthusiasm when the ship cleared the harbour entrance and retired to the comfort of the bar. Later he would make a brief musical appearance, to the quizzical stares of the seagulls off Flamborough Head, before returning to the bar, finally emerging in time for the grand musical entrance into the harbour at the end of the trip. Then the flags and the bunting flew from the mast, the siren blew, the accordion reached heights of melody previously unknown, the gangway managed to secure itself to the pier and the crowds bustled ashore looking for fish and chips and candyfloss. Bridlington was having a whale of a time.

One of the London dailies sent their man 'Lobby Ludd' to the summer holiday resorts. You needed to have a copy of their newspaper in your possession and then challenge him, if you could recognise him from the photo and his description in the paper. If correct in your challenge you received the sum of £5. It didn't help that the picture in the newspaper looked more like an identikit than a photograph. Anyway I was more likely to be at the pictures than looking for him. The Winter Gardens and The Lounge on the Promenade, the Roxy in Quay Road, and the Palace, all received their fair share of my pocket money. Except, that is, the part saved for my summer romance. Grandpa had kept in touch with some of his retired colleagues, one of whom, very considerately, had a pretty granddaughter about my age. The family lived in Scarborough, and Gloria came down with them when they stayed in Bridlington for a few days each summer. We went bathing, walking and had a wholesome seaside fun time together over two or three summers in the late thirties, keeping up a correspondence for many years afterwards.

Mother had a school friend who lived at Withernsea and we spent odd days and weekends there; my bedroom looked out towards the water tower, a dominant feature and a necessary one in that low lying gently rolling landscape. Railway excursions were run to Blackpool during the autumn illuminations and we made the journey a couple of times, going up the Tower and watching the afternoon tea dance in the ballroom before taking a tram ride along the promenade to view the illuminations, the train arriving home around midnight.

In 1934, and again in 1936, we spent a week in the Lake District at 'Eagle Cottage' in Glenridding, on the edge of Lake Ullswater. (Some seventy years later the cottage looked just the same). My bedroom overlooked the flower garden at the back of the cottage where a small mountain stream gurgled away and whose sound filled my dreams. We climbed Helvellyn, following the track that ran past the cottage, walking along Striding Edge and looking down onto Red Tarn, brooding, cold, dark and ominous beneath us on the one side, a steep slope of shale falling away on the other. A steamer took us from Patterdale to Pooley Bridge, and a rowing boat was hired to venture far out on the still waters of the lake. We waited on the platform for the local train that was the start of our journey home, being deafened by the shriek of the whistle as an express train came down Shap Fell, thundering through Shap station on its way south, the platform shaking as it shot past leaving a trail of steam and smoke in its wake.

In early 1938 my great grandmother Elizabeth lay dying at the home of her son George; she was 98. The family assembled at her bedside in the house in Exmouth Street, including 'Phyllis's boy' as I was called by the d'Andilly side of the family. My memory of her, as I stood at the bedside, is that of a frail tiny white-haired lady, almost lost amongst the white pillows and sheets, yet still able to take our proffered hands in hers and raise a smile. It was the era of children being 'seen and not heard', but what would I not give, now, to have heard from her own lips the story of that adventure which ended so mysteriously in the Confederate countryside of Louisiana.

5: WAR CLOUDS GATHER

It was the summer of 1939 when we started to lose the England we had grown up in. Dan was at Bridlington, staying in the small terraced house in Ollinda Road and together we walked all over the town until we knew it well enough to have moved around blindfold. Most of my time was spent at the bungalow, where grandpa, a kindly old gentleman in plus-fours, smoked his pipe, tended his sweet peas, staked out his raspberry canes and sallied forth each lunch-time to his local, the Seabirds, near the railway bridge at Fortyfoot. He told me that one day in the mid-thirties he had been in there across lunchtime as usual, when he fell into conversation with an aircraftman from the RAF rescue launch base in the harbour who turned out to be Lawrence of Arabia. This was before the days when children were allowed anywhere near the smell of beer, so I never went with him on these daily excursions. He had eventually retired from the G.P.O. with the traditional gold watch and the Imperial Service Medal.

Dan and I sometimes waded in the harbour at low tide near to the RAF base and once egged each other on to follow the Gypsey Race, from its outfall into the harbour, to Beck Hill. The stream rises to the north-west of Bridlington and meanders along until it disappears under the town streets, emerging out of a tunnel through a forbidding high brick arch in a corner of the harbour. The rush of water was strong in the winter with the snow-melt from the Wolds, but in the summer was little more than a trickle. We got a hundred yards or so past the entrance, it was pitch dark and the tunnel seemed about to take a turn just ahead of us. Our trousers were soaked, it was dank, eerie and the gentle trickle of water sounded like Niagara Falls in the confined space. We knew that, going around the next corner, we should lose sight of the daylight coming from the harbour behind us and were unsure whether any compensating daylight would guide us towards the other end, so we turned back, promising ourselves we would go all the way one day; but we never did.

Having started school at the same time, Dan and I did many things together, including having a scrap near the school swings in Ringrose Street. It was always 'scraps' at school, never fights; school finished at four o'clock and everyone turned out to watch because it was usual to have one big scrap a week after school. We set-to; Dan was the heftier and the outcome was a foregone conclusion, it was just a case of how long I lasted. With these gladiatorial contests it didn't matter who won, what mattered was what sort of a fight you both put up; after all, you couldn't send a blood-thirsty crowd of kids away disappointed when they'd been looking forward to it all day. After I had picked myself up off the concrete a number of times, Dan was declared the winner. We shook hands and became mutual best friends for the rest of our lives. What the scrap was all about I have no idea.

Although we enjoyed Bridlington in the summer, when there were shows, entertainments of all kinds, long days on the beach and the harbour to explore, we enjoyed it even more in the winter. During the Christmas holidays we felt that Brid. belonged to us, the holidaymakers and the minstrels had long departed and the town was deserted. It seemed always to be cold in those late-thirties winters, with snow on the ground or just around the corner. The winds howled and the seas crashed angrily into the corner where the South Pier meets the Spa, it was wild and exhilarating and we would go home to tea all psyched up. One stormy winter's night, when we were alone in the house at Ollinda Road, the lifeboat rocket went up, lighting the sky above the town. We scrambled into our waterproofs and ran all the way to the sea front, just in time to see the lifeboat launched amid lots of shouting, storm lanterns, men in yellow sou'westers, and the boat on its cradle crossing the darkened beach into the surf until it was lost from sight amongst the waves.

We were there when the old Mauretania steamed past on her last voyage to the breaker's yard; what a stately vessel she looked with her red and black funnels and classic lines. Ocean liners, British, French, Italian, Dutch and German vied with each other for the Atlantic passenger trade in the '30s, and Blue-Riband records were a source of national pride. The voyages of these great ships were part of the passing scene and it was sad to see such a beautiful vessel on her way to the graveyard. One summer, the Royal Navy cruiser *Leander* anchored in the bay as part of a showing-the-flag exercise. The pleasure boats and fishing cobles ran special trips out to this seemingly huge man-of-war, getting as close to her as they could. War was indeed drawing ever nearer. A black cloud was gathering over the horizon, affecting everyone at every level, the newspapers were subdued and their language sombre. Trenches were dug in the parks, sandbags were stacked around important buildings and air-raid shelters began appearing everywhere. Strips of sticky paper criss-crossed windows to minimise flying glass and gas-masks in cardboard boxes were piled up in Council depots ready for issue.

But life went on as usual, there was no alternative; you placed your misguided faith in the politicians and hoped for the best. Many books have been written and TV documentaries produced, often with the benefit of hindsight, about the run-up to the war and the early war years, one of the best being Peter Fleming's 'Operation Sea Lion'. Another is 'And Hell Followed', by Odette Keun which was written at a time when things looked blacker than black and all our thoughts were on how we could survive the war, let alone think of winning it, nor dare we imagine the horror and the consequences of losing it. She told it like it was, as it was happening, with a furious intensity, sparing no one's reputation. Both books reflect life in Britain as it was for ordinary people in those confused early days.

Before all that and still at school, I became interested in stamps and had started to collect them. In Waterworks Street, towards the Paragon Street end near Little Chariot Street, there were some old buildings, several storeys high. Near Fowlers Café there was an entrance and a well-worn wooden staircase led from floor to floor, until you came to the top landing where a door with a glass panel announced, 'A. Rassmussen', and the inviting words underneath, 'Stamp Dealer'. Opening the door was like stepping back in time; here was peace, quietness and gentility. In the centre of the room stood a long table with a glass-topped case, displaying stamps from all over the world, more sheets of stamps covered the walls and there were well-thumbed albums stacked side by side that could be taken down from their shelves and perused at leisure at a small table. Here was the fascination with travel and far away places, where African warriors with clubs and shields stood steadfast, where exotic blooms flowered in colours previously unimagined, and great liners, and aeroplanes with two wings and lots of engines could take you there. Beyond the horizon, that's where I wanted to be, and stamps took me there. Over the weeks and months of my occasional visits, the old gentleman with the black cap and the grey whiskers came to know the young enthusiast, smiling as we conducted our 2d and 3d worth of business with all the courtesy of another era. At home the stamps were sorted onto the correct album page, British Empire, Argentina, Trinidad and Tobago, Van Diemens Land, (where on earth was that?), Abyssinia, Brazil, Panama, the very names stimulated the imagination. One day, yes one day, I would go and see these places for myself.

Mr Rasmussen was visited on the days when dad went into town to have his hair cut. This ritual took place at the barber's in the basement of the Prudential Tower in Queen Victoria Square. We would cycle into town on the tandem, which was then chained up in the passage by the side of the tower and I went along to choose my stamps. Dad often said that he could equally read a map as read a book and his outlook must have rubbed off on me, because the desire to see faraway places was there from an early age. However, people in our position didn't travel abroad, they had neither the money nor the opportunity.

The first time I saw Hull City was in the early thirties when they were playing at the Anlaby Road ground and enjoying one of their tenuous spells in the 2nd Division. Dad took me to the ground on Saturday afternoons when there was a home match, the excitement and anticipation mounting as we walked along Anlaby Road, past the wooden hoardings that bordered West Park and onto the cinder track that gently curved by the side of the railway track. LNER Clerks had a neat little cricket square just before you came to the wide expanse of the Circle and, when the seasons overlapped, we paused to watch a few minutes of cricket on the way to football. I was seven or eight when dad took me to the East Stand, where we stood amongst the crowd under a shaky roof, about level with the halfway line. Patterning shows, because for many years I was to be found standing beneath a suspect roof on the East Stand about level with the halfway line, only this time at Boothferry Park and, even later, sitting opposite the halfway line in the East Stand at the KC Stadium, but this time under a secure non-leaky roof.

Bunkers Hill, at the Anlaby Road ground, was a mound of earth at the southern end of the pitch. The Best Stand was a draughty barn of a place with a curved corrugated iron roof from which panels regularly blew off, landing on the adjoining cricket pitch. A local brass or silver band played at half time, collections being made for them, or a charity that they supported. The collection was made by four men, each taking a corner of a canvas sheet, walking round the touchline inviting people to throw pennies into it. This was fine if you were at the back of the stand but could be painful if you were near the touchline, when it was advisable to look straight ahead and keep your collar turned up until the sheet, sagging with copper coins, had passed by. On crowded days like Cup matches, small children would often be passed down to the front of the stand, where people made room for them. George Maddison was the first-team goalkeeper, and as the goal at the north end was tight up against the low white wooden fence, Maddie would converse with groups of us youngsters whilst the forwards were busy up field, the aroma of Moors' & Robson's best bitter adding zest to his forthright comments on football, the world in general and referees in particular. The 3rd North was a tough division, a memory of honest down to earth football played with skill, passion and sending offs on a grass pitch which turned to a quagmire in winter. City never had any money, regularly selling their best players in order to survive; to kick-off with a new ball was an event worthy of comment on the terraces. If the match ball was booted over the stands during play, the game could be held up whilst it was retrieved. Visiting supporters were not segregated, mingling freely with local fans; there were no stewards, one or two policeman at most and hardly ever any trouble.

City's young reserve goalkeeper was Billy Bly, probably the best keeper never to play for England; he was acrobatic, fearless and seemed to break a different bone in his body each month. The manager was Haydn Green; he had superseded Bill McCracken who lived at the top of the Avenue and whose son attended Wheeler Street School. Bill was famous, or infamous, for his use of the offside trap. City always played in black and amber stripes, home and away, and any other strip seems to me an irrelevance; they got their nickname of the 'Tigers' because of those stripes, which are unique in the Football League and to be cherished.

In the thirties, the Champion magazine gave away a cardboard league table and sheets of press-out tabs with team names and colours on them; these slotted into the four tables for the 1st and 2nd Divisions and the 3rd North and 3rd South. The football results came through on the wireless at half past five on Saturday evenings, at which time the nation sharpened its pencils. Those who wouldn't know their Arsenal from their Everton listened to see if they had correctly forecast their 3 Draws or 4 Aways on Littlewoods Pools. The tables were usually adjusted from the Sunday newspapers and, at the end of the season, teams were moved up or down the leagues as appropriate. Our league table was pinned to the wall, but was taken down at the end of 1939 when organised football ceased. In the '30s there was 1st Division football to be seen at Blundell Park, and dad sometimes took me across on the ferry to watch Grimsby Town, where Hall, Betmead and Buck dominated the midfield.

The winters were bitterly cold, snow came early and hung around for weeks and months. The icy slides in school playgrounds often lasted from November until early spring, being polished assiduously by boys' jackets to keep them in prime condition. City's ground hosted other events besides football and one chilly night we all sat in the Best Stand, watching a troop of mounted Cossacks thundering up and down the touchline in front of us. Riding almost upside down on their horses, they picked up pieces of cloth the size of a handkerchief from the ground with their teeth as they raced along. It was dusk as they performed this and many other dangerous-looking tricks with swords and flaming torches, all of which looked most inadvisable to me.

6: CRYSTAL SETS AND FOUNTAINS

Our first wireless was a crystal set, housed in a handsome square wooden box with a hinged lid. We took it in turns to put on the headphones and delicately adjust a knob, to which was attached a fine wire, colloquially known as the cat's whisker, which played on the surface of a crystal. If you were lucky enough to live near a local broadcasting station you received a decent signal, any station further afield being usually weak and difficult to hear. It was wonderful to pluck voices out of thin air, no matter in what language and the following morning people compared notes about which stations they had picked up the previous evening. Valve receivers made their appearance but were initially expensive, needing proper aerials, batteries and maintenance, so most people opted for the Broadcast Relay Service, later Rediffusion, which sent programmes down wires to your home. On Sundays, when the BBC under Lord Reith fed the nation a diet of religion and dirge, you could also listen to Radio Luxembourg and sometimes Radio Normandie. These were the first commercial stations we had heard and it was a new concept for us, Carson Robison and his Pioneers, a cowboy singing group who toured the music halls, became Carson Robison and his Oxydol Pioneers when broadcasting from Radio Luxembourg.

We learned other important things such as 'Friday Night is Amami Night', and that toothpaste could turn children's teeth into 'Gibb's Ivory Castles'. Not many children round our way aspired to toothpaste anyway, salt being a cheaper alternative. The first soaps reared their heads, Stella Dallas being one of the earliest. It was all good stuff and I rose early on Sundays to switch on the Rediffusion speaker in its brown plywood case, listening to the programmes whilst making the fire, sifting the ashes for cinders and breaking the nutty slack in the coalhouse into lumps small enough to feed our narrow grate. By the time Al Bowley was warbling away, the fire was beginning its losing battle trying to warm the room and Sunday was well and truly under way.

There were some regular feature programmes on the BBC such as In Town Tonight at seven-thirty each Saturday night, when famous visitors to London, (whom no one had ever heard of), talked to the interviewer about themselves. Then there was Monday Night at Eight, a magazine programme with loveable characters, (sic), like Sid Walker the rag and bone man who told stories of his adventures on the streets, and Valentine Dyall, 'The

Man in Black', who told spooky tales in a sepulchral voice. Straightforward news broadcasts were read on the Home Service at regular times, 1300, 1800 and 2100, by men who spoke the King's English, possessed good vocabularies and breath control, didn't drop their voices or run their sentences together. There was classical music to be heard, though little of it filtered through to our house because dad preferred the Light Programme, which featured tame pianists like Charlie Kunz and a fat xylophone player called Teddy Brown.

Two or three times a week, at 10.25 in the evening, a dance band programme was broadcast from a London club or hotel, Lew Stone, Harry Roy, Ambrose, Carrol Gibbons, Geraldo, Maurice Winnick, Oscar Rabin, Nat Gonella and many other bands being featured. Most popular music of the day was bland and inoffensive but there were occasional rhythmic tunes bordering on jazz. Although usually in bed before ten o'clock, the living room door was left open at my request so that the music floated up the stair-well until the programme finished at eleven o'clock. Generally the wireless broadcast healthy moralistic programmes, innocent, free from innuendo and smut and it was what we were all brought up on. It can't have been all that bad either, for it shaped the nation's morale and character at a time when those qualities were about to be severely tested.

Sunday mornings saw the occasional Church Parade, complete with band, passing along the streets. These processions could be heard approaching from a distance and there were usually a few small boys and dogs lining the road to watch them pass by, polished instruments glinting in the sunlight and the colourful standards fluttering in the breeze. Most often came the Salvation Army band with its banner and followers walking behind, the Boy Scouts, the Boys Brigade and sometimes the Hesslewood Orphanage band. Other street music came from hand-turned barrel organs, hurdy-gurdies pushed along on wheels which set up at different places in the street, the organ grinder, often a disabled ex-serviceman, hoping to receive some coins tossed into his up-turned cap from passers-by. There was something romantic about barrel organs when they played under the gas lamps in the evenings as men were coming home from work; one used to set up across the road from us, underneath the lamp post at the corner of Carlton Villas. Other transient street-traders were the knife-grinders with their equipment on the front of a bicycle, using pedal power to turn the grindstone; rag and bone men with their horses and carts, and chimney sweeps carrying rods and brushes on their backs or in a home-made trailer behind the cycle. Knockers-up went along the streets in the early hours with a long bamboo pole, gently tapping on the bedroom windows of workmen, rousing them for work or to meet tide times down on the dock. I wondered what happened if they knocked up the wrong house.

Role models were wholesome ones, boxers like Joe Louis, Jack Petersen and Len Harvey, aviators Amy Johnson and Amelia Earhart, cricketers, footballers, explorers, adventurers, racing drivers like Malcolm Campbell in Bluebird, Tommy Lipton in Shamrock, Stanley Woods winning the TT Races; people who displayed skills and courage, who actually achieved something and warranted admiration rather than adulation. Memories of the Great War were still vivid in the thirties. Dad had served in the West Yorkshire Regiment during the war, being gassed whilst serving in the front line and spending time in hospital in France. He had also been hit in the thigh by a sniper's bullet, a cigarette case in his thigh pocket saving him from serious injury; the damaged and distorted case being still with the family. Each November we went to the packed British Legion gathering at the City Hall to remember the fallen and still in my mind's eye are the hundreds of poppy petals fluttering down from the balcony, with the music and the flags creating a sombre, unforgettable atmosphere. It had been a dreadful war, as all wars are, yet here we were once more with the war clouds gathering. For many families, still grieving for loved ones killed in France and now with young ones of their own, it must have been a grim time indeed as they contemplated the future.

It was pleasing to captain the football and cricket teams, but not so welcome to be made Head Boy and Head Prefect in charge of twenty Monitors. The honours were appreciated, but four o'clock was surely the time for other pursuits, not for staying behind for meetings with teachers. The time could be more usefully employed kicking a ball about, or practicing romantic manoeuvres in somebody's front room.

Yorkshire cricket epitomised everything that was good and wholesome. Winning record numbers of Championships whilst at the same time supplying half the England test team, was something taken for granted, and it was commonly said that if Yorkshire was short of a fast bowler they need only shout down the nearest pit shaft for one to answer the call. Hutton, Sutcliffe,

Bowes, Verity, Yardley, Sellars, Leyland, Turner, Wood and many other famous names came to The Circle and were duly hero-worshipped by hordes of schoolboys clustered around the white wooden boundary railings on the long summer evenings after school. Hull Cricket Club had its notables too; Charlie Flood, a gangling wicket keeper and hefty hitter, had also played for City at inside-left and scored a couple of dozen goals for them. Bastow, a gents-outfitter with a shop in Jameson Street, was a medium-paced bowler whose style intrigued me, when he reached the wicket his arms and upper body opened up like a flower and he looked so graceful that I tried to emulate him, but without success, so I stuck to my batting. Hicks, of the Hicks' confectionery firm, was a team member and Hopper another notable bowler; he was double-jointed and his arms came over together as he delivered the ball. This was confusing to watch, so what it was like for the batsman at the other end can only be imagined.

School Sports Days were held once a year on The Circle, when sports teams from every school in the city competed for prizes. Reasonable over the hurdles but useless at anything else, athletics was not me; neither was I into school concerts or plays. If there was nothing going on that interested me I preferred to stay home and read a book, seeing no point in doing things just because I was expected to. At home we played card games when there wasn't anything worth listening to on the wireless, Rummy and Whist were the most popular, matchsticks being the usual currency; we kept a book with our scores in it until we got fed up of keeping track and the book was lost. The most popular board game was Sorry, where feelings could run high, tensions later being relieved by Ludo, table-tennis or blow-football on the kitchen table.

Entertainment in the thirties was dominated by the magic of the silver screen, every neighbourhood having its own cinema, often referred to as the local 'flea-pit'. Some 200,000 people went to the pictures in Hull every week, the warmth the smoke and the sharing together of the cinema experience cost anywhere from 6d upwards. Whilst still watching Flash Gordon going round the universe in a converted bath-tub at children's matinees, I persuaded my parents to take me with them on their regular evening visits into town, to the first-run cinemas like the Dorchester, Cecil, Regal, Tower or the Regent. The black and white newsreels were increasingly showing film of Hitler's latest rant, and seemingly endless columns of German soldiers and tanks filled the screens. During the interval before the big film the usherette walked up and down the aisles spraying perfumed air-freshener over everyone, whilst at the front the ice-cream girl stood under the spotlight with her tray. Any conversation with her was drowned out by the racket made by the Mighty Wurlitzer organ which rose from the depths nearby, to the applause, or apathy, of the audience. It was the era when the stars of the films being shown on screen would sometimes make personal appearances. Dan and I met Lon Chaney Junior at the Criterion and came away, slightly awed, with signed photographs. The auditoriums of the cinemas, full of people, really seemed to become palaces of dreams. The Langham was the largest cinema in the city, seating well over two and a half thousand people, the Holderness Hall being not far behind.

Theatres were more expensive, the Palace had two shows nightly, 6.20 and 8.30, and occasional visits were made there and also to the Tivoli. One visit to the Palace with some other lads and our girlfriends saw us perched uncomfortably on wooden benches in 'the gods', with the stage looking an awfully long way down and far away. The shows were Variety programmes featuring a big name at the top of the bill supported by acts ranging from dancers, vocalists, comedians, ventriloquists, conjurors and acrobats to performing dogs. When the Alexandra theatre staged the pantomime Dick Whittington and his Cat, my parents took me to see the show. Afterwards we went backstage to meet the Cat, but I was more impressed by Jean Forbes Robertson, the Principal Boy, who had very nice legs. More often though, we went to pantomimes at the Grand Theatre in Leeds, which were lavish productions and, along with other northern pantomimes, were said to outshine their London counterparts.

Dad played billiards every Wednesday evening at Sloans Billiard Hall, on the first floor above the shops in Little Jameson Street. Occasionally mother would take me into town to meet him and we would all come home together, catching the tram from Waterworks Street. One night in the late '30s, when we were in one of the private rooms overlooking Jameson Street, the building opposite belonging to the Co-op Society, caught fire. We had a grandstand view of the fire engines and the ensuing activity, until we thought it better to retreat because the heat threatened to crack the windows on our side of the street.

The Wilberforce statue stood on Monument Bridge and when you walked past it towards Whitefriargate, crossing the lock gates that divided Princes Dock from Queens Dock, there were ships on either side. In the mid-thirties Queens Dock was closed, the road and pavement between the two docks being widened and surfaced. After they had filled in the dock, moved the statue and laid out the gardens, the fountain in Queens Gardens had its inauguration, when seemingly the whole town turned out for the event. We were on the outskirts of the crowd so dad hoisted me onto his shoulders to give me a better view over the heads of the people. The fountain offered a magnificent display of light and colour, with large and small coloured water jets, lasting about half an hour without repetition. The cascades of coloured water and the varying heights of the jets produced a display that couldn't have been bettered anywhere. 'Tourism' wasn't a word used in those days, but this spectacle would have brought them in by the busload.

The Guinness clock was a focal point in the city centre and at night its illuminated face could be seen the length of Ferensway as you walked along.

7: THE OPEN ROAD

In August 1938, dad took me on the tandem for a holiday in London. We caught the train to Leicester, leaving there in the early afternoon and got as far as Kettering by teatime, reaching Bedford on the first night and staying at the Fox and Hounds pub. As we cycled further south through Luton, the roads became increasingly busy; there were B&B cards in many windows and we chose a house in Elmer Gardens, Edgeware, for 2/6d each for the night. Dad thought that Stanmore would be more convenient for the tube and bus services so we moved the next day to a house on the corner of Marsh Lane, staying there the next three days, travelling by tube into London each morning after breakfast and returning late in the evening. We sat in Hyde Park one afternoon listening to the band of the Queen's Cameron Highlanders, walked up Knightsbridge to a Lyons Corner House for tea, and hired a boat on the Serpentine. The weather was perfect for the whole week and there was a trip on the Thames, visits to the Ritz cinema in Edgeware, Primrose Hill, the War Museum, the Zoo, the Science Museum and, on the last night to see Lupino Lane in 'Me and My Gal' at the Victoria Palace where 'The Lambeth Walk' was the current hit song.

We walked everywhere, eating at snack bars and consuming numerous milk-shakes at Express Dairies and ABC milk bars, all shiny chrome and glass and high stools; if our feet hurt we took an hour off and sat in the Monseigneur news theatre near Piccadilly Circus, watching the black and white newsreels, the 'March of Time' and Donald Duck, Mickey Mouse or Goofy cartoons. It surprised me how close together some of the famous London land-marks were; the Houses of Parliament, Downing Street, Whitehall, the Cenotaph, Trafalgar Square, were all just names heard on the radio and could have been miles from each other for all I knew, but here they were, within a few minutes walk of each other. It was fascinating to watch the trams disappearing underground into the Holborn Tramway tunnel. We both liked London and I think it did dad a lot of good as he couldn't chain smoke and steer the tandem at the same time, particularly as I was in the slipstream, complaining bitterly.

Leaving London for home, we had lunch at the Tudor Café in Biggleswade, mended a puncture near Alconbury Hill, ate at a transport café near Peterborough, went to a cinema in the town and stayed at a B&B in Cromwell Road for 4/- each. The roads, once clear of London, became less busy, and it was a real pleasure to cycle along the A1 enjoying the scenery, breathing in the clean air. My legs, tired at first, had strengthened as the trip progressed, and on the return journey they put in their fair share of the pedalling. We left Peterborough after breakfast, had lunch in Sleaford, passed through Lincoln, where the cathedral never seemed to get any farther behind us as we travelled down the unrelentingly straight Ermine Street, headed for New Holland and the ferry across the Humber. We were both tired out but felt fit and healthy and pleased with what we had achieved in the week. Whilst we were busy cycling up and down England, Prime Minister Chamberlain was also busy, flying back and forth to Germany, eventually landing at Heston waving a bit of paper for the newsreels and assuring us of, 'Peace in our time'. So much for him.

Apart from fountains, another thing the East Riding did well was to produce perfect drinking water; it came straight out of the chalk of the Yorkshire Wolds by courtesy of the Springhead Pumping Station, or Springhead Waterworks as known locally. A narrow path bounded by wooden railings skirted two sides of the building, with fields on one side of the path and the waterworks with its tall chimney on the other. Looking through the tall arched windows you could see the large wheel turning as it drew water out of the ground. Run the tap and the water came out pure and ice-cold, even in summer, and tasted wonderful.

In the later school terms, groups of senior school-children visited local businesses and factories, ostensibly to broaden their views of commerce, industry and the world of work in general, but also for the firms concerned to project themselves as good places for school-leavers to take up work in the months ahead. We came away from these interesting afternoon tours of factories with booklets and souvenirs, welcoming the change from the classroom. My first cycle was a present on my thirteenth birthday, a Raleigh sports model with a curved cross-bar and Sturmey-Archer 3-speed gears. It was about the same time that the change to long trousers occurred but, not appreciating all the messing about with cycle-clips I continued cycling in short trousers for some time.

A decent football was another present; this had oblong leather panels and a bladder that you pumped up, lacing the outer casing to keep it in and give the ball its shape. If you headed the ball on the laces it left a dent in your forehead, but that was nowhere near as painful as the scars left by the studs of the soccer boots of the period. These studs were hard circles of leather stamped together and hammered by three nails into the sole of the boot; they frequently came out during a game and stuck in the mud, or in an opponent's shin. As they cost 3d each to purchase and have them hammered in at the cobblers, you would see lads searching the pitch after a game looking for free studs. The boots themselves were made of coarse leather and laced round the ankle. The toe-caps were made of what, steel, lead, concrete? If you got a kick from them you knew about it. Running around for an hour in heavy boots clogged up with mud left you dead beat at the end of a game. Unless you'd won, in which case the boots felt like ballet shoes as you clumped home in them. We played our home matches on Saturday mornings or the occasional evening, on the school field that ran along the bottom of Northfield Road.

Street games were common. Marbles made of clay were 50 for a penny, glass ones 12 for a penny; these were rolled along the gutter, aiming to hit your opponent's marble and thus capture it. Sometimes the game was played against a shop frontage, but the marbles could roll down the gentle slope into the gutter and extra skill was needed. Cigarette cards were placed at an angle against a wall and were won by flicking your own card to dislodge them. Cards placed flat down against a wall had to be covered by your own card to be won, and great were the arguments as to what constituted 'covered'. Conkers were popular in season, those pickled in vinegar usually lasting the longest. Hide and Seek was popular with everyone except the neighbours, whose gardens were often trampled in the rush to find a hiding place. Whips and tops, kites and yo-yos came and went, Mexican jumping beans cocooned in silver paper from cigarette packets could be used for races and betting. Balsa-wood aeroplanes with rubber bands for turning the propeller had their day, as did gliders sent on their way by catapult. Cap guns, and automatics with pockets of tiny explosive powder on a paper roll were popular but more expensive. For the musically inclined there were mouth-organs, jew's harps, kazoos and, if all else failed, combs covered in tissue paper.

My aunt gave me a diabolo as a present; it was the only one in the neighbourhood but never attained the popularity of the much cheaper yo-yo. Bogies, however, were much prized. These consisted of a wooden box nailed or screwed on to one end of a broad plank of wood, with two wheels up front and two at the back. The de-luxe models had a seat inside the box. The front wheels were often fixed but could be on a swivel, in which event the contraption could be steered by rope from the driving seat. Wheels from prams were ideal, sometimes being removed from the original vehicle before its legitimate life had run its course. Someone had to push, their reward being a ride later on. These desirable status symbols were invariably home-made, vastly unsafe and liable to come to grief at any time, though the element of danger and possible disintegration only added to the fun. They were generally frowned upon by grown-ups due to the hazard they presented to people on the pavement; even passing mongrels snarled at them. There were hardly any scraps or gang fights other than at school, after all it was bare-knuckle fighting and it hurt. Nevertheless if you didn't stand your ground you were branded a sissy. Scraps at school took place on the small playing field nearby, which accommodated 3 or 4 swings set in concrete. Adjoining the swings area was a large field with a small farm at the far end; at our end of the field was a pond which froze over in winter on which we made slides. There wasn't much hanging around on the streets, if youngsters banded together it was more for mutual support, for example when they went to dances hoping to meet girls, than for scrapping with each other.

The school year was punctuated by the two weeks of the Easter holiday, the four weeks of the summer holiday, Hull Fair week,

Bonfire night and the two weeks holiday at Christmas. Hull Fair, the largest travelling fair in Europe, was a big event in our year; free to everyone, brassy, gaudy, tatty, exciting and smelling of smoke, cinders, chips and vinegar, noisy and sometimes scary, an annual event when the true citizens of the town let their hair down. You could go there in a gang and be sure of meeting groups of girls amidst the lights, the noise and the excitement. The Steam Yachts, Figure of Eight, the Circus and the Wall of Death were popular, together with the Waltzers, Dodgems, Cakewalk, Caterpillar, Moon Rocket and the Big Wheel. The power for most of the rides was provided by steam traction engines; everywhere there was steam and the music of calliopes, and you went home stuffed full of candyfloss, brandy snap, Carver's chips, and with cinders in your hair. The side-shows included boxing booths where challengers were offered £5, about two week's wages, if they could stay in the ring for a couple of rounds with one of the resident boxers. I'll bet it was seldom claimed, judging by what you saw of the bruisers who stood in their trunks and dressing-gowns at the front of the booths. The lights lit up the sky over the city and I would lie in bed late at night, the window slightly open at the top, listening to the noise of the fair and relishing the smell of the fish dock if the wind was from the south. And all of this for free.

Bonfire Night was another big event, wood and rubbish being gradually assembled on waste ground for weeks before the big night. Pocket money was squandered on rockets, jumping-crackers, Catherine-wheels and the like. Before I was old enough to be allowed near a proper bonfire, dad bought small boxes of indoor fireworks and we sat around our square living room table with its oil-cloth covering, staring at the wonders of the Volcano and the Trails of Fire. With money short, birthday and Christmas presents were often combined, and in this way came my first train set, a Hornby clockwork tank engine with passenger coaches and a circle of track. Some years later a move up-market was made to a Bassett-Lowke Flying Scotsman set, with signal standards, trackside bits and pieces, platforms, signal boxes, cross-overs and points added as pocket money allowed. Meccano was the popular metal construction toy of the thirties and one year there were hints that a construction present was in the offing. On the big day expectations were dashed, the hoped-for Meccano turned out to be a book with thick cardboard pages of shapes which could be pressed out and fitted together. By this time I had come to realise the value of money and that there wasn't much of it about, but the disappointment lingered.

In the spring of 1939, Senior School pupils went around local streets putting ARP leaflets through every door, advising people what precautions they should take in the event of air-raids, such as sand-bagging one room, blocking the ventilation bricks against gas, gluing thick paper or material in criss-cross patterns across windows to minimise flying glass and storing bottles of water and tinned food as emergency rations. That is what we did to our back room sometime that summer.

On Sundays, tandem rides to the coast were interspersed with taking one of the numerous excursion trains to the coast instead. Withernsea was a popular destination, where a turntable at the end of the line was an added bonus. Hordes of small boys would open the carriage doors and leap on to the platform before the train had stopped, charging along the platform to make sure of the best position to watch the engine being turned round ready for the return journey. Sometimes, instead of a proper train, Sentinel steam coaches were running the line; there were lots of trains in both directions, so if you missed one it didn't matter much. Paragon Station was crowded, with families queuing at one of the windows of the Victorian ticket office, or clutching their thick green cardboard tickets ready for clipping at one of the ten or more platform gates. On Sundays a dozen main line and excursion platforms could be in use at peak times, each train consisting of anywhere between six and a dozen coaches. Excursions extended further afield with the advent of Runabout tickets and other special ventures by the railway company, when days out at Bridlington, Scarborough, Filey, Whitby and as far as Staithes became possible. The coast lines travelled over the viaducts at Whitby, Sandsend and Staithes and were quite a sight to see as trains steamed across them.

A feature of the thirties was the annual Empire Air Day, when RAF aerodromes put on flying displays and exhibited aircraft on the ground; these events assumed added significance as the decade took us ever closer to war. Dan and I paid our 6d and visited the aerodromes at Leconfield and Driffield, our last visit being in May of 1939 when the planes on view included a Hawker Henley, Avro Anson, Armstrong Whitley and a Spitfire on the ground at Leconfield. There were ropes around the planes to keep them safe from eager hands...but... We rounded off the day by smoking his dad's cigars in the front room at Newington Street, making ourselves quite ill.

Reassuring, but depressing at the same time, we watched Herbert Sutcliffe make an unbeaten 234 against Leicestershire at the Circle. In almost the last match of our School Cricket League that summer I got a hat-trick, which our sports master Mr Thomas noted in his match report to the green Sports Mail; this was very curious as the opportunity rarely happens to an opening bat. In July 1939 I left Wheeler Street school, aged 13¾, two months before the outbreak of war, and in August we went by train to London for a few days. Trenches were being dug in the parks and sandbags were stacked against important buildings. We took a boat trip along the Thames, spent a day at Hampton Court, getting lost in the maze, and on our last night in London saw Arthur Askey and Tommy Trinder at the Palladium, travelling home the next day on the Yorkshire Pullman. In those days the trains had character, the stations smelt of smoke and energy instead of disinfectant and cancellations, and a single ticket took you anywhere in Britain, cheaply. It was to be our last family outing for some time, grim reality was about to take over all our lives and the world of the thirties was to become no more than a treasured memory.

Mam with her parents,
Colonial Street, 1905

Lucien Ludovic Camille
Roubier d'Andilly

Stanley Close, 1923

Phyllis Constance d'Andilly, 1920

with Mam & Dad at Burton Pidsea, 1926

Grandparents, Aunt Mabel and
Uncle Les, Bridlington 1926

with Mam at Burton Pidsea,
1926

with Mam & Dad at
Anlaby Common, 1928

Fashionista, 1928

1930

Mam and I in Prospect Street,
Hull 1930

with Josie, 1929

Mam and I at Grandpa's
allotment, Anlaby Common,
1930

with parents, grandparents, Uncle
Les, Aunt Mabel and Aunt Agnes,
Bridlington, 1932

Bridlington Harbour, 1936

Grandparents Close,
Bridlington, 1936

St. Chad Road, Bridlington, 1933

Mill Farm, Burton Pidsea, 1933

The well-travelled tandem

Dc 00568
LONDON(Croydon)
AIRPORT

6d.

To be shown always or given up on demand.

The Air Council will not be responsible for any damage, injury or loss, however caused.

Available on day of issue only. Not Transferable

T.86   D.2633   Wt.4106
110,000   2/38   D.B.,P.
51—1233
(SEE OVER

The Dragon
Rapide
Flight

Wheeler Street A.F.C.,
1938

Tennis Club, 1939 - Boys' playground
Juniors and seniors' classrooms at left, Domestic Science block at right

PART 2

THE
WAR YEARS

1: THE EARLY DAYS OF WAR

The schools across the city were closed when war threatened. Some re-opened at the end of August but Wheeler Street remained closed, everyone transferring to a new school in Priory Road. Our Report and School Leaving Certificates were written by a Headmaster who had no prior knowledge of us as pupils; he did his commendable best, but we all wished that our reports could have been written by our teachers at Wheeler Street. On the first day of September, amidst the general chaos of a country preparing for war, began the evacuation of over a million schoolchildren to the safety of the countryside and into the care of the billeting lottery. They were assembled at their schools, taken to the railway station by bus, and farewells said. On the morning of the 3rd of September 1939 we sat at home listening to the wireless whilst Neville Chamberlain told us we were at war with Germany. Hitler had sent his troops to invade Poland, calls had been made by the international community for them to withdraw, but Germany refused to halt their advance and Britain and France, treaty bound, immediately declared war. Little was said in our house but there was an air of sadness and it was very quiet; along with everyone else we had realised that war was inevitable. The RAF began dropping millions of propaganda leaflets over Germany. That would surely teach them not to mess with us. Germany's answer was to torpedo the nearest passenger liner.

Hitler had the effrontery to tell the world some years earlier: 'Even if we could not conquer, we should drag half the world into destruction with us, and leave no one to triumph over Germany... we may be destroyed but if we are we shall drag a world with us - a world in flames'. Even though forewarned by word, and confirmed by deed, the League of Nations proved ineffectual in confronting Germany throughout the '30s when they should have led the field; Britain had been let down by its politicians, was woefully ill-prepared for war, and it seemed that few, other than Churchill, had realised the extent of the evil on our doorstep. At school we had little contact with politics, the outside world only coming to our notice when we were handed a tin box for the Silver Jubilee of King George V and Queen Mary, although we couldn't escape all the business about the abdication of Edward Vlll.

We soon had our first experience of the eerie wail made by air raid sirens; it was a sound that would send a shiver down the spines of generations of people for the rest of their lives. Cinemas closed, anti-aircraft guns were installed within a ring of sandbags at Costello playing fields and we all went to have a look at the thin gleaming steel barrels and be reassured. There were some false air raid warnings where nothing happened and most cinemas opened again after a few days. A universal blackout was imposed. Heavy curtains were fitted behind doors to prevent light shining into the street when the doors were opened, and extra curtains and black paper blinds were put up at windows. All illuminations, including street lighting, were switched off. In the darkened streets people stumbled about trying to avoid lampposts or bumping into each other. Torches and candles quickly disappeared from the shops and Air Raid Wardens went around the streets telling people to, 'Put that light out', a phrase that soon caught on, and was used in radio comedy sketches to raise a wry smile.

Cars and buses were also trying to avoid bumping into each other, the metal grill placed over their headlights casting a beam of light downward onto the road only a little way ahead of the vehicle. Drivers' eyes were strained looking for the white paint marks on the kerbs, and traffic accidents accounted for more casualties in the first few weeks of war than did enemy action. The street lighting near us was by gas lamps, a man arrived in the early evening carrying a long bamboo pole with a hook on the end, opened the glass door of the lamp and turned up the flame under the mantle. Now, when darkness fell, the streets stayed dark and, had we but known, would remain so for many winters to come. The winter of 1939 was the coldest for half a century. In addition to the usual snow and ice, fogs blanketed the city, some of them very thick indeed as the outpourings from household chimneys mingled with those of factory chimney stacks. The mournful sounds of fog-horns on the river only added to the atmosphere of foreboding.

Dan and I cycled to Brough, where we lay in the grass at the edge of the airfield with a pair of his dad's binoculars and studied the planes on the tarmac at Blackburn Aircraft's camouflaged factory; there were flying boats, a few Bristol Beaufort torpedo bombers also a new aircraft that Blackburn's were developing, and it was a wonder that we weren't apprehended and interned for the duration. At home we were making balsa-wood models of aircraft, laying out airfields and engaging in dog-fights between Hurricanes, Spitfires and squadrons of ME-109s. When tired of that we made models of warships and fought great sea battles, in which the entire German fleet was sunk whilst all our ships returned safely to the harbour in a corner of the bedroom.

By the early '40s railway stations had their names removed or painted over and all country signposts had been taken away in case of invasion. Cycling along the road through Ottringham, you came across a group of concrete buildings on the south side of the road, enclosed by a wire fence. The buildings housed powerful wireless transmitters, also within the enclosure was an assembly of masts and aerials. We conjectured that amongst the transmissions beamed from Ottringham into occupied Europe, could be coded messages to the Resistance organisations. Great power would be needed to force transmissions through the jamming from German radio stations, and the station was indeed reputed to have been the most powerful medium and long-wave station in Europe at the time.

Grandpa was taken into Sutton Annexe hospital and I cycled out to see him a couple of times, little knowing that my own life was to be forever linked with this particular hospital. Air raid warnings became more frequent, and films with titles like, 'I Was a Captive of Nazi Germany', began appearing in cinemas. The black and white newsreels were almost wholly devoted to war pictures. We went to the Alexandra Theatre to see Harry Korris in 'Arcadian Follies'. Of all the theatres in Hull the Alexandra was my favourite, it had an air of faded grandeur, the sweeping entrance steps took you into the richly carpeted foyer then into the auditorium where the red velvet seats wrapped themselves around you, making you feel snug and comfortable.

The 'Andy Hardy' series of films began to appear, and my fickle heart was now betrothed to Judy Garland. In November some of us were called back to school for a gas-mask drill; how I hated the smell and the clinging rubber round my face. God, how we hoped it would never come to this. Scout evenings had started again at Transfiguration and we all returned after its temporary closure, but Duckie had volunteered as an Army Padre and it wasn't the same without him. I started borrowing books on all manner of subjects from the Carnegie Library which nestled amongst the trees in West Park. It was peaceful inside, and simply being amongst books and the centuries of wisdom and knowledge on the shelves was comforting in a world that seemed suddenly to be turning on its head.

Barrage Balloons appeared in the skies over the city. Some were floated from a fixed site, others were tethered by a steel cable to a winch on the back of a lorry and could be moved to positions likely to be most effective. The balloons were sent up when enemy aircraft were approaching, intending to make the bombers fly as high as possible in order to make accurate low-level bombing more difficult. Hull, being situated on the bank of a wide estuary, was a sitting duck anyway because the river stood out like a silver ribbon at night, guiding the bombers to where the city lay, waiting and virtually defenceless. That wasn't our only bit of bad luck. Bombers that had been on raids inland and had bombs left over from their original target, dropped them on Hull on their way back to Germany, so we had our own raids plus leftovers from everyone else. Then there was the bonus of an air raid warning when the planes went over, and another when they returned. The siren alerts, the broken nights' sleep and the bombing raids were to test the city to the limit in the years to come, but the war at sea had started on the first day and didn't finish until VJ Day some six years later. It was to be the longest battle campaign of them all and arguably the most crucial. Both my uncles were called-up into the army, leaving wives and children behind to cope as best they could. The future was black, unknown, and each day became a little life in itself that you hoped to get through safely. December came, it snowed and the year ended in darkness fear and apprehension.

After the confused ending to 1939, armed with my School Report and Leaving Certificate, I was ready to go forth into the world and earn a living. In the early part of January 1940 it snowed, then it froze and remained bitterly cold, snowed again, and for good measure fog blanketed the city. These were sombre days, with not a ray of hope on the horizon. In the evenings we sat around the fireside making rugs by hooking strips of material into rectangular pieces of hessian, whilst listening to the news or to Sandy McPherson playing interminably on the BBC theatre organ. Normal programme scheduling had all but ceased, and the theatre organ was the easiest option to fill the airwaves between frequent interruptions for government announcements.

I commenced a night class in engineering drawing at the school near the top of the Boulevard, two nights a week from half past seven to half past nine; goodness knows why because I don't recall being at all interested in the subject. The job that appealed to me most was working on the barges that plied up and down the Humber and the Trent, carrying grain and all manner of interesting cargoes, but it was a popular job and despite frequent enquiries at the local shipping offices, there were no vacancies.

Towards the end of January 1940 I joined a number of other boys for an interview at Wm. Cussons Ltd., where the position of office boy had been advertised in the local paper. The job paid nine shillings a week for five and a half days with Saturday afternoon off and was pleasant enough, working amongst the aromatic smells of a large grocery store. The offices were above the ground floor shop at the corner of Beverley Road and Norfolk Street, surrounded by storerooms full of crates of tea, bags of coffee, boxes of cheese and other commodities. My job was to carry out all the menial tasks expected of someone on the bottom rung of a commercial career but swiftly decided that it wasn't me.

This was a strange period in the war, not a lot happened apart from false air raid warnings, the building of concrete pill-boxes, cordoning-off of beaches, erection of air raid shelters and preparations against invasion. Food and fuel shortages began to bite and the shortage of fuel meant that there were fewer vehicles on the road. It was the lull before the storm and was later referred to as the 'Phoney War'. By contrast, the war at sea had already become a war for the survival of our island, U-boats continued to sink alarming numbers of merchant ships with the loss of men and cargoes and there seemed no answer to the blockade of our shores. Starvation loomed and the government urged everyone to 'Dig For Victory' by utilising any spare bit of land to grow vegetables.

2: TELEGRAMS IN THE BLITZ

Whilst working for a few weeks as an office boy, I had applied to the Post Office in Alfred Gelder Street for the position of Telegraph Messenger, delivering telegrams by cycle all over the city. The job carried more prestige and more money, but was harder to land. Although applying in early January, it was March before all the medicals and interviews were completed. At one of the interviews, the Postmaster unexpectedly required me to name, in order, all the streets on the right hand side of Anlaby Road going into town from Hawthorn Avenue, then all the streets on the opposite side of the road coming back again. I missed one, Perry Street, but he seemed satisfied. The starting wage was 12/6d per week, of which 5/- was kept for myself and 7/6d contributed to the family budget. The winter was dragging on and snow, ice and fog were not the best conditions in which to start a new job cycling around the city in the black-out. Nevertheless I was very pleased with myself, and my prospects seemed to have improved noticeably.

For the first few days I was taken round by a senior Messenger; after that I was on my own. On arriving for work you signed on, took a blank docket from a pile, wrote on it your name, number, (T44), shift times, and handed it in to The Box. An Inspector would place your docket at the bottom of the pile of other dockets belonging to Messengers sitting on wooden benches waiting for their turn. The Box was a glass-sided cabin where the telegrams, or 'wires', came hurtling in cylinders down a brass pneumatic tube from the Instrument Room on the top floor. The yellow envelopes were sorted by the Despatcher into pigeon-holes, each covering a different part of the city, called 'runs'. There were also the occasional Greetings Telegrams intended for birthdays, weddings and the like; these came in decorated golden envelopes and were in effect a second class wire. Ordinary telegrams, particularly any hand-marked 'Urgent', took priority, very few people possessed telephones so telegrams were the fastest form of communication. For an additional payment of 9d you could pre-pay a reply.

When a pigeon-hole filled up with wires, the Despatcher pulled them out and entered the number, given to each telegram by the Instrument Room, on to the top docket of the pile in front of him, also noting the time of despatch and the estimated time of return of the Messenger. He called out the number of the Messenger concerned, who then took over responsibility for the wires, sorting them into the order in which he expected to deliver them. An average time for an outlying estate like Preston Road or North Hull, with twenty or thirty wires, could be 70 minutes, for Bilton Grange 75 minutes, but if railway gates closed off the road at one of the numerous points in the city it could take much longer. The gates were closed by hand, the gatekeeper emerging from his hut by the rail side, waving a red flag by day and a lantern by night. Some of the railway crossings had foot-bridges and, if you felt strong enough, you carried your bike up and down the steps rather than wait for the gates to open. It was often touch and go whether you got to the other side before the last of the hundred coal wagons went through, the gates opened, and you were overtaken by hordes of cyclists. Walking turns to nearby locations were much prized, particularly in bad weather, these generally took about 20 minutes and when you returned to the office your docket went to the bottom of the pile, thus affording longer time in the office before you were sent out again. Also, if it was around lunchtime and a market day, a walking turn enabled you to fit in a call at Carvers canvas-covered stall in the market to buy chips and peas in the firm's time.

Walking turns were particularly enjoyable, wandering about Land of Green Ginger, Exchange Court, High Street, Crown Chambers and The Avenue, where doors opened off the labyrinth of corridors on to offices that were straight out of Dickens, with well-worn wooden counters, the standard pendulum wall clock, wood and glass partitions and long sloping desks where clerks on high wooden stools scratched away at ledgers. The offices were mellow with age and dust; not cheap current dust but quality dust, matured over centuries, and were warm and cosy on a snow-laden day. Sometimes the foot-soldier got as far as Humber Street or Wellington Street, where the boxes of fruit and vegetables spilled onto the pavements outside the warehouses, and where the horses, shackled up to their rullies, eyed the apples and wondered if it was worthwhile trying to pinch one. The occasional squashed fruit added its own aroma to the scene. Some of the produce came across the river by the early morning ferry and everything was hustle and bustle, lively and interesting.

Back at the ranch, those Messengers setting out on a run descended the steps to the basement, where the heavy red cycles waited in the long rack to be selected. Choosing the best of the cycles available you pushed it up the long slope into the garage area, out into Alfred Gelder Street and away. Over the next couple of years, as the bombing of the city intensified, there came some very sad days. As you got off your bike at the top of a terrace down one of the crowded streets of the city, the people talking on their doorsteps, or hanging out washing on the clothes-lines that criss-crossed the terrace, would fall silent and you could feel the pairs of frightened eyes watching you to see which house you were going to. People almost never sent wires to each other in those days but the War Office did and the Admiralty did, and their telegrams seldom contained anything but bad news. All too often it was... 'Regret to inform you... killed in action... missing in action'. We never knew the contents of the wires that we delivered, however our instructions were to wait whilst the telegram was being read, in case there was a reply to be made. To stand there and unwillingly watch whilst somebody's world fell apart in front of your eyes was tough, and it was these sad personal experiences that stirred emotions new to me, those of hatred and helpless anger. And to have to go through it day after day seared it into your soul like nothing else could.

The morning after a bad raid the streets were covered with debris, ARP Wardens and neighbours scrabbled about in the wreckage looking for survivors in what, the night before, had been somebody's home. Sometimes people were still trapped underneath the rubble, often there were bodies laid out nearby. Over everything hung the smoke, the smell of brick-dust and smouldering timbers. The power lines and telephone wires were almost certain to be down. Water from damaged pipes coursed through the gutters and across roads. Fractured gas pipes presented another problem. To help fight fires when the water mains had burst, a number of large water tanks had been sited at the end of streets and at other strategic points. When there was a telegram for an address that had been bombed, you had to ask people nearby if they knew about the occupants: were they dead, had they survived, were they in hospital, living at a different address, this information being written on the envelope so that the telegram could be forwarded. On a pile of bricks there would sometimes be a wooden board giving an address where any surviving occupants could be found, having moved in with a relative or were in hospital.

We were provided with a serge uniform that had to be kept neat and tidy and was regularly inspected. It consisted of a navy blue jacket and trousers with red braiding, black boots and leather leggings into which trouser bottoms were tucked; a pill-box hat with a shiny brim and a numbered brass badge. A leather belt with a brass buckle went round the waist, and onto this was slotted a leather pouch for the telegrams in their yellow envelopes. In a separate compartment of the pouch were spare telegram forms and, (for new recruits), a 3d copy of a compact Hull Street Guide. All the brass needed polishing daily, including the buttons on the jacket; a length of brass with a narrow slit for slotting the buttons into was very useful for keeping polish off the material.

There were about 50 Messengers, ranging from the new

recruits aged 14 to the seniors of 16 who were ready to move inside the office to clerical jobs, or to become postmen. Our week's duties were taken from The Board, which was changed and put up on the wall every Friday. We were divided into groups of six or eight Messengers, who worked different shifts that were rotated on a weekly basis. One week you could be on duty 0700-1500, the next 1200-2000, then 0900-1700, then 1100-1900 or a split duty, which everyone disliked, 0900-1200 and 1500-2000. Within these times twenty minutes was allowed for meal breaks. We usually brought sandwiches from home and these could be supplemented by peas and chips or a 3d fruit pie from Ma Bellis' bakery shop down Chapel Lane. There was a canteen in the office itself but we didn't earn enough, and rarely had time enough, to patronise it. We ate our meals in a large square recreation room adjoining the delivery room. There was a stove on which stood a large kettle, always on the boil, rows of small wooden lockers dotted around the walls, a few wooden chairs and, in the middle, a full-sized billiard table. This was little used and was covered by an oilskin cloth and a worn and warped plywood cover which formed a convenient table during the daytime. The plywood was stained with chip grease from the packages of chips and peas dumped on it whilst locker doors were opened to seek an enamel tea mug.

The billiard table was available in the evenings but by the time you had cycled to work, then cycled round Hull for eight or ten hours in all weathers, you wanted to get home more than you wanted to play snooker. Occasionally, if there was a night-class on the premises and your shift finished at a time when it wasn't worth going home and returning to the office, then it might be feasible to have a game, if you could find an opponent.

Night classes were held in the basement and were intended for those who wanted to move further up the ladder. The primary lessons were English, Maths, Geography and Mensuration, (measuring), emphasis being placed on clear and legible handwriting. Classes were held in a room in the basement on Mondays, Wednesdays and Thursday evenings from seven to nine and after these finished, half a dozen of us often went to the YPI in George Street, or to the Custom House in the Market Place. At both these places, the caretakers were relatives of one of the Messengers and we used to lark about in the basements amongst bags of musty files and, strangely, bales of hay. The Messenger with a relative at the Custom House was Jed Croombe. Before the war each office building in the city had its own caretaker who lived on the premises, usually on the top floor. At night, as you walked round the Old Town, the attic windows would be lit up and the streets seemed friendly places to be. But now, like the rest of the city, the windows were blacked-out, dark and fearful against the night sky.

There was a Crown branch office, South Newington, at the corner of Westbourne Street and Hessle Road, which was staffed by two Messengers from Head Office on a rota basis. They covered the hours from 0800 to 1830 and delivered to the area from Manchester Street to West Dock Avenue, including the kipper smoke-houses and the crowded streets and terraces on both sides of Hessle Road. 'South Newy' was very handy for me as it was only five minutes from home, being virtually at the bottom of the avenue. We had mild flirtations with Miss Sullivan, the young office assistant who was nominally in charge of us. Next door to the office lived a young girl who was very friendly, wore black silk stockings and was quite a distraction. In retrospect it is a tribute to our sense of duty that we didn't deliver all our telegrams to her house. Most of the wires went to the fish houses in the nearby streets or to the bookmakers in a house at the top end of Manchester Street, where the narrow passage that you pushed your way along was always full of nervous smoke and hopeful punters waiting to make a killing on the 3.30 at Kempton.

As if cycling all day for six days a week was not enough, a group of us often cycled to Bridlington or York on Sundays. On the strength of getting a drink when we arrived there, one Sunday I headed an all-star cast to see Gloria in Scarborough. She had no prior notice of our arrival and was so flummoxed at seeing a bunch of virile sweaty young males descending on her without warning in the middle of a quiet Sunday afternoon, her parents being out to boot, that she gave us all glasses of neat cordial without diluting them first. She so bedazzled the lads that they drank it anyway, there being an unusual number of stops on the way home.

The better shifts that were allocated to senior Messengers came my way in due course, the pay also increased, and I graduated from Woodbines and Gold Flake cigarettes to de-Reske Minors. The vagaries of war dictated what hours you worked, and when Germany invaded Holland and Belgium we put in some very long hours indeed. Sundays were worked on a rota basis and were usually easy days because there were few wires to take out, and none at all to the Corn Exchange, the Pacific Club or the city offices.

Cycling was pleasant in the summertime, but when winter set in greatcoats were necessary, and when it rained there were thick unyielding black Macintosh capes to cope with on top of everything else. Somewhere in this regalia you were supposed to find room for your gas-mask in its square cardboard box. Fat chance. Within a couple of months of gas masks being issued, very few people on the streets carried them, and we certainly couldn't cope with them. Snow fell and was shovelled into the gutters where it became slush and then froze into grubby ruts and mounds. The available road surfaces became narrower, and increasingly slippery with ice, as the cold intensified and the winter wore on. Your hands became so cold that fingers froze and you couldn't feel the handlebar, so you steered with your hands clenched and used the heel of your hand to guide the bike in the right direction. Messengers would come in, their hands aching with the cold and have to be persuaded not to put them on the warm radiators. We did wear gloves but they made little difference and after a few minutes on the road your fingers were numb once more. Tramlines were a constant hazard; a trap for the unwary at any time, they were lethal when the piles of snow filled the gutters, nudging cyclists towards the ribbons of steel in the middle of the road. There was the sideways manoeuvre, swerving across the lines at an angle before resuming your course, but you wouldn't attempt this with ice on the road.

3: FISH WITHOUT CHIPS

Night raids became more frequent and intensive, with bombs and incendiaries raining down from the darkness in sticks and clutches on a regular basis, sometimes specifically targetted, often indiscriminate. People began sleeping in the Anderson shelters in their gardens, others took refuge in the dank communal street shelters, and some lucky ones left for the countryside each evening to stay with friends. It was dark by teatime and we were often delivering wires when the sirens sounded. The streets were cleared and Air Raid Wardens shouted to people to take shelter. Sometimes the bombs quickly followed the sirens, at other times there were a few minutes of dread between the bombers being spotted approaching the coast and arriving over the city. AA guns opened up in conjunction with the probing beams of the searchlights as the drone of the engines became louder, and you had to make your mind up quickly whether to make a dash for the office, continue delivering wires, or take shelter. Invariably we carried on delivering wires until the first bombs fell, which helped to focus the mind remarkably quickly. As with every street, avenue and terrace in the town, we knew where the nearest air raid shelter was. When you cycle around a town all day, every day, for month after month, there's not much you don't know about its topography, and street shelters were your main resort when you were out and about. These were usually at the top of densely populated streets or near blocks of flats; they lacked ventilation and sanitation and could be death-traps if hit by a bomb so I didn't go into them if it could be avoided. As much of the city is below water-level, the shelters had to be built at street level because the sub soil became water-logged only inches down.

At home we had no outside shelter. The room directly behind the shop became our refuge room, with the chimney, the ventilation bricks and the door bottom all blocked-up or taped over against possible gas attacks; strips of fabric criss-crossed the window to minimise the risk of flying glass. Tins of food and bottles of water were stored to see us through until the gas clouds dispersed and we could venture outside again. And if the worst came to the worst we could go out in style, listening to the jazz records stored in the corner cabinet. There were stirrup pumps operated by Air Raid Wardens which drew water out of a bucket and could direct a trickle of water onto a fire. How inadequate it all was. Faced with a nation that had built up a large war machine throughout the last decade, then tested it out in the Spanish Civil War before attacking its neighbours, all we could do was wait to be bombed, gassed or invaded, with virtually no hope of preventing or surviving any of them.

Leaflets headed 'Chemical Warfare Notes' advised us about the different gas smells, the effects of gas on people and its treatment. This detailed information cheered us up no end. A sombre reminder of the threat of gas was not only the mask issued to all civilians, but also the small oblong box with a tiny window that was for your baby if an attack came, air being pumped into it by hand. As well as the night bombings, the threat of invasion hovered over the country and even as late as 1942 had not gone away, leaflets being issued saying that in the event of invasion, emergency rations for one person for five days could be purchased for 6/-, comprising: 1lb corned beef, one tin baked beans, one tin condensed milk, 2oz tea, 1lb sugar, 4oz margarine, and biscuits.

The war overseas was going badly, with most of Europe now in German hands. In May 1940 the British Expeditionary Force, BEF, was evacuated from the beaches at Dunkirk by the Royal Navy and a fleet of little ships which put out from English harbours, it being a miracle that so many troops were saved. However, much equipment was inevitably left behind for the Germans to utilise and, in the understandable euphoria at getting our soldiers back safely, Prime Minister Churchill had to remind the nation that evacuation did not constitute a victory. Only the white cliffs of Dover seemed physically and symbolically to stand between us and invasion.

Volunteers were forming groups to defend their factory or workplace. Initially called the Local Defence Volunteers, LDV, the name was changed to the Home Guard after a couple of months. There was an early move to start such a group at the Post Office and everyone joined up. There were no rifles, hardly any ammunition or even uniforms to spare, but little things like that were no deterrent and many groups were formed. In August 1940 they actually let Home Guard Private Close, J., complete with tin hat and itchy khaki battledress, near a proper rifle, a 1914 'Lee Enfield' model. Some of us were taken in a Post Office van to a firing range on the coast at Rolston, where we lay spread-eagled on the grass and shot at stationary targets.

Organised sport was suspended, all fit young men were in the forces or in the process of joining up. Maurice Leyland, Yorkshire's middle order left-hand batsman brought a scratch team to The Circle, and a group of us went along to see the match. The local amateur soccer leagues were also depleted, the stronger amateur teams like Kingston Wolves had been decimated when practically the whole team was called up. Attempts were made to carry on some semblance of league fixtures and I turned out for Wolves on a number of occasions. But some things didn't change and as the summer wore on, Hilda and I were back together. Schooldays behind us, the attraction, despite frequent interruptions, was plainly still there. She went away with the family and sent letters and postcards from Scotland. When she returned there were cycle rides to Little Switzerland, a wonderland of overgrown woodland trails amongst the hills of Hessle foreshore, complete with disused mill. And there were more walks to the meadows near the waterworks. Throughout that summer we were meeting every other day and by October I was going round to her house and her parents were visiting mine. We seldom went to the cinema, maybe thinking it was time wasted that could be devoted to more enjoyable outdoor pursuits.

The air raids continued, the sirens sounded practically every night and the bombing raids intensified. What manner of people sent aeroplanes to kill and maim defenceless women and children who had never done them any harm? Answer came there none. Night classes had started up again after a short lapse. Billy Thorburn and his Band came to the Tivoli and we went to see the show. Hilda and I seemed to have decided that the warmth of theatres and cinemas was preferable to the cold outdoor November nights. Regular shifts were being worked at the fish dock, where the busy time on the market was in the early morning and the duty hours were from 0630-1230, the rest of the eight-hour shift being worked at South Newington. Naturally all of this, being right on my doorstep, suited me fine.

Head Office covered Alexandra and King George Docks, where the merchant ships berthed. These were wonderful exciting runs, taking wires to the men just in from the Atlantic convoys who had brought the materials we desperately needed to go on fighting, and the food without which we should have starved. The sights and sounds of the ships, the men of the merchant service who were such heroes to us all, the hustle and bustle of the docks, all probably helped shape my future and character more than I realised. Tramp steamers can often have their own individual smell, a mixture of distant cargoes, oil, hot steel, rope. The police boxes at the entrance to King George Dock and Queen Elizabeth Dock were the first stop in order to find out where the various ships were berthed, and climbing aboard these wonderful vessels with their clanking winches and bustle everywhere was only the preliminary to finding the man you wanted. If the wire was for a seaman he could usually be found on deck, but if it was for a stoker or boilerman then it was down into the depths of the ship, along alleyways, past the galley with its appetising smells, down iron companionways into the heat of the engine room and then wandering about until you found somebody to ask. If the man you wanted was busy in the bilges straddling the propeller shaft, then down to the bilges you went, crouching along through the tunnel until you found him. Merchant ships were sitting ducks for U-boats in 1940 and to make the carnage worse, Admiral Doenitz ordered that no survivors were to be taken from sinking vessels.

In that summer 274 ships were sunk for the loss of 2 U-Boats, so easy was it to shoot the fish in the barrel and tighten the blockade of our island.

Unfortunately, dock runs down Hedon Road were infrequent. The major routes for telegrams were along the main roads and on to the outlying estates of North Hull, Preston Road and Bilton Grange, so I was happy to be allocated more and more frequently to the fish dock roster. There were two sections to Saint Andrews Dock; the eastern end nearest to the lock gates into the river was the North Sea market, and the western end, of similar size, was the Iceland market. The names signified little, as fish from anywhere could be landed at either market. A bomb had landed on the North Sea market early in the war and most of it lay in ruins. At the end of the Iceland market were some slipways where trawlers were pulled up and repairs carried out. Further on was the cod farm of Hampshire Burrell where fish was processed by female workers about whom alarming tales were told to new recruits, enough to make the bravest think seriously about slipping any cod farm telegrams they had into someone else's pouch. Of course they were only stories. Well they were, weren't they? Separating the Iceland market from the North Sea market was a strip of land which housed the Post Office, where we had our telegram sorting room, kept our cycles and ate our sandwiches. On the south side of the dock, called the 'dry' side, was the ice factory where trawlers filled up their fish-rooms with ice for the next trip, also a fish meal and oil works, a rope works, numerous small engineering works, some fishing companies offices, the dock surgery and the fishermen's stores.

There were usually two Messengers on duty, whose job it was to walk along the length of the North Sea and Iceland markets, delivering telegrams to the fish merchants in their Boxes at the back of each Stand. The Stand was a narrow strip between the Box and the quayside, where the trawlers landed their fish. It was always cluttered with kits, boxes and barrels of fish, filleting stands and people moving about in all directions. As well as being continuously wet underfoot with water and fish guts swilling down into the dock, hosepipes snaked everywhere and it became particularly congested when a trawler was unloading. When the trawlers came alongside, the catch was hauled up from the hold in baskets and swung onto the quayside ready to be auctioned, Dutch style. The fish were then cleaned and filleted at large wooden benches, with running water coursing through a well in their centre, before being open boxed, or taken in kits on barrows and loaded into the railway wagons or onto horse-drawn rullies waiting at the back of the market. The work of the Stands was directed from the row of concrete Boxes, perched like eyries behind the filleters. A prominent board on the front of the Box identified each merchant by name, and access was gained to these glory-holes by iron rungs leading up to a narrow doorway.

Telegrams came into the office by teleprinter, direct from the head office in town. You were given a bundle of wires and quickly sorted them on the table into the order in which the Stands came up. Some of the merchants and businesses had registered a specific name for their companies, thus reducing the cost of a lengthy telegram address, and you needed to know these code names, for example that wires addressed to 'Iceberg Hull' should be delivered to Hellyer Brothers, sorting them into the correct order of delivery before stuffing the whole bunch into your pouch and sallying forth onto the market. There were perhaps a couple of hundred fish merchants names to remember plus each of their telegraph addresses and the number of their box in the order they came up as you set out from the office. Woe betide you if you mis-sorted a wire and had to deliver it on your way back from the farthest end of the market; eagle eyes had seen you pass by on your outward journey and knew that the wire should have been delivered some minutes previously. Time was crucial to a merchant and a lost sale could result from the late delivery of a wire.

As you walked along, threading your way between the filleting benches, avoiding the barrow-lads and their barrows, the bobbers unloading a trawler at the edge of the quay, the mess of guts washing down the quayside into the dock, you were trying not to trip over the snaking hosepipes as you went. Especially did you try to avoid the lethally sharp filleters knives laid casually on the edges of benches that you might automatically clutch at if you felt yourself slipping. And, of course, there were seagulls everywhere, screeching at each other as they fought over the entrails. The men who worked on the fish-dock wore heavy boots or clogs and were sure-footed, whereas our footwear was intended for walking or riding bikes and was much less secure. Also, you needed to have a ready riposte for the barrow-lads, filleters or bobbers if they called out to you; it didn't do you any good to be labelled as snooty in that environment. I loved it, every bit of it, took to it like a duck to water and knew that I would be back amongst it all, someday. Extra hot soapy baths, in the regulation 5" of water, were needed when reaching home, girlfriends lacking appreciation of the healthy smell of the fish dock; at close quarters anyway.

Getting to the dock from our house presented two options. The first, and shortest, was to hump my cycle over the long narrow footbridge at the bottom of Liverpool Street that spanned the dozens of railway lines servicing the dock. The second option was to cycle further along Hessle Road to West Dock Avenue and then through the subway on to the eastern end of the dock, coming out near the end of the North Sea market. The subway was long and paved with cobblestones, had a low ceiling, ran beneath a mass of railway lines and was ill lit and forbidding. When the rulleys came through on their metal-rimmed wheels, the horses' hooves added to the noise and the tunnel echoed with the din, the horses shied with fright, became difficult to control and were a danger to cyclists and everyone around them. The downward slope into the tunnel saw the drivers struggling to control the momentum of their load before they came to the sharp bend in the road at the tunnel entrance. At the other end of the tunnel the horses strained to drag their loads round another bend and up the slope into the daylight. It was all a bit daunting. Most cyclists dismounted at the entrance to the tunnel and walked their bikes along the narrow footpath rather than try to ride through, the road being only just wide enough for two rullies to pass. The roof dripped water and the white glazed tiles that surfaced the tunnel amplified the noise. Many years later there was a serious accident in the tunnel when a load struck the low roof, causing an explosion, after which the subway was closed for good.

Appetising smells wafted from the canteens of Cullen's and Stanton's when you passed by them; there wasn't any rule that Messengers couldn't go into the canteens but it was understood that you didn't go into public places when on duty and in uniform, except on business. Anyway we never had the time. The fish-dock office in those days was the busiest in the country, both by number of telegrams and for the Messenger/telegram ratio. You got back to the office from one run to find another big stack of wires waiting to be sorted into order, turned round and went straight out again, the shift being virtually non-stop for the two of you.

In the summer and early autumn of 1940 the RAF flew high over the fields of Kent, pitting their Hurricanes and Spitfires against the Dorniers and Heinkels on their way to bomb London.

With London bombed into submission, the way would have been clear for Germany to invade England, and only a few young men and aircraft stood in their way. Britain was totally alone and isolated by now, Germany having over-run and subdued most of the Continent. If the RAF were beaten, we too would have been invaded and overwhelmed. Church bells, silent since September 1939, were to be rung as a signal that invasion was considered imminent and they were rung once, on the 7th June 1940, fortunately without a landing, but that must have been a very serious situation. Also in that June, Mr Churchill prepared us for the Battle of Britain that he knew must come soon.

It came in September, when Field Marshall Goering assembled some 2800 planes for the task of bombing London into submission. Britain had developed radar in the thirties and, aided by this invaluable tool, Air Chief Marshall of the RAF, Sir Hugh Dowding, masterminded a tactical strike plan for the meagre 700 fighter aircraft at his disposal, his plan proving to be the key factor in the battle. In the middle of September 'the few', though out-numbered and stretched to the very limit, defeated the Luftwaffe in the skies over southern England. Hitler knew that he could not launch an invasion without command of the skies, and postponed Operation Sealion, the invasion of Britain, until a later day. For the RAF it had indeed been their finest hour. We rightly remember those brave young men in their Spitfires and Hurricanes but sometimes overlook Dowding and others who made the victory possible.

The annual Post Office Messengers' Dance came and we all took our partners for the hokey-cokey and the last waltz, hoping to finish the evening cuddling up rather than diving into a shelter. The war news was continuously bad, Europe was subjugated and helpless and only Britain was still flying the tattered flag of freedom, waiting to be overrun. But life went on, with dances and visits to the pictures providing a brief escape from reality. In mid-December, looking to escape the cold, Hilda and I played table tennis at her house; it was fun, but not to compare with the cornfields of summer.

On Christmas Day I worked from 0730-1530, a good duty as things went, and at least the family could wait for me to join them for Christmas Dinner. In the evening Dan and I walked into town to the Cecil Milk Bar by way of celebration and walked home again to listen to records. One record that found its way into the collection about this time was Glenn Miller's Sunrise Serenade backed by Moonlight Serenade as the B side. Issued on the cheap Regal Zonophone label at 1/6d it shows how difficult it can be to assess a tune's potential. It was bought for Sunrise Serenade, but who remembers that now compared to Moonlight Serenade, that most haunting of wartime melodies.

4: BOMBED OUT

In early 1941, visits to the pictures were extremely popular, as people sought to escape the grim reality of life around them. You could go into the town intending to see a film at the Tower, fail to get in due to the lengthy queues, try the Regent, Cecil, Regal, Central, Dorchester, Criterion, Princess Hall and not find a seat in any of them. Most of the films were escapist, as were the lyrics of the popular songs of the day. In peacetime there is time for all manner of irrelevances, but when the reality of war takes over you go back to the basics of love, partings and hope for the future, for hope is all there is to hold on to. Vera Lynn sang the mood of those years and earned the loyalty of servicemen by her visits to entertain the troops on the front line in Burma.

Working in an all-male environment, girls seemed to be temporarily off the menu, being supplanted by the gang culture of the period. But we were young and knew what lay around the corner for all of us, so fighting each other seemed junior grade stuff. Instead, we did pointless things like up-rooting the Time of Closing notice board outside the West Park gates. Dan helped me carry this unwieldy trophy home one night and we were just about to take it up to my bedroom when mother saw us and made us take it back to the park.

In the middle of March 1941, a couple of very heavy raids saw a resurgence of preparations to resist invasion, which seemed to be presaged by the intensified bombing. We watched and waited, whilst the situation overseas went from bad to worse. Britain and the Empire stood alone, nobody looked like coming to our aid and we felt that the rest of world was waiting to see what happened to us before taking sides. The odds were staggeringly against us. The biggest asset we had was Winston Churchill, who held the nation together in those awful days when there was no one else remotely capable of doing so. Without his strong leadership at that momentous period in our island history everything could have fallen apart; and with Britain gone there would have been little or no hope for an enslaved Europe. Perhaps the biggest contribution

Britain made in the war was its refusal, under Churchill, to give up the fight, even though the situation looked hopeless. Eventually things did turn in our favour, the USA was provoked by Pearl Harbour into joining the battle, and Hitler made the massive blunder of invading Russia. Today everything is laid out in the history books with the benefit of hindsight, one event following another in documentaries, war conveniently fitted in between Coronation Street and News at Ten. But at the time, you lived through each day with a confusion of emotions; thankful you were still alive after last night's bombing, tired, hungry, fearful, angry, determined, not daring to think what tomorrow might bring.

At two minutes before three in the morning of Wednesday the 7th of May 1941 a landmine dropped in Stirling Street, about fifty yards from our house, killing many people and injuring many others. Where houses had once stood there were only masses of rubble with the all too familiar smell of brick dust hanging over the scene. Landmines drop by parachute so you don't hear them coming, and are indiscriminate in their targets, being blown by the wind. The raid had been going on for some hours and when the landmine exploded we were sheltering under the stairs, structurally the strongest part of the house, where a couple of make-shift beds were permanently on the floor in the cramped space. The blast blew the windows in, flying glass was embedded everywhere, doors were blown off, the roof was lifted and the tiles blown away. Soot and plaster covered everything, the curtains were in shreds, the ceilings had either collapsed or were hanging down, the wallpaper was in strips, the furniture overturned, ornaments blown away. We just sat there, suffering from shock, hugging each other and crying. In relief that we were still alive? Because the home and its contents that had been lovingly put together over the years was gone forever? Wondering whether more of the overhanging debris, or indeed the house itself, was about to fall on us, we picked our way through the wreckage onto the street where our neighbours were doing the same. Little groups came together but nobody spoke. Bombs and incendiaries scattered the town centre and the firelight reflected on our faces as we stood there, in shock, unable to take in what was happening. Hull must have looked like one huge bonfire; across the river in Lincolnshire people were said to have been in tears as they watched the city burn.

Hawthorne Avenue was impassable for bricks and rubble, and

with glass scattered everywhere we had to step carefully. Our faces were blackened, there was no electricity and the possibility of gas leaks precluded the use of naked lights to see our way around. All communications were down and with bombs still falling and the town centre ablaze, there was no likelihood that the Fire or Ambulance Services could help us; with so many incidents all over the city they were overwhelmed. We dragged some of the rubble to the sides of the road to make a passage for any rescue vehicles that might eventually get through, the bombs continuing to fall. Rescue work was going on in Stirling Street with people using their bare hands to remove the bricks and rubble to get to people trapped underneath. People helped each other to get over the shock and bandaged wounds as best they could. All this, beneath the fiery red sky and with the sound of the bombers still circling; it was what you imagined Hell could be like. The smell of brick dust, wood and plaster persisted as the whole town suffered. Gradually, as daylight came and the bombers departed, the long night ended and a long day began to unfold. The fires in the centre of the town were brought partly under control. Where sticks of bombs and incendiaries had fallen on houses, groups of people combined to quell fires and dug to rescue people buried in the rubble of their homes.

Looking at our house, its shell still standing and propped up on either side by other shells of houses, we wondered if it would be condemned. Some time later it was examined by the Council and was indeed condemned, along with adjoining properties. We received £27 compensation for the damage. However, the scale of damage to houses throughout the city quickly became apparent, necessitating a total re-think on the need to re-house thousands of homeless people, and any properties remotely saveable were re-assessed as repairable. Ours was one of those reprieved and was eventually patched up sufficiently to operate the shop as lock-up premises, but it was much longer before it was repaired sufficiently for us to live there once more.

That day the scene in the middle of town was chaotic. Shells of buildings in King Edward Street and Jameson Street stood like skeletons with their guts spilled out onto the street. Fires were still burning, the fire-fighters battling to bring them under control. In parts of the Old Town the wooden sets in the streets were on fire. Phones, gas, water, electricity, you would be lucky to have any of these. Paragon Station was out of action and there were no trains in or out of the city. We all turned in for work, but amongst the chaos few telephone lines were functioning and we felt as if the city was cut off. The telegrams that did get through we delivered through streets strewn with hosepipes, tenders and ambulances. No buses or trams ran, many streets were blocked with debris and hundreds of fires continued to burn throughout the city. The fire-fighters were stretched to the limit, water had become scarce and an assessment was made of water in the basements of bombed buildings in case it could be recycled.

Photographs of the bombing often show the streets after they had been cleared of debris, but it was quite different immediately after a raid, with people still buried beneath collapsed and smouldering buildings, acrid smoke hanging over the scene and the rubble strewn across the street making the passage of fire engines, ambulances or other rescue vehicles impossible. Rescue teams would be working amongst the tottering shells of buildings to get to those trapped beneath the wreckage. Fractured gas mains and unexploded bombs posed a threat. Death lay in wait even though the bombers had long departed the scene. The Post Office functioned to the best of its ability and all Messengers were on overtime; we often needed to carry our bikes on our shoulders over the piles of rubble blocking the roads. Barely on its feet, the town was still recovering from the night's ordeal when the bombers came over again the following night. On the first night they had apparently intended to bomb Liverpool but had been diverted to Hull. The second night their target was Sheffield but they were again diverted to Hull; or as the government communiqué called us on the BBC broadcasts, 'A north-east coast town'. How daft can you get?

More than 400 people were killed on the two nights and many more injured. Some of the worst incidents were in the street shelters, Regent Street, St. Paul's Street, Nornabell Street and South Parade. Again, everyone turned in for work, all of our runs taking us twice as long as usual. Likewise with Home Guard duties, a massive effort was put in to keep things functioning as near normal as possible. The Alexandra theatre was destroyed along with the big stores, Thornton-Varley, Edwin Davis, Hammonds and Powolney's restaurant and nightclub. Messengers would depart with a pouch full of telegrams and return much later with half of them undelivered and covered with pencil notes as to re-directions obtained, or a note saying that the premises were a bomb site and the occupants could not be traced.

On the second night, the Telephone Exchange in Mytongate,

the Central Fire Station, the Corporation bus garage, Rank's Mill, Eagle Oil Mill and Holmes Tannery were destroyed, together with buildings along the banks of the River Hull, hundreds of tons of grain, flour and seed falling into the water along with the masonry. The grain smouldered for days, its aroma mixing with the smoke from other buildings still burning. Statistics show that in these two nights there were 20 scatterings of incendiaries, 120 tons of bombs dropped including 180 landmines and 300 individual bombs; the raids started about eleven at night and ended about five in the morning. If you went through it, it is hard to describe the terror and the helpless anger of those unending nights. A brass plate set into the pavement in Queen Victoria Square commemorates those who died in the basement of the Prudential Tower, where they had sought shelter from the bombing.

Rescuing trapped people was everyone's priority, but amongst the chaos pets and animals were also suffering. Mother was very compassionate towards animals and belonged to NARPAC, the National ARP for Animals, doing her best to help any animal in strife, in war as in peace. We were often trotting off to the PDSA with some animal in a box to be treated, most often by the Chief Vet., Mr Doutre, and I still have a 1941 book of hers, 'First Aid to Dogs and Cats', that she used during the war.

Our shop was open to the street. All the cash, stamps, postal orders and other valuables were locked in the safe, but the premises needed to be made secure. As the phone lines were down, dad set off to cycle into town to appraise head office of the situation. Someone came to assess the damage and it was decided to board up the property as soon as possible. Meantime, dad stayed with the property whilst mother and I went to live with my grandparents in Elsiemere Walk, Anlaby Common.

Dad had been a Rifleman in the Great War but was considered too old to fight in this war so served as a Fire-Watcher, where his usual station on the night-watch roster was the tower of the church at the top of Hawthorn Avenue. When the tower was declared unsafe after suffering damage from the Stirling Street blast, he was transferred to a look-out post on top of the Carlton cinema, which also housed our nearest siren; the next one being on the Priory cinema. When an air raid was imminent, the sirens throughout the city started up independently and a hush fell over the darkened streets. As the last sirens' wail died away you could feel the tension spreading over the city.

With the post office in Hawthorn Avenue boarded up, we settled in with my grandparents at Anlaby Common. My bedroom was at the front of the house looking towards the main road, and contained some of my possessions, the many carefully crafted balsa-wood ships and aeroplanes inevitably not amongst them. There was now a much longer journey to and from work. When it was decided that the office could be re-opened as a lock-up shop, mam and dad cycled there on the tandem in the morning, returning to Anlaby Common in the evening. Shortly after re-opening we found that someone had looted the house, taking, amongst other items, my sets of lead soldiers, farm animals, numerous Dinky Toys, the Bassett-Lowke Flying Scotsman, its carriages, signals and track, also many smaller toys bought from pocket money over the years.

Hull suffered from German air raids more than any other English city; so said Cabinet Minister Herbert Morrison, who also observed that, 'Hull seems to be a kingdom of its own, with an identity of its own. It is a remarkable place with an individual character'. Out of 192,000 houses in 1939, 186,000 were damaged during the war. Hull had seventy bombing raids over four years yet was never specifically named on the radio or in the newspapers, as were London, Coventry, Southampton and others, simply being referred to as a 'North East coast town'. The Germans knew which town they were bombing so why the secrecy? After the war everybody naturally enough remembered Coventry. But Hull? 'Never heard Hull mentioned'.

The atmosphere was of a city besieged; we were all trapped, waiting to be bombed gassed or invaded, and this engendered a community feeling of everyone being in it together. My cycle, which was at Jordans in Prospect Street for repair, had been destroyed, no compensation was available for its loss so another cycle had to be bought, this time a Sun Lightweight with racing handlebars, which cost £10/12/6d including derailler gears and dynamo. Finding that much money wasn't easy, but we were working ten or twelve hours a day as the number of telegrams gradually increased, and the overtime helped.

At South Newington we continued to see a lot of the girl next door. Looking back I am grateful that my courting days occurred before tights came into vogue, it was all much more interesting then. Being at the top of the ladder, my duties were semi-permanently at the fish dock, or South Newington, and I was a familiar face to the merchants on the dock, sometimes being gifted parcels of fish.

It was now June, and teams were made up to play cricket on East Park or Pickering Park, until we acquired a permanent pitch on Beresford Avenue when we decided to call ourselves Beresford United. Long cycle rides became a regular Sunday fixture as the days lengthened. Gordon Hazell cycled with me to Filey and back one Sunday, leaving home at eight in the morning and arriving back at ten that night. The following Sunday 'the club' cycled to Scarborough to see Gloria and her younger sister Mary, a round trip of about 100 miles.

The roads outside town were very quiet, with hardly any vehicles on them other than those of the military who must have had their own maps, because all signposts had been uprooted. You could hear the songbirds, smell the meadows and the cornfields baking under the sun, take in the beauty of the wild flowers on the verges and in the fields, watch the butterflies and bees whilst you ate your sandwiches and drank from your water bottle, as nature continued to ignore the human stupidity taking place all around it. Butterfly bombs were later to be scattered by planes over this peaceful countryside. These were small explosive devices which, landing in grain fields, were intended to make the gathering of harvests a dangerous occupation. Wooden posts and other objects remained standing in fields for a long time, like silent sentries, deterring gliders from landing invasion troops. A few roadblocks manned by the army had to be negotiated, otherwise we had the countryside to ourselves, petrol being restricted to the military and other essential vehicles. Lonely stretches of beach were guarded behind rolls of barbed-wire, concrete pill-boxes appeared on the cliffs and at strategic places further inland; the first serious line of defence against invasion.

Came July and Hull got another pasting from the Luftwaffe. We were now working 12-hour days, turning out for Home Guard duty all night and attending evening classes, all of it involving the four mile trip from Anlaby Common and sometimes I didn't get home for a couple of days, sleeping on a bunk in the basement at Head Office. It didn't leave much time for anything but work and sleep, with most of the latter interrupted by sirens and bombs falling. Later that month the GPO received a bomb squarely on the garage entrance, next to the cycle ramp that came up from the basement to street level, so for the next few weeks we were humping our workman-like red cycles up and down some internal steps in the office, through doorways, past the sorting office and out onto Alfred Gelder Street via the Staff Entrance.

A number of Royal Mail delivery vans were destroyed in the bombing, some of them being ancient sturdy vehicles of the model T Ford lineage that had been kept going past their retirement date due to the war shortage of commercial vehicles. In my pre-school years the drivers had given me lifts when they came three or four times a day to clear our pillar-box in Hawthorn Avenue. After clearing the mail from inside our office and emptying the box outside, the vans went on to clear the box at the corner of Cecil Street further down the avenue, before returning and dropping me off outside the shop. The vans had an angular framework with a split windscreen, the doors were half-doors, wood at the bottom with brass door handles and a rolled-up canvas screen for the top half. The driver's seat went across the draughty cabin and consisted of a wooden bench with a couple of well-worn, horsehair cushions; the gear levers came up through the wooden floorboards and you could watch the road passing underneath through gaps in the floor. The horn was brass with a rubber bulb and gave off an imperious honking sound. It was a smelly, noisy, bone-shattering ride and cold in winter, but exciting if you were four years old.

5: WOODEN RIFLES

Sunny weekends tempted everyone into the countryside and my small roll-up canvas tent was again brought into use. Having organised our Saturday and Sunday duties in advance by bargaining with other Messengers, a group of us set off one Friday evening after work and cycled to Forge Valley for the first night's camp. We reached Whitby the next morning, finding time for a kickabout with a tennis ball on the sands before going through Pickering to York and turning towards home, camping at Millington Springs on the Saturday night and returning on the Sunday in time to go on duty for the late shift. Most of our summer weekends were spent playing cricket on various grounds around the city, popular venues being the Hull Brewery ground on National Avenue, Ideal Standard's on County Road North, Pickering Park, Beresford Avenue, Chamberlain Road, Costello Playing Fields and the land next to the railway sidings west of Calvert Lane, adjoining Smith and Nephews' sports ground, where matches were played on a Sunday.

Dan and I cycled to Harrogate and Knaresborough for a few

days, camping by streams, the rippling water sending us to sleep in no time. The rest of the holiday was spent at the pictures and a visit to the New Theatre to see Ralph Lynn in 'Rookery Nook'. During that summer a friend and I took out two girls from Pulman Street; this went on for weeks and was a strange interlude, the four of us being mutually compatible and swopping partners frequently. This period was memorable because of the frequency with which our courting in the tenfoots was interrupted by 'the buzzers', as the air raid sirens had come to be called. What would it have been like to have experienced normal teenage years I wondered? My generation was bombed through most of ours and then went into the Forces to get shot at; if you were fortunate enough to come through it all unscathed, when you came home you were not only older and a different person, but the fun years of youth had passed you by. They say what you never had you never miss, but I wonder. Maybe it was a subconscious feeling of being deprived of something that sent me out later on, to make up for the lost years and find some fun for myself.

By October Hilda and I were together again, but now seeking the warmth of the back seat of the pictures rather than the cold draughty doorways and passages of Hawthorne Avenue. The bombing continued, the sound of the sirens intruded into the cinema, making the flashed-up warning of an air raid on the screen superfluous. Some people left to seek the nearest shelter but others stayed in their seats, the performance usually continued anyway. Becoming frustrated with something at work, I argued with an Inspector, landing myself with three hours extra unpaid work for shouting at him. Hilda consoled me at the night-time; she was very good at consoling was Hilda.

Night classes had resumed now that autumn had arrived, and sessions of general horse-play in the basement of the YPI expending male energy, resumed with it. There was a group of us who naturally gravitated together, Ken Priestman, T26, (Kadie, because he always wore his hat at a rakish angle), Gordon Hazell T15, (Acker), Frank McGee T46, (Trigger, due to his volatile temperament), Harold Wilson T16, and me, (Jake, T44). George Tebbs, (Tibby, T13), and J.E.D. Croombe (Jed, T50) also joined in from time to time. We did runs together that stretched the boundaries of the art like combining deliveries to Bilton Grange with telegrams for North Hull. It was all about timing. If two of us were going out at the same time, one east and one north, we would set off together up Holderness Road, sharing the East Hull deliveries between us before making our way over roads, lanes and fields to Beverley High Road to deliver the North Hull wires, returning to the office along Beverley Road. There, we ended up breathless, exhausted and hopefully within the time allocated on our dockets. If you were over the estimated time by a noticeable amount there were awkward questions asked, and stories needed inventing in order to avoid the consequences. The Inspectors were aware of these escapades and would occasionally take a cycle ride along one of the main roads to try and catch us in the act. Sneaky maybe, but it was doubtless in their Civil Service job description. However, no one was ever brought to account, so perhaps the Inspectors did what they had to do but turned a blind eye and entered 'nil sighting' reports in the book.

The group organised the weekend cycle rides and were the nucleus of the football and cricket teams, the latter complicated by Trigger, whose glasses frequently fell off at crucial moments when chasing a ball into the outfield. If there was a Messengers Dance or other social occasion we banded together for mutual support, in the office as well as out of it, and Authority viewed us with disquiet at times. Following my bust-up with the senior inspector, Trigger thumped the night class teacher and he and Harold were called to the inner sanctum of the Head Postmaster and given the sack. Probably I came near to it, but there didn't seem to be anything definite to pin on me so they sacked some of us to set an example to the rest. It was approaching Christmas 1941 and I was becoming increasingly fed up.

My duties at Head Office now had early finishes, 6-2, 8-4, 9-5, 10-6, and as much of the work was on the fish dock where it was always an early finish, my evenings and Sundays were free.

Although our group had been split up, we continued to meet for matches and weekend cycle rides. Trigger lived out at Benningholme Cottages near Skirlaugh and was hard to keep track of, but Acker Hazell had got a job coaling on the railways, much to everyone's envy; we all thought that working around steam engines a far better job than delivering telegrams. Meantime I was working on my own agenda. The counterpart of boy Telegraph Messenger was girl Probationer, and they worked on the top floor of the building, on the telephone switchboard or in the Instrument Room. The latter was full of teleprinters and patrolled by female guards, or Supervisors as properly known. Sometimes the girls delivered messages to other parts of the building and would pass by The Box where the lads were sitting around waiting for their next turn and there would be muted whistles, followed by black looks from Despatchers and Inspectors alike. Occasionally we took messages up to the Instrument Room, with the possibility of a clandestine meeting in the corridors, or better still, in the lift. It all added spice to a day's work.

Jean Cutting was a year or so younger than I; lovely and vivacious, she worked as a Probationer Telephonist and lived in nearby Hamlyn Avenue. We started going out together and were regarded by everyone as a couple, waiting for each other after work and cycled home together. We went to cinemas and dances and snuggled up in the ten-foot behind her house, until her parents took pity on us and brought us in out of the snow. When our group of lads went to the pictures Jean was always included; she had two younger sisters, Susan and Gloria. Jimmy Cutting, my holiday friend from Burton Pidsea, was their cousin.

By now the Home Guard had kitted us all out with the standard army battle dress with a 'Home Guard' flash on the shoulder and there were occasional platoon forays to a firing range at Rolston where a proper army instructor shouted at us. We learnt how to drill and fire a rifle, though there were few of the latter available at the time and the drill was often carried out using wooden rifles instead. More than once the Staff Entrance steps at the Post Office found themselves guarded all night by a 16 year-old holding a piece of wood. Guard duty at the office came round regularly and we slept on bunk beds in the basement between stretches on guard, larking about there when not on sentry duty outside in the dark, waiting to skewer German parachutists. Restless, my friends gone, I was at the top of the tree seemingly going nowhere. Entering the Forces and returning, (hopefully), after the war to be a clerk, postman, or a sub-postmaster didn't appeal. Jean and I were very young and God only knew what the war was yet to deal out for both of us. Meantime, the golden evenings of spring and the high grass beyond the waterworks awaited before the nightly sirens sounded; the future would have to take care of itself.

Jean spent periods in London and other towns, where she had volunteered to help staff the Exchanges, which were under extreme pressure in those dark days. On one of these occasions I went out with Sheila, a lovely doll of a girl with an impish face and a sense of humour to match. We cycled a lot, lay in meadows and laughed a lot. Once, looking for the site of Meaux Abbey, all we found was a pile of stones in a field, but we probably had more fun there than the Monks did. Visits were made to her house in Braemar Avenue and she spent time at our house. As with Jean, maybe it could all have been different, one day, without a war. Then Jean returned from her travels and it was back to normal. At the beginning of Willerby Road there were two back-to-back telephone boxes which we used for special things that we wanted to say to each other, often to the amusement of a gang of urchins who had twigged what we were doing and pressed their noses to the glass. Jean came to our house frequently, meeting my parents, and we kept in touch in the years ahead, when I was to be away. Meantime things had taken a sudden turn for the worse at the good old GPO.

One particular Messenger was ostracised by everyone because he told tales. Edicts issued by the Inspectors appeared on our notice board, forbidding this or that practice, matters that only another Messenger could have known about. He was duly taken to task by a group of us and the result was foreseeable, we were paraded upstairs before the Assistant Postmaster and advised that it might be a good idea if we left before we got the sack. For some time I had been writing to various firms to be taken on their books, to C.D. Holmes, Amos and Smith's and George Clark, the brass founders, with a view to becoming an apprentice marine engineer. Letters were also written to the Shipping Federation and various shipping lines about becoming an apprentice deck officer; all of it without success. With everyone turning me down at sea I even turned to the RAF at Cranwell, but my heart wasn't really in aeroplanes, all I wanted was a ship. Then I caught wind of an avenue previously unsuspected.

6: MORSE CODE AND RHYTHM CLUBS

How about going to sea as a marine Wireless Operator? I knew nothing about wireless and had hitherto not been particularly interested in the subject, but if it provided a passport to finding a ship then let's go for it. There were wireless colleges dotted around the country; the college at Colwyn Bay was well known through advertisements in the national press, and it may have been through seeing one of their adverts that I learned of their existence. There was even a wireless college nearby at Bridlington; but all of these were fee-paying private colleges, so in addition to paying for board and lodgings there would be tuition fees to find, financially beyond my reach. However, investigations led me to the unbelievable reality that there was a wireless college right on my doorstep, which meant that I could live at home whilst taking the course. Not only that, but the courses were provided at a municipally funded Technical College, meaning that no tuition fees were involved. Things seemed to be looking up.

The college was in Park Street at the junction with Londesborough Street, opposite the long low Artillery Barracks with its old canon on the forecourt. I had already paid a couple of visits to the wireless department there by the time I was declared persona-non-grata at the GPO. The entrance level for the course was that of Secondary School or above; an interview and a couple of test papers disposed of that problem and I was accepted for the next term, commencing after the summer holidays of 1942.

My parents were willing to support me for however long it took, and the few short weeks between leaving the Post Office and commencing the wireless course passed in a state of contentment not felt for some time. At last I was going somewhere, the course was charted and now it was all up to me. The summer passed with cycle rides, sojourns in the meadows and playing cricket. A local man, Lester Atack, had put out feelers with the idea of starting a Jazz Club, or Rhythm Club as they were known then; we talked, and soon afterwards the Hull Rhythm Club was formed with a handful of members. What we had in common was a love of jazz; which didn't mean dance bands, cocktail pianists, crooners, or any of the peripheral stuff often referred to as jazz, just the basic, mainly black, American music that we had come to know from our fragile shellac 78 rpm records.

The Rhythm Club met on Sunday afternoons in the front room of a house in Hinderwell Street, a motley crew, including some airmen from Leconfield, a couple of Messengers, a lad with a guitar, and Lester, who played the drums whenever he could lay his hands on any. We grew in number, each pleased to talk to someone who spoke the same language. A membership card was issued, the annual subscription being 2/6d. Lester and his wife Judy lived in the top flat at 49 Pearson Park, where we met regularly to talk and play records until the early hours. In August the club moved to larger premises at the corner of De Grey Street on Beverley Road, where we could continue listening to our records, hold discussions and enjoy jam sessions on Sunday afternoons, as by this time we had attracted quite a few people with assorted instruments. There were to be many changes of venue after that, and most of them were to be visited over the ensuing years, including a room over a cobbler's shop in Salthouse Lane, a large room at the YPI, and the Windsor Hall in Argyle Street.

At last on course for sea-going, I absorbed all the news about the merchant navy. It was June 1942, and one of the worst-ever months for Allied shipping losses, with 627,000 tons sunk along with their crews. The German plan to isolate our island and starve us into submission was well on course, and it was touch and go whether we were going to survive. Everything was scarce and becoming scarcer; people saved scraps of material and bits of wood, straightened out old nails, planted vegetables in any square yard of earth, re-used anything they possibly could and threw nothing away. The Germans were still busy bombing people, setting up extermination camps, turning Europeans into slave labourers in factory, mine and field and torturing or murdering anyone they didn't like, and only the English Channel stopped them from trying it on us.

An elementary book about electricity and wireless was purchased from Brown's Bookshop in George Street and studied at home. The cinema was still high on everyone's escapist list and in the twelve months of 1941 I made over 100 visits. This would have to slow down pretty sharply, and soon, because the wireless course, as outlined at the interview, consisted of lectures and practical work during the daytime, the notes from which had to be written up in the evenings ready for the next day. Also there was no longer any money coming in. The course was normally twice its current length, but had been condensed in order to turn out qualified Operators as quickly as possible to replace those lost at sea. It looked like a lot of hard work and was just the challenge needed after the non-mentally taxing job of delivering telegrams.

After three years, by the middle of 1942, the threat of invasion seemed to have diminished but still hung in the background like a dark cloud. The bombing raids continued to hit 'a NE coast town' on a regular basis and people came to recognise the sound of the aircraft engines in the darkness, particularly the labouring engines because these were the laden bombers, and you tried to separate the Junkers, Dorniers and Heinkels coming one way from the Lancasters, Halifaxes and Wellingtons going the other.

All able-bodied men were fighting overseas or were on ships, in camps, in barracks or on airfields dotted all over England. The streets were populated by children, the middle-aged and the elderly, predominately women, but with a scattering of youngsters like ourselves. The call-up age for military service was 18 to 41; I was 16 when the wireless course started again after a brief summer break. The blackout descended nightly, the shops were virtually empty, except for the sparsely-stocked food shops which had the inevitable queue of housewives, holding their ration books containing the coupons for their family's weekly food allowance. The ration for one person for one week was 4oz bacon, 8oz sugar, 2oz tea, 2oz butter, 4oz margarine, 4oz cheese, 2pts milk, meat to the value of $^1/_2$d and one egg per fortnight. 'Spam' and dried egg powder made their appearance. Everything outside rationing you got when and where you could, bread was still un-rationed and continued so throughout the war. Government subsidised British Restaurants provided a meal for about a shilling to supplement the lack of nutritional meals available at home, also some fish and chip shops remained open, dependant on a few of the older vessels braving the mines and dangers of the North Sea to fish the inshore waters. Beer was rationed, chalked notices on boards were placed outside pubs to let customers know that some barrels had been delivered and that they were open for business. We were short of raw materials and street rallies were organised, at which people donated frying pans and aluminium pots to build Spitfires. Railings outside private houses and in the parks were cut down to make guns and tanks.

The teachers at the college reflected the war-stretched situation. The head of the wireless department was a genial, portly man in his '50s, H. Redvers Smith. His assistants were an ex-RAF man and a MN wireless operator, both released from the services as unfit, the latter a bag of nerves from his war experiences. The other member of the team was Mr Kauffman, a retired GPO telegraphist. He was about seventy and sent the most beautiful morse you could wish to hear, steady and rhythmic, sure and confident, free from errors and pure joy to listen to. If morse was music, it was he who would write the symphony. We didn't realise it at the time, but he was the most important of all our teachers. Earlier in the war the college had trained members of the Royal College of Signals, some of whom had gone on to Bletchley Park for intelligence gathering, listening to enemy wireless messages and passing them on to the ENIGMA de-coders. In peacetime, students could study for the 1st or 2nd Class PMG Certificate of Proficiency in Wireless Telegraphy, and there was also a simplified Special Certificate suitable for smaller craft, which placed less emphasis on the technical side but carried the same Morse Code requirements. It was the latter, the Special Certificate, which was the only one issued during the war when training Wireless Operators for merchant ships and was the one we were studying for.

Merchant ships in wartime did not break radio silence to send messages when at sea, to do so would have been to give away their position to listening U-boats, who could use their Direction-Finding equipment to pinpoint the ship's position and that of its convoy. The only exception to this radio silence was an SOS. Operators were not required to send morse, although they obviously needed that capability, but they were required to listen. And to listen well, because the traffic addressed to their ship individually, or to their convoy as a whole, was broadcast blind. This meant that you had to take messages down correctly, the first, and often only time that they were transmitted; you couldn't call the station back and ask him to repeat a bit that you'd missed. Also, you were standing by the receiver five minutes before the broadcast was scheduled, not five seconds after it had started. Reception was crucial and was given priority over the technical and practical side of the job; ships were being lost in numbers, their crews with them, and it was imperative that Operators be made available for sea-going as quickly as possible.

It takes time to learn Morse up to speed, it comes gradually, week by week, month by month, so every day at college there was either a full morning or afternoon's practice. Morse is not sent by the fingers or the hand but by the wrist; if you didn't get that right at the outset it was uphill all the way. The first advance in speed to 10 or 12 words a minute comes easily, but after that progress becomes slower. A 'word' contains five characters and the exam requirement was 20 words a minute for plain language. Figures and letters mixed together, 'code', were also grouped in fives, the speed required being 16 groups a minute. It is easier to send morse than it is to receive it at the same speed.

Our classroom was on the corner of the first floor of the college. From our windows we looked across Londesborough Street to where the sick children lay in their beds on the balcony of the Children's Hospital. The beds were wheeled out into the sunshine when the weather was good; we waved to the children from our half-open windows and they waved back. The morse room contained four wooden tables, each about 12ft long and 3ft wide, with a wooden bench on either side. At intervals along each side of the table were morse keys, the traditional Post Office standard key, nicknamed the 'bone-crusher', each one connected to two brass strips going the length of the table. At the end of one of the benches sat Mr Kauffman at his master key, quiet, gentlemanly, a little stern. The keys were wired up so than anyone could practice with headphones on his own key or switch over so that his keying could be received at any other position in the room. We listened to Mr Kauffman sending the morse characters and did our best to emulate him, each in turn. The rest of our day not devoted to morse practise was taken up with theory lessons on electricity and magnetism, concentrating on short and medium wave marine transmitters and receivers, direction-finding equipment and lifeboat transmitters. We also learnt practical maintenance and fault finding on transmitters and receivers so that the practical work tied in with the theory lessons. References were made to the two text books used on the course, the Admiralty Handbook of Wireless Telegraphy, which looked as if it had been produced in the Crimean war, and the periodically up-dated Technical Instruction for Marine Wireless Operators by Dowsett and Walker, always referred to as 'Dowsett' and recognised as the profession's bible.

We attended classes from 9 to 4.30 with lunch from 12 to 1.30. Sometimes I went home to lunch on my cycle, but more often took sandwiches and sat with others on the long wooden bench at the back of the big arched shed on Corporation Field. Except on hot days, when it smelt. Once a week I took my sandwiches to grandma d'Andilly's house in nearby Guys Terrace, Colonial Street, stepping back in time amongst its aspidistras, horse-hair sofa, Victorian ornaments, gas mantles and cats curled up everywhere. There were some nubile girls around the college, but I was still going out with Jean and, by the look of things, spare time was going to be at a premium, leaving little time for any extra-curricular activity.

Each Friday morning there was a Morse test, during which Mr Kauffman sent to us for three minutes in plain language, then in groups of five-figure code and finally in groups of figures. Our papers were marked during the next couple of days, anyone not keeping pace with the class would receive individual help. Following the receiving test was the individual sending test, where we each sent a piece of prescribed language text, code and figures, the rest of the class taking this down for practise. It came to my turn and after I stopped sending there was a silence in which Mr Kauffman brought out a purse from his jacket pocket, took out a sixpence and, without a word, pushed it across the bench with a smile. Nothing like this had happened before and he seemed as pleased as I was. Morse is a language of character and rhythm and enjoyable to listen to when well sent. It is also like riding a bike, once learnt you don't forget it.

There were thirty lads in the class, all about the same age, however, there were three of us who naturally gravitated together, George William Cherry, Geoffrey Robinson Corlyon and me. We studied together, drank together, listened to jazz together, took out girls together and went away on weekends together. George's father owned Fretwells Printers in Scale Lane, Geoff was the son of a car-dealer and entrepreneur of some style, whose business premises seemed to be the Calvert Club. Known as the '3Cs', even to The Establishment, we studied alternately at each others' houses in the evenings, our mothers providing sandwiches, roast potatoes and cups of tea. (My great aunt, Cecilia Louisa Roubier d'Andilly, married a George William Cherry, a seaman, in 1898, and George and I speculated about us being distant cousins but never got around to resolving the matter). George lived in Harland Way, Cottingham, and Geoff in Calvert Lane, but the problem at my house was the record collection, which was in the room where we were studying, consequently some of these evenings saw little work done. The collection eventually numbered about six hundred 78s and had probably reached half that number by 1942. By unanimous agreement we voted, 'I wish I could shimmy like my Sister Kate', by Muggsy Spanier's Ragtime Band, as our signature tune. More jazz was listened to, analysed, discussed, criticised, admired and joyfully accompanied, at the expense of our studies, than was good for us. The records were played on a wind-up gramophone which had no volume control, and rolled-up socks had to be stuffed in the sound box after midnight in deference to my parents trying to sleep in the bedroom above. College work was hard going as the twelve-month course had been condensed into two terms, covering the period from early September 1942 to April 1943 and my time was divided between studying and Jean, with little time for anything else.

The Americans, now involved in the war in Europe, were also fighting the Japanese in the Pacific. A crucial battle was being fought on the island of Guadalcanal in the Solomon Islands where, in atrocious jungle conditions, they halted the advance of the Japanese towards the northern coast of Australia. Australian forces were fighting the Japanese in New Guinea. On the Russian front, the Germans were advancing on Stalingrad in one of the most bitterly fought campaigns of the war, a million Soviet soldiers dying in defence of their city. Nearer to home, convoy ON127, comprising 32 merchant ships, was attacked by a pack of 13 U-boats in mid-Atlantic, twelve merchant ships and one escorting destroyer were lost with only one U-boat being damaged. The war news was discussed daily at college as well as at home. There was a victory at last when Montgomery's 8th Army broke through against Rommel's Africa Corps in the North African campaign at El Alamein, and the normally silent church bells were rung in celebration.

7: CAMPBELTOWN

1942 turned into 1943 and, as spring came to England, the war in the Atlantic gradually turned in our favour. The valiant efforts of the Canadian Navy and Air Force in reaching further and further out into the Atlantic, plus the support of American forces and the ever-extending range of RAF Coastal Command, meant that air cover for convoys now stretched across the ocean from England to the States. The air war over Europe also turned in our favour and we suffered fewer air raids as British and American bombers began to dominate the skies, flying deeper and deeper into Germany. The last Jews in the Warsaw ghetto were rounded up and sent to Treblinka, where the bitter weather, starvation and beatings would see them systematically worked to death as slave labour. In the Pacific the Americans, including future President Lt. John F. Kennedy and his crew of PT109, were fighting their way around the islands of Kolumbangara and Gizo in the Solomon Islands.

Whilst the war raged over the globe, we were sitting our exams, preparing to set out on a sea-going life; if we lasted that long. A leaflet headed 'Wartime Opportunities for Holders of the Special Certificate in Wireless Telegraphy' was handed to each of us, giving the pay for 'Radio Officers in the Merchant Navy' as £9/17/6d per month plus War Risk Money of £5 per month and Differential Pay of £2/-/- per month whilst on Ships Articles', noting that 'Radio Officers in the Merchant Navy rank as Officers and are required to wear uniform'. On the day that we were presented with our certificates, enabling us to apply for jobs with

Marconi, Siemens or one of the shipping companies, a resplendent figure in Royal Naval uniform, cap at a jaunty angle, epaulettes bright, light reflecting off badge and buttons and with gold braid everywhere, swept into the room and perched himself nonchalantly on the edge of a table at the front of the class. This was Colin Matheson, an officer in a branch of the Royal Navy that none of us, up to that moment, had ever heard of. This was about to change, pronto. Having been granted permission to address us he made the most of it. Mr Matheson represented one of the 'Special Agreement' groups set up by the Admiralty to cover activities of the RN normally outside their remit. When the war began there were virtually no ocean-going salvage and rescue tugs in Britain. As the war progressed and the number of convoys increased, such rescue vessels were urgently needed to tag along behind the convoys, assisting stricken vessels by putting out fires, rescuing men from the water and towing damaged ships to a safe port where they could be repaired.

Mr Matheson told us that we were presently building more than one class of very powerful ocean-going rescue tugs, not only for convoy work but also for other special operations. It all sounded good stuff, 'Boy's Own Paper' material. He didn't minimise the risks, though you could see some of them without his help; circling around in the water like a sitting duck whilst trying to secure a rope to a ship struck by a torpedo ten minutes earlier, was one of them. Another problem, we only learned later, was that Admiral Doenitz had instructed his U-boats to target the tugs first; if you sink a tug towing a disabled ship you kill two birds with one stone.

The job was basically the same as that on merchant ships and the Agreement to be signed was headed: 'T.124T AGREEMENT BETWEEN ADMIRALTY AND A MERCANTILE MARINE OFFICER OR RATING FOR SERVICE IN HIS MAJESTY'S COMMISSIONED RESCUE TUGS'.

Merchant Navy discharge books were to be issued under the agreement, the terms of pay and conditions were those of a merchant seaman, including membership of the Merchant Navy Officers Pension Fund, (how about that for faith in the future). As far as George and I were concerned, it all added up to being in the Merchant Service but sailing under the White Ensign, with the bonus of a bit of action thrown in for good measure. So we joined up in May 1943, two eager 17 year olds, never been away from home before and with no real idea of what we'd let ourselves in for. Geoff had meantime decided to go on salvage vessels with Rizdon Beazley. We all agreed that we didn't mind what happened to us as long as we got one voyage in first.

Having been issued with RN travel warrants, George and I travelled up to Glasgow by night train a few days later, arriving at some ghastly hour in the morning, having had no sleep on the journey. We walked from the station, carrying our bags and looking for somewhere to have breakfast, but nowhere seemed to be open. Eventually a terrace of tall Victorian grey stone houses appeared in view, one or two of which advertised themselves as private hotels, in one of these there were signs of life. The door was opened to us by an elderly man struggling into a waiter's black dress jacket. He served us breakfast, starting with porridge laced with salt, which pulled us up sharp and was surreptitiously covered with lashings of sugar.

Making our way to the departure point for the MacBraynes bus service to Campbeltown, we left Glasgow at eight in the morning and spent the whole day on the road. The vehicle had seen better days and shook us up something chronic as the journey progressed. The roads were decent in Glasgow but as we wound our way round the edge of Loch Lomond they went from A roads to B roads and meant it. The scenery was wonderful, but neither of us fully appreciated it as we were feeling distinctly queasy from the bone-shaking ride over the pot-holed surfaces. There was a brief stop at a place called Rest and Be Thankful, from where there were views down the valley, and this gave us an opportunity to exercise our seized-up limbs. Down by the side of Loch Fyne we went, stopping at picturesque Inverary to walk down the main street, restore our circulation and look for something to eat.

At Lochgilphead another brief stop, and by this time we wondered where we were going, the winding and almost deserted roads, the glorious scenery, but what lay at the end of it all, and where was the end anyway? The road from Ardrishaig to Tarbert seemed almost to dip into the Loch in places. There was time for a walkabout at Tarbert, then along the road to the edge of the West Loch until we came out onto the Atlantic seaboard near Gigha Island. Here was wild scenery indeed, the Atlantic breakers dashed themselves against the low shore and there was evidence that the sea had washed over the road in places. We drove south towards the Mull of Kintyre and Campbeltown, feeling tired, sick and not a little apprehensive. In later years I have made trips to

Campbeltown on metalled surfaces and on roads that have been straightened and widened, but the journey still evokes the memory of how it was that first time, in the middle of a war, with George and I en route to the ends of the earth, the bus, the roads and our stomachs all giving us a hard time.

An alternative route from Glasgow to Campbeltown entailed a train ride to Weymss Bay, then boarding one of MacBraynes paddle steamers across to Tarbert and continuing by bus for the rest of the journey. Whichever way the journey took me in the years ahead, the coast road down the length of the Kintyre peninsula always awaited. It seemed to go on forever, past the lonely graveyard set on the edge of the ocean, its iron railings and gravestones enveloped in the swirling mist and spray of the breakers and looking like something from a Victorian melodrama; on and on until suddenly the road turned inland and drifted down into a small town, miles from anywhere, as isolated as you're likely to find, and you were in Campbeltown, the base and headquarters of His Majesty's Rescue Tugs.

Straightening our stiffened bodies, we retrieved our cases from the bus, dumped them near the Royal Hotel at the end of the jetty and surveyed the scene before us. There was a neat little harbour in the shape of a square; a few fishing boats nestled up to the quay and a steam yacht with graceful lines was moored at the farthest arm of the harbour. The bay stretched out towards Davaar Island, which guarded the entrance to the sheltered waters. The 'wee toon' nestled under the shadow of Beinn Ghuilean, rising steep and austere to the south. From the harbour a pleasant promenade stretched away into the curving distance and was lost in the evening mist. The main street climbed gently towards a couple of hotels and a scattering of shops. It all seemed pleasant, picturesque and agreeable enough to two weary travellers.

Adjacent to the Royal Hotel on the seafront was the Victoria Hall, the administration headquarters of the Rescue Tug service. We reported there and were directed to the vessel we had seen lying at the head of the harbour, the yacht HMS *Minona*. Presenting ourselves to the Duty Officer on board, we were shown to a cabin containing two bunks. We tossed a coin, George lost and took the bottom bunk. The cabin was long and narrow, so getting dressed and using the washbasin required some ingenuity. It was late, we were tired and hungry, a steward brought sandwiches and shortly afterwards we collapsed into our bunks.

In peacetime the yacht had belonged to Coates the cotton

people, and had been commandeered by the Admiralty for use as a base ship, subsequently undergoing minor alterations for her new role. She was a handsome little vessel, built in 1908, wood and brass in the saloons and cabins, scrubbed wooden decks, and was a delight to wander over and explore. We stayed on board for a few days whilst being interviewed in the Victoria Hall, where we noted that there were lots of WREN clerks and typists. Life suddenly seemed brighter. One of the Officers in Charge of the base during our time at Campbeltown was Lt. Commander Lionel Greenstreet. He had been the 1st Officer of the Endurance, Shackleton's vessel, on the 1914 expedition to the South Pole when she became trapped in the ice and was one of those left on Elephant Island, whilst Shackleton and others made the journey by open boat to South Georgia to seek help.

The interviews, including medicals and morse tests, were spread over a few days. We were told to leave all personal items at home; diaries were under no circumstances to be kept and no cameras were to be taken on board ship. Apparently satisfied, they issued us with 1st Class travel warrants, plus a chit on a naval outfitters in Glasgow, instructed us to get kitted out and report back in Campbeltown in a week's time. George and I travelled back to Glasgow by the trusty MacBraynes bus the following day, located a naval outfitters, Paisley's in Jameson Street, and were measured for our uniforms. And lovely stuff they were, of soft doeskin, likewise the greatcoat. Two white shirts and 'half a dozen collars, stiff' with studs, uniform cap and badge, gold braid with green insert for the jacket sleeves, epaulettes for the greatcoat, black shoes and socks, plus a raincoat; leather gloves and a white silk scarf. Leaving these to be altered as necessary, we went on leave for five days, pleased to have got through the preliminaries and been accepted as officers into the Royal Navy. I signed the T.124T Agreement on the 25th May 1943 aged seventeen years and eight months, holding Merchant Navy Discharge Book No. 269688 issued by the Ministry of War Transport. It all seemed a long way from taking telegrams out on a bicycle, barely a year before.

After a few days at home visiting friends it was goodbyes all round. Looking back, it is hard to imagine what my parents must have been feeling, seeing their only child going off to sea in wartime, but there were no tears or drama, though maybe they came later. There were some difficult moments saying goodbye to Jean because we had been going out for some time and were very fond of each other. George and I set off back to Scotland, stopping in Glasgow to visit Paisley's for a final fitting and donning of uniforms before travelling back to Campbeltown. There were bound to be pitfalls along the way and, sure enough, we arrived in Campbeltown to the accompaniment of smirks all round. The uniform cap had a wire ring inside the crown to make it stand out, and this branded you as a rookie straight away, so the first thing was to take out the wire, relaxing the cap, and with a bit of jumping on and pulling around, it soon looked worn-in. We were back on the *Minona*, but now we belonged there, not just as guests of the Navy.

The daily routine varied little. After breakfast in the saloon, the rest of the morning was spent up top in the converted bridge, where some benches with morse keys had been installed. We were taken through RN wireless procedures, which varied from those of the MN, one difference being in the use of Naval Code. All RN vessels carried two yellow code-books with which to communicate with Admiralty or other RN ships as need arose. These books had lead-weighted covers, ready for throwing overboard if the ship was threatened with capture. We spent a good deal of time coding and de-coding messages from these books, then sending messages via the morse keys and it was becoming clear why they wanted MN operators for these RN-directed vessels. On the one hand we were under Admiralty orders, flew the White Ensign, and were to work with RN Fleet Escort Groups; on the other hand, most of the work we were intended for was the rescue of merchant ships; consequently a comprehensive knowledge of both wireless procedures was required.

The food was excellent, particularly after the past couple of years of rationing at home, the sun shone in that early summer in the west of Scotland and all was well in my world. Homesick? There was too much going on, all of it new and exciting, but there was the time George and I spent in the fo'cstle with a wind-up gramophone and a pile of 78 records. We sifted through the usual military bands, operatic choruses, comic monologues, pale-blue pianists and general corn, and then we found it, Artie Shaw and his orchestra playing 'Frenesi', backed with 'Adios Mariquita Linda'. It was a favourite record back home, and we played it and played it, so maybe we were a bit homesick after all. There were two small cinemas on the promenade, the Rex and the Picture House, which showed films all week except Sunday, with programmes changing midweek. George and I didn't frequent the pubs or the clubs so we did spend a deal of time in the smoky escapism of the cinemas. These visits plus writing letters home and to girlfriends, took up most of our spare time whilst we waited to be appointed to a ship.

At the entrance to Campbeltown Bay lay Davaar Island, reached from the mainland by a causeway which was covered at high water. Depending on the tide, you had to move quickly across it and be sure of your escape route over the rocks and shingle, otherwise you could find yourself cut off, spending a cold and hungry night on the island. We walked across the causeway to have a look in the cave where there is a drawing of Christ, done many years before. The RAF had a base at Macrihanish, some miles away on the western side of the peninsula, but we seldom saw any RAF or WAAF's in town, Campbeltown in those days was the undisputed capital of the Rescue Tug empire.

8: FIRST TRIP

Two of the grey-painted rescue tugs had anchored in the bay and then departed as silently as they had come. From these brief glimpses of our future, we formed the opinion that they were beautifully proportioned vessels and handsome in appearance, but that you had to be mad to think about going across the Atlantic in one. They were powerful vessels with lots of pulling power, crewed by about 30 officers and men, with a gun on the fo'cstle and a few Lewis guns dotted around. They varied in length between 150 feet and 200 feet, which didn't seem to us anywhere near big enough to cross an ocean. We were becoming accustomed to being saluted and to returning the salute; it was the uniform that was being saluted, not the person. At the foot of the ship's gangway the sentry came to attention and you saluted him, once on board you saluted the Officer of the Watch and then turned to salute the quarter deck, where the White Ensign was flying. In retrospect it was a strange induction into the Royal Navy, we were given no drill, no instructions, no guidance as to how an officer was expected to behave, not even how to return a salute properly. Perhaps they reckoned that whether or not you could salute, or march properly, it wouldn't make you a better wireless operator. And anyway there was a war on.

The *Minona* housed the occasional deck or engine room officer, but catered mainly for Operators awaiting drafting between ships and in this situation you found groups emerging. A few of us obtained the use of a WREN's typewriter in the Victoria Hall, producing a news-sheet entitled the 'T.124 Times', full of dreadful jokes and observations on what was going on around us. This was soon imitated by another group bringing out the 'Minona Moaner', a gutter-press publication as evinced by the title. These attempts at livening up the place were frowned on by Authority when it got wind of what was going on, for we spared no one in our observations. We were all shipped off to sea before any further editions could appear.

The *Minona* was a beautiful vessel, and it came as no surprise to learn, much later, that she had been purchased after the war by Richard Burton and Elizabeth Taylor, renamed *Kalizma* after their three children, and was the ship on which Mrs Burton was presented with that famous diamond. But in 1943 all we had was a dodgy wind-up gramophone, one decent record, and not even a glass bead in sight. In 1944 the *Minona* was to be joined by another requisitioned yacht of similar size, the Majesta, which moored alongside her.

George and I were anxious to ship off to sea to find out what it was really like, and on the 10th June 1943 I was allocated my first ship, H.M.R.T. *Allegiance*. She had been built earlier in the year by Cochrane and Sons at Selby, displaced 700 tons, was 156 feet overall with a speed of 13 knots and had a crew of 31. Her armament was a 12 pounder, more for reassurance than menace, and half a dozen AA machine guns. She carried two wireless operators of which I was the junior and wet behind the ears. Bidding farewell to George and the life aboard a comfortable yacht, I packed my bags and set out by rickety bus for Greenock. We both wondered whether we should ever see each other again.

The *Allegiance* had just come in from sea and lay, grey and workmanlike, alongside the quay at Greenock. There was urgent activity to get her refuelled, provisioned and off to sea again. Still partly attached to the shore by an umbilical cord and hesitant to let go of my security blanket, I heard that Morton had a home game, so I was off down to Tapilow like a shot. And what a wonderful sight awaited me, a team playing in black and amber stripes on a run-down ground almost identical to the one back home. Morton became my adopted team and I have followed their fortunes ever since, purely on the strength of those black and amber stripes and the memory of visits to that forlorn little wartime ground that reminded me of home.

We moved into the river to box compass and test the degaussing protection against magnetic mines, before proceeding down the Clyde. My cabin was shared with a Warrant Officer who was awaiting placement as 3rd Officer; it was cramped and contained a washbasin, chest of drawers, two bunks one above the other and a small padded bench. The door opened outward onto the port alleyway of the main deck, which ran aft to the open towing deck, and inboard to other cabins, the wardroom and the galley. On the after-deck were the powerful winch and the manilla towrope, 120 fathoms long and 18" in circumference. The door-sill from the cabin was high, about a foot or more, a situation much appreciated once we were out to sea and the alleyway became ankle deep in water sloshing in from the after-deck. Directly across from the cabin was the companionway leading to the boat deck, where the wireless room was situated. Diagonally across the alleyway was the toilet, a refuge I came to know well in the days ahead.

Although not a naval requirement, many of us had chain bracelets which showed our name, rank and service number, enabling a body to be identified if other means failed; mine was worn round the wrist, others wore it round the neck. My cabin was on the port side; the wireless room was on the starboard boat deck above, immediately forward of the funnel and had its door opening outward, exposed to the weather. Depending on which side the weather was coming from, there was a choice of routes to take from cabin to wireless room. The preferred one was straight across from the cabin, up the port side companionway, out on deck, make your way past the ship's boat, behind the funnel and into the wireless room. The alternative route took me along the internal alleyway, past the accommodation, the wardroom and the galley and then up the starboard companionway which lead onto the boat deck almost opposite the wireless room door.

Leaving Greenock, the trip had been calm down the Clyde, past Arran and Ailsa Craig, but leaving the lee of the Mull of Kintyre she rolled a lot and I felt distinctly unwell, spending much time in the toilet being sick. This wasn't helped by the mistaken notion that my stomach should be kept clean at all costs, and to this end I took frequent doses of Andrews Liver Salts, which worsened matters considerably. It's one way of losing weight, that's all I can say in retrospect. We joined our convoy in Loch Foyle, Northern Ireland, and even after we had left the Irish coast and headed west into the Atlantic, my stomach was still playing up.

After a couple of days moving further out into the Atlantic we began the wide sweep to turn south. The sun shone, the weather became warmer and I gradually came to life again. Discarding the bucket which had been clamped between my knees during the four-hour watch periods, I stood upright once more, looking out to sea in appreciation of feeling normal. My re-appearance in the wardroom was greeted with ironic cheers. We knew that there were U-boats in our vicinity because we received periodic wireless messages from Admiralty and C-in-C Western Approaches about their estimated locations, but so far we hadn't seen any, and all in all it was time to feel good about life once more.

A first trip to sea is different from other firsts. A first kiss for example is an experience, hopefully wonderful, within an established framework, but a first trip to sea has no such framework. Everything is new and there's nothing you can relate to, so you just get on with it and try to make as few mistakes as possible along the way. We plodded on behind the convoy, now far out in the Atlantic, on a course which took us well away from the French coast with its hostile ports and U-boat pens, but also took us closer to the U-boat packs that lurked in mid-Atlantic. We learned later that the majority of ships in our convoy were carrying supplies connected with the forthcoming invasion of Sicily. One of the troop transports broke down and we put a line aboard her, taking her in tow whilst she sorted out her engine problem. We proceeded well astern of the convoy, feeling vulnerable at slow speed, until she had repaired her engine, when we cast off and made speed to resume our station with the convoy. Shaping in past the Azores, we made for the Straits of Gibraltar, and my first glimpse of foreign soil.

Whilst we were busy in the Atlantic, in the Pacific the airfield at Munda in the Solomon Islands was taken by the Americans as they prepared to drive north through New Georgia. In the Mediterranean, General Eisenhower was preparing to invade Sicily using Montgomery's 8th Army and General Patten's US 7th Army. In the Atlantic, Admiral Doenitz was ready to try out new strategies with larger U-boats. Statistics later showed the tide beginning to turn in the Allies' favour in the Battle for the Atlantic and in May, 41 U-boats were sunk, a further 17 being sunk in June. On the Russian front a huge Russian-German tank battle was fought at Kursk, which the Russians won at the cost of a quarter of a million lives, and was later seen to have been one of the major turning points of the war.

As our convoy moved through the Straits, my first sight of Gibraltar was of this mass of rock on the horizon, getting ever bigger as we approached. It stirred me at the time, this was the famous Rock, besieged in history, always triumphant, a symbol that lived up to its billing. Most of the convoy continued into the Mediterranean but a few ships turned off into the Bay of Gibraltar, the *Allegiance* with them. The merchant ships anchored in the bay; we entered the harbour and went alongside in the trawler base, joining a host of Hull trawlers requisitioned by the Admiralty, mainly for minesweeping, and now flying the White Ensign. The air was warm and vaguely scented, the atmosphere seemed full of tension as it hung over the rock that towered above us and dominated the scene. The harbour was full of shipping, battleships, cruisers, destroyers, submarines and small craft. Having wanted for long enough to get into the war, into the real stuff, it seemed that I'd got there; but how to stay there, become a part of this atmospheric exciting place, that was the question.

9: THE ROCK

One of our Rescue Tugs, the *Salvonia*, was based at Gibraltar. Seeking out her Operator, it transpired that he had served a prolonged spell abroad and was glad to swap places and return to the UK. The exchange being approved by the two Captains, I joined the *Salvonia* as 2nd wireless operator in mid July 1943. The crew of the *Allegiance* all thought I was mad to stay in Gibraltar instead of returning to England with them. The *Allegiance* had been modelled on the *Salvonia,* an ocean-going tug of 1939, and didn't differ from her markedly in outward design.

At the beginning of the war there were only some half dozen tugs capable of carrying out the ocean-rescue operations needed by the Admiralty, the *Salvonia* being probably the best of the bunch. They were all requisitioned along with many smaller river and harbour tugs. At that time it could hardly have been foreseen how desperate would be the need for ocean-going rescue tugs, or the part they were destined to play in the war, but a building programme had been embarked upon in those early years, commencing with some twenty Assurance class tugs, of which the *Allegiance* was one. Six slightly larger and more powerful tugs, the *Envoy* class, were to follow later. In 1943 this build-up was being supplemented by two dozen newly built American diesel-electric ocean-going tugs of the *Eminent* class, released to the UK under the Lend-Lease Agreement. The most powerful rescue tugs of all were the eight British *Bustler* class with a speed of 16 knots.

The *Salvonia* was the duty Rescue Tug based at the western entrance to the Mediterranean; her duties were wide-ranging and she could be called out to ships in trouble in the Atlantic or the Mediterranean. There were now rescue tugs stationed around the world, in Singapore, Trincomalee, India, South Africa, Dakar, Newfoundland, the Mediterranean and in home waters. The *Salvonia* left harbour at dusk, patrolling in Gibraltar Bay all night and returning alongside at early light, her job being to counter the piloted torpedoes and the swimmers with limpet mines who came out under cover of darkness from Algeciras on the Spanish side of the bay. Spain, although ostensibly neutral, was Axis-friendly and turned a blind eye to activities along her coastline opposite Gibraltar. There was known to be an Italian tanker alongside in Algeciras harbour, the *Olterra*, which had been adapted for the use and concealment of underwater craft and swimmers, from which attacks were carried out against Allied shipping at anchor in the bay. As night fell, Italian frogmen left the *Olterra*, swimming under cover of darkness, their targets being the ships laid at anchor in the bay, to which they sought to attach limpet mines. The *Olterra* also launched 'chariots', piloted by two men sitting astride a steerable torpedo-shaped craft.

Commander Crabb was the RN Mine and Bomb Disposal Officer in Gibraltar. When I joined *Salvonia*, he and his team were engaged in countering the undersea menace in the Bay of Gibraltar and, as new ideas were developed, they were put into practice. The story of Lionel (Buster) Crabb is told by Marshall Pugh in his book, 'Commander Crabb', and also in the film, 'The Silent Enemy', which covers this period of the war in Gibraltar. We left harbour at dusk, patrolling between the anchored merchant ships, trying to spot anything suspicious in the water, dropping anti-personnel charges or light depth charges overboard if suspicions were aroused. We also carried rifles on board. Working without lights and as close in-shore to Algeciras as possible, we patrolled the bay all night. Periodically an underwater explosion would shatter the peace of the bay as anti-personnel mines were tossed into the pools of light cast by searchlights, the explosions pinging against dozens of ships' hulls, killing innocent fish and waking seamen from their dreams. We did this all the time I was in Gibraltar, working in conjunction with fast motor launches also patrolling the bay and engaged in similar activity. The area covered on some nights was considerable, particularly when a convoy arrived, or when ship numbers were reaching the stage of final assembly before a convoy sailed, at these times the ships at anchor could cover an area up to three miles long and a mile across.

Meantime, Gibraltar was living up to expectations. Main Street was full of cafés opening directly off the street, with small tables set around a tiled dance floor, and girls, who looked considerably younger than I, performing Spanish dances with swirling skirts and flashing limbs to the sound of clicking heels and castanets. And all this whilst you drank Muscatel and nibbled peanuts. It seemed to me that Hessle Road could do with a bit of this. In need of a haircut, I walked up the hill to visit a Spanish barber. After the haircut he suggested a shave, advancing towards my chair with a cut-throat razor and I had visions of never seeing England again. It all turned out well, but I was quite relieved to walk out into the sunshine afterwards.

Dress was casual on board ship, both in port and at sea, but we had to put on uniform when going ashore, Gibraltar being very much a pukka Royal Navy station. Once a week I donned a clean set of tropical gear, 'whites', consisting of uniform cap with a white cover, white open-necked short-sleeved shirt, white shorts, long white socks and white shoes, and went ashore to change the ship's Confidential Books, CBs; these books being my responsibility on board. This was a regular weekly jaunt and with the code books signed out to me, I breezed down the gangway and set off to walk through the busy dockyard to the CB office, situated deep inside the Rock and approached through an entrance to a large limestone cave, guarded by heavy security. There was some distance to walk through the cool rock-hewn corridors before reaching the CB office, where WREN's were working at desks or attending to other officers also there to exchange their ships' code-books.

The large RN code books remained on board ship at all times, but a weekly supplement was issued to all naval ships giving the rotational coding details for the following week, and it was this supplement that I had to collect, at the same time returning the previous week's issue. In addition to the main code, there were minor local codes and these also had their weekly supplements. The minor codes were LOXO, FOXO and MEDOX, which always sounded to me like a music-hall turn. Having safely negotiated these transactions with the duty WREN Officer, I signed my life away for another week before walking through the dockyard back to the ship with the documents, thinking that any German agent worth his salt could very well be following me with evil intent. Although Gibraltar was theoretically a secure base, there was a daily influx of dockyard workers from across the border with Spain, amongst whom it would be easy to infiltrate. Enemy agents were known to operate on the Rock, so a firm grip was kept on my briefcase, just in case.

Regular cinema shows and Tombola nights were held in the dockyard and there were lots of bars and cafés in town, so there was always plenty going on ashore. However, we were most often on our way out through the boom at the harbour entrance as darkness was falling and everyone else was going ashore, so when we did have nights free we took full advantage of what was on offer. An ENSA show came to town with the wonderfully mad Beatrice Lillie and the dainty Vivien Leigh, fresh from her success in Gone with the Wind, and we all made sure that we saw that show. There was an officers' bathing beach at Rosia Bay, where Nelson's body was brought ashore after the Battle of Trafalgar in 1805. I went there once and wished I hadn't bothered. All togged up in whites, rolled up towel under arm, I set off down the gangway humming happily to myself, intent on a laze around in the warm waters of the Mediterranean, enjoying a relaxing afternoon. No sooner had I waded into the water than I was stung on the calf by a jellyfish, spending the next two, very painful, days in the naval hospital. It has always seemed to me that water is not a natural element for right-thinking people. On it yes, in it no.

My first letter home from abroad was posted in a red pillar-box in the main street in Gibraltar, on the night the *Allegiance* arrived from England. Anxious to let my parents know that my first trip abroad had been made safely, I walked down the main street of Gibraltar looking for the Post Office. It was late at night and the office was closed, but there was a stamp machine outside. The trouble was that it only issued halfpenny stamps, which presumably was the rate for local postage within the Rock. Feeding the machine with coins produced a string of stamps, which were plastered all over the envelope until reaching the required sum for mail to England. Amazingly enough, the letter did get through, although it was heavily censored. The letter has long since disappeared but the envelope survives.

The rescue tug personnel were a disparate assembly drawn from all walks of life, a hardcore of trawler and small ship men predominating. A dislike of authority and a grudging adherence to law and order characterised the service, the officers being no exception. We conformed when necessary in order to placate the Admiralty, otherwise we went our own way, quietly proud of the job we did, which, by its very nature, was often carried out in the worst of conditions and in the knowledge that we were frequently somebody's last hope. This approach to life I absorbed gradually, though it had been evident early on that H.M. Rescue Tugs was far from being a quiescent branch of Admiralty. There was usually an air of truculence bubbling away below the surface, even amongst ourselves sometimes, as witness the ditty directed at some luckless tyro issuing orders from the bow, which begins:

'They stand on the fo'cstle and shout,
They shout about things they know nothing about'...
(substitute own words)

A signal came aboard one bright morning to proceed to Bougie on the North African coast. We tagged along behind a convoy bound for Malta and hived off to our destination, where we picked up a large mesh target float and towed it to a rendezvous some miles east of Gibraltar. There we were met by the French battleship, Jean Bart, a massive vessel, 35,000 tons, 800 feet long and with 8x15"guns and 20x5"guns. Launched in March 1940 in Loire, she had sailed to Casablanca in an incomplete condition in June of that year to prevent her falling into enemy hands as the Germans advanced across France. In November of 1942 she had been disabled when, under Vichy French jurisdiction and currently immobile in Casablanca, she engaged the US battleship *Massachusetts* which was shelling her from seaward, being gutted and suffering many casualties as a result. She was now an addition to the Allied fleet having been re-fitted, re-armed and brought back to life.

Anyway, she wanted to test her guns and we had been designated to tow this latticed contraption up and down for her to try her luck. The morning was bright and sunny as we exchanged messages about speeds and distances and then she opened up with her 15" guns. It was like Hull Fair but more dangerous. There were big red flashes and an awful lot of noise whilst we looked on and waited to see where the shells would land. The first salvo was wide of the target but also wide of us, though we drew only scant comfort from this. We had about half a mile of towrope out and everyone on board was immediately in favour of increasing this to several miles. However, you increasingly lose control of your tow the more rope you pay out, so half a mile was as good as it was likely to get. After a while we became quite involved, and started placing bets as to where the next salvo would land. The shoot took up most of the day, and we breathed more easily when it was all over.

Home again in Gibraltar, it was back to the routine of night patrols and trying to grab some sleep in the hot stuffy cabin in the daytime if you could. The ship obtained its allocation of booze and cigarettes from Saccone & Speed in the town, one of my jobs being to keep track of these items in the ship's Bond. Cigarettes were cheap, about 6d for 20, and spirits were likewise at rock-bottom prices, 5/- for a bottle of gin. Tins of loose tobacco came from a firm called Ticklers, of Grimsby. Everyone was into the duty-free stuff, cabins full of bodies, thick with smoke and drinking gin out of cups when there weren't enough glasses to go round. You literally did not know what tomorrow would bring, and 'eat drink and be merry' seemed more apposite in wartime than it ever had in peacetime. There were noisy parties, especially when we met up with other tugs that were passing through, renewing friendships, exchanging news of tug exploits and misdemeanours and, inevitably, convening the court of 'Cardinal Puff', a popular wardroom drinking game in which mistakes were penalised by having to start all over again. More mistakes naturally meant more alcohol imbibed, usually rum or gin, and the more befuddled you became the less chance there was of completing the complicated sequence correctly. Two Grand Masters of the Order are required to convene and oversee the issue of a Certificate, mine being signed and sealed with the top of a Gordons' Gin bottle stuck on with sealing wax.

10: CURRY AND MARMALADE

In August the Italian chariots got through to a Norwegian tanker in the bay, breaking her in two; on the same night there was a large explosion from limpet mines attached to the 7,000 ton Liberty ship *Harrison Gray Otis*. 2-0 to the enemy. In September Italy capitulated; the thorn in our side that had been the *Olterra* was taken into Gibraltar harbour and that chapter of the war drew to a close.

We made a trip to Algiers where some shipping needed moving around. Expecting to stay there for a few days I took a room in the Allied Officers Club in the Hotel Aletti on the harbour front. This was very pleasant, and I took kindly to Algiers, bathed in intrigue, sunshine, red wine and the aroma of Galloise cigarettes, spending my time wandering the city and drinking coffee at sidewalk cafes. One afternoon was spent strolling round the native quarters on my own looking for the casbah. North Africa was still in turmoil after its recent liberation and there were people rubbing shoulders with you in the streets and bars who could belong to either side. There were probably more spies per square mile in Algiers at that time than anywhere else. Intrigue and suspense were in the air and you could almost smell the tension as well as feel it.

Leaving a local cinema one night I was jostled and my uniform cap snatched from my head. Giving chase, I grabbed hold of the culprit, an Arab lad of about 15, and had just succeeded in getting a hand on my cap when one of his mates came up, pushed me, and together they made off again. Chasing them, I eventually grabbed my cap and hung on to it. A number of youths gathered around me, but by then we were, luckily, in a well-lit street with lots of people about and the youths melted away into the darkness of nearby alleyways. Probably there was a market for uniforms and they would have got money for my cap. It was not safe on the streets at night, you could taste the danger on your tongue, as somebody once remarked. A carved wooden box in a shop window took my eye and I bought it to take home, doubtless paying too much for it, being unfamiliar at the time with the practice of bargaining.

Back in Gibraltar, a destroyer came in from sea bearing evidence of battle about her decks, with torn and twisted metal and her rails askew. She had dead and wounded aboard and we went alongside her to transfer the bodies to *Salvonia*. A naval Shore Detail came on board us with equipment canvas and flags, to attend to the bodies. We moved out to the deep water off Europa Point and shut down our engines. The Padre conducted a brief service, and 'Abide with Me' was sung by everyone on board, including some crew members from the warship, there to say goodbye to their comrades. As we lay still and quiet in the water, the Mediterranean sun shone down onto the half dozen bodies laid on wooden planks on our after-deck, each draped with a Union Jack. After the Lord's Prayer and a Blessing, the bodies were raised one by one and the plank rested on the ship's rail. The Padre said some words over each body in turn, the plank was tilted and the body slid from under the canvas and into the water. When all the bodies had been consigned to the deep, a few flowers were scattered on the water and we returned silently to harbour.

The RAF base was nearby; the airfield was adjacent to the sheer face of the Rock and aircraft were continuously taking off and landing. General Sikorski, the Polish statesman and Prime Minister-in-exile, was killed in 1943 in an air crash when his Liberator plunged into the bay just beyond the runway. It happened whilst we were berthed only a couple of hundred yards away, but it was all hushed up and there were said to be mysterious circumstances. Larry Crabb had the job of recovering scattered documents from the sunken plane before they floated off on the currents towards Spain. The incident was a well kept secret and I didn't learn about it until after the war, which is not surprising, because there was always so much going on around you that you accepted it all and got on with your own job. Only much later would it be possible to piece events together and put them in perspective.

One thing I did know, that I was young, healthy and that the sap had not only risen, it seemed to be approaching bursting point, so when we were detailed to proceed to Oran I felt my moment had arrived. We went alongside in the harbour and much to my delight Oran was a perfect example of a seaman's port, cafés, girls, music, bars, cabarets and more girls. We went ashore in groups from the ship and wandered from bar to bar along the waterfront, trying out the various North African wines, enjoying the music, the bright lights and the ambience of people having a good time. In many of the bars there were brass models of ladies and gentlemen in unusual positions and these were studied closely by all of us from an artistic point of view. Our stay in Oran was not long enough, but everyone seemed much happier by the time we left.

There was a board game in the wardroom called Dover Patrol, which was popular despite being a busman's holiday. My regular opponent was the Mate, a Red Sea Pilot before the war, who used to retail distracting stories about the mysterious East into my receptive young ears whilst sinking all my pieces. One bit of advice he gave me was to have marmalade with my curry; I still do when at home, but have given up asking for it in Indian restaurants as you get some funny looks. And they never have any anyway. A young singer called Frank Sinatra was the new kid on the block and opinions were aired as to whether he was the new Crosby. The younger set mostly favoured Sinatra, acknowledging that they were both great vocalists, but the times they were achangin' and the audiences also. A new voice was needed and it belonged to the greatest ballad singer of them all, Francis Albert Sinatra.

In early October we sailed east along the North Africa coast looking for the *Hiram S Maxim*, a US Liberty ship in trouble. We found her near Tenez, where she was beached in a cove, safe and sound for someone else to attend to later on. Relieving her of some bags of sugar, her holds being full of it, we went off to Algiers for orders, arriving there in the dark and anchoring in the harbour to await morning. Someone told us that there was a Customs post operating in the port, (did nothing ever stop these people, didn't they know there was a war on?) Upon hearing this, the Chief Steward became alarmed at the unaccountably large quantity of sugar in his storeroom and decided to get rid of it over the side into Algiers harbour whilst it was still dark. We all lent a hand, pushing bags and shovelling sugar out through the porthole. Fine, until the dawn revealed that a barge had moored alongside us during the night and was now covered in a thick layer of best American white granulated. Panic set in, and all hands, me included, scrambled down rope ladders and hose-piped it all into the harbour. The Customs never did come.

In late October 1943 we left Gibraltar as part of an Escort Group, shepherding a large convoy back to England. *Salvonia* was being returned to her commercial owners, now that sizeable numbers of purpose-built ocean-going rescue tugs were coming on stream. We docked at Barry after an uneventful voyage and were glad to be back on British soil again, looking forward to some leave. I met a very pretty dark haired girl called Betty Jones, who lived in Cadoxton at the far end of the tram line, and for the next week all my spare cash went on fish and chip suppers for two and tram fares. The ship moved up to Liverpool, then to Garston, where we spent some time kicking our heels, eager to go home on leave. It wasn't until we put out the final mooring ropes in mid-November that we could head for home, replete with a wealth of stories to dine out on whilst the Admiralty contemplated its next move.

There was great rejoicing at home, my parents probably

thought they would never see me again when I'd left them six months earlier. Copious quantities of duty-free cigarettes kept dad in the manner to which he was accustomed, and Jean folded into my arms as though we had never been apart. Leave lasted from 10th to 26th November and seemed to shoot by; just as I had got used to home life I found myself back on the *Minona*. Campbeltown was much the same and a couple of weeks were spent writing letters and seeking refuge from the cold winds in the warmth of the cinemas. In mid-December I was sent on a few days leave before joining the *Eminent* in Glasgow on the 20th December 1943.

11: THE EMINENT

The *Eminent* was an American built vessel, of all-welded construction and one of a number of ocean-going tugs now beginning to arrive from the United States. Her Chief Radio Operator was taken ill just before Christmas and was replaced by Bill Nicoll. Bill lived in Glasgow and took me home for meals and also to meet Marjorie, his fiancée. Most evenings I made my way to Green's Playhouse Ballroom to listen to Joe Loss and his Orchestra, who played many American tunes and had a good rhythm. The vocalist with the band was Elizabeth Baty. The dance floor was thronged with uniforms, and couples huddled close together in the smoke dimmed spotlights, but I was usually tight up against the bandstand savouring the musicianship and getting a headache. The weather was very cold and after six months of Mediterranean sunshine it didn't go down too well. There was a good choice of variety theatres in Glasgow; most of them were visited, as was a small cinema in the Gorbals to see 'Night Must Fall', an excellent film. Having been ashore on ship's business I was still in uniform and, under a host of curious but friendly stares, felt as much an event as the film.

Early in the New Year of 1944 the *Eminent* moved up the Clyde to Campbeltown, where we swung round a buoy for a few days on Duty Watch. We were called out into a turbulent Atlantic to the *Loch Geary*, to tow her in and beach her, but she had been too badly damaged and sank on us before we could do anything useful; all the crew was taken off safely. Back at the buoys, we contented ourselves with taking the liberty-boat ashore for visits to the cinema, trusting that the screen stayed clear of recall messages and the ship's siren remained quiet. Ships' sirens were sounded in port to alert any crewmen ashore to return to their ship immediately, ready for sailing. Sirens at night echoing around the bay made an eerie sound, the whole town becoming involved whether it wanted to or not.

The cinema newsreels gave us better tidings from the war overseas. The Solomon's campaign came to an end with the Japanese being driven from Gualalcanal, and a fierce sea battle took place off Vella Lavella. Nearer home, some of the launching sites being prepared by the Germans for their flying bombs, V.1's, were identified and attacked. In Russia the severe winter conditions came to the relief of Leningrad; besieged by German forces for more than two years; 200,000 Russians were killed defending the city and another 600,000 died from starvation, cold and exhaustion.

In the middle of January orders came to proceed to Loch Foyle in Northern Ireland, to join a convoy forming for Gibraltar. For someone who wanted to see the whole world, and as soon as possible, this was mildly frustrating. On arrival in Loch Foyle we anchored off Moville, put the boat down and set off for an evening ashore. We were all in civvies, Ireland being neutral territory, and proceeded up the main street, settling in the snug of the first general store we came to, staying until it was time to go back on board. The Guinness was strong and the ambience of the store with its well-worn wooden settles, the smell of ale, tobacco smoke and laughter, cast its spell over us and we were all very jolly by the time we left.

Gale force winds sprang up during the night but the convoy left on schedule. A sister ship, the *Aspirant*, took up station with us astern of the columns of ships, the destroyers and corvettes settling into their defensive pattern around the convoy. Progress was slow in the heavy seas and the *Aspirant* and ourselves were tossed about like corks. We could see the full length of *Aspirant's* keel as she was buffeted and thrown about by the massive waves and it was no consolation to realise that we were doing exactly the same. When our bow was thrown out of the water the whole ship shuddered before she buried her nose deep into the next wave, it felt as if we were slamming into a brick wall. Next she would roll wildly from side to side until her stern was thrown up in the air, the screw would thresh frantically as it came free of the water and the whole ship vibrated from stem to stern as if she was going to shake herself to pieces, and us with her. Her final trick was to emulate a ping-pong ball on a fountain, but by this time no one was amused.

Everything aboard was lashed down, except the crew. We were thrown from side to side, fore and aft, up and down. Going down an alleyway was like being on the Cakewalk at Hull Fair, eating and drinking was an adventure in timing, climbing the companionway to the bridge an exercise in muscle control. Sleep was nigh impossible, but after a day or two exhaustion took care of that. Your best bet was to lie flat on your stomach with arms and legs out to the four points of the compass and hope that you weren't thrown out of your bunk. At first you ached in every muscle, but after a week of it you emerged from that phase into one of mild pain and then into a toned-up sense of fitness. You were still browned-off with the constant shuddering and being thrown about day after day like a shuttlecock, but had become fitter now to cope with it.

The weather gradually improved, but had its downside. The gales and choppy seas, which had previously shielded us from the attention of the U-boats, gave way to fair weather and calm seas, enabling the U-boats to see us through their periscopes once more, and normal service was resumed. Some ships in the convoy were bound, like us, for the Mediterranean, others for the Far East, and the remainder for South Africa. As we passed the Azores we went our separate ways, with parting messages on the Aldis Lamp for good luck and safe voyage. On the thirteenth day out from Loch Foyle we reached Gibraltar, the convoy intact, the sun shining. Things were looking up.

The *Eminent* was built by Defoe/General Motors in Bay City, Michigan, being completed on the 14th September 1942, my 17th birthday. She was 143 feet long and bounced about like a cork in a fountain even in calm weather. My cabin was on the main deck, being shared with three others, Bill, and the 3rd and 4th Engineers. There were four bunks, two on one side, one above the other, and two on the opposite side of the cabin, which was about 15ft square. There were two metal wardrobes, two washbasins and two chairs, which could be secured to the deck when at sea. The door had a kick-out panel and opened onto a small area adjoining an alleyway, which ran fore and aft between the chain-locker and the main thwart-ship alleyway. This main alleyway housed the galley and the companionway to the crew's quarters on the lower deck. At the business end, where British tugs had towing hooks and manilla towropes, the American tugs had an electric winch and a 5" steel cable.

My bunk was the top one nearest the cabin door, which was

always left on the hook when at sea. As we were all watch-keepers there was a lot of coming and going throughout the 24 hours, and one or other of the cabin lights was on all the time. The large red alarm bell that rang for action stations was immediately above our cabin door, six feet from my pillow, was loud enough to be heard all over the ship and half way across the Atlantic. It rang frequently when we were at sea so mild heart attacks were commonplace when roused from deep sleep in the middle of the night. Sleep was always at a premium and it was only exhaustion that allowed you to sleep at all. Bill and I discovered the delights of toast and marmalade and mugs of tea at two o'clock in the morning when we changed watches. The wireless room was on the deck above our accommodation and was reached by a steel companionway in the centre of the ship. Everything about the ship was metal with hardly any wood anywhere. Also on the wireless deck were the wardroom, the Captain's cabin and the companionway to the bridge, but more importantly there was a small pantry with a toaster, hotplate and an electric kettle and these were put to good use in the early hours, raising morale when it was at its lowest.

The wireless room was a revelation. Where the *Allegiance* had workman-like Marconi gear, the *Eminent* possessed an Aladdin's cave of delights. Each piece of equipment was sophistication itself, black and chrome, moulded and smooth, rounded, functional, a joy to behold and to operate. It worked and it worked well; all honour to the name of Scott. In addition to the receivers and transmitters, there were auxiliary receivers and miscellaneous equipment at head height on the bulkhead in front of you. The operating position had been thought through, the morse key was in exactly the right place and all the controls were within easy reach. The whole set-up exuded friendly efficiency and was a real pleasure to work with.

Having left Gibraltar only a matter of weeks previously, there was not much I wanted to do ashore except visit the dockyard cinema and write letters home. The bathing area at Rosia Bay was not on my list of places to visit. We were tied up alongside the *Aspirant* so there was a great deal of climbing aboard each others' ships and partying. We stayed alongside for a few days, catching up on sleep and preparing to leave Gibraltar as part of an escort group shepherding a convoy back to England.

12: U-BOATS

On the round trip UK/Gibraltar/UK, we were to be at sea for 28 days out of 31. Needing to maintain a continuous wireless watch between us, Bill and I worked five hours on and five hours off for the 28 days. In convoy it was multiple-frequency watch keeping including the basic 500 kc/s (W/T morse) and 2410 kc/s (R/T telephony). The concentration required to monitor different frequencies and receive messages over a five-hour period was demanding and, compounded by the continual lack of sleep, meant that both of us were mentally and physically exhausted to the point of sickness, well before the end of the trip.

We left Gibraltar on the 1st February 1944, bound for the UK as part of an escort group to a sizeable convoy. Two aircraft carriers and some corvettes also took up station with us and there was an unusually large amount of aircraft activity as the ships formed into columns and headed out through the Straits of Gibraltar into the Atlantic, the *Eminent* bringing up the rear. Information had been received, via the coded wireless U-boat Situation Report, that there were submarines in the vicinity, and the bell for action stations rang a few times without anything eventuating. On the 9th of February the convoy was well out in the Western Approaches, preparing to shape in for the Channel, when we received an urgent signal from Admiralty advising that we were being stalked by a U-boat pack. Our escort group responded to the threat, and the following is a brief extract from the 9th February wireless log of the *Eminent* as I recorded it at the time: 'Between the hours of 1520 and 1718 the escort group took up action stations. Using the R/T code-words, Matapan, Playbill, Jessica, Waterhouse, Pilot, Fantasy, Hopkins and Roseport, the attack formations were co-ordinated and a series of depth charge attacks were made near the convoy. Log records show that 3 U-boat kills were made by the Group in these attacks and this was advised to Admiralty. Our convoy suffered no casualties'.

It was riveting, listening to the messages passing between the corvettes and the destroyers then hearing the depth-charges projected overboard a few yards from us. On the convoy frequency we heard the orders as they were given, acknowledged, and acted upon; we knew when the depth-charge throwers would be in action, then heard them fired in patterns from their cradles, followed a few seconds later by the 'crump' as they detonated, seemingly right beneath us. Most of the time you sit on watch and the airwaves are silent, but when you are under attack there is no need for radio silence or coded messages as the enemy knows exactly where you are and is about to present his calling card, then, the airwaves suddenly explode into life with urgent messages in plain language. Through the wireless room porthole we saw the destroyers and corvettes manoeuvre in tight circles and watched the depth charges thrown and explode. The shrill sound of ships' sirens and the instructions shouted on loudhailers from bridge to bridge dominated everything around us as the corvettes took up attacking positions, re-grouped and attacked again, explosions banging against our hull. For everyone in the convoy it was a 'them or us' situation.

There were further suspected kills as the corvettes and destroyers continued their attacks, now astern of us, accompanied by the sound of more depth-charges as the convoy continued its course towards home. This total of three kills and three possibles in a single defence of the convoy was a huge success, with not a single ship being lost. Particularly was it a triumph for the tactics of the Walker-trained groups of corvette sub-hunters that he pioneered and which, in the end, cost him his life through overwork, strain, exhaustion and simple war-weariness. Johnny Walker died at the early age of 48, like countless others in the war, burnt out serving his country, perhaps having done more than any other single person in helping defeat the enemy at sea in the Battle of the Atlantic. The story of his war is told in the book, 'Walker R.N.' by Terence Robertson, which contains an account of an attack on a convoy between the 7th and the 9th of February 1944, both from the British side and from Hartwig Looks, the Captain of U-264. 'He, (Looks), knew there were 20 U-boats in the vicinity with more arriving at regular intervals and decided to launch his attack on convoy SL147 on the night of February 8th/9th. It was a large convoy and he had hopes of more than usual success.' Details of the battle follow, with this coming at the end: 'With 81 merchant ships depending on him, (Walker), two aircraft carriers hoping he would protect them, a close escort screen of six warships...he had faced one of the most dangerous 'pack' attacks of the war and ripped it apart by killing three of the enemy...without loss in ships...' The dates and the facts correspond, so maybe it had been the big man himself looking after us on that trip. I'll probably never know for sure but I like to believe that it was.

An American LST was having difficulty keeping up with the

convoy. She had been involved in the landings at Anzio, had been badly knocked about and was on her way to England for repair. We dropped behind the convoy, threw a rope aboard and took her in tow for the rest of the trip home. The convoy was met by covering aircraft as we entered the Channel, and a comforting feeling it was too as they flew low over us like a mother hen gathering in her chicks. We made landfall at Plymouth and stayed alongside for the next week or so, catching up on sleep and evening entertainment. It was mid-February and still very cold, but there was warmth and bright lights on offer at the Palace theatre where Harry Parry and his Sextet headed the bill. One of his vocalists was Doreen Villiers with whom I was in love at the time, but she proved fickle and married an American airman before she even knew I existed. Also on the bill at the Palace that night, were the singing duet Ted Andrews and Barbara; at the end of their act they brought on stage a diminutive Julie, who sang in a clear sweet voice that had everyone applauding.

The *Eminent* now began a series of exercises in the Channel. In the area between Portsmouth and Lands End we towed lengths of hardware and strange-looking objects with platforms. We towed them in good weather and in bad weather. We towed them one way then we towed them the other way. We anchored them, berthed them, joined them up, docked them, cursed them. It made no difference, they were still there the next morning, waiting to be towed up and down the Channel again. This went on for weeks. Nobody knew why we were doing this or what the contraptions were for, nor what their eventual purpose might be. The Captain sent in his daily report on their handling, then we did it all again the next day, through February, March and into April. Towards the end of April one of our tugs, the Dutch *Roode Zee,* was torpedoed and sunk by an E-Boat whilst similarly engaged at the eastern end of the Channel.

Between trips, we spent time in many of the ports along the south coast, particularly Portland Dockyard, where the Operator on the *Lariat*, Archie Gibson, joined me for excursions ashore to the local hostelries or to the cinema. We played a lot of chess, sometimes all day, once becoming so absorbed in a game that I became stranded on board *Lariat* when she moved out to anchor and had to spend the night aboard her. At the end of March I went home for five days leave from Southampton to find that Dan was also home, as was Joyce, a previous girlfriend, now about to join the ATS, and the three of us spent some good times together, being joined by Lester for late night record sessions. A day's stopover in London was put to good use, enjoying the atmosphere, checking out the latest edition of 'Revaudeville' at the Windmill and dining in Soho, before catching the late train to Southampton.

In late April, whilst we were busy in the Channel, the disaster of Slapton Sands was unfolding nearby; American soldiers training in Landing craft offshore were fired on by E-boats, resulting in considerable loss of life. There were E-boats buzzing up and down the Channel all the time we were performing with our experimental hardware, but the Germans were perhaps as baffled as we were as to what we were doing, and left us alone in order to seek more promising targets. After the war, recovered documents revealed that they thought our strange objects were connected with harbour defence and so posed no direct threat to them.

One dreadful night when we were trying to anchor in gale force winds in Start Bay, instructions were shouted from the bridge to the fo'csle to lower the anchor on seven lengths of chain. However, as chain length number six disappeared into the water and nothing else followed, it became clear that someone had literally dropped a clanger and that an anchor and six lengths of chain now reposed on the sea bed. A few unkind words passed between the bridge and the fo'cstle, and we spent the rest of the night dodging round the bay with our tow attached. Quite why the sixth length of chain had not been shackled onto the seventh length, and so to the securing bolt in our chain locker, was never satisfactorily explained. At early light we entered harbour and sheepishly owned up to losing bits of the Admiralty's hardware. Nobody passed Go and nobody collected £200.

Leave came along in short spells, usually when repairs were needed. On these occasions a few days were spent in London staying at a Service Club, or at the Regent Palace Hotel if there was a room available. London was now a turbulent mass of uniforms, the crowded pavements in the West End overflowed onto the roadway with servicemen and women. Every taxi had Yanks in it or spilling out of it. Queues for theatres and cinemas became longer and you queued for just about everything, cafes, milk bars, tubes, taxis, buses and trains. But the atmosphere and excitement you would not have wanted to miss. Everything was vital and larger than life. It was clear that we were on the verge of invading Nazi-held Europe and the very air seemed charged with tension. Apart from the Americans, there were uniforms of every

Allied nation on the streets, including our own Army, Navy and Air Force, ATS, WRENS, WAAF, Free French, Polish, Canadian and other Commonwealth forces. The darkened streets gave up a babble of voices in different tongues and it was difficult to identify some of the uniforms, unless there was a flash on the shoulder. A real-life melodrama was unfolding all around us, and fate was handing out walk-on parts for the most momentous event of our lives.

Spells of leave allowed for swift trips home, but the travelling took up so much time that the period at home was all too short. When going on leave and expecting to return to the same ship in the same place it was permissible to travel in civvies, but when attached to base or joining ships it was regulation to travel in uniform. A visit to Ye Old White Harte to see if anyone else was on leave, a night out with Jean, a night at home and that was about it before it was time for the long journey back again. The trains were crowded with uniforms of every kind, kit-bags were everywhere, noise, smoke, compartments filled with sleeping bodies, inert forms stretched out in the corridors and often in the toilets, people sleeping in every known position. The 1st Class travel warrant issued by the Admiralty was only a nominal passport to a seat; in reality all it meant was that you were authorised to board the train.

There were other Hull men on the *Eminent*, and when one or other of us had a few days leave he would be off to Hull carrying parcels and letters for delivery to families in various parts of the city. Upon returning aboard he would bring back letters and packages from home, plus local newspapers which were circulated around the ship. One of these lads was Jim Williams, a young seaman-gunner whose life was to run some way parallel to mine in the years ahead, leading to a friendship which blossomed again in the winters of our discontent.

Waiting on the platform at York or Doncaster, particularly at night, was an event in itself. Sometimes the buffet was open, sometimes not. But there was always the Women's Voluntary Service doing sterling work on one of the platforms dispensing tea and buns, if you had the time between trains to locate them and were travelling light. However, if you had all your changing-ships suitcases and kit-bags with you then tough luck, because you were anchored to your luggage and could slowly die of thirst. None of the wartime trains had any refreshments on board, or if they had I never found them. When the train stopped, you opened the nearest carriage door, pushed your bags and yourself inside and stayed where you landed. The LNER A4 Pacific's were magnificent, even wartime dirt and grime couldn't hide their pedigree as they came thundering through on the centre tracks at York or Doncaster. At the end of the journey it was a privilege to walk down the platform at Kings Cross and touch these powerful living creatures, maybe exchanging a few words with driver or firemen. It always seemed to be 'Silver Fox' or 'Silver Link' that ran between Waverley, Edinburgh and Kings Cross when I travelled so much.

Dan had joined the RAF as an aircraft engine fitter and was undergoing induction and training at an RAF camp near Kirkham in Lancashire. On one of my brief leaves, I fiddled the travel warrant and routed myself through Kirkham on my way back to the south coast. We met outside the barracks in the afternoon and went looking for a meal and a pint; I was only there until the next morning, having to catch the mid-morning train to London. We had a couple of drinks in a local pub before it was time for Dan to return to barracks that evening. When we reached the barrack gates I hung back whilst Dan went inside, re-appearing with an RAF uniform in a brown paper parcel. Naval officers were allowed to wear civvies ashore when on leave or off duty, as long as they carried appropriate identification, and I was presently wearing a sports jacket and flannels. I wrapped these in the brown paper after changing into the RAF uniform in a nearby public toilet. We went through the barrack gate, carrying my civvies in a parcel and saluting as we went, walked to Dan's hut and stayed talking until lights out. Next morning, after breakfast in the Mess, I walked out of the barracks in my civvies. When I told people that I had worn two uniforms and been in the Royal Air Force during the war, nobody, except Dan, believed me. Three uniforms if you count the Home Guard. How on earth would the Allies have coped without me.

13: D-DAY - 1944

Returning to the south coast was to enter a restricted zone; once inside you were not allowed out again. It was May and the tension was palpably mounting. We were about to launch the Second Front to liberate Europe and help take some of the pressure off the Russians on the Eastern Front. The coastal area and for some miles inland was crammed with men and equipment, the roads were full of columns of tanks, jeeps, Bren-carriers and anything else that moved on two wheels or four, aircraft in quantity were everywhere, on the ground and in the air. Sometime in this period I remember sitting on a hill overlooking the sea and the south coast, writing home about my feelings and what England meant to me. Bombed, hungry, we were all, servicemen and civilians alike, living in an emotionally charged environment, and if you're going to win a war you need to be psyched up.

If we thought we had seen it all in the way of strange tows we were mistaken. We were sent round to the Thames where, waiting for us, was a hollow concrete caisson weighing some 6,000 tons. It was one of a number of caissons that had been constructed on the banks of the river and was daunting in its uncompromising mass, rising out of the water like a block of flats and looking just as unwieldy. There was a walkway around the base and bollards to which towropes could be secured. Our orders were to tow this monstrosity out of the Thames, through the Straits of Dover, and deposit it at Dungeness. At this juncture people started writing long letters home. We all thought the whole idea was mad and the more we thought about it the madder it seemed. The caisson was oblong, flat fronted, only a little smaller than the Hull City Hall and looked about as difficult to tow. It was so huge that the German guns on the cliffs overlooking the Straits couldn't possibly miss us as we crawled along at two or three knots in the narrow channel, presenting the easiest of targets and with no escape route. Although the caissons were code-named 'Phoenix' units, we immediately dubbed them 'concrete coffins', as being more appropriate.

We set off, crawling along at a snail's pace, speculation abounding that this was going to be our last voyage and got as far as Dover, the narrowest part of the Straits, where we expected the guns to open up. However, all remained quiet and we proceeded slowly on our way, waiting for disaster to strike any second, passed Folkestone still holding our breath and neared Dungeness, where the *Roode Zee,* had been torpedoed by an E-Boat whilst doing similar work a week or two earlier. When we reached inshore waters at Dungeness, army personnel put out in small boats and directed us where to position the tow. Men scrambled up the iron rungs and climbed down inside the Phoenix to open the sea-valves in the base. The unit slowly flooded before settling into the shallow water on the eastern side of the Ness, coming to rest on the sea bed with just a few feet of the concrete rim showing above water.

We were not the only tug towing concrete coffins and assorted hardware around the Channel. During May the sea-lanes along the south coast had become increasingly busy, bordering on the congested. Having earned full marks for managing our first trip successfully, we were sent back into the Thames to collect another coffin and do it all over again. This time we were in company with two sister ships, *Lariat* and *Destiny*. The three of us hitched up to large Phoenix units in Tilbury and set off for Selsey Bill, a longer tow than the previous one. Once again the guns remained silent as we passed through the straits; it seemed that not only were we baffled by what we were doing, but the enemy also. Our guess was that they were keeping a watching brief and as long as we didn't turn towards the French coast, they left us alone and observed events with interest. Why they didn't sink us and effectively block the Dover Straits we never knew.

It took us the best part of two days to make the trip, crawling along at a couple of knots, much of the time waiting for the guns to blow us out of the water, sink the Phoenix, or both. When we reached Selsey we handed over our 'coffin' to the Royal Engineers and were glad to anchor off Newhaven for a few hours, before returning to Tilbury. Dover and the Straits were nicknamed 'Hell Fire Corner' for good reason. It was only months later, in September, that the Canadians silenced the guns which had shelled Dover and shipping for most of the war. We were not long in Tilbury before being sent to Dover, where we went alongside for the night. In the evening, ourselves and *Lariat* were invited to sample the hospitality of the Sergeants Mess, which overlooked the harbour, and I well remember that as a most convivial evening. The next day, still in the company of *Lariat*, we proceeded to Ramsgate, where we picked up another Phoenix and towed it to join the growing collection of units at the eastern side of Selsey Bill.

In all, there were six different sizes of Phoenix, ranging from 1672 tons to the King Size 6,044 tons. The latter were 204 ft long, about 60 ft high above the water line and 56 ft wide. The larger Phoenix took six months to build, mainly in the Thames and along the south coast, with smaller units being built on the West Coast and at Goole and Middlesbrough on the East Coast. Some of the builders' names are still familiar all these years later: Balfour Beatty, McAlpine, Laing, Costain, Mowlem and Taylor Woodrow. The main assembly points were off Dungeness and Selsey Bill for those units manufactured on the East Coast, and Portland Bill for those arriving from the West Coast. Other sections of assorted hardware that we had towed around earlier in the year were also being assembled in the Solent. And a strange sight they presented: ribbons of floating roadways bobbed up and down on the swell and platforms with stanchions sticking up at each corner, swung at anchor. About this time, speculation gave way to realisation of what our efforts of the last few months had been all about, and the code name 'Mulberry' was first heard.

We tied up alongside the liner *Aorangi,* laid in the Solent, and I climbed aboard her to buy razor blades and a tub of Brylcreem from the NAAFI stores. You don't go on an invasion every day of the week so you might as well look your best. I had sent in a record request to the BBC Forces Requests programme and they duly played Muggsy Spanier's 'Sister Kate' whilst I happened to be listening-in. We were sent on a local job and became literally stuck up a creek without a paddle. Whilst attempting to pull off a landing craft which had drifted onto a mud-bank in a creek near Southampton, we ourselves became stranded in the shallow water and had to wait until high tide to float off.

Shore leave around this time was a game of cat and mouse. Leaving the *Eminent* was one thing, finding her again quite another; if she had moved in the interim she could be anywhere along the south coast doing anything at all, legal or otherwise. On one such occasion in Portsmouth I had been ashore to the pictures only to return and find that she had vanished, but where to? There was nothing for it but to report to the naval barracks in Pompey, an RN Patrol jeep being prevailed upon to take me there. The Duty Officer found me a cabin for the night which overlooked the large square of the parade ground, and a happy evening was spent in good company in the Officers Mess. This pleasant occasion was somewhat marred the next morning when, hangover and all, the combined bands of the Royal Navy and Royal Marines struck up below my window. Matters improved when a pert little WREN brought me a cup of tea in bed. After breakfast an RN jeep took me down to the jetty, from where the duty boats and liberty boats plied back and forth to the hundreds of ships now gathering in the Solent. A launch took me out to the *Aorangi*, a graceful passenger liner more accustomed to cruising the southern oceans on her voyages to and from New Zealand in peacetime, than playing mother ship to rescue tugs. After reporting to the Duty Officer on board I wandered around the ship until a launch became available to take me to the *Eminent*, now lying at anchor in the Solent amid some 70 other ocean-going tugs, masses of landing craft and assorted vessels. It was early June and that was to be my last trip ashore for some time.

Early in 1944 a thick patch of discoloured skin had gradually formed on my calf, it didn't hurt but was rough and as hard as leather. Not knowing what it was, it worried me that lack of treatment could see it worsen; on the other hand if the M.O. said that it was serious it might mean hospitalisation. Not on the verge of this lot I thought, and stayed well clear of doctors. It went away about a year later, still a mystery, but was most likely associated with the jellyfish sting in the same area that had hospitalised me in Gibraltar. The crew was making the ship ready for sea, whilst in the Captain's cabin and the wardroom, papers and charts were spread out and heads bowed over them as they were studied and discussed. The wireless orders giving the frequencies, special signals and codes were also studied, the two main frequencies to be used were 500 kc/s and 2410 kc/s. The guns were cleaned and oiled once more, the American 3" AA gun on the bow and the 20mm Oerlikons on the bridge. Sailing Orders stated that 'Whilst on passage you may engage, by day, any aircraft flying below 1,000 feet if not recognised or identified as friendly; and by night when it is clear that you are being directly attacked, and then only with close range weapons'. A comprehensive list of Allied aircraft and markings was attached. Fire drills were carried out. The Chief had been worrying about his generator lasting out, but no one doubted that he would triumph over adversity and that his engines would get us to the other side and back. When D-Day was postponed for 24 hours due to bad weather, the mounting tension gave way to a feeling of anti-climax and it became boring just hanging around, wanting to get on with it. On the 5th of June we sent our last mail home, expecting that letters would be delayed until after the assault before being forwarded to their destination. An officer came on board with last minute orders and a message of encouragement from General Eisenhower. We had a lifeboat drill, a fire drill, a gas mask drill, another briefing on the Oerlikon and the rifles nestling in their case in the Captain's cabin. Rifles; entrusted to rescue tug personnel, what were they thinking of?

Whilst the Allies assembled an armada to invade and liberate Europe, the Nazi death camps continued murdering and burning 10,000 people a day. The Russians, helped by 150,000 Yugoslavian partisans, launched a massive attack in Belorussia, trapping a German Army Group of 350,000 men. In the Pacific, the island of Saipan was invaded by 20,000 U.S. Marines, who sustained heavy losses. The Australian and New Zealand forces, triumphant in the terrible battles in the jungles of New Guinea, were now deployed to SE Asia. Nearer home, Polish troops fighting with the British Army took part in the capture of Monte Cassino and moved on towards Rome. The war in the jungles of Assam saw the march of the Japanese towards India halted by General Slim's forces in Burma.

The shipping in the Solent stretched in all directions as far as the eye could see, from battleships to landing-craft full of men and equipment, riding uncomfortably at anchor in the gale force winds. Everything and everybody was ready, but the weather wasn't. The hours dragged on until, with Eisenhower's understated phrase, 'OK let's go', the biggest amphibious invasion ever seen got under way, with an estimated 7,000 ships, 11,000 aircraft and nearly 3,000,000 fighting men.

The surface optimism barely obscured the valid reservations about the possible success of the whole D-Day operation. Only twice before had an amphibious assault on enemy territory been attempted, neither of them had gone well, and neither was remotely on the scale of this one. Firstly, at Salerno, five days into the operation Eisenhower had reported: 'We have been unable to advance and the enemy is preparing a major counter-attack'; the Air Force having eventually to be called in to save a desperate situation. Secondly, at Anzio, a landing was made without encountering enemy opposition and complete tactical surprise was achieved, but the very first German counter-attack threatened to throw the Allies back into the sea and re-capture the beach-head. The omens were not good.

Yet here we were, preparing to attack a heavily defended shore, the 'Atlantic Wall' strengthened over years of occupation, guarded by minefields and unpleasant underwater obstacles, with heavy guns and machine gun nests covering the beaches, and the enemy waiting for us. Gloom and anxiety apparently abounded in the offices of the Allied staff and, as we now know, Eisenhower had prepared a second statement along the lines of, 'The Allies have been thrown back into the sea'. The element of surprise was paramount, and major diversionary operations had been carried out over many months, notably in Kent, in order to keep the enemy guessing as to the date and place of the invasion, whether it was to be Normandy or the Pas de Calais. The Germans reasoned that the Pas de Calais was the most likely landing place because it was the shortest sea crossing and would provide the Allies with maximum short-range air support. This seemed to be confirmed by what they were led to believe was a build up of forces just across the straits in Kent; so they kept their Panzer Divisions behind Calais and waited.

Meantime, Eisenhower had expressly forbidden all mention of a harbour in D-Day communiqués, and extended the ban for some time afterwards, fearing that its very existence, and more importantly, its destination, would reveal to the enemy that Normandy was indeed the targeted landing place, and not the diversionary landing that some German strategists thought it might be. The maximum secrecy accorded the Mulberry Harbours doubtless explains why there are no photographs of the hundreds of sections of the harbour being towed across the Channel, or of the hectic assembling of the harbours off the beaches immediately following the landings. Michael Harrison put it succinctly in his book 'Mulberry' 'It is clear that events conceived and born in silence tend to remain undiscussed and unknown'.

Aircraft and gliders had been passing overhead all night, full of British and American parachute troops heading for their drop zones inland from the beaches. Now, under cover of darkness, the first invasion ships moved off towards France. Masses of aircraft in large formations continued to thunder overhead. We received orders to make ready for 1000 hours on the 6th June and await orders. It had seemed at one time that you could almost walk from deck to deck across the solid mass of ships assembled off Spithead and in the Solent, but now the anchorage was gradually emptying as the spearhead landing craft left silently for France.

The code-name for the invasion of Normandy was 'Overlord'; the naval operation within Overlord was code-named 'Neptune', and the section of Neptune that we were engaged in was code-named 'Mulberry'. All rescue tugs had a large 'M' painted on the side of their funnel. The mine-sweepers had been busy in the Channel and the ships at the sharp end of the assault were now proceeding down the mile-wide swept channels towards the beaches, whilst everyone held their breath and waited. The long awaited invasion of Europe was under way at last, but it was still some hours before the world would awake that morning to hear the first communiqué from SHAEF, Supreme Headquarters Allied Expeditionary Force: 'Under the command of General Eisenhower, Allied naval forces, supported by strong air forces, began landing Allied armies this morning on the northern coast of France'.

Once the initial invasion force had passed through the swept channels we could get into the act with our strange-looking tows. Our activities over the past few months now made sense. An amphibious assault on this scale needed a harbour, and nothing was more certain than that the Germans would disable any harbours they held along the French coast long before we could seize them. Invasion troops needed a huge diversity of supplies and they needed them there and then. Some of these supplies could be transported over open beaches during an initial assault period, but not the heavier equipment. Harbours adjoining the landing beaches would be the ideal solution to the problem, because they could ensure continuous landing facilities for supplies and heavy equipment right where and when the troops needed them. Such a harbour would need to be the size of Dover harbour and be built and operative in a couple of weeks. It sounded impossible, (and still does), but the planners thought otherwise, and now we were at the sharp end trying to prove them right.

14: THE SECRET HARBOURS

The answer to the urgent supply problem was to take a harbour with us across the Channel, something never before attempted. Chester Wilmot, the war correspondent, observed after the war that, 'When the D-Day operation was planned, there was no evidence that a supply chain could be sustained over open beaches. The possession of a harbour gave the planners freedom to choose their landing place. Without this psychological advantage the whole venture of D-Day may never have been undertaken'. To build a harbour you first needed some joined-up floating roadway sections, 'Whales', from the beach extending out to seaward. Then you needed a floating pier-head platform, 'Spud', to attach to the seaward end of the length of roadway, the pier-head being capable of rising and falling with the tide between the corner stanchions which anchored it to the sea-bed. With this assembly in place, ships could berth alongside the pier-head platform, discharge their cargo and have it transported down the floating roadway to the shore. All good stuff so far, but you couldn't envisage a floating pier stuck out in the Channel lasting very long in any sort of weather, so some manner of outer protection was called for. Enter the 'Phoenix' units, which could be sunk to form the outer wall of the harbour, thus providing sheltered water for the inner harbour. Some redundant merchant ships, 'Gooseberries', were sunk to act as a breakwater, and floating units, 'Bombardons', were anchored further out from shore to break up wave formations and help provide calmer waters in the approaches to the harbour.

To manoeuvre massive blocks of concrete into position in bad weather, and to do it off a hostile shore, didn't sound much like a piece of cake, but that was something to look forward to. In the wireless-room there was no watch-keeping that day or in the days to come, we went on watch and stayed on as long as necessary, snatching sleep whenever we could. On our first trip, on the 6th June, we took six lengths of roadway through the boom and into the swept channel allocated to us. There were ten channels leading to the Normandy coast, four of them for the Americans going to Utah and Omaha beaches and six for the British and Canadians going to Gold, Juno and Sword beaches. These channels branched off from an assembly area 20 miles SE of the Isle of Wight named 'The Spout', which quickly became known as 'Piccadilly Circus'. Wave after wave of bombers roared overhead, as one group disappeared towards France another followed, until at times the sky seemed full of planes and the noise was deafening. The warships bombarding the beaches and the replies of the German coastal defence guns could be heard all the way across the Channel.

As we progressed southward down our allocated channel, a hospital ship passed us going northward in an adjoining channel, her bows had been blown away and she was being towed stern first back to England, probably having struck a mine. A number of landing craft also passed us in the same channel, most were empty but some had wounded lying on their decks. Everyone managed a wave. Struggling at around four knots, we were passed by two battleships of the *Royal Sovereign* class, going south at great speed. A corvette that we worked closely with on the south coast also passed us, its Aldis lamp flickered, the message said, 'come back safe'.

At the end of the first day's fighting, all five beachheads had been secured at a cost of ten thousand casualties. General Montgomery's invasion plans had included securing the high ground between St. Lo and Villers-Bocage, in order to protect the site of the projected harbour from shelling by the German artillery batteries at Merville. Sixty-odd years later, after walking along the invasion beaches looking at the remains of the harbours we had built, and trying not to get emotional about some half submerged blocks of concrete, we went around the remains of the Merville Battery. Stepping in the footsteps of those men of the Airborne Division who captured the Battery that night, brought home the sacrifices that countless ordinary men made on that momentous day. One incident, typical of countless others, of young lives sacrificed to liberate the continent; in this case to destroy the guns that threatened our harbour assembly area. By 2100 on D-Day the Hampshire Regiment had taken Arromanches on Gold Beach and secured the site for the British harbour which, at that moment, was being towed in sections across the Channel.

In addition to the miles of roadways and the pier-head units, there were some 150 Phoenix units to be towed across the Channel by about 100 ocean-going tugs. Forty or fifty smaller tugs waited off the French coast to nudge the various units into place for settling. The logistics of the overall invasion plan were staggering. The conception and planning, the men and supplies, the ships and the aircraft, the deception plans, the assembly of everything in the right place at the right time in the right order, yet still maintaining the element of surprise, was a feat with no parallel in modern times. Looking back now, at the small part of it that we were involved in, it still seems little short of amazing. For centuries, wars had consisted of men and machines battling it out against other men and machines, but the idea of floating a harbour across a 100 mile stretch of water and placing it on a defended beach was revolutionary; a master stroke that caught the enemy by surprise and turned the tide of the war. Albert Speer, German Minister for Armaments, later said of the harbours: 'By means of a single brilliant technical device, the Atlantic Wall defences became irrelevant'.

We continued down one of the swept channels. At midnight there was a beautiful moon tinged with red, but we had little time to appreciate it. In addition to coping with our own heavy wireless traffic, the enemy had by then located our invasion frequencies and was jamming our signals, making reception almost impossible for much of the time. In the early hours of the morning, a haze made it difficult for the bridge to keep an accurate lane position. It was crucial that we kept to the swept channel, not only because there were likely to be mines to either side of us, but also because there were hundreds of ships, big and small, coming and going all around us. They could see that we were unable to manoeuvre and kept well out of our way, but there were other ships which had been damaged, couldn't manoeuvre, and these presented a real hazard to us.

A lead-weighted canvas bag was wedged amongst the wireless gear, ready to receive the code books and be thrown overboard in the event of our being boarded or captured. The dimmed and shaded lights over the wireless gear radiated a calm and serenity which was at odds with the noise of the jamming from the powerful German transmitters which now blanketed all our frequencies. Most of our wireless traffic was from the beachhead to the control ships off-shore. Our wireless control ship was the cruiser HMS *Scylla* and we had three frequencies to monitor, though so far there had been little directly affecting us. This was not surprising as ours was just one of the myriad specialised jobs that needed doing that day, and everybody was busy trying to put their own particular piece of the jigsaw into place.

The noise of the bombing and gunfire increased as we neared the far shore. Approaching the beach landing area we passed close to the *Rodney* which was firing her 16inch shells continuously. The battleships *Warspite* and *Ramilles*, which had overtaken us earlier, had joined the cruisers *Belfast* and *Diadem* in bombarding targets inland. The shock waves from their guns could be felt through the air and up through the ship's hull. E-boats were reported in the area. A ship to starboard of us was set on fire, probably a tanker judging by the size of the explosion. Wireless messages from the beach to the ships offshore were coming thick and fast, in plain language.

It had taken the best part of 24 hours to make the crossing to Manvieux and somewhere along the way a small infantry landing craft, an LCI, had lashed herself to us with ropes, she was badly damaged and would probably have sunk otherwise. When we arrived offshore we could see beach obstacles sticking up out of the sand and debris everywhere. Battleships and cruisers were bombarding targets just inland, their guns emitting belches of flame as the shells sailed overhead. Rocket launchers fired off their missiles in batches, accompanied by a rushing sound and sheets of flame; awe-inspiring in the daytime, they became even more dramatic as darkness fell. As far as the eye could see in any direction, there were battleships and heavy cruisers bombarding the shore and landing craft weaving their way through the confusion of shipping off the beaches. The smell of cordite filled the air, the noise was deafening and smoke blanketed the whole area.

The weather had fallen away to a light wind and moderate sea. There was no evidence of enemy planes, but there was some activity on the cliffs above the beaches, where we saw planes landing and taking off. As we moved closer to the beach we saw abandoned tanks and equipment lying near to the Landing Craft which lay beached at all angles, their doors open, just as they had hit the beaches that morning. Debris of all kinds lay around in confusion and bodies floating in the shallow water were being washed up on the beach. Some craft had not got as far as the beaches and were caught in the underwater sea defences, or had been damaged by mines. An explosion shook the nearby small seaside town of Arromanches, the blast being felt on the ship. This turned out to be our troops blowing a hole in the concrete sea defences to provide a route off the beach for vehicles. The enemy, initially caught by surprise, was now re-grouping. Air activity was starting up and we also experienced the first of the German glider bombs, which screamed round the anchorage just above sea level, hoping to hit a random target. These were quite alarming and it was like taking an unwilling part in a game of Russian roulette.

We stayed off the beachhead for the next 36 hours, holding on to our tow and keeping out of the way of the Landing craft and other vessels passing us on their way to the beach, waiting until working parties and small craft had cleared sufficient space to allow the securing of our roadway onto the shore. Dusk was falling when we left, the battleships and heavy cruisers were still bombarding targets just inland and the rocket launchers continued to send their screeching tracers of fire towards their targets. The chatter of small arms fire came from the beaches and beyond. E-Boats were now active in the anchorage and bursts of tracer bullets sped low across the water as sporadic engagements took place. Picking our way through the shipping that was milling about off-shore, we set off for home along the northbound channel. Midway across, we came upon an American coast-guard vessel that had broken down and was drifting; we threw her a line and towed her back to England. We were otherwise unhindered, made good speed of 10 knots or more and reached the Solent as dawn was breaking.

Shackled up to another strip of floating roadway, we joined other tugs for a second trip, leaving on the 11th June. The trip south was uneventful, the whole Channel seemed to be wall-to-wall shipping, with vessels of all shapes and sizes coming and going, whilst the bomber formations continued to roar overhead. Our roadways could only be secured to the beach if the area had been cleared of obstacles and the approach had been cleared of underwater mines and defences; and when we reached the beaches we were ordered to lay offshore until signalled to move in closer. There was more than one pier being laid in the harbour now being formed. Wireless messages were coming through our control ship, but nearer in-shore messages could also come via Aldis-lamp, loud-hailer or urgent gestures from ships and beach alike. After our length of roadway was settled in position we turned for home, making good speed through the swept channel, taking about eight hours for the crossing and reaching Lee on Solent on the 14th. Our second trip had been quicker than the first, when there had been chaos and confusion in the aftermath of the landings and we had needed to hang on to our tow for much longer.

We waited with other vessels to take our turn for the next tow. Letters home were hurriedly scribbled, minor repairs carried out and we left the Solent on our third trip at 0330 on the 15th in company with a number of other tows. We cleared the boom at 0800, bound for the American sector at Omaha. In the afternoon, halfway across to France, we broke down. Feeling very vulnerable, we drifted slowly with the current, losing our position in the marked channel, watching the other tows pass us as they continued their way south. Fortunately the weather was good, the engine repairs were soon completed, and after a couple of hours of slowly drifting towards a minefield we were underway again. The tug *Cheerly* was a little way ahead of us with her tow when she was attacked by an E-Boat, which fired a torpedo at her, the missile passing in front of her bow.

15: FLARES IN THE NIGHT

There were two harbours to be constructed simultaneously. One was in the British and Canadian sector off Arromanches on Gold Beach and named 'Mulberry B', ('Port Winston'), which was to serve Gold, Juno and Sword beaches. The other harbour was in the American sector off St. Laurent, named 'Mulberry A' and was to serve Omaha and Utah beaches. Each harbour would stretch along the coast for a couple of miles, with names like St. Laurent and Port en Bessin figuring large in our sailing orders. In those first days everything was an unknown quantity to us, the planners obviously knew what the hoped-for outcome was going to look like but we simply carried out orders, positioning our tows at the locations or co-ordinates to which the sailing orders directed us. Sixty or more years allows for a lot of hindsight, the harbours have been covered in books and television documentaries, and D Day itself has passed into recent history, but at the time we were involved in that history it was organised confusion. When we reached the French coast all we saw was a few miles of beach. The code names, sectors and village names were pinpointed on maps after the war, but by then it wasn't easy to relate the names to where we had actually been in those early days. At the time, we were more concerned with avoiding beach obstacles, dodging other shipping, keeping a lookout for drifting mines, wondering whether a glider bomb was going to hit us or an E-Boat single us out for special attention, and above all was the problem of controlling an unwieldy tow in a congested anchorage. Our first two tows with roadways were to the British sector, the third was to Omaha.

When we reached Omaha on the third trip it was crammed with ships large and small. The bombardment was continuous, with the *Glasgow*, *Texas* and *Arkansas* firing at targets well inland. There were swarms of landing craft and small ships busy inshore as we anchored off the beach in the darkness. At daybreak we moved up to start positioning our roadway, this took us nearly all day because of the low-water obstacles which were still being cleared and the amount of congestion on the beach. Glider bombs continued to whistle around at ship height and there were sporadic sorties by E-Boats off shore, but these were beaten off and were not a serious threat. The Navy and the RAF were providing umbrella protection over the Channel and for the beach operations, so we saw relatively little of the Luftwaffe in those early days of harbour building. Barrage balloons were flown over the harbour to deter low-level attacks. German mine-laying submarines were reported off the beaches.

We left Omaha beach to return home and were about ten miles offshore when an intensive barrage started up. Flares were being sent up all around us and the nearby cruisers were firing their smaller weapons continuously. It was a pitch-dark night and the whole scene was threatening, most of the flares being right above us. The activity continued for some time and at about one-thirty in the morning two E-Boats shot out of the darkness straight across our bows. As we were at continuous action stations all our guns were manned, and we opened fire. The Captain said that he felt certain we had hit one of the E-Boats before they vanished into the darkness as swiftly as they had come. There was a lot more hostile activity around us in mid-Channel throughout the night, the enemy had by now recovered from their initial surprise and were hitting back wherever they could. We reached Lee on Solent on the 17th around midnight and made ready for another tow.

There was fierce fighting in the coastal strip where our troops had secured a foothold, and what was urgently needed was back-up in men and materials. Every soldier needed food, ammunition and equipment to the extent of about a ton a month and all the vehicles required fuel and spares. The beaches could receive 2,500 vehicles a day, a figure which would gradually increase, but the completion of the harbour to the stage where the first supplies came down its roadways was extremely urgent. It was a race against time to get the harbours operational before the enemy, with his greater mobility of road and rail networks, concentrated his forces against our beach-head and pushed us back into the sea.

News of one of our ships filtered through. During December 1943 whilst on stand-by in Campbeltown, the Rescue Tug *Sesame* had been fitting out in Princes Dock in Hull and I had been assigned to her as 2nd Operator. Shortly afterwards this posting was cancelled and I was sent to join *Eminent* instead. At the time I was very disappointed, because joining *Sesame* would have given me three weeks at home over Christmas. As things turned out it could have been my last Christmas anywhere, because she was torpedoed by E-Boats and sank on her way to France on the 11th June. *Sesame* was one of our group of vessels that had left at 0330 that morning and was somewhere ahead of us in the line of tows going south. There were some survivors but I don't know whether the wireless operators were amongst them. They were towing the same lengths of 8-road-units as we were and, according to witnesses, these were still afloat after she sank, with the tow-rope disappearing into the water where she had gone down. This was on the same night that the *Cheerly* had been attacked just ahead of us. The ocean going tug USS Partridge was also sunk that night, so it looked as if the E-boats were attacking the tows as easy targets, because we were slow moving and vulnerable. Or maybe they were simply attacking any targets they encountered.

Sections of the harbours were now beginning to function, the roadways and pier-heads were in place and the outer breakwater protection was taking shape. LCT'S, LCM'S, Rhino Ferries and DUKW'S that previously needed to find space on the congested beaches to unload, could now come alongside the floating pierheads, and the discharge figures rocketed. Tanks, heavy artillery, troops, vehicles and mountains of supplies began to stream into Normandy. The harbours enabled ships to unload in an hour what it could take a beach landing half a day to accomplish. Not only were the rapid turn-round and discharge times an immense bonus, but they came on stream just in time to solve another problem. The beaches had begun to wear out due to the heavy traffic that had passed over them in the first days of the invasion and could no longer cope with tanks and heavy lorries, which increasingly became bogged down in the soft sand. The harbours were proving to be everything their designers could have hoped for, even though not yet fully functional.

On Sunday the 18th we left Selsey Bill on our fourth trip across; the weather was good and we had a large Phoenix in tow, heading for Omaha, but as we proceeded slowly south the weather began to deteriorate. We were in company with about ten other tugs, some of which subsequently lost their tows as the weather worsened. If a tow of this magnitude turns sour, the Captain has to make a quick decision; shackled to a heavy object which shows signs of going under and dragging the ship down with it, you slipped the tow otherwise it was time to abandon ship.

There was a great deal of wireless traffic concerning the renewed enemy action in the Channel. We were constantly passing through the aftermath of skirmishes and the remains of smoke screens as we got further south. At night, flares lit up the sky and we did not feel at all comfortable about these because we were not sure who was sending them up, or for what purpose. Being suddenly illuminated by flares in the middle of the night makes you feel very vulnerable. One of the two bridles on our tow snapped, placing an excessive strain on the remaining bridle, so we hove to. The wind had reached 30 knots and the sea was too rough for any small craft to come to our assistance. We tried to get a wireless message through to *Scylla* to advise her of our situation, but the Germans were still jamming all our frequencies and I doubt that they received it. No one could have helped us anyway, but it was important that other ships knew of this unexpected hazard in the middle of one of the swept channels. So

134

passed Monday the 19th, hove-to in mid-Channel, half-connected to 6,000 tons of floating concrete, the storm increasing and the ship out of radio contact with the beachhead.

Tuesday the 20th wasn't much better, but we made slow progress towards France, arriving offshore during the morning. We could not bring our half-connected and unwieldy mass of concrete close in-shore because, if matters took a turn for the worse, we were capable of destroying Mulberry A and half the shipping in it single-handed. We were doubtless not the only ones to feel apprehensive about the situation. It must have been alarming for large vessels like the *Arkansas*, *Texas* and *Glasgow*, busily engaged in bombarding targets ashore, to see a small concrete mountain apparently out of control bearing down on them. We received a number of frantic messages, both on the Aldis-lamp and by wireless, all of them curt and unfriendly, telling us to keep clear.

To make things more interesting, the Chief rang the bridge to advise that we were running low on Luboil and that he would have to shut down one of our engines. The tenuous grasp that we had on controlling our tow disappeared at this juncture. We had 6,000 tons of dead-weight concrete only partly attached to us, were now working on one engine instead of two and were bearing down on a very congested and busy anchorage in choppy waters, with gale force winds from seaward making matters worse by the minute. We could tell our friendly neighbourhood battleship about our misfortunes and induce instant apoplexy, but there seemed little point. The shore line was a jumble of Landing craft mixed with chunks of the battered harbour, and other wreckage bobbed drunkenly around the anchorage, so their pointed advice to us by lamp to keep clear of all shipping in the anchorage went straight over our heads. We were largely hostages to fortune, no longer in control of our own destiny, nor theirs either had they but known.

We badly needed good weather, but instead got a strong NE wind with waves six or eight feet high driving us on shore. It was also around the time of the full moon, which brought the spring high tides with it and, already disabled, we didn't need any of this. The Commanding Officer of a British warship inside the Omaha 'Mulberry' wrote of the situation there on this very day: 'The scene inside the Mulberry was one of unutterable chaos; literally hundreds of Landing craft were ashore, piled one upon another. The floating roadways had vanished. The bombardons were chasing one another madly round the bay. The Phoenixes had cracked and what little sea-room remained was packed with wreckage. DUKW's, Landing craft, coasters and barges were dragging their anchors steadily toward the beach'. ('Operation Neptune', Cmdr. K. Edwards R.N.). Enter the *Eminent* from left stage, half-connected to 6,000 tons of concrete and breathing heavily. It was a perfect SNAFU situation.

During that long tense day we battled through the area north of the breakwater line, slowly and majestically moving ever westward whilst endeavouring to keep our head to wind to allow us some semblance of control over the tow, however slight. Our target area of Omaha Beach was now well behind us. We entered new territory in the shape of Utah Beach and encountered a fresh set of problems, one of which was that we had no detailed map of the sector because we were not supposed to be anywhere near it in the first place. The American battleships Tuscaloosa, Quincy and Nevada were firing their heavy guns in the direction of Ste.-Mere-Eglise, all was noise and confusion and they were probably as surprised to see us as we were to see them. The Saint Marcouf Islands loomed up ahead, about four miles offshore, commanding the approaches to the Carentan Canal. We could imagine that this would be strategically fortified and hoped that some of our troops had already sorted it out. The weather showed little sign of abating as we continued our unsteady way slowly westward, hoping that the weather would relent sufficiently to allow us to regain control of the situation. There were some small craft taking shelter close inshore and one of these, a plucky little American tug, ventured out to help us but after making some valiant attempts to get a line aboard the Phoenix it became clear that the weather was too bad for her to do anything and she had to give up.

We hove-to all the night of the 21st about a mile offshore, probably opposite Ste.-Mere-Eglise. We had tried to get closer inshore to find shelter, but it was all far too dangerous so we came out to sea again. Apparently we were the only rescue tug from the last group still holding on to its tow. During daylight on the 22nd we struggled towards Omaha beach, avoiding obstacles and trailing our caisson behind us. There were two Phoenix units and two floating breakwaters washed up on the beach, well away from where they must originally have been placed. The Bombardon breakwaters were another outer defence of the harbours that the storm had dislodged from their moorings, some of them were busy acting like battering rams, breaking down the concrete sides of the caissons and adding to the chaos that the storm was creating. We held on to our tow throughout that troubled day whilst the storm increased until, during the evening of Thursday the 22nd, we finally manoeuvred our Phoenix into position in what was left of the harbour wall and turned eastward to locate the entrance to a channel which would lead us back to England. This had been our longest and toughest trip, spending five days off the French coast in dreadful weather and horrendous towing conditions.

In his own Report, General Eisenhower said of the storm, 'the Mulberries themselves began to disintegrate, particularly the U.S. installation, which was in an even more exposed position off St. Laurent than the British one at Arromanches. The Phoenix caissons shifted and the angry seas poured through the gaps, pounding craft against the piers and smashing them to pieces. Only the blockships saved the situation from becoming one of complete disaster, with consequences so serious as to imperil our very foothold on the Continent'.

Shortly after midnight, as we headed north in mid-channel, flares lit up the sky over the ship and a plane circled around us four times, flying very low. It failed to respond to our recognition signals so we opened fire, Jim claiming that he scored a hit on the plane and, as there was a red flash low over the water in the direction of its eventual departure, it may well have been forced to ditch. We reached Lee-on-Solent just after dawn on the morning of the 23rd of June, the anchorage was almost empty save for damaged ships, various mother ships, and assorted small craft.

By now we were all shattered and living on our nerves, continuously short of sleep, physically exhausted, mentally stressed and generally punch-drunk. The *Eminent* was little better, she was to take us across that hostile stretch of water five times and bring us back safely, towing objects she surely never reckoned on seeing in her lifetime. Her builders would have been proud of her. Now all we wanted was to settle in a quiet creek and go to sleep for a month. The soldiers in the ditches of Normandy doubtless felt as exhausted as we did, yet had to go on fighting. But everyone who survived those first days was luckier than those who stayed on the beaches that first morning. Back in England the *Eminent* had developed a number of minor defects and we spent two days at anchor in the Solent as reserve duty tug whilst these were fixed. Everyone caught up on sleep and also took advantage of the facilities on board the *Aorangi*, sending the ship's boat across frequently for the crew to buy writing materials, soap and other necessities, and to enjoy the luxury of walking round the decks of a large vessel as a change from the cramped space we lived in aboard the *Eminent*.

On the 29th of June we set off for France on our fifth trip, towing a concrete coffin. The storm had damaged the American harbour so badly that they had probably abandoned any idea of patching it up. On the way across we received orders to take our Phoenix to help bolster the sea wall of the British harbour. We positioned our tow successfully along the outer edge of the harbour and set off for home. There was a lot of enemy aircraft activity as we crossed the Channel, but neither aircraft nor E-Boats singled us out for attention and we returned to the Solent on the 2nd July, where we stayed at anchor for six wonderful days, catching up on sleep

On the 8th of July we left with another tow but received a wireless message when part way across, recalling us due to an increase in E-Boat activity in the Channel.

16: FIRE ON BOARD

The American Mulberry had been virtually destroyed in the storms of the latter part of June, but the British Mulberry, with its standard caissons, was a little further advanced in construction and survived in better condition. It was more sheltered, better assembled and better planted, as Eisenhower later acknowledged. Although greatly reduced in handling capacity by the storm, the British harbour serviced a steady 7,000 tons of supplies a day, including much heavy equipment that could not be landed by any other means. The harbour continued to function well into the winter, until the capture of Antwerp finally provided the Allies with a major mainland port through which to channel supplies. Mr Churchill later said of the Mulberry Harbour: 'This miraculous port has made possible the liberation of Europe'.

The harbours had been built, our part in the overall scheme of things was accomplished, and it had all gone better than expected. Rescue Tug casualties had been estimated at 25% by official sources before Operation Neptune began, but of the hundred or more ocean going tugs that took part in the D-Day operation, the British *Sesame* and the American *Partridge* were the only casualties. We felt the loss of both vessels, with shipmates on one and working with the other before D-Day. Other ships that we had worked closely with were the destroyers *Onslow* and *Onslaught* and they both came through safely.

Our only casualty occurred in the engine room, where a motor starter-handle kick-back struck a young boilerman on the head, killing him instantly. This cast a gloom over the whole ship; it was sad to think that we had come through the invasion without a single casualty only to lose him through an accident. Throughout the period when we were building the harbour, the whole area was subjected to whatever attacks the Germans could muster; mines were a hazard anywhere and at any time, as were the random low flying bombs. Marauding E-Boats came and went, sometimes in groups. An occasional U-boat had been reported in the Channel. Human torpedoes were another problem, they were much the same as those in Gibraltar Bay. The aircraft that attacked and sank the *Lawford*, two days after D-Day, were constrained by the RAF, who kept the skies above the beaches virtually clear of enemy aircraft throughout the invasion period. The Navy kept both ends of the Channel bottled up against incursion from any large German surface vessels and also restricted any U-boat activity.

All the tugs involved in Mulberry had been run to a standstill. No repairs had been allowed over the June/July period other than those essential to keep vessels at sea, and now it was time to catch up instead of patch up. In July we sailed up the Thames to the repair yard of Green and Siley Weir at Blackwall for a scheduled month's refit. We also sailed straight into the line of fire of the V.1 missiles, or 'buzz-bombs' as they came to be called. Blackwall, Silvertown, Canning Town and the East India Docks suffered heavily as these missiles came over in increasing numbers and there were more shattered homes and piles of rubble every time we went ashore. The buzz-bombs came over every few minutes, the menacing drone of their engines the only warning of their approach. When the engine cut out as its fuel supply ran dry, there was a period of suspense and an ominous silence as the explosive began its descent.

American Flying Fortresses by day and British Lancasters by night were increasingly making sorties deeper into Germany, attacking strategic targets and giving support to the Russians, who continued to bear the brunt of the land fighting. After years of being bombed we were at last able to take the air war to the enemy, the mood in the country being in favour of dumping bombs on any part of Germany that could help shorten the war, and as quickly as possible. Brief spells of leave came along whilst we were undergoing repairs and there was lots to talk about at home, everyone being amazed to learn about the harbours. The newspapers had printed the authorised daily bulletins about the air and ground fighting but there was never a word about Mulberry. General Eisenhower had indeed done a good job.

We visited various pubs in the East End, making friends, some of whom came back aboard with the crew, including the boxers Jack London and Eddie Phillips. I sought out Collins Music Hall and The Angel at Islington. The Elephant and Castle, the Prospect of Whitby and Dirty Dick's were all well supported. When the thick fog descended, all the villains I'd ever read about seemed to lurk in every corner.

The need for deep-sea rescue tugs had now lessened, we had the upper hand in the Atlantic and had towed the harbours to France. But the war in the East still raged and when the *Eminent* had completed her repairs we were ordered up to Methil in Scotland. From there we were to go to Iceland to collect AFDIT, a floating dock, and tow her halfway round the world to Sydney, Australia. On this escapade we were to be accompanied by our sister ship *Lariat*. We left dock together and proceeded up river into the North Sea, but had not gone very far when flames were seen coming out of our engine room. Efforts were made to extinguish the fire, but it could not be contained. There were fuel tanks just beneath the deck plating, above the engine room itself, consequently the danger of an imminent explosion loomed large and the order was given to abandon ship.

Being on watch at the time, I was called to the bridge and received instructions from the Captain to send a distress signal. After sending the SOS on 500 kc/s, I joined the rest of the crew who were scrambling over the side into the Carley Float, the ship's boat having already filled up and pulled away. We drifted about in the water for a while getting our feet wet, before willing hands hauled us aboard the *Lariat*. We circled the *Eminent* for some time and, as the fire seemed to be no worse, a volunteer boat party put off from the *Lariat* to go aboard her. After an hour or so the boarding party managed to bring the fire under control and the rest of us returned on board. The *Lariat* put a line aboard and towed us into Harwich. We spent a day alongside whilst an examination of the damage was carried out and were then towed back to East India Docks, to be greeted with cries of, 'Not you lot again', from the dock workers as we came alongside. This was another major refit job for the *Eminent* as the damage caused by the fire was extensive. A skeleton crew was left on board her in East India Dock and the rest of us were sent on Survivors' Leave before being dispersed to other vessels or shore bases.

By this time the Rescue Tug Service was approaching what was to be its full strength, over 150 vessels in all, and a second shore base, HMS *Badger,* had been established in the Great Eastern Hotel, Harwich, near to the harbour entrance. After a brief home leave, a kind-hearted Admiralty sent me there on the 9th of September 1944 to live what was, for wartime, a life of luxury. I had a pleasant and spacious bedroom, all meals were served in the elegant dining room which was furnished in all the grandeur of the Victorian era. The food was excellent, the entrance hall stately, the grand staircase was in keeping with tradition and I was wakened every morning with a cup of tea by a WREN in a white blouse, navy blue skirt and black silk stockings. Now what more could you ask for. Well, yes, but let's leave that. It was all better than towing blocks of concrete to France. The Three Cups pub was next door, and the Pier Hotel was only a short distance away, so we were well catered for. There was also a small cinema nearby, with others further afield at Dovercourt and Parkestone Quay. The hotel was full of Operators and there was a lot of social activity, including parties with the WRENs in our accommodation.

After a fortnight of lotus eating, a signal came from CCRT directing me to Portsmouth barracks and from there to the liner *Empress of Russia*, which was anchored in the Solent doing duty as a mother ship for small craft. The launch that took me out to her came alongside some submarines that were tied up to this stately vessel and I had to clamber over three or four of them, lugging my gear with me, in order to reach the foot of the gangway. By the time I had climbed up to the deck, seemingly hundreds of feet above me, I was worn out and ready for bed. After a few days on board I was sent to the *Enticer* as relief for an Operator going on leave. The *Enticer* was one of a slightly larger class of vessels than the *Allegiance* and I joined her on the 27th of September when she came into Portsmouth. We meandered along the Channel to Falmouth, staying there a few days before moving to Swansea, where there were plenty of theatres and cinemas. After a few days we were banished to Milford Haven, where *Enticer* was to become duty rescue tug on station. Thankfully the Operator returned from leave, and I was glad to give him his ship back. The return journey to base was tedious and the train took ages to reach Swansea, but this was compensated for by spending time in London before catching the train to Harwich.

Life continued sweetly at Harwich, and a couple of weekends at home were engineered. Also, when it seemed propitious, I took off for London in mid week for the occasional day out. Another relieving job turned up, this time on the *Superman*, where else but Milford Haven, a journey with numerous changes, slow trains stopping at every station on the way and when you finally got there: nothing. Relieving jobs were a real bind, you had to take all your gear with you each time in case the ship you were joining put to sea. It was the middle of December 1944, cold, and a long miserable crowded and wholly uncomfortable journey lay ahead of me. In London a visit was made to the 'Windmill' as a token farewell to civilisation before lumping my baggage onto a GWR train bound for the West Country and beyond, endeavouring to sleep it all off in a corner seat. The journey was as slow and tedious as expected, particularly west of Swansea. When the train reached Milford Haven at some ghastly hour in the morning everywhere was freezing cold, blacked out and steeped in gloom. I walked some distance, carrying two heavy suitcases, in order to find a taxi which could help me locate the *Superman*. We stopped to enquire her whereabouts at every police box at every dock we came to, eventually locating her hours later and miles away, at Pembroke Dock. By that time, cold tired and hungry, after a wretched journey, lugging my bags everywhere, a freezing taxi ride and dawn just breaking, it felt like the end of the world. Her engines were shut down, there was neither heat nor light on board, she was cold, cold, cold and covered in damp layers of coal dust. 'Miserable' a didn't even come close.

The gallant old *Superman* had been called up for service early in the war when the situation was really desperate. She was a river tug, happily plying her trade up and down the Humber for the United Towing Company of Hull, but the war arrived and changed everything. One of the original tugs hastily requisitioned when war broke out, she performed much dangerous and courageous work in those dark days of 1939 and 1940. She was pushed to the limit, and I guess that even when they gave her a prestigious White Ensign to fly, and put a 20mm AA gun aboard her, she would much rather have gone back to nudging ocean-going ships into their berths. She'd done her bit and now there were lots of big powerful tugs out there so why not go home? But no one was listening to her and she was put out to grass here, at the end of the line.

Nevertheless she was a happy little ship; we never moved from the quayside and my sojourn aboard her was only long enough to find out where the local NAAFI was and to board the *Stormking*, which also had the misfortune to be there, before packing my bags once more and hyping myself up for the journey back to Harwich. Taking leave of the card group on the *Stormking*, with whom I had been playing Crib and Newmarket for the past ten days trying to ward off insanity, I left the *Superman* on New Year's Eve, travelling by bus to Johnston to catch the London train, celebrating the New Year of 1945 in a blacked-out crowded smoky train somewhere along the way. Paddington was reached early on New Year's morning and, after a railway buffet breakfast, the morning was spent buying records in Woolwich, the afternoon in Foyle's book shop and the evening seeing 'Kismet' at the Empire, Leicester Square. The slow train from Liverpool Street got me to Harwich well past midnight and to an extremely welcome bed in the Great Eastern.

17: GUARDING THE THAMES

In January 1945, CCRT appointed me to the St. Mellons, lying at Tilbury. Her Captain was Lt. Arthur Godfrey Hawkins, OBE, RNR, of *San Demetrio* fame, better known to all on board as 'Hungry Hawkins'. In November 1940 convoy HX84 out of Halifax, Nova Scotia, had been intercepted by the German pocket battleship Admiral Scheer, the ensuing action witnessing the gallant sacrifice of the Armed Merchant Cruiser *Jervis Bay*, when she tried to divert enemy fire from the convoy she was protecting. This action also saw the shelling of the tanker *San Demetrio*, which was carrying 12,000 tons of petrol, setting her on fire. Two boats were launched from the tanker, these later becoming separated in the gale and heavy seas, 2nd Officer Hawkins being in charge of the second boat. The following morning the vessel was still on fire and spewing petrol but remained afloat, so the surviving crew re-boarded her. Without any aids to navigation, under enormous difficulty and in danger from further attack, 2nd Officer Hawkins and the crew brought the *San Demetrio* through 1,000 miles of North Atlantic hazards safely into the River Clyde.

Back in 1942, when at wireless college, we practised sending morse to one another from newspapers or any available book to hand, the book that I carried around with me for this purpose was a 6d paperback, 'The Saga of *San Demetrio*'. I still have the book, with the pencilled ticks denoting the division of the sentences into groups of five letters still evident. The book was made into a film in 1943, *'San Demetrio* London', and little did I imagine that I would be sailing with the hero of that epic voyage before the war was out.

The *St. Mellons* was alongside at Tilbury having some minor repair work carried out. It was clear that she wasn't going anywhere in a hurry and Lt. Hawkins gave me 48 hours leave. Returning on board, I was made Duty Officer whilst others went on leave and soon afterwards I was granted another 48 hours leave. These brief periods at home were spent at the cinema, seeing Jean and any friends who were also on leave, the bush telegraph being very effective. Arrival times at Paragon Station seemed invariably to be 3 or 4 in the morning and I kept awake from Kings Cross to Doncaster in order to avoid missing my connection and getting carried on to Newcastle. Approaching Hull by train during the night, one thing to look out for in the darkened countryside was the large revolving metal cylinder of the Earles Cement works near Brough. Even with the blackout precautions, there were always a few chinks of light from the furnace to be seen and you took your bearings from these, knowing that it was almost time to get your luggage down from the rack.

Tilbury was a good base from which to reach many places, particularly the West End, where I joined the jostling crowd of Americans and others of the Allied Forces in the Forces Clubs, cinemas and theatres. A trip was made to Chatham to see a WREN friend from Campbeltown, but she had been transferred elsewhere at short notice, as indeed had the *St. Mellons* during my absence, having sailed from Tilbury to Southend, so another train was needed to rejoin her. We stayed at Southend as Thames Guard Ship and Duty Rescue Tug for some weeks, anchored unhappily off the end of the closed and deserted longest pier in the world. Quite what we were supposed to guard we weren't sure, but London would doubtless sleep more easily knowing that we were on station. Occasionally we went alongside the pier-head, where the dilapidated peacetime fun fair was tastefully decorated in army camouflage and barbed wire. It was bitterly cold from that January through to March and the only consolation that we had, shared by an army detachment and a Boom Defence Unit billeted at the pier head, was the exclusive use of the 'tiddly railway' that ran the mile and a half between the pier head and the shore. The buzz bombs continued to drone overhead every few minutes on their way to London.

I was to be further depressed that bleak winter. Most of the Post Office Messengers were in the forces and we wrote to each other to keep in touch. Nothing of importance was written about, all mail passing through the censor, and we had enough sense not to comment on war matters. Ken Priestman, who lived at 36 Kelvin Street, had joined a tank regiment and he wrote to me on the 3rd January 1945 from 'A' squadron, 5th RIDG, BLA (British Land Army) in reply to a letter of mine he had just received, bemoaning the fact that we were both miles from home at Christmas. He wrote 'We'll have to see what (next) Xmas brings, and make up for all this balls'. The envelope was marked, 'On Active Service', and had been opened by the Censor. I wrote back to Ken on the 23rd of January. A little while later my letter was returned with a rubber stamp on the front, which read: 'IT IS REGRETTED THAT THIS ITEM COULD NOT BE DELIVERED BECAUSE THE ADDRESSEE IS REPORTED DECEASED'.

On the back of the envelope, which had been opened and sealed again at the APO, Army Post Office, someone had written 'Return to 'Jack', H.M.R.T. *St. Mellons*, c/o GPO London'. And that was Ken, gone forever; an only child, never to return home to Kelvin Street and never to see that next Christmas. For what? Why? Like millions of other young men across the world, his only crime had been that he was in the wrong place at the wrong time. Hardly a day has passed since that I haven't thought of him, a fine lad whose life was ended before it had begun.

Towing trips to Brightlingsea and back to Southend were followed by a rail trip to London to take CB's to the Admiralty. Another spell of leave at home followed, during which I travelled to Sheffield to see Gloria who was at University there, and we reminisced about happy days on the sands at Bridlington and Scarborough. The Rescue Tugs that had taken part in the Invasion had been refitted, their crews rested, and most were being sent to the Far East to continue the war against the Japanese. For others it was rest and prop up the sea wall for a while, which made a pleasant change. The war seemed to have been largely taken out of our hands now and was down to the aircrews and the soldiers fighting on the Continent. The ship was undergoing minor repairs so mother came down to London for a few days. We stayed at the Euston Hotel and packed a lot into her visit, seeing Anne Shelton at the Finsbury Park Empire, frequented Lyon's Corner House cafes, Express Dairies, ABC and Fortes milk bars and the Monseigneur News Theatre in Leicester Square. We also saw Kay Hammond at the Apollo Theatre in 'Private Lives', visited Madame Tussaud's, the Zoo, and travelled everywhere on red double-deckers or Green Line coaches. After her departure I collected some CB's from an office in Admiralty Arch and returned to the ship at Tilbury.

The film 'Western Approaches' was released about this time; it was an excellent portrayal of the Merchant Navy at war and was made on a shoestring by the talented (ex GPO) Crown Film Unit. Its cast were all serving officers and men of the Merchant and Allied Navies and it portrayed a realistic account of the merchant seaman's war. Unfortunately it was overshadowed by 'In Which We Serve' which received all the publicity, having the money and the big names. We moved up river for compass adjusting before returning to anchor off Southend Pier, where the buzz bombs continued to drone overhead every few minutes, day and night. If you wanted a definition of indiscriminate terror bombing you couldn't do better than a buzz bomb.

In mid-March the *St. Mellons*, built by Harland and Wolff at Govan in 1918 and showing her age, moved up to Sheerness for bunkers. Bunkering meant that the whole ship was covered in coal dust and the crew with it. In November 1944, a matter of weeks before I joined her, she had been towing barge BK6757, loaded with liquid explosives, from Spithead to Dover when a gale forced her to take shelter off Newhaven. The barge broke adrift at the height of the storm and ran ashore near the West Pier where it exploded, killing 19 people and injuring 13. After this episode, the old girl probably needed a little peace and quiet off Southend Pier.

My cabin was on the starboard side, up for'ard and off the saloon/wardroom. It was very cramped, contained a bunk next to the hull with a porthole above it and drawers underneath. There was an ancient washstand with a mirror and a tip-up basin that emptied into a can beneath; doubtless the washstand was the last word in ablutionary luxury at the time she was built. A tiny settee was squashed in at the narrow end of the cabin where it followed the curve of the ship's hull towards the bow. There was hardly room to turn around, let alone swing a cat. The cabin was probably 8' by 5' and was one of six that opened off the saloon, where a square dining table took up most of the space. The only exit from the saloon was a narrow doorway that gave on to an enclosed deck leading aft. It was a classic death-trap situation, especially as my cabin was in the farthest corner, diagonally across from the doorway. I had already calculated that I could leap across the cabin table to the door in one bound if the need arose.

18: VICTORY IN EUROPE

Towards the end of March we left Southend in convoy towing a landing craft, bound for the Schelde and Antwerp. The number of U-boats in operational condition had now reached 463, the highest figure of the war, but despite this, mines continued to take a greater toll of shipping than did the U-boats. German surface vessels from west Holland were still active off the Dutch coast, attacking our shipping in the approaches to Antwerp. We saw recent evidence of this on the way across the North Sea in the form of wrecks sticking up out of the shallow water. Buzz bombs droned overhead every few minutes. The Mulberry Harbour continued to supply the troops as they battled across France and Germany, maintaining the Allied supply line when there was no other port able to do the job. Its planners had hoped that it would outlast the first crucial month following D-Day when the battle for Europe hung in the balance, but it had functioned well past that, on into the winter months, and it was only with the capture of the port of Antwerp in 1945 that the load was lifted from its weary shoulders. Rear Admiral Edward Ellsberg wrote in his book, The Far Shore: 'So, without fanfare... long vanished from that blood-stained beach, Operation Mulberry, that fantastic conceit which had made the Normandy Invasion stick, faded into oblivion.'

By March 1945, some 6,000 V.1 flying bombs had crossed the Channel, killing over 6,000 people and seriously injuring three times that number. A further 2,800 people were to be killed by the thousand or more V2 rockets which had now started to fall on London. Nearly all these weapons were aimed at greater London and were fired over the Channel and the southern North Sea between mid-1944 and March 1945. Having been in that corridor virtually all of that period I count myself lucky not to have become a statistic. The Germans were now increasingly desperate as they were driven back towards Berlin and were throwing everything they had at London and southern England in a last ditch attempt to turn the tide in their favour. And it so nearly succeeded. It was touch and go right to the end as to whether the V-weapons would inflict the devastation that would lead to the capitulation of Britain that Hitler hoped for, before we could locate and destroy them and their launching sites.

There was a slim chance of destroying a flying bomb in flight because they were visible, followed a steady course and flew at a pre-determined height at around 400 mph before the fuel ran out, but the V2 rockets were a different kettle of fish altogether and there was no defence against them. They could be launched from fixed or mobile sites hidden in forests, carried a ton of explosives, reached a height of 50 miles and fell faster than the speed of sound, so there was no prior warning of approach and no interception was possible. The threat was only overcome after many months when the Allies had fought their way into Holland and over-run the last of the launching sites. Even at this late stage the Germans were working on an inter-continental missile capable of reaching the cities of the eastern seaboard of America. In 1945 how very nearly could defeat have emerged from the jaws of victory.

The *St. Mellons* picked her way carefully up river and berthed in Antwerp docks. There was ample evidence of the ravages of war all around and we could hear sounds of battle not far distant. A group of us walked around the devastated centre of the town, which was deserted and quiet. In the evening we visited Skipper Street, where the small cafes were putting on a brave show of 'business as usual' with bread and wine and not much else, whilst the violins and accordions played in the background. We moved on to the Navy House, the RN Barracks, and ended up in the NAAFI canteen which was full of all ranks and nationalities, drinking and exchanging experiences with other servicemen long into the night

There was much work to be done in Antwerp, clearing the docks so that supplies could land near to the front line, finally lifting the strain off the lone Mulberry Harbour that had continued to channel supplies for the last nine months. One day, a few of us hitched a lift with some soldiers in the back of an army lorry to Gent, and then on to Bruges. There was not much to do there so we wandered amongst the bombed buildings, stopping at any small cafes that we found open. There was little food available, but the wine seemed plentiful so we pooled our money on the table in the approved fashion and proceeded to sample the local vintage. We were joined by a couple of girls and the afternoon passed most agreeably, though seldom have I seen money disappear from a table so quickly. We were all very happy and pleased with ourselves by the time the army collected us later that evening to take us back.

The following day we hitched a lift in an army lorry to Brussels, which was full of jeeps, half-tracks, tanks and vehicles of all kinds. Military personnel from every allied country thronged the streets and it was as though London, immediately pre-invasion, had been transferred en masse. The occasional sound of gunfire could be heard as we were not many miles from the fighting. We saw the film 'Henry V' at a NAAFI cinema and had dinner at the NAAFI Officers Hostel, afterwards travelling by train, (free to servicemen), back to Antwerp. Our last night there was spent at the Onyx Café and the Central Bar before moving up river to Terneuzen. With the exception of a few days working at Flushing, during which we wandered round the wasteland of shattered buildings, we remained at Terneuzen as Duty Rescue Tug, Schelde, for the next few weeks. Watch was now being kept on V/S (visual) for shipping and signal stations instead of wireless watches, so there wasn't much for me to do except read, write letters, or join in the card games which proliferated all over the ship. The sound of distant heavy gunfire continued and large formations of bombers thundered overhead day and night, followed by the sound of bombs exploding as they found their targets further inland.

We went alongside the rescue tug *Sea Giant* in Terneuzen for a few days, she was one of two American mercantile tugs serving with the Royal Navy and was a hotchpotch of superstructures, very interesting to explore. Some mail arrived to brighten things up. What a great job the Armed Forces Mail Office did to maintain the flow of letters to and from home throughout the war, considering all the movements of armies and ships and later the chaos in Europe, all the while maintaining the essential secrecy necessary. As we moved up and down river, doing all manner of odd jobs, we passed close to sandbanks with the debris of war cast up on them, including some German helmets, some said with heads still inside, although I didn't see any. What I did see however were packs of rats running around, so I drew my own conclusions. Things livened up when we were sent to escort some landing craft from Ostend. We took them across the mouth of the Schelde and out through the swept passage in the minefields into the North Sea before returning to Terneuzen. Always uncomfortable, going through minefields. The minesweepers had done their job and the swept channel was well marked by buoys, but mines have a habit of wandering off on their own sometimes, especially when bad weather detaches them from their moorings on the seabed.

Terneuzen is at the head of the Albert Canal and most evenings groups of us went for a walk along its grassy banks towards Gent; the peaceful water, wild flowers and bird-song contrasting with the sounds of war in the background. The Seaman arrived in the middle of April and we had fresh faces to swop yarns with. There were yet more attempts by the uncertified to attain Cardinal Puff status and, being in possession of this valuable document, I could afford to sit back and enjoy the fun. One day we acquired a horse-drawn Hansom Cab; the horse was docile and we took turns with the reins, driving around Terneuzen. The army and RAF had plenty of transport and this was always available for a free lift. We travelled in a covered RAF lorry to Salsate, visiting various cafes, and I bought a mirrored jewellery box from a shop which had nothing else in its window; the people were probably selling their possessions to buy food and I paid the asking price.

On 4th May 1945 the Germans surrendered in northern Europe and VE Day was declared. Everybody climbed aboard everyone else's ships and joy, mingled with relief, spread over Terneuzen, its citizens, the Army, Navy and Air Force alike. The long, long nightmare had finally come to an end. War is dreadful and surely a last resort, but this was one war that had to be fought. And it had to be won, or Britain would have gone the way of the continent, and a second Dark Ages would have beset Europe. The *St. Mellons* was presented with a cake by the citizens of Terneuzen who regarded her as part of the scenery, having propped up their sea wall for so long; also some of us had domestic contacts ashore.

In the period following the end of the war, much became clear to the Allies as the German war machine was dissected, and it was seen just how close run the victory had been. The V2's had been stopped only just in time when the sites were over-run by our advancing troops. Another secret weapon, the V3, was being readied in the hills above Calais, a giant gun 350 ft below ground and with a 400 ft barrel, trained on London; fifty of these were planned, each firing a large shell every 12 seconds. Another few short weeks and it could all have been very different, with the 'Nazi Pestilence', as Churchill called it, resurging at the eleventh hour. As slave labourers were released, stories of their treatment were eclipsed only by the horrors of the camps and death ovens at

Treblinka, Auschwitz and Bergen-Belsen. When the black and white newsreels of the camps and the 'March of Time' documentaries appeared on cinema screens people fell silent; I remember being in cinemas over this period, and the chill that spread through the audience. Even after the reports on the radio and in the newspapers, nothing prepared people for the stark reality of film, the depths of human depravity laid bare, and the realisation that it could have happened here. On a personal note, the conflict had lost me three friends, a school friend, Kenneth Simpson, had been killed, Ken Priestman from the Post Office had been killed as also had Jed Croom, another Messenger. Dan, George, Geoff and I never took life for granted from then on, indeed we often told each other that every day was a bonus.

A signal arrived ordering us to proceed to the Downs for onward routing to Plymouth. We made our way down river, past the submerged fields of Walcheren, where the Allies had opened the dyke gates in order to flood the land prior to invading the area, and joined up with a convoy to go through the minefield. As we moved south there were flashes and the sound of explosions from the direction of Calais and Dunkirk. Whether these were isolated units still fighting, we knew not. We anchored off Deal due to fog, eventually arriving at Plymouth, where George was on the Reward and other friends were on the *Growler*, so there was a combined all-night party before we sailed next day for Falmouth.

The *Allegiance* was laid alongside in Falmouth and there was yet another round of parties to survive and cinemas to visit. It was the heyday of Hollywood escapist musicals and the cinemas were full of uniforms and girls. Apart from being despatched in the middle of the night to locate and tow in a gunnery target that had broken adrift, we spent an untroubled couple of weeks in Falmouth. The atmosphere was one of immeasurable relief, a huge evil cloud had been lifted after five long, long years of war and menace. The dark days and uncertainty had lasted right until the end and we could scarcely comprehend that it was finally over. We told ourselves that it was indeed over but didn't dare to believe it. Five years of living through war is not shaken off easily and the reality of peace was going to take time to sink in. The strain lifted from everyone, the coming together in time of threat that had united the nation now relaxed, total strangers hugged each other and the euphoria of escape from danger floated like a bright cloud over the whole country.

We were called out in the early hours one morning to locate the

Marie Flore, a French vessel in trouble in the Channel, towing her into Falmouth. Our next job was to assist the *Enchanter* in the Bristol Channel, where she was having difficulty with a large dry dock tow in bad weather. The following day we moved to Portsmouth to become Duty Rescue Tug, taking turn about with *Resolve*. A fun fair was nearby and a crowd of us joined in the first such activity seen for a very long time, sailors and girls all enjoying themselves. And the lights! Wonderful, after years of darkness. No more blackout, no more stumbling over kerb edges or bumping into people and lampposts in the dark.

The *St. Mellons* had been named after a village in South Wales. Some forty years after the war I visited the church there and was made welcome by the Vicar, who showed me the ship's ensign, tattered and worn, hanging above the aisle, and her port navigation light resting in an alcove. It was pleasing to see this tangible evidence of times past being treasured and respected; at peace now in the church, it was still capable of stirring memories. The people of the village had adopted the *St. Mellons* during the war and it seemed fitting that a part of her had come to rest in their midst, now that her long and eventful life was over. We were presently moored at the King's Stairs, Portsmouth, alongside the battleship *Renown* which dwarfed us and whose deck we had to cross to go ashore. A group of us went aboard the Victory, and were brought face to face with history. We owe our freedom to our forefathers who fought and died for it, and we should guard their legacy well. Freedom can be lost by the pen as well as by the sword. Lose your freedom and you lose everything.

The battleships, *Renown*, *Malaya* and *Ramilles*, the cruiser *Jamaica* and the monitor *Eribus* were at adjoining berths, the port continuing to fill up with destroyers and corvettes whilst pinnaces and liberty-boats swarmed like water beetles across the water. At the end of the war Portsmouth was a very busy place, and a very happy one. Our next job was from Portland, 'Operation Bombardon' and entailed towing unused roadway sections of the Mulberry Harbour, still on our side of the Channel, out to sea, sinking them in eighty fathoms off the Channel Islands. We worked in tandem with Justice and others, making a number of trips, but were frequently hampered by the weather. Waiting for it to improve meant that we couldn't go far from the ship, our time being divided between playing cards on board, a nearby cinema and visiting the pubs hard by the Portland Naval Base dock gates; particularly the Green Shutters which was noted for its strong cider.

A group of us went for a walk around Portland Bill, past the Borstal, through Easton, Wakenham, Fortuneswell and Chesilton, after which we slept like logs. We must have enjoyed this novel venture, sailors walking, whatever next, because we were joined by others and repeated it the next day, even extending it to include Chesil Beach. After a couple of weeks propping up the sea wall the ship became scheduled for a boiler clean, the end of June seeing me once again on leave. Some of the lads had also arrived home on leave and lunchtimes were often spent in the Old Town pubs exchanging experiences.

Joyce came home on leave from the ATS and matters became complicated. I was still going out with Jean, though our relationship was presently in limbo, and was also seeing her friend Betty and taking her to the cinema. Three girls seemed too much to handle and a strategic retreat was implemented by watching cricket at the Circle, playing snooker with dad, visiting the New Theatre with friends, record sessions and cycling. It was good to be back on a cycle again and the tandem was brought out one Sunday for a family jaunt to Spurn Point. The well-used family cricket bat was also brought out of retirement and sent away to Gunn's to be re-bladed. New bats were something you could only dream about just after the war, so any old ones that could be found were resurrected. It was returned some three weeks later and was used when batting for Milners over the next two or three seasons, before eventually being bequeathed to the club, which was perpetually short of gear.

Having spent the greater part of July on leave, I departed for London towards the end of the month, looking for lodgings at every Servicemen's Club and the usual haunts such as the Regents Palace, only to find them bursting at the seams with uniforms. A pea-souper of a fog didn't help in the search and the night was eventually spent at a B&B in Brunswick Square. I arrived there at midnight complete with two heavy suitcases, to be appraised at the door by a wary proprietor. This stranger, appearing out of the fog, banging on the door at midnight waking everybody up. The next day I saw Phyllis Dixie at the Whitehall Theatre before travelling back to Portland Dockyard and the *St. Mellons*. Nothing much was happening aboard and visits, accompanied by liquid refreshment and a pack of cards, were made to surrounding ships. The outcome of one of these trips was that I found myself part of the cricket team of HMS *Attack* one perfect summer's afternoon, travelling in an RN bus with a crowd of sailors to Bovington Army Camp. The match was drawn, but that was incidental to an afternoon fielding in the sunshine and a slap-up tea in the Sergeants' Mess, before returning to Portland dockyard.

19: A WORLD AT PEACE

Dan arrived on short leave from RAF Stranraer and knocked us up at six one morning whilst I was at home enjoying a couple of days leave. A busy period followed, snooker at the Wellington Rooms, cinemas, evenings in town and listening to records. Returning to Portsmouth, the *St. Mellons* was now laid outside the cruiser *Frobisher*, so there was her deck to cross as well as the cruiser *Diadem* in order to get aboard. A wireless broadcast announced that Japan had capitulated on the 14th of August 1945, 'VJ Day'. This was the dawn of the atomic bomb, a dreadful way to force a conclusion to a war, but faced with the alternative of invading mainland Japan that could cost America an estimated million lives, there was little choice. 'The Second World War was over. It had killed at least 50 million people, and scarred forever the minds and bodies of fifty times that number'...Len Reid.

The world had ceased its madness, the senseless killing had stopped and the guns were silent, but it would take some time to adjust to peace. Surrounded by victory celebrations, bonfires, church bells, street parties and general rejoicing, I went to the Odeon at Southsea to see 'Henry V' once more; it seemed an appropriate film for the time, and the following day I saw it again. Films, books, music, if you find something you like, stick with it. I trust that 'Casablanca' will be showing in my afterlife, otherwise I may have to get up and leave. During this period my spare time was spent writing for small, limited circulation jazz magazines, many of which flourished during the war, mostly amongst servicemen. Research into the origins of jazz had whetted my appetite to visit New Orleans one day to see the places I'd written about. The entry of the States into the war had increased jazz coverage in the UK through the American Forces Network, AFN, and there was so much good music and musicianship around at that time that you couldn't pick out any particular band above another. Two memorable songs were Glenn Miller's 'Moonlight Serenade' and the shared 'Lili Marlene'.

Meantime we went into dry dock to have our rudder repaired and half the crew went on leave, including me. Catching the overnight train from King's Cross landed me at Doncaster Station at three in the morning. The war might have finished but I continued to end up there regularly once a month at three in the morning, hungry, with the buffet closed, a mouth like the bottom of the proverbial birdcage and my connection not due for hours. Uncle Les was home on Long Service Leave from Burma where the army had had a rough time fighting the Japanese. Before being sent to Burma he had served with the 8th Army in North Africa and had not seen his family for seven years; his two young sons, David and Geoffrey, didn't know who he was when he came home. The family gathered in the Silver Grill to celebrate our safe return, this being about the only café, on the corner of West Street and King Edward Street, still standing in the centre of the town and occupying an upper floor of a bomb-damaged building. Food was still rationed but cafes were granted special licences, although their menus were very limited. Early in the war the government had introduced British Restaurants, where people could get a two course meal and cup of tea for 1/-, there was the Prospect Cafeteria and a restaurant at Victoria Pier. The war years had seen the petrol companies amalgamate, and only 'Pool' petrol was sold at petrol stations, when available. The supply of petrol had gradually diminished as the war progressed and some vehicles took to the streets with a large balloon of gas on the roof as their main source of fuel. We may have won the war, but many more years of shortages and austerity lay ahead. Compared to the big cities, the rural population had survived the war reasonably well, being spared the heavy bombing, and with access to country fare to supplement the official rations. Mother had some friends in the East Riding and occasionally we obtained eggs from their farm.

Returning to the ship through London, I had arranged to meet the ship's Bosun, who wanted to show me around his home stamping ground, centred on the 'Elephant and Castle'. After an eventful evening in the company of a number of hard gentlemen who all wanted to buy me beer, we caught the midnight train to the south coast. Back in Portsmouth there were visits to see Harry Parry and his orchestra and the RAF Dance Band at the South Parade Pier in Southsea, a palace of dreams with a wooden floor. We were out of dry dock by this time, undergoing minor repairs, so there was little for me to do, my time being spent in Portsmouth town centre or travelling on the bus to Fareham or Gosport, enjoying the surrounding villages and the countryside.

In order to collect our wages and purchase any 'slops', (clothing and general requirements), we needed to board the *Marshal Soult* which was laid in a corner of Portsmouth dockyard. She was officially a monitor, a dying breed, but had been retired from that job some years previously. Her big guns had been removed and she was now sequestered peacefully in a corner of the harbour, seeing out her days as a supply ship. Built in 1915 she was not designed for comfort, most of her 6,400 tons seemed intentionally obstructive below decks as you clambered around trying to find your bearings. Her main armament had been 2x15" guns in a single turret, and the supports for these massive guns took up most of the available space below deck, stretching from beam to beam. To get from fore to aft below decks necessitated lying almost flat on your stomach on a gently rounded steel slope of large dimensions, then shuffling along until you were past the narrowest part. This was feasible going one way empty-handed, but more difficult coming the other way laden with shirts, socks and a large green suitcase. Perhaps it was all part of an Admiralty keep-fit campaign.

Early October saw me leaving Pompey for Campbeltown, via Hull. It was very convenient living halfway up the country, all north-south train journeys could be broken at York or Doncaster and a few hours spent at home without asking permission or anyone noticing. Being moved around more than my fair share, this facility was very welcome. Including a 24-hour diversion to Hull, it took from 1400 on Wednesday until 1400 on Saturday to make the journey: Portsmouth-Waterloo-King's Cross-(York-Hull-York)-Edinburgh-Glasgow, train to Weymess Bay, ferry to Tarbert and bus to Campbeltown. The base at Campbeltown was in the process of winding down, preparatory to moving to Harwich. The thoughtfulness of the Admiralty in furnishing the Rescue Tug headquarters with a secretarial pool of WREN's had been much appreciated over the years, probably by both sides. There was a WREN's Halloween Party at Ardnaig, followed by the *Minona's* Farewell Dance at Lochend Hall to which I escorted two (2) WREN's; it included free beer, supper and whiskey galore. There was an ENSA show at HMS *Nimrod* which was best un-remarked, but then, who would want to travel to the ends of the earth in a cold November to entertain a bunch of sailors, so full marks to them for effort. Campbeltown had much in common with Hull, being a fishing port isolated from the mainstream and with its own independent clan. Two months were spent on board the *Minona* before the intrepid MacBraynes bus took me back along the Mull of Kintyre for the last time, to join the *Bustler*, lying alongside at Greenock.

The *Bustler* was the largest type of ocean-going rescue tug at 1120 tons, 205 feet long, a speed of 17 knots and a crew of 40 instead of the usual 30. After dumping my gear on board, I went to see a jazz friend who lived in a tenement block in Clydebank; we played records till three in the morning and at breakfast the family shared their precious egg ration with me. I made my way across Glasgow to see an exhibition of Matisse and Picasso, emerging baffled but open-minded, then went to see Marjorie in Dumbroch. She had also joined the LDV when it was first formed, and when it later became the Home Guard she had entered the Signals Branch, maintaining communications and tending carrier pigeons. If the telephone lines were down and your wireless was kaput how did you get messages to HQ? The humble pigeon triumphed again, as Dastardly and Muttley knew well.

Orders came to proceed to Campbeltown, where else. There was mail for me to collect from Mrs Black, who ran the dairy on the seafront. We had become good friends over the years when I used to receive parcels from home c/o her shop, it by-passed the official channels and was quicker; we corresponded for quite a while after the war. The family lived in one of the tenement flats above the shop where beds were set into the wall and closed off by sliding wooden doors, very cosy in cold weather. Back on board I was landed with the job of Duty Officer. The *Bustler* was moored to a buoy at the farthest point in the bay so it looked like being a dull night, until the 4th Engineer returned on board with two WRENs. We were having an interesting evening which looked like getting even more interesting, when we were called out at short notice and despatched to Loch Ryan, scrambling to get the girls ashore in the duty boat before we sailed.

20: DEADLIGHT AND DUBLIN

When the war in Europe ended, all enemy shipping was ordered to surrender and make for the nearest Allied port. A total of 138 German submarines from the Atlantic had arrived in Loch Ryan and it was quite a sight for us to see them at close quarters. An agreement had been reached amongst the Allies that the U-boats were to be disposed of, and 'Operation Deadlight' was mounted to tow them out to sea and pull the plug.

The ships involved in Deadlight were divided into two groups. Group A was under the control of the destroyer *Onslow* and Group B, our group, was headed by the destroyer *Onslaught*. The Rescue Tugs involved were *Masterful, Saucy, Earner, Freedom, Enforcer, Sea Giant, Enchanter, Prosperous* and *Bustler*. The Polish destroyer *Crakowiak* joined later, as did *Mendip* and *Piorun*. A few of us went aboard a U-boat, and it was surreal to experience the claustrophobic atmosphere and the smell of stale air and diesel fumes that lingered. Recollections were stirred many years later by 'Das Boot', a German TV re-creation of U-boat life in wartime.

Our first tow from Cairnryan was U-2363, which we took 188 miles out into the Atlantic WNW from Loch Ryan and sank in deep water. We steamed back to pick up and dispose of U-100, an ocean-going type, before a force 8 gale warning sent everyone scurrying for shelter in Campbeltown Bay. We stayed at anchor for five days until the gale blew itself out, before returning to Loch Ryan where we collected U-485 and sailed in company with six other tugs, all with similar tows. U-485 was cast off at an arranged rendezvous in the Atlantic to be used as a target in bombing practice by the RAF. Our next tow was U-997, another of the large ocean going submarines. *Emulous* had arrived and was towing alongside us. After this tow we proceeded to Campbeltown as the weather had deteriorated.

In the worst of the gale we were called out to the rescue of the Saint Merriel, on fire off Port Patrick. A line was put aboard her in terrible conditions and it was a struggle to tow her into Loch Ryan. When the weather abated we shackled up to U-1301, towed her out to the graveyard and sank her, returning just before the gale once again curtailed operations. When it eased off we set off towing U-637 but she began to sink on us in choppy seas, taking water through the open conning-tower. We had to pay out the tow-wire from our winch as she sank, otherwise we could well have been dragged down with her, which would have been ironic to say the least. Another irony was that the number of British merchant seamen lost in the war, 32,000, was about the same as the number of U-boat crew lost; the Merchant Navy's wartime losses of 25% were said to be a higher proportion than any of the other services.

After Operation Deadlight was completed we proceeded to Greenock where, being Sunday, there were no cinemas open. A couple of days later, Christmas Day 1945, I watched Rangers beat Clyde 3-1 at Ibrox, followed by a solitary tea at the Grand Central Café to celebrate a solitary Christmas. Shortly after Boxing Day we left Greenock for Falmouth, towing a large Landing Craft Train Ferry. We greeted the 1946 New Year whilst alongside the *Samsonia* in Falmouth, before moving back to Greenock, where I watched Morton beat Hearts 4-2 on their war-neglected little ground. The *Bustler* moved to Partick and there was time to go home for a few days. Back in Glasgow the ship was playing games, moving from Marisbank Quay to Meadowbank Quay to Plantation Quay, and one gloomy Saturday teatime after watching Rangers beat Queens Park, I had a marathon walk trying to locate her. Alarm bells rang when she wasn't where I'd left her and I began to wonder if she had gone to sea, being quite relieved when she finally loomed into sight.

The Admiralty decided that, as the *Bustler* carried an early form of radar, I should attend a course of instruction. This was a six-week radar course crammed into three and a half days and was held in a large house on the outskirts of Glasgow. At Hampden Park, to watch Scotland play Belgium, fog closed in during the match and towards the end none of us could see the other side of the snow-covered pitch. What a massive stadium Hampden was, a place of legends and the hallowed scene of many battles, akin to Wembley and Odsal. Morton drew 4-4 with Rangers at Ibrox with me and a handful of Morton supporters isolated in a shivering bunch on acres of terracing, placing our hopes in Garth scoring the winning goal.

After phoning Marjorie to make sure she was in, I took a tram most of the way to her house, followed by a walk in the freezing cold. Unfortunately when her parents had gone out that evening they had locked the door, taking the key with them, so Marjorie opened a front window for me to climb through. We had a great evening, talking about the *Eminent* and her D-Day experiences, looking at photographs, drinking numerous cups of tea and catching up on news since we last met. Her parents were not a little surprised to find me there when they returned home.

In early February 1946 we left Plantation Quay in Glasgow for river trials, then moved back to Greenock and the next day sailed to Campbeltown for orders. From there we were sent across to Lisahally, where we anchored, a few of us catching the bus into Londonderry to visit pubs and sample the local fish and chips. The frigate *Tremadoc Bay* was anchored nearby, she was to tow U-2326 and we were to tow U-2518 to Cherbourg when the weather improved. We moved to anchor off Moville, where the trip ashore followed the same pattern as the previous visit on the *Eminent*, a group of us spending the evening ensconced in a snug enjoying the Guinness.

Tremadoc Bay and ourselves set off towing our U-boats down the Irish Sea, but the weather again freshened, the submarines became difficult to control and we took shelter in Dublin Bay. Entering the harbour at Dunlaoghaire, we moored alongside the jetty with our U-boats. Going ashore I had a look around before taking a tram to Dublin and immediately loved it; after the rigours and privations of wartime Britain it all seemed as wonderful as a toyshop might seem to children; I bought chocolate, face powder and lace-edged tea towels. After a walk around the city centre the tram took me back to Dunlaoghaire, there to find a small crowd of people gathered on the quayside gazing at these unusual arrivals in port. The following morning the quayside was swarming with people; photographers, reporters and onlookers by the score, all clustered around the U-boats and us. Apparently we were the first British warships to enter Dublin harbour since 1921, a quarter of a century earlier. After we left, a girl sent me a newspaper cutting of an article about us that had appeared in a Dublin newspaper. The weather improved and we set off for Cherbourg, handing U-2518 over to the French navy on arrival. A sortie ashore revealed a much battered and derelict football stadium, and a match was arranged between the *Bustler* and *Tremadoc Bay*. On returning to Falmouth the Admiralty took me off the *Bustler* and sent me to Leith, (via Hull), to join the *Envoy* in Rosyth. When I arrived the *Envoy* was under repair and going nowhere, so it was not difficult to obtain leave and Scotland was traded for a week at home.

With the war over, there were large numbers of servicemen and women with no jobs to return to in civvy street. To release them from the forces simultaneously would cause all manner of social problems, so a demobilisation system had been set up to control the gradual release of all service personnel. Everyone in the forces was given a number determined by age, length of service, marital status and other criteria. Those with the longest service were given low numbers and were due for release first. With a demob number of 63 I was sent into the outfield but didn't mind, I was happy at sea and hadn't planned on going anywhere. Government leaflets giving information on training for jobs were circulated, though the only one that appealed to me was forestry because it seemed to promise fresh air and freedom. We would have to wait and see how things turned out.

160

21: BERMUDA

It was back to Scotland and the *Envoy*, after a few days leave, only to find that someone had stolen my gear. I wasn't in Leith long before being recalled to Harwich, (via Hull), and had barely settled into the Great Eastern before a signal came to join the *Restive,* a sister ship of the *Allegiance*, lying at Meadowside Quay in Glasgow. The *Restive* was 165' long, weighed 597 tons and had a crew of 24 plus 7 officers. So it was back up to Scotland again, this time staying at the St. Enoch's Hotel in Glasgow. The hotel also housed the local Rescue Tug headquarters, and a conference was called with the Captain of the *Restive,* Lt. Guy Gibson, of Woodcock Street, Hull, the Captain and Radio Officer of the *Emulous* and me. We were all delighted to learn of our respective destinations, the *Emulous* to return to the States for de-commissioning, the *Restive* to take up station as Duty Rescue Tug at Bermuda of all places. Both ships left Glasgow in company for Plymouth and the following day left Plymouth for Bermuda. For some time I had been established as a Chief Radio Officer, and on the *Restive* was the one and only.

Bermuda was one of the world's fantasy destinations, like Rio de Janeiro and Honolulu. The image of these places had been nurtured by cinema travelogues and Hollywood musicals and was a dream far beyond the reach of ordinary folk, so we looked forward to our posting with great enthusiasm. However, illusions of a pleasant passage were shattered as the weather deteriorated when we got out to sea. What had looked like a leisurely, 'Report weather, position, course and speed' trip, turned into a hectic voyage instead. Single-operator watch periods flew out of the porthole and it became a 'go on and stay on' situation. The wireless equipment included a Direction Finder, two receivers, three transmitters, an emergency spark transmitter and a domestic receiver. Two days into the bad weather the coil of the main transmitter burnt out, the D/F went on the blink, and the next few hours were spent improvising repairs and soldering components in place whilst being flung around at the same time.

The gale continued and the cabin was in turmoil, with papers, clothes and bits of wireless equipment all over the deck. It can be difficult enough to diagnose problems and to repair wireless gear at any time, doing it in a rough sea added another dimension. Our bow was slamming into the waves, the sea crashing over and swamping the bridge, followed by the ship being tossed into the air and slammed flat down onto the sea a few seconds later. Food, except sandwiches, was out of the question and sleep likewise. If you were in your bunk it took you all your time to stay there and not be thrown out of it. This time we were fortunate as the gale eased off after a few days.

By the time we passed Barca Point in the Azores, the weather had calmed down and everything was perfect except for the wireless gear, which continued to give trouble throughout the trip. My time was divided between the wireless room, the bridge, snatched meals in the wardroom, and sleep, which averaged about 3 hours out of every 24. Now that we had left the UK Area Station at Portishead behind us, wireless messages were being received from the North Atlantic Area Station in Halifax, Nova Scotia. The British marine wireless world was being divided into 9 geographical areas, some of them sub-divided, and whichever area you were in, you dealt with that Area Station for all your traffic. The new 'Empire Long Distance Areas' used the wartime Admiralty network, with headquarters at Portishead near Bristol and area stations at Halifax, Capetown, the Falklands, Ceylon, Singapore, Sydney, Wellington and Vancouver.

After a week at sea we made radio contact with Bermuda and also picked up the local radio station, where Duckie was commentating on the Boat Race for the BBC. What a pleasure it was to hear his voice again, and for him what a joy it must have been to return to a normality he must have thought he would never experience again. As Padre to the 2nd Cambridgeshire Regiment, he had refused to leave the wounded of his regiment when Singapore was captured by the Japanese in 1942, and was interned in Pudu jail for the rest of the war. Russell Braddon told his story in his 1955 book 'The Naked Island', immortalising him as 'a name which tens of thousands of Australians, Englishmen and Scotsmen will always remember till the day they die'. In January 1946 he wrote to me from his home in Raskelf saying 'I do realise that you have been thinking of me and I cannot say how much it has meant to me both away and when I have come back'. My thoughts had been of him, though without realising where he was. That he had thought of me whilst in that hellhole made me feel very humble. He returned to Cambridge shortly afterwards to become Chaplain of St. John's College.

Bermuda is a group of islands that sits on top of a three-mile high submarine volcano. Only a few of the islands are inhabited, the largest containing the capital, Hamilton. The weather was freshening again and the bridge needed the D/F to get a fix on this dot of land. And what a beautiful dot it turned out to be. The weather was warm, the air tropical, the moon magical and it was easy to see what all the fuss was about. A drawback was the high cost of living but we found means of modifying this, even if only slightly, and eased ourselves into the islands' way of life by availing ourselves of the facilities open to us. All officers were automatically honorary members of the Royal Bermuda Yacht Club, the RN Officers Club, the RN Commissioned and Warrant Officers Club, the RN tennis club and the golf club at the Mid-Ocean Hotel. It was still a very costly place, but with free bed and board on the ship, the cheap railway that ran from one end of the island to the other, a bicycle, and all that wonderful free scenery we scraped by, and all in all the *Restive* began adapting to Bermuda style living very well indeed. The Admiralty was looking for something to occupy her surplus men and ships, all of them released overnight from the need to wage war, hence the sending out to grass of the *Restive* to Bermuda. But what to do with her now she was there? We parked ourselves in the naval dockyard on Ireland Island and waited to see what turned up.

What turned up were the cruisers, *Bellona, Diadem* and *Birmingham,* part of the West Indies Squadron. After berthing them we found ourselves taking regular parties of their liberty men across to Hamilton in the morning and bringing them back again, suitably refreshed, at midnight. The trip from the dockyard was some four miles across the Great Sound, passing through the Fairy Islands, before reaching the quay running adjacent to Front Street in Hamilton. The buildings on Front Street, painted in the colony's traditional pink and white, housed top quality clothing shops, small department stores and exuded an aura of money with a capital M. There was a constant stream of Lease-Lend vessels returning to the States and calling in at Bermuda to refuel, the majority of them were landing craft but there was also a scattering of rescue tugs, so our social lives were enlivened by wardroom parties during their stay. Shipmates last seen in distant waters were embraced, and the health of Cardinal Puff enquired after many times.

A legacy of the visit of some of the large battle-wagons was the disposal of their surplus ammunition, left in a pile on the quay. We took 500 tons of lethal-looking shells and canisters on board and dumped them in deep water off the Point. On the whole we preferred taking liberty men across the Sound. The two cinemas in Hamilton were a bit pricey, but free films were shown twice weekly in the Warrant Officers Club in the sail loft, and were popular with all ranks; as was the weekly tombola also held there. The frigate *Ballinderry* had arrived and taken up general duties in the dockyard, an outcast like ourselves. Sometimes the place was full of American and British warships; at other times it was quiet and empty for days on end. Doubtless it was this lack of regular employment that germinated the seed of an idea in the minds of our superiors ashore and we found ourselves allocated to the 'school run', taking a dozen or so of the dockyard workers' children to and from school in Hamilton. Some days we breezed over to Hamilton in the morning, returned to the dockyard and went back to collect the children at teatime. More often we deposited the children and stayed alongside in Hamilton all day, taking them home again in the evening. There was great amusement when a couple of park benches were put on board for the children to use during the trip across; we were also adept at putting them to good use.

Having so much spare time saw us travelling the length of the island by the colonial style narrow-gauge railway, or exploring our surroundings on bicycles. We walked all over Ireland Island, Somerset Parish and Southampton, sunning ourselves on the almost deserted club and hotel beaches or bathing in the warm sea. The clubs and hotels, most of which had been quiet because of the war, were now gearing themselves up to receive the anticipated influx of peacetime tourists. The *Fort Amherst* and the *Fort Townend* were British passenger liners which ran a regular service between Hamilton and New York in the absence of the *Queen of Bermuda*, which was being fitted out for the needs of peacetime after returning from her wartime duties. All manner of activity was increasing day by day as the islands moved from war to peace. Days drifted into weeks and then into months as we continued our idyllic tropical island lifestyle. Letters were written home weekly and to girl friends, with lots of mail being received in return. Lunchtimes were usually preceded by a cycle ride in company with Harry Knight, Eric Rae, or others from the ship, to Somerset parish, where we sampled rum and coke and other interesting drinks on the shady veranda of a wooden café called Joe's. Sometimes it was hard to tear ourselves away from Joe's hospitality, and lunchtimes would often slip away unnoticed in the sunshine.

As part of the Lease-Lend agreement concluded between Churchill and Roosevelt earlier in the war, Britain had received some ancient four-funnel destroyers from America; in return Britain leased land in Bermuda to the USA for an air base. The US forces brought their radio station with them and, as the East Coast radio stations also came belting in direct from the States, there was plenty of good music to be heard. It was therefore a loss, to some of us anyway, when the King's Point AFN station departed in May 1946, being replaced by Radio Bermuda ZBM, a much more sedate operation, sans jazz programmes.

22: JAZZ AT THE RECTORY

We embarked on a series of picnics by ship's boat to nearby Ports Island, one of the Fairy Islands group, about three miles distant across the Great Sound. Like the majority of these small islands it was uninhabited. There were some graves of French sailors, who had contracted yellow fever in the late 1800s and been isolated there until they eventually died on the island. A note made at the time reads: 'Equipment landed on the island for two days and nights included 4 officers and 10 ratings, 28 eggs, 14 loaves of bread, 2 hams, 8 bottles of rum, a dog called Yip and an accordion, all taken by ship's boat and collected again a couple of days later'. There were the remains of buildings on the island and, although we had a happy time there, we gave a thought to those sailors who would have looked out over these same waters, wondering about their lives and suffering and what their thoughts would have been. Yip however was untroubled by any thoughts whatsoever, taking up station alongside the grub and refusing to move until we returned to the ship.

Having gone through the war unable to swim, I decided Ports Island was a good place to start, envying the others who were having fun in the water. It was literally sink or swim time. Finding a quiet spot I pushed off strongly from a coral outcrop expecting to sink like a stone, but found it possible to flail around and actually keep from drowning. Memories were revived of the instructor whose idea of teaching a group of 8yr olds to swim was to watch them jump in the baths to see whether they showed any 'aptitude', (i.e. drowned or not), thereby putting most of them off swimming for life. The happy summer passed by, lazing at Mangrove Bay and Cambridge Beach, now with the added enjoyment of swimming. There were games of tennis with the

Captain and invitations to tea with the dockyard foreman and his daughters, June and Kathy, both about school-leaving age and amongst the group of children we took across to Hamilton.

The *Patroclus*, a sister ship of the *Eminent*, was one of the vessels being repatriated to the States. George was on board her, and we had a lot to talk about during her short stay; he would see friends at the White Hart again before I would. After the departure of an unsteady George and the *Patroclus* for New York, a venture was mounted to visit the nearby coral and marine gardens. We borrowed the ship's boat and drifted in the sunshine all afternoon, gazing over the side and swimming amongst the coral reefs and tropical fish. A diver came aboard, bringing with him an assistant and his pumping gear. We took him to the other end of the island to lay some navigation buoys in the channel off St. George's and it was fascinating to observe him at close quarters, donning his helmet and equipment and watching the pumping gear being organised.

This was the period of the big fights at Madison Square Gardens and we listened to AFN to hear Tony Morielli knocking out Bruce Woodcock in the fifth round and Joe Louis beating Conn in the eighth. Whilst we were living in the lap of luxury and eating real eggs instead of re-constituted dried-egg powder, bread rationing was brought in back home. Odd jobs were found for us such as putting to sea to assist the *Reward, Warden* and *Enforcer* who were towing a large floating dock, AFD5, from Alexandria to Bermuda. A very swish luxury yacht, the *Stella Polaris*, passed us on her way into harbour, a little reminder that the world was returning to normal. There was a ripple of excitement when we heard that the *Enigma* was paying off in Singapore; we took this to be a sign that the Rescue Tug service was disbanding and that demobilisation was near. Nonetheless we continued ferrying school children and dumping ammunition, trying not to confuse the two.

A Roman Catholic priest came on board for lunch one day and, amongst other things, talked about jazz. Father McPherson was a genial Canadian from St. Joseph's church in nearby Somerset parish. He had a collection of 78rpm jazz records and this was the start of a friendship that was to last many years, entailing exchanges of records, books and correspondence from all parts of the world. On most of my free evenings I cycled to the Rectory, where we talked and listened to records together until well after midnight; the only reason we packed it in then was because he had to be up early to take Mass. There was a spare bedroom in the Rectory, where I slept occasionally, getting up in the mornings in my own time. The Bermudan girl housekeeper cooked eggs and bacon for breakfast and whole days were often spent at the Rectory on my own, playing records or reading books from the extensive library.

Our record sessions sometimes turned into jam sessions, with Frank, a guitarist from the nearby air-base at Kings Point, a couple of GI's who played the piano, one of them being particularly good at boogie-woogie, Father Mac on his full set of drums and me doing my best with a pair of maracas. When sleep finally won out, some bedded down on settees, others with more stamina made their way back to Kings Point. If you have not heard boogie-woogie with a maracas accompaniment you have not missed anything.

The shops on Front Street sold American Jazz and Race Records, and a small collection was accumulating in my cabin until, eventually, I took them to the Rectory to store and play them. Their weight and vulnerability to breakage presented a problem, as did the possibility of paying Duty when arriving back in England, nevertheless the unlimited access to US dollars that Bermuda afforded saw me ordering quite a few records direct from Don Leary Ltd. in Chicago. It seemed I must have bought a sufficient quantity of the Apollo label to attract attention, because a letter from that company followed me to England offering me the sole distributorship in the United Kingdom. The label featured black artists, small groups and blues singers; in the immediate post-war period labels appeared under the catalogue classification of Race Artists or Race Records and, due to contractual restraints, many well-known musicians recorded for them under pseudonyms, although most were recognisable from their style of playing.

Charlie Osberg, the Chief Engineer, who hailed from Falmouth and had a rich Cornish accent, came with me on the train to Hamilton and then on to St. Georges to see the aquarium, the Devil's Hole and the Crystal Caves. The engine broke down halfway to St. George's so we all got out and walked along the track the rest of the way. Life continued its demanding round of sunbathing, cycling, picnics, boat trips, swimming, meals and tennis with June and Cathy, cinema visits, shipboard parties, days and nights of reading and records, visits to Joe's. And all of it in a sub-tropical paradise, blessed by the ambience of peace after war.

A Canadian destroyer, the *Mic Mac*, berthed alongside us and contact was established, leading to an exchange of visits and the acquisition of more records. Whilst we were off-station having a boiler clean, an emergency call came to locate a flotilla of LCI's that had lost its way. They were calling at Bermuda to re-fuel on their way back to the States and had strayed off course. Being small craft intended for landing infantry on beaches, they had no D/F and only one wireless between them. As the *Restive* was temporarily unavailable, about twenty of us took over a medium sized harbour tug, the *Empire Tessa*, throwing some gear and grub aboard, plus a TCS6 Tx/Rx for me to try and contact them by radio. We set off in the early dawn like the US cavalry riding to the rescue, established radio contact, and eventually located the scattered flotilla about 200 miles out, some of the more ambitious amongst them apparently heading for Greenland. Fortunately the weather remained calm, they were all rounded up by the third day and brought safely into port. Some years later the *Empire Tessa* was renamed *Eminent* and worked in naval dockyards.

In early August we heard that we were paying off and leaving the *Restive* behind in Bermuda, but before that we had to enter dry dock so that she could be inspected, hull cleaned and handed over to the local marine authority in good order. Although the *Restive* was sizeable by tug standards she was small by ship standards, nevertheless, walking about on the bottom of the dry dock beneath her she seemed pretty big to me.

The annual cricket match between the parishes of Somerset and St. George's was due to take place and we were given invitations to seats in the best tent. This was a Caribbean style match, with the locals enjoying themselves hugely and the children, all decked out in their best clothes, looking delightful. There was a lot of rum and Coca Cola in our vicinity, also plenty of ice cream and hot dogs. By early afternoon the sun and the drink had combined to foster a feeling of immense goodwill all around the ground and only a desultory interest was taken in what was happening on the field. The blue Atlantic sparkled in the distance, the awnings gave shade and the crowd subsided into somnolence until a batsman caused a flurry by sending the ball in their direction.

The *Restive* paid her crew off, and as there was no officers' accommodation at the shore base, HMS *Malabar*, we were given Lodging and Provision Allowance, L&PA, and left to fend for ourselves until a vessel hove into sight that could take us back to the UK. Fortunately there was the spare room at the Rectory, and Father Mac invited me to stay there, gratefully content amongst the records and books; efforts at keeping in touch with *Malabar* to see whether a homeward bound ship was in the offing were, at best, half-hearted.

The crew departed in ones and twos on various vessels and in various directions, but I stayed on, left to enjoy my ham and egg breakfasts. Frank, the sailor from Kings Point, continued to bring his friends along for jam sessions or to listen to records. A pleasant couple of weeks passed at the Rectory until a visiting Bishop appeared on the horizon, needing the bedroom. Looking around Hamilton, accommodation was found in the 'Winnona' guesthouse, across the street from the cathedral. Soon afterwards the Admiralty found me a berth on board the frigate HMS *Ballinderry,* which was sailing direct to the UK. Father McPherson and I bade each other goodbye; apart from enjoying jazz together we loved books and literature and he had been instrumental in introducing me to the 'New Yorker' magazine. In appreciation I sent him a subscription to the British literary magazine, 'Jon O'London's Weekly' and we continued to exchange books, records and letters for some years afterwards. We may have left the *Restive* but she hadn't left us, some years later a film called The Key appeared, in which she featured as a war-time rescue tug, alternately manned by two Captains, Trevor Howard and Oscar Homolka, the romantic interest being provided by Sophia Loren. There were some shots of the *Restive* at sea, not enough to satisfy anyone who had sailed in her, nevertheless it was good to see her again.

23: CIVVY STREET

Aboard the frigate *Ballinderry* with her 140 crew, I shared a cabin with a Midshipman Jellicoe, from the family of the same name. He was a likeable lad and one could imagine him doing well, following the distinguished Navy tradition. We had some good yarns and a lot of laughs, sharing a rifle when there was a routine small arms practice at sea using the ship's disc thrower. It was expected that we should take about ten days to reach the UK, however the second day out from Bermuda a seaman developed appendicitis, so we had to alter course and proceed at speed to Halifax to put him ashore. Our speed was about twenty knots in uncomfortable weather and it took us 36 hours from the point of deviation to reach port. In Halifax we berthed alongside two Tribal class Canadian destroyers, our old friend the *Mic Mac* and the *Nootka*, so we went aboard to renew acquaintances. We stayed in Halifax for a couple of days, leaving for Chatham in choppy weather which turned into a force 8 gale, but was hardly noticeable aboard a vessel twice the length of a Rescue Tug.

A cable came via the *Ballinderry* wireless room from my parents on the occasion of my 21st Birthday. My hope had been that they wouldn't do this, sending me a card instead, but now there was no chance of keeping the event quiet and it was inevitable that the spotlight would be upon me in the wardroom that evening at dinner. A speech of sorts would be expected, but the edge was taken off this ordeal by accepting numerous congratulatory tots during the day, and I was very relaxed by the time the Captain, an RN Commander, called on me to say a few words. Although I have no clear memory of the speech, it was probably in the best traditions of the Royal Navy, and it all passed off well enough.

A film was shown in the wardroom each night on an 8mm projector and rifle practice was held on deck when the weather cleared up. The passage down the Channel was uneventful and we anchored off Sheerness before disembarking at Chatham. I went through the demobilisation procedure at Chatham Barracks before proceeding to HMS *Badger* at Harwich, where leave was granted almost immediately. At home there was great rejoicing and a very large birthday cake. Gloria was home from Sheffield University and a day was spent with their family at Scarborough. After a busy week of record sessions, and meeting friends who had also returned from overseas, it was back to Harwich. I got as far as London but missed the train to Harwich, spending the night at the Three Nuns Hotel in Aldgate.

Officially demobilised, I signed off HM Rescue Tugs at the shipping office in Dovercourt on the 4th October 1946 after three and a half years under the White Ensign. The 'Order For Release From Naval Service (Class A)' form granted me 3 days SOSL leave plus 56 days resettlement leave, expiring on the 2nd December 1946. Travelling to London a free man, I watched Charlton beat Bolton 2-0 at The Valley, followed by an evening at the Garrick Theatre to see Beatrice Lillie, before catching the midnight train home from Kings Cross. My war was over; at 21 the whole world was before me. Bridges had been burnt at the Post Office and I felt no desire to drop anchor. On reaching home one of the first things I did was to take off the metal identification bracelet, worn around my wrist since 1943.

Geoff was home, and we were shortly joined by George, as our demob numbers were the same and came up simultaneously. George and I, accompanied by our mothers, went by car to collect our demob suits from the Fulford Barracks in York. I was kitted out in Montague Burton's government-issued blue and white single- breasted pinstriped suit with narrow trousers, black shoes and trilby hat. The late '40s and early '50s were to be marked by wide trousers and double breasted suits with a pleated back so the de-mob issue probably didn't last long as a fashion item. On the way back from York we stopped for a meal at the Londesborough Arms in Market Weighton. At home, the suit was consigned to the wardrobe in favour of slacks and an open-neck shirt, feeling that I'd had enough of collars and ties to last me a lifetime.

Hull Fair was in full swing in October, and what a welcome sight it was after the drab years of the blackout. The fair was crowded with returning Forces and the atmosphere was exhilarating. Jean and I resumed our long-term on-off relationship. My first visit to the races, at Doncaster with Geoff, resulted in financial disaster and was also my last visit to the races. Over the next few weeks there were frequent visits to the cinema, Boothferry Park and to see friends and the parents of friends still overseas. Time was also spent in YOWH, yarning away with friends not seen for a long time, Josie, the blonde barmaid, eventually limiting George, Geoff and me to three 'Black and Tans' apiece at lunchtimes. After lunch there, or upstairs at the Lord Collingwood, we drifted on to the Blue Bell or the Corn Exchange then flirted mildly with the waitresses upstairs in the Kardomah café in Whitefriargate, until such time as we felt we ought to go home. Occasionally we sought out a billiard hall for an unsteady game of snooker, arriving home late in the afternoon, greatly pleased with ourselves.

Dan and I set off one evening on his Norton to visit a Jazz Club in a pub in Leeds where the Yorkshire Jazz Band was playing. It was a beautiful mellow autumn evening and the ride on the back of the bike was a joy, the countryside at its best and the wind in our hair, no crash helmets or leathers, just Harris tweed sports jackets and flannels. We were made welcome at the pub and the evening passed merrily amidst glasses of ale and the enthusiasm of the audience. The tuba was well to the fore as the band drove its way through all the good old numbers and we were very happy when we set off home about midnight. A straight hill took us gently down a well-lit road on the outskirts of Leeds and we were merrily singing along to some jazz tune when the string of lights suddenly ceased. We continued straight ahead in the sudden darkness but unfortunately the road had veered to the left, the bike and contents ending up in a hedge on the opposite side of the road. I clearly recall being upside down in the hedge and hearing a man's voice in the darkness saying, 'Silly buggers', as he walked past with his dog. We were both shaken, not stirred, but it put me off motor bikes for quite a long time.

Geoff was keen on backing horses and occasionally enticed me into the Old Town Club on Queens Dock Side. This crumbling establishment opened in the afternoon when the pubs closed, providing ale and betting facilities in the days before the betting laws became civilised. A favourite outing was the weekly bill of wrestling at the Madeley Street Baths on Hessle Road, where the atmosphere was rowdy, raucous, heaving with bodies and an absolute hoot. The knowledgeable ones, George, Geoff, Dan and I, ignored the seats and made for a standing place on the balcony, leaning over the rails. The arena was hot and sweaty, with a noise-level measurable on the Richter scale, and it sure had atmosphere. Top favourite was Bert Assiratti, the British heavyweight champion and originator of the 'Boston Crab' submission hold. 'Black Butcher' Johnson and the 'Farmer's Boy' were other favourites. The shouts of encouragement, or outrage, were deafening as they echoed round the hall and bounced off the glazed white tiles of the swimming baths. The gladiators in the ring, barely visible through clouds of cigarette smoke, sweated profusely and were spurred on by shouts of 'killim' from the crowd. Bert always managed to subdue his villainous opponent with the 'Boston Crab' hold and win the bout in the last minute, sending everybody out on to the streets happy, the pubs on Hessle Road doing a good trade after the wrestling turned out. Many servicemen were in the process of adapting from Woodbines to Turf cigarettes and from Pusser's Navy rum to Lemon Hart but experienced no difficulty in adapting to Hull Brewery or Moors' & Robson's ales. Saturday afternoons were spent at Boothferry Park watching the Tigers or the Reserves; such was the enthusiasm for all things to return to peacetime normality that even Reserve matches attracted 10,000 or more. Boxing also returned and Geoff and I stood amongst the crowd in Wenlock Barracks to see the long awaited fight between Frankie Jackson and Sammy Shaw.

George and I were going out with two sisters at this time, myself with Audrey and George with Joyce, whom he subsequently married, and we motored all over the quiet roads and by-ways of the East Riding in George's car. Jean and I were still friends, she belonged to the Amateur Operatic Society and was rehearsing at the YPI in George Street, where we met afterwards and travelled home together. Some time later she joined with her sisters, Susan and Gloria, to form a vocal group, 'The Joybells', which then became 'The Jeanettes', and later 'The Marten Sisters', touring variety theatres, cabarets and appearing on television. They also entertained American Forces at bases overseas, sailed on Atlantic cruise ships in shows starring David Whitfield, George Formby and Shirley Bassey; Jean later going solo.

Now that the Armies of Occupation were established in Europe they brought their own radio stations, and the flow of good music continued. Some war surplus equipment had found its way onto the commercial market and an RAF 1155 aircraft receiver was purchased so that I could listen to the American Forces Network station in Munich. A favourite programme was 'Midnight in Munich' which came on at eleven every night for a couple of hours. Continental radio stations were starting up after the war, including Hilversum where the music was good and the female presenter had a very sexy voice, only edging the WREN on the R/T channel at Appledore in the Bristol Channel by a whisker. I tuned in to Appledore when my ship was nearby, listening to her giving out navigational warnings and weather forecasts, and probably knew the positional changes of every buoy in the Bristol Channel, all the local shipping movements and every vestige of coastal fog for miles around. If she'd talked about what she had eaten for supper I'd have hung on her every word. The girl from Hilversum was probably telling me what she had eaten for supper anyway, as I couldn't understand a word she was saying,

Jean and I welcomed in 1947 at a New Year's Eve dance at the Regal ballroom in Beverley. Despite going with Geoff to a course of dancing lessons at the Harry Brandon Studio in one of the large houses opposite the Carlton, I seemed to have two left feet and was rubbish at transferring the lessons on to the dance floor. Jean, however, was a great mover and it was a pleasure to hold her whilst she danced. Dan and I went to Brid for a couple of days during the time when The *Archibald Russell,* a four-masted barque and reputed to be haunted, was laid alongside the South Pier. We jumped from the quayside onto the deck and had a look around her before the watchman caught up with us. RAF launches were still stationed at the end of the harbour, and now the cobles were offering fishing trips and pleasure cruises to visitors as life gradually returned to normal. We played bowls on the two outdoor greens at Beaconsfield and walked around the town just as we had done before the war robbed us of all those years. January drifted into February, Jean and I spent a lot of time together and it was becoming make your mind up time. There wasn't any overwhelming demand on dry land for a ship's wireless operator, so was it another career, or drifting into the sub-post office when dad retired? I wasn't ready to settle down ashore, or think of marriage, or contemplate sub-post offices, not whilst a whole world waited to be explored. The winter was bitterly cold, snow piled up in the streets, the countryside was feet deep in it and snowploughs were needed to keep the trains running. There was a stirring in the blood, telling me that I wanted to be off, away from the cold, the shortage of food, empty shop shelves, make do and mend, restrictions, queues everywhere and an atmosphere of post-war weariness that was understandable but depressing.

TELEPHONE:- 35901 (4 LINES)
TELEGRAMS:- "HERSA" HULL.   *Registered Office:* 18-30, BEVERLEY ROAD.

HULL, 25th Jan 1940.

Memo from

WM CUSSONS LD.

GROCERIES | GREENGOLD | PROVISIONS
REGD. FOODSTUFFS

FBT/MV.

Master Jack Close,
43, Hawthorn Avenue,
HULL.

Dear Close,

I am writing to tell you that you
have been successful in your application
for the post of Office Boy, about which
you saw me yesterday.

Your commencing wage will be at the
rate of 9/- a week, and at the age of 16
you will come onto our standard wage scale.
Until then you will have every opportunity
of earning such increases as your work
justifies.   Your normal half day will be
Saturday, but there will be a periodic
transfer, about once in four weeks, to
Thursday afternoon.

I look forward to seeing you make
good progress in this work, which will give
you plenty of opportunities of learning
office routine.

Yours faithfully,

[signature]

Secretary.

GPO Telegraph Messenger,
1940

Jean, 1940

Lester and Judy at Pearson Park,
1940

HULL
RHYTHM
CLUB.

Meeting Sunday Afternoon
2-30 p.m.

H.M.R.T. *Allegiance* on trials off Hull, June 1943

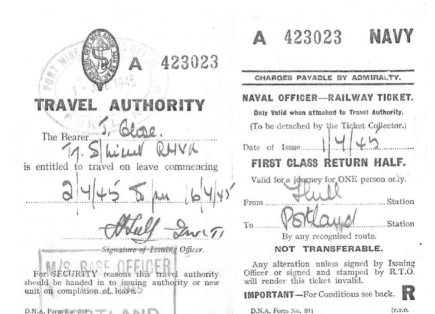

Rail Travel Pass, issued for all journeys, 1943-46

H.M.R.T. *Eminent*
1943

Phoenix units positioned as sea wall defence of Mulberry Harbour,
Normandy, June 1944

H.M.R.T. *Salvonia,*
Algiers, Summer 1943

Portsmouth, 1945

H.M.R.T. *St. Mellons* - Antwerp Dock Pass, March 1945

H.M.R.T. *Restive* in dry dock
Bermuda 1946

Captain (right) and hard-working
crew of *Restive*

The *Restive's* park bench

Ports island picnic

Joe's Cafe, Somerset, Bermuda

S. 1601 A. (Established—May, 1945.)

ORDER FOR RELEASE FROM NAVAL SERVICE (CLASS A)

Personnel Serving on Agreement T.124 and Variants including the Commissioned Cable Ship Agreement.

(This form of Release Order is to be used for both Officers and Ratings.)

H.M.S. MINONA.

Date of Dispersal 4 - 10 194 6

To I. CLOSE. (Name).

Radio Officer. (Mercantile Capacity).

Official Number

1. You are being released from war service as a Class A Release. (See Note 1.)

2. You have been granted :

Delete this line if no foreign service leave has been granted.

* 3 days' foreign service leave, expiring on S.o.S.L.

and 56 days' resettlement leave, expiring on 2 - 12 - 46.

This latter date will be the date of your final discharge. (See Note 2.)

3. You are free to take up civil employment from the day following the date of this Order, which is also the date your reinstatement rights become effective.

4. You may wear civilian clothing while on leave, and you are to cease to wear Naval uniform after the date of your release.

5. You should carry this Order with you until your Discharge Book is received and you are to produce it when required.

(Rank)

4 - OCT 1946

Commanding Officer.

HARWICH

NOTES.

Note 1.—Class A consists of individuals released from the Forces, under the Plan for Re-allocation of Manpower, during the interim period between the defeat of Germany and the defeat of Japan, in priority of age and length of war service.

Note 2.—The 56 days' resettlement leave includes the 14 days' notice of discharge to which you are entitled under the terms of your Agreement.

with Geoff and George on demob leave, December 1946

with Dan on demob leave, 1947

Sheila

Audrey

PART 3

BEYOND
the
HORIZON

1: CALM BEFORE THE STORM

Geoff and I felt we needed some time ashore. As re-training was necessary in order to upgrade the wartime Special Certificate if we were to continue at sea, the spring of 1947 saw us embarking on a six month Course at the Technical College. The morse requirement for the higher certificate was the same as for the Special Certificate, however the technical paper and practical work sections meant starting from scratch because the wartime certificate had only touched lightly on both these subjects.

The summer was a good one, Sheila and I went for cycle rides in the countryside, searching out quiet grassy meadows and woodland glades and spent time at each others' houses. Mam and dad were keen on Leeds pantomimes, and later in the year we stayed overnight at the Queen's Hotel to see Roy Barbour in Jack and the Beanstalk at the Theatre Royal. Food was still rationed and would remain so for some time to come; whale steaks appeared in the shops, as did Snouek. And there was 'Spam'. Any food at all was welcome, and fish and chips were always there to fall back on when other food was scarce. Horsemeat, ostensibly for pets, was sold from a shop at the corner of Marlborough Terrace. Bread rationing continued and you queued for most things, being grateful for what you could get. Many shops had empty shelves; it was only during the next couple of years that goods gradually became available as factories changed over from wartime production. There were queues for the pictures too, cinema-going in the post-war years was hugely popular and at one time there were over 30 cinemas in Hull; my cycle took me to all of them. Bertram Mills Circus came to Walton Street fairground, Yorkshire came to The Circle, and Geoff and I went by train to Headingley to see Hutton and Washbrook open the England innings against South Africa.

In August, college broke up for the summer holidays, so there were more cycle rides, walks, cinemas and cricket. Grandpa, having been in the Post Office for many years and now retired, took over the office at Hawthorn Avenue for a week whilst the three of us went on holiday to Campbeltown, travelling by train to Glasgow, staying at St. Enoch's Hotel overnight. We caught the train to Gourock, boarded the MacBraynes ferry to Tarbert and then the bus to Campbeltown. The buses and the roads had seen great improvements since my last visit. We stayed at the White Harte hotel in the Main Street, made trips to Southend and Carradale and walked over the causeway to Davaar Island. Where once there had been an air of tension and menace, now all was peaceful and serenity reigned; the fishing boats jostled each other alongside the jetty under a watchful cloud of seagulls and the town gently slumbered in the sun. Campbeltown over the years seemed another home to me; comfortable to be there and to sit quietly on the sea-front, surrounded by memories. My parents were pleased to meet up with Mrs Black, cementing a friendship which continued for many years. On our return journey we stayed at the same hotel in Glasgow, dad and I going to see Rangers in the afternoon, after which we all had tea with Marjorie and Bill, caught the tram back to the hotel and returned home the following day.

College commenced again in the autumn, as did the concert season. Polish pianists came to the Queen's Hall in Georges Yard, a traditional brass and mahogany concert hall with atmosphere. The first pianist I heard there was Meirowski, the second was Pouishnoff, after whom all other pianists playing Chopin paled by comparison. The third pianist was Blaszczynski and he never stood a chance.

At the end of October, forty of us sat the PMG exam at the Technical College. One of the class was George Hobson, whose parents conveniently ran the County Hotel in Charles Street; some of our studying was done there, helped by a steady supply of beer. On passing the exam I went hotfoot to the Shipping Office in Posterngate and from there to the Marconi office in Albion Street to get things moving. They got moving all right; I had decided to go trawling and was in for a rude awakening.

On a cold dull day in late November 1947 I signed on with Marconi to join the *St. Stephen,* an ancient trawler of the St. Andrew Steam Fishing Company fleet. The following day I checked in at the firm's office on St. Andrew's Dock and was told to present myself at the doctor's surgery for a medical and was also given an authorisation paper for me to draw sea boots, jersey and other gear from the Fishermen's Outfitting Store on the quayside. The Store smelt of oilskins, rubber thigh boots and fish. Gutting knives, mittens, palliasses and guernseys were on sale along with other items not previously encountered. The fish dock was familiar territory, the sights, sounds and smells were the same as five years previously, but as for what followed it was quite unlike anything I had experienced before.

2: FISHING AND LIVER BOILING

I climbed aboard the *St. Stephen,* complete with kitbag, rubber thigh boots, a seaman's jersey and a positive demeanour, ready for what fate would throw at me. It threw everything, and pretty swiftly too. No sooner had we left the shelter of Spurn Head than a gale force wind struck the ship and she began to roll, pitch and try to stand on end. After passing the routine 'TR', (name, position, course, speed and destination), to Humber Radio, I felt free to be thoroughly sea-sick as we got out into the North Sea, taking to my bunk and praying for death all the time we were running off, eventually surfacing near the top of Scotland, a shadow of my former self.

The *St. Stephen* had been built in Beverley in 1928, was 140' long and 355grt. Originally the *St. Romanus,* she had seen war service as the minesweeper *Oak,* returning to fishing in 1946 as the St. Stephen, was later re-named *Lady June* and ended her days as the Recepto. No provision for wireless communication had been made when she was built, but by 1946 a couple of pieces of radio gear had been lodged in a corner of the skipper's cabin as an afterthought. This cabin was reached by a narrow wooden ladder leading vertically down from the wheelhouse.

My bunk was one of a number in the communal cabin aft, above the propeller shaft, and was the only space, about 6ft by 2ft, for myself and my belongings. The narrow bunks were ranged in pairs, one above the other, around the cabin, each enclosed by sliding wooden doors. The bunks and mattresses were unhygienic and most of us took a cheap straw palliasse, 'donkey's breakfast', to put on top of the grubby mattress. The cabin was always noisy, with men coming and going throughout the 24 hours when we were fishing. No fresh air dared intrude on the cigarette smoke and general fug. We ate at the central table around which the bunks clustered. Fiddles, the slats of wood fastened to the table to prevent the crockery sliding off in bad weather, were a permanent fixture. Apart from the first few days after leaving port, once on the fishing grounds we had fish and chips for most meals, interspersed with helpings of stew, 'shackles', from the deep pan in the galley, and there was always the massive kettle full of tea and condensed milk boiling away on the range in the galley, a meal in itself. A continuous bench-seat followed the contours of the central table, the bunks being directly behind it. The cabin, with its narrow companionway leading up to the after deck being the only way in or out, was cramped, claustrophobic, and another certifiable death trap, similar to the *St. Mellons,* only worse.

Somewhere off the Orkneys I ceased praying for death and found my sea legs. It was still blowing a gale but it no longer mattered, I was still alive and actually felt hungry. We reached the West Coast of Iceland and rode out a prevailing blizzard by sheltering in Dyra Fjord, then managed about 10 days of fishing as allowed by the weather, which always seemed to be in a bad temper with itself in those parts. For our efforts on that trip we landed 730 kits of fish, 350 of them flatfish, the most profitable, and made £3,702 on the market just before Christmas 1947. My pay slip showed total earnings of £19/12/11d from which £8/10/- was deducted for Income Tax, leaving me with £11/2/11d for the week's work. It had been unrelentingly awful, whether operating the wireless gear in cramped conditions, boiling livers, or simply coping with the cabin, and I wonder now why I didn't sign off after that first trip. Perhaps it was the challenge, or simply being bloody-minded, that made me sign on for another voyage, or maybe it was a rite of passage, something I had to do to come to terms with myself. Everyone in West Hull seemed to be on trawlers, had been on trawlers, had relatives on trawlers, or had something to do with trawlers; it was a way of life all around you as you grew up and I needed to be a part of it. Or maybe I thought things could only get better; if so how wrong can you be. I bought myself a Longines watch to mark the occasion of the first trip and prepared to have another go.

Trawler Skippers depended on their hard won knowledge of those icy northern waters; relying on their own judgement where to trawl to get the best catch, they seldom shared this knowledge with others. The owners, naturally enough, preferred to employ the most successful Skippers, so it was a very competitive business and any 'insider knowledge' of fish movements was kept close to the chest. There was no noon position entered in the ship's Log, as there would be on a merchant ship, and only the Skipper, Sparks and sometimes the Mate, knew where the ship was at any time. After the standard notification of, 'Sailing for Bear Island/White Sea/Iceland', neither the owners nor the crew knew the vessel's position from the time she reached the fishing grounds until leaving them ten or twelve days later, when a message would be sent to the office giving the number of kits of cod, haddock and flats caught and which day's market the ship expected to catch.

Roy, the Skipper on the St. Stephen, was on his first command. It was the Christmas trip, which nobody liked and everyone wanted to have ashore; the boat was getting to the end of her life, was probably uneconomic to run and the weather was seasonably foul where we were heading. But that was the way it was with Mates and Skippers, you took what chances you were given by the owners in order to get a foot on the ladder. As for me I was in at the deep end and didn't realise how deep it was.

The Operator's job on trawlers was quite different from that on merchant ships. On the latter, the hours of work were laid down by international agreement and the main preoccupation was the safe passage of the vessel as provided by regular watch-keeping, weather reports, navigation warnings, telegrams to and from the owners or their Agents concerning ports of loading and discharge of cargoes etc. Operators on trawlers carried out similar duties, but their main job was to listen to other Skippers and Operators who had yarns bent on, and try to suss out where they were fishing and what sort of catches they were getting. The hours of watch keeping were long and flexible and when the fishing grounds were reached you went on watch at breakfast, staying on until well after midnight.

On my second trip we were trying our luck in scuffly weather on the 'Hindenburg Line', the 100-fathom line down the middle of the Denmark Strait between Greenland and the NW tip of Iceland. It was so-called because it had been heavily fished for many years by German trawlers. We were caught in a gale coming at us from the north, which was upon us so swiftly that we had no chance to run for cover into one of the fjords that make up that jagged corner of Iceland. To do so would have exposed the *St. Stephen* broadside to the massive waves and swell that were building up and could have rolled her over. As the hours went by, the storm worsened, until what we were seeing, and surviving, was truly unbelievable. We lived every head on collision, every swamping of decks and wheelhouse, every violent shudder and shaking of the ship, knowing that our only hope of survival was to keep her head on to the waves.

There were four of us marooned in the wheelhouse and we spelled it at the wheel, two of us at a time trying to keep her steady. The sea was a never ending vista of huge walls of boiling green and white water bearing down on us, dwarfing the ship and tossing us about like a cork. Ton after ton of angry water hit the ship, breaking over the bows, often giving the bows a miss altogether and slamming straight into the wheelhouse. The continuous shrieking of the wind and the darkness accentuated the feeling of helplessness we felt in the face of the storm. In all my time at sea I never saw such monstrous green and angry seas. The broken wave crests, as we saw them from the bridge, were well over the top of the mast, the Skipper reckoning they were anywhere over 100ft high from the depths of the troughs, but who knew, who cared, any one of them could have been the last one we would ever see. The storm and the fury of the water channelling its power into the narrow funnel of the Strait continued for hour after hour with no sign of letting up, the threatening sky blended with the night and only the bridge clock gave you a sense of time to hold on to. The old hands on board said they had never seen anything like it, and how we eventually came through it, God alone knew. When you are in a terrifying situation your world contracts and all you can take in is what is happening around you; the outer world ceases to exist and you live in a microcosm that could end at any moment.

We all thought we'd had it, though no one said as much until later. The four of us, Skipper, Mate, the decky at the wheel and myself, were bruised from being violently thrown about the wheelhouse, without food or sleep and were hungry and exhausted. The wind gradually slackened off from a full-blown storm to a strong gale and we hoped that it would continue to decrease. There were no weather reports for that God-forsaken place so we had no warnings of storms approaching or departing. A volunteer was called for to go aft and fetch some sandwiches because none of us had eaten for 24hours. Death-wish Close responded. Manoeuvring myself onto the port wing of the bridge, momentarily shielded from the worst of the gale by the bridge door, I climbed down the iron rungs of the vertical ladder and nearly broke my ankle landing on the deck. All best judgements notwithstanding, the deck was coming up as my foot was going down and there was quite an impact. Good start.

A narrow metal rail ran along the engine room casing at waist height, I grabbed this and set off to go aft as quickly as possible.

When I was halfway along the deck a wave came over the fo'cstle and a solid wall of water swept down the port side, hitting me in the back and completely immersing me. My thigh boots filled with water and my legs and body were swept out parallel with the deck as I clung to the rail with both hands. It took all my strength to hold on, until, after what seemed an eternity, the clutching water drained away from around my body and out of my boots, the pressure eased, my feet touched the deck and I scrambled aft to the cabin. So much for that. But there was more.

On the way along the deck I had caught a glimpse of the steering chain, which lay along a chain race in the scuppers, linking the wheelhouse to the rudder. The chain had snapped and the loose ends were thrashing about. A work party was hurriedly assembled and a hasty repair made by two of the lads, one lying on the deck working whilst the other lay on top to hold him down. Walls of green water were swilling along the deck and it was a miracle they were not swept overboard. None of us could imagine how it had been possible, in those seas, for the ship to keep her bow into the weather with a broken steering chain and surely it could only have been like that for the very briefest of time. Judging the ship's movements in conjunction with the waves, my return dash along the deck was made with sandwiches stuffed down my jersey, arriving in a heap at the foot of the bridge ladder before scrambling up to the relative safety of the bridge. Over the next few hours the weather gradually eased and we brought her bow round towards the land very slowly. Getting broadside on to the heavy swell left behind by the storm was not the best of scenarios even at this late stage. Back in the shelter of the fjord, out of the storm, with many fishing days lost, we licked our wounds.

The least appealing part of the job was boiling the livers. This was easier on the larger and more modern vessels, but on the antiquated *St. Stephen* it was hard going. On vessels out of Hull the liver boiling was traditionally the job of the wireless operator, and was carried out when sufficient livers had accumulated in the baskets on deck to warrant a boiling, this being fitted in between periods of listening out on the radio. Liver boiling was simple in theory, but years of exposure to salt water and arctic gales, plus lack of use during five years of war, had resulted in a corroded boiler and seized up pipes, and I never achieved a satisfactory return from the ancient contraption on the *St. Stephen*.

The fish were caught by shooting the trawl over the starboard side and towing the net along the sea-bed for anything between thirty minutes and two hours. When the ship's engines were stopped, the vessel lost way and the net with its catch floated to the surface. The net was hauled inboard by the winches operating the gilson, a rope hoist attached to the derrick on the foremast, and when the bag of fish was hanging suspended over the deck, the Mate ducked underneath it, released the rope around the cod end and quickly dodged out of the way as the fish flooded into the pounds. The pounds were deck boards arranged in squares to contain the fish, and stop them slithering all over the deck. The fish were gutted and the livers thrown into wicker baskets. The Sparks, cook and galley-boy could all be called on to help with the gutting if the fishing was heavy; I had a go at it once, standing in the pound cutting out livers and entrails, but wouldn't have made a living at it.

The basket of livers was dragged along the deck to the liver-boiler, an ancient work of art worthy of inclusion in any fishing museum. This masterpiece of Victorian technology was shaped like an egg timer, and was about as much use in producing oil from livers. It sat on top of the port side engine room casing, near the funnel. The basket of livers was hoisted up, the livers tipped in through a small porthole and the lid screwed down to stop them spilling out again. The next bit was pure Heath-Robinson. A thump on the engine room casing with a spanner was intended to alert someone in the engine room to release steam into the pipe leading to the liver boiler, where an arrangement of handles and stopcocks fed the steam into the boiler.

After a while, some oil would show through the small glass set in the neck of the boiler and lots more lovely cod liver oil would flow into the bottom half of the boiler. Not so. Half the time nobody down below heard the wake-up call, more often than not the levers became stuck, resulting in under-cooked livers blocking the system. I came to like unrefined cod liver oil, sampling whatever dripped from the uncooperative assortment of pipes and machinery. The settling at the end of the voyage included a percentage based on the amount the ship received for the cod liver oil. The *St. Stephen* would doubtless have come bottom of any Cod Liver Oil League Table, so I was probably not the most popular Sparks on the fish dock. I blamed the fish, saying that they were constipated, but found little support for the theory.

3: THE NORTHERN FJORDS

The NW corner of Iceland has a number of deep narrow fjords cutting into it from seaward. The walls of these fjords are dark where the granite shows through the snow and ice, rising sheer out of the water to 1,000 feet or more. 'Forbidding' is a word that comes easily to mind, with 'claustrophobic' not far behind. However, when you've come out of a storm ravaged Denmark Strait you look upon these sheltering walls as friendly faces, ask no questions and voice no criticisms. Once inside most of the fjords, the engines had to be kept running because the water was too deep to afford anchorage. There was little or no habitation in these inhospitable places, except in Patrixfjord, where there was a small fishing village with a few houses, limited supplies of food and fuel available from a timbered general store, and the luxury of a small jetty to tie up to.

A group of us from the ship were standing around on the jetty in Patrixfjord talking to some local fishermen, when a large Husky dog that was fussing around us bounded onto the overhang of frozen snow along the edge of the jetty, falling into the icy water between the jetty and the ship. There was only a foot or two of space for the dog to move about in, and had it stayed there for only a few minutes it would surely have frozen to death. An Icelander climbed down a rope ladder, grasped the dog and hauled it back up the six or eight feet to the quay. The dog was soaked and must have weighed half as much again as its normal weight. The man went off to seek medical attention, but the dog shook itself as though it was all part of a day's work and started frisking about. We spontaneously applauded the man for his act of bravery and then moved away from the edge of the jetty before the dog got any more bright ideas.

When the ship's deck and rigging had been put to rights after the storm damage, we put our nose outside to test the weather before resuming fishing. On the way home I reflected on the voyage and concluded that there were much easier ways of making a living; but if none of them appealed then it hardly mattered. And there was I, like the rest, down on the dock after a couple of days of high-pressure living, signing on for another trip. And for another after that, four trips in all on the *St. Stephen,* in that severe winter of 1947/48. We passed through the Vestmannaeyjar Islands and watched Hekla, Iceland's largest volcano, in eruption, the glow in the night sky following us for a long time on our journey south. The trip had been a difficult one with gales all the time we were fishing and on the way home. Running short of coal, we put into Scrabster in the Pentland Firth, where the whole crew, including the Sparks, disappeared into the nearest pub whilst coaling took place. There was a hectic 48 hours at home before we set off for the White Sea, hugging the coast, but had to put in to Aberdeen for winch repairs, whereupon the Sparks went to the pictures and everyone else went to the pub.

The next day we made for the Norwegian coast, coming inside the lee at Traen in the Lofoten Islands before proceeding to Lodingen to pick up the pilot, who took us through the narrow seaways to Harstad. This was maelstrom territory and we passed some ominous looking whirlpools close to the ship. Twelve hours were spent alongside at Harstad and, having no local money, I bartered some cigarette papers and a Mars bar for a ticket to the nearby cinema. We had barely set off again through the fjords when we hit a submerged rock off Ramnesgr. Although it felt to be only a slight scrape it warranted an inspection by a diver, so we put into Hammerfest, billed as the most northerly town in the world. The hull was duly examined and given the all clear so we carried on to Honningsvaag, where we dropped the pilot and entered the Barents Sea. There are some voyages that stand out in the memory; the trips through those desolate northern fjords in winter, the steep sides of the mountains covered in snow and ice glistening in the pale sunlight; breathing in the icy cold air and watching the lonely villages sparkle in the evening light as dusk falls, must count amongst them.

Fishing was good for cod and haddock about seventy miles NxE of Helesness and there was something of a 'fish-shop' going, with many ships trying their luck. In the years after the war, fish was plentiful everywhere, the grounds having been only lightly fished during the previous five years. Dan's father was there in the Victrix; he had been a trawler skipper for many years and we talked on the R/T about Dan, football, home matters, about anything except fishing. By this time I had fathomed the vagaries of the liver boiler and it was producing acceptable quantities of cod liver oil, to which, worryingly, I was becoming addicted. Nothing tastes quite the same as unrefined, first-boiling, cod liver oil from fish straight out of the sea. I know you will take my word for this.

Back home, the ship had to go on the slip due to her recent brush with bits of Norway, so Sheila and I had a week together instead of the usual 48 hours. It seemed a good time to grow a beard. Having tried it once before in warm climes and finding the process itchy and uncomfortable, I thought it might be less irritating in a cold climate but was wrong; it was still itchy and uncomfortable, and after a couple of trips it was shaved off. Wartime innovations in technology were filtering through and I bought a 'Plus-A-Gram', which needed no winding handle or rolled-up socks, and sent our steam gramophone into storage. The 78rpm records took on a new lease of life, blossoming in the full range of electronic sound, no less. The vinyl era had also arrived, with LPs at 33rpm, followed soon after by 45rpm singles; there were also records at 16rpm, mainly for dialogue, but they didn't catch on.

Lester, Dan and I sat in front of this wonder machine, now installed in our back room, playing records until two in the morning, when I had to tear myself away to get a taxi down to the fish dock. We left on the morning tide for the Norwegian coast via Lodingen and Harstad, where we went alongside to take on ice for the fish room. By the time we had reached Honningsvaag the weather had deteriorated and we anchored for the night. Hampered by the weather again the next day we laid-to, after trying a couple of hauls that yielded very little. There were some ships still fishing off Cape Tereberski and we steamed to join them. It was freezing hard, ice covered the ship and we had to chip it away from the deck gear each haul in order to continue fishing, and also to prevent the ice building up which would eventually make the ship top heavy and cause us to capsize.

The weather gradually improved as we pushed further and further to the east and once more shot the trawl to try our luck. We were far from the other trawlers by now, alone in a sea that shone azure blue in the clear arctic light. We passed the Cape Kanin pursuing a lonely search for flatfish off Kolguev Island. Novaya Zemlya was visible on the horizon, its icy profile glinting in the low sun and reflected in the steely blue water. We seemed to be at the end of the earth. In those latitudes, at certain times of the year the sun never sets, balancing on the horizon in the evening and rising again around midnight. The opposite occurs in mid-winter and then you are fishing in constant darkness except for a brief glimmer of daylight about noon when the sun appears above the horizon, disappearing again a few minutes later.

We steamed to Scalpen Bank and shot the trawl for the last time at Makur, before clewing up and making for the fjords and home. At Tromso we went alongside to take on supplies and I wandered around the shops, buying sealskin slippers and provisions. Food was still rationed in England and everyone regularly bought tins of lard and tinned meat from the local stores to take home. We coaled at Lodingen, picked up some mail and telegraphed the gaffer that our tally was 1300 kit including 200 of flats, then set out for home aiming to land for Thursday's market. It was 30th March 1948 and I should have been Best Man at Dan and Bunty's wedding, but instead was heading into a SW gale off the Norwegian coast. I signed off the *St. Stephen* when we docked, receiving £26/6/9d for the three-week trip.

York City were coming to Boothferry Park, the black and amber bills on the hoardings were plastered over with a strip saying 'Carter will play' and we all went along to see Raich Carter, the greatest player ever to don a City shirt, weaving his magic. He combined with another great ball player, Willie Buchan, and later, Eddie Burbanks, to produce some of the most sublime soccer I've ever seen in a City shirt. After a weekend thinking things over I decided that a spell ashore was called for, and resigned from the trawler section of Marconi. The record collection numbered about 600 by this time and on two or three nights a week our house became a jazz club in its own right, friends dropping in for coffee, sandwiches and music, often staying until the small hours.

The winter had been a harsh one, with trains held up by snowdrifts, villages and farms cut off and transport disruptions commonplace, but it eventually gave way to a beautiful spring. Tennis was played each morning on the courts at West Park with Pete Wilson, a school friend, and anyone else who turned up. We worked up quite a thirst, which was duly satisfied at the Newington pub, more often called 'Parkers', at the corner of Walton Street, where the bitter was kept to perfection, cool, clear and like nectar to exhausted tennis players. We were pretty hopeless and spent more time laughing than playing tennis, but we were young, we could still hardly believe our luck at being alive, the lights were on, there were no bombs falling on us, life was good and was to be lived to the full. After the first few months of meeting returning friends and exchanging experiences, there was hardly any talk of the war, it was still too fresh in the mind and we'd had enough of it. But it was a long time before the memory and the trauma of it began to fade; even then it only slipped as far as the subconscious, settling there as a backdrop to the rest of our lives.

4: ROLLING DOWN TO RIO

I went to the Marconi office in Albion Street for an interview, after which I was sent to Dr. Grieves for a medical, prior to being taken on their books again. I also joined the Radio Officers Union at their first floor offices in Percy Street, ready for new experiences, merchant ships, tramp steamers, the rolling deep, whatever. Sometime during the war an almost unnoticed name change took place and we all became Radio Officers instead of Wireless Operators. To my delight I was assigned as 1st and only Radio Officer on the *Grainton*, lying alongside at King George Dock in Hull, preparing to sail for Rio de Janeiro. What a place to go! I could hardly get my bags on board fast enough. Rolling down to Rio, Betty Grable, Alice Faye, Copacabana Beach, Sugar Loaf Mountain, rumbas, sambas, congas, bathing beauties, I knew all about Brazil.

But first there was the ship, and being my first merchantman there was a different environment to assimilate. Our cargo was coal and by the time we left the loading berth the whole ship was covered in coal dust. Once out into the river, the breeze blew most of it away and hosepipes washed away the remainder. Articles signed at the Shipping Office in Posterngate were for a single round-trip to South America and return to the UK, at merchant navy rates of pay and 'all found', i.e. bed and board. The *Grainton* had been built in 1929 and was a typical large tramp steamer of the period, with solid no-nonsense lines ending in a counter stern. She had a straight-up funnel, the top section of which had a walkway around it to facilitate dismantling for passing under low bridges. Of 6341grt, she belonged to 'hungry' Chapman's of Newcastle, so-called because of the tightness of the crews' rations in the depression days of the '30s, and the nickname had stuck. Happily, the food was fine on this trip.

We left dock at 0400 GMT and single-operator watch periods, 0800-1000, 1200-1400, 1600-1800 and 2000-2200, were commenced. The weather was perfect, and by the time we passed Madeira and the Canary Islands a routine was well established whereby the 2nd Engineer and I played chess on the after hatch in the afternoon and again in the evening. We passed the Cape Verde Islands, shrouded in mist, entering the doldrums to a glassy calm sea and hardly any wind. It was hot, and sunbathing on the hatches was the order of the day. It is well over 5000 miles from Hull to Rio and after we had covered about half of that, the

European and African radio stations gave way to those of South America, Latin rhythms filling the wireless room by day and well into the evenings.

The NE trade winds brought short heavy showers and it was a pleasure to lie in the sun, on top of the hatch, get soaked, then dry off in the sun, all without moving. As we ran gradually westward, the watch-keeping periods changed, so that sometimes my day started at 0600 ship's time, other times at 1000. Meals were taken at awkward times, sometimes hurriedly. In between watches the Automatic-Alarm was set. This unit responded to the morse characters of the distress signal, SOS (...---...), setting off alarm bells and alerting the Operator to return immediately to the wireless room. Unfortunately, the high level of static experienced in the tropics triggered off those early AA's more often than did any distress signal. Technological improvements eventually solved the problem and they became more effective.

The biggest drawback to an otherwise pleasant trip was the ancient transmitter. In the early days of wireless telegraphy a signal was sent across space by means of an electric spark, generated at high voltage by a spark transmitter. This was superseded by an electro-magnetic signal generated by a valve transmitter, all ships being gradually equipped with such transmitters during the 1930s. All of them, that is, except the *Grainton,* which still proudly sailed the world's oceans, wars notwithstanding, carrying the grandfather of all spark sets as its main transmitter. The rest of the equipment was a mishmash of Marconi receivers, Lodestone D/F, AA, and was reasonably up to date. It would have surprised me to learn that there was another ship sailing the oceans in 1948 that had a spark set as its main transmitter; as far as I knew they were long banned from marine use, except in lifeboats.

One of the drawbacks of a spark transmitter is the signal band, which is very wide. A valve-generated signal of 1,000 cps can be transmitted alongside a similar signal and both can be heard separately and clearly, without interference from each other. This is not the case with spark signals, which spread themselves across a wide band of frequencies, blotting out other signals for miles around. This was emphasised the hard way when I tried to contact a coastal radio station in Brazil and received in reply the Q-Code signal 'QRT' which means 'stop sending'; or 'belt up' in plain language. It was clear that the spread of my signal was interfering with other stations operating nearby, so for the rest of the voyage it was necessary to be circumspect as to the times and frequencies used to get messages through. I began to develop a guilt complex and resorted to using the transmitter in the middle of the night when the airwaves were quiet. The snag to that cunning plan was that, not only was the ether quiet, but so was the ship, and nobody was very pleased to be woken up in the dark hours by the spluttering sound of a spark transmitter at full throttle. With valve transmitters you can adjust their power gradually as required, but not spark sets.

Nearing the coast of Brazil we passed some whales with flocks of birds hovering around them. Before long we smelt the land, saw the faintest smudge on the horizon, and anticipation ran through the ship at the thought of going ashore. The weather had turned cooler now as it was winter in South America. Low on the horizon there appeared a row of tiny matchboxes which grew in size as we drew nearer, magically turning into hotels lining the beach at Copacabana, their windows glinting in the early morning sunlight. We glided past the Sugar Loaf Mountain at the entrance to Rio harbour and came to anchor off Niteroi, 25 days after leaving Hull. The Agent climbed aboard with the mail and money and no time was wasted in going ashore with two other lads from Hull, spending the rest of the afternoon at a table outside the Florida Bar sampling the local beer and watching the girls go by. Moving on to the Flying Angel club, we met up with others of the British community including Mac, a clerk from the British Embassy, who took us on a tour of the town. The evening progressed wonderfully under his experienced guidance, the ambience of Brazil enfolded us, and the next day we woke up on the floor of his flat in Filamenco to find the sun already high in the sky.

The *Grainton* spent ten days laid at anchor off Niteroi, served by a regular supply of small boats plying as ferries between the ships at anchor and the quayside at Rio. Some evenings were spent ashore, returning to the ship the following morning to see how the discharging was progressing before going ashore again. After a week or so the money ran out, and the last couple of days in Rio were spent playing snooker, reading books and chatting to other sailors at the Mission to Seamen. But for that week, Rio was my oyster. One evening, I took the cable car to the top of Sugar Loaf Mountain; the trip was in two stages, at the first stop you could linger and admire the view from the café, before catching the second car to the top. The view from both stages was wonderful in daylight, then at dusk and finally at night, with the lights strung out round the bay and along the beaches, the floodlit statue of Christ that looks out over the city seeming to float isolated and high in the night sky. Lots of places look like their postcards when you get there, but Rio was better than that, and had an atmosphere that caressed you like no other. I have heard Rio called 'achingly beautiful', and you can't argue with that.

A lot of time was spent just walking around, sitting at café tables, admiring the girls, absorbing the street scenes and feeling the energy and the bustle of the city. The trams went to all parts of the city and were very cheap; a ride of about an hour costing less than a penny. The tram that took me to Ipanema ran alongside the beach at Copacabana, which looked a wonderful place to be. The trams were very popular and always full, late joiners having to cling to the outside like flies. When two trams passed each other there was a simultaneous shrinking in to the handrails to avoid being swept off and scattered in the road and it was easy to imagine that not all the people avoided this fate all of the time. The clingers-on must have travelled for free because there was no way anyone could have collected their fares.

'The Brazilian girl, being utterly feminine, considers inconsistency a right; if caught out, then the lie of a beautiful woman ought to be treated as whiter than white. There is about Rio, a sensuality encountered in no other city; desire embraces the place like a cloud about a mountaintop', observed one traveller. I loved Rio and the time there passed too quickly for me. Some places are better in the anticipation than the reality, but not Rio. As Francis Albert might have said, 'It's my kind of town'; and in ten days enough memories were stored to bring a smile to my face for some time afterwards. Discharging completed, we sailed at midnight to Montevideo for orders. The trip from Rio to Montevideo should have taken five days, but we ran into a southerly gale, and one day on the noon-to-noon position, actually went sideways for a hundred miles. We were a big ship and an empty one, standing high out of the water, and were blown about like a balloon. On the way to Montevideo we received a wire directing us to Rosario in Argentina, to load grain.

We picked up the pilot at the entrance to the River Plate. Once the pilot is aboard ship the Radio Officer's work is usually over and he can shut up shop until the ship returns to sea, so I had a superb view of the countryside on our river journey over the next few days. We passed Buenos Aires and reached Intercession. The next stage took us up the Rio Parana to Rosario, a large port that was the centre for the grain harvest coming down from the Pampas. As we made our way through the countryside it was evident that the phrase 'pampas moon' was no misnomer, the moon just sat there in the evenings, a huge red-tinged ball balanced on the horizon.

At Rosario we anchored in the river to await berthing instructions and the usual flood of people came aboard. The Ships' Agent was the most important of these in our eyes because he was the contact between ship and shore, supplying us with provisions, money, mail, medical services and general information. Next to board were the Customs and the police, the latter armed with daggers and revolvers. Not being accustomed to this from our own authorities back home it all seemed a bit over the top, but best go along with it; when in Rome etc.

The Argentine Immigration authorities issued all visiting seamen with a 'Certificate of Identification', similar to a visa, complete with photo and fingerprints. The photographer who came aboard had a large wooden-framed camera on a tripod, covered his head and shoulders with a cape and everyone took turns to sit in front of him on a chair in the sunshine. My photograph resembled a black and white cameo of a Sicilian bandit. This document had to be carried at all times, under penalty of castration or death, probably both, and I still have mine just in case the Argentine police want to question me about something.

Twelve days were spent in Rosario, walking around the town during the day and visiting shows and cabarets in the evening, until the money petered out. Late one evening whilst wandering around Rosario on my own, I came across a small cinema just outside the town centre. There were the usual black and white photographs in a glass-fronted case, which seemed to indicate some sort of Spanish language musical, so I bought a ticket for the cheapest seats and went inside. The film turned out to be the life story of Albeniz, the composer and pianist, and was the beginning of an appreciation of his music, 'Triana' thereafter reminding me of Rosario, as 'Espana' reminds me of Gibraltar.

There were many ships of various flags waiting their turn to load grain and it was common for crews to visit other ships; apart from the friendships struck up with other seamen at these times my stamp collection also benefited from these jaunts. A casual meeting ashore with an Operator who had also been at the Tech. in 1942, led to us joining forces for visits to shops, cafes, bars, cinemas, and cabarets. Meantime, the elevators moved up and down the quayside, discharging grain into our holds through metal and canvas chutes and sending up clouds of dust in the process, the smell reminding us of harvest fields. Loading completed, we sailed for Bremen. A few days out into the Atlantic we experienced engine trouble and hove-to for twelve hours whilst it was fixed. There was patchy fog around us so we kept a good lookout and listening watch, our ship's bell and siren being sounded frequently. The *Grainton* had no radar; if we had it would probably have been spark operated.

In mid-Atlantic we discovered a cat that had been living in the bunkers. Ships' cats are a law unto themselves, they live on one ship for a while, get fed up and move along the quay to another ship where the grass seems greener; just like people. Once a week it was dhobi day and my washing was dumped in a bucket of hot water with half a packet of Persil thrown in. Persil, Oxydol and Rinso were among the first of the new wonder soap powders and were a boon for sailors and housewives alike. No longer was it necessary to scrub away with a brush and a thick bar of Sunlight soap, all that was needed now was to dump the clothes in a bucket of soap and water and leave it overnight. On my first attempt, too much powder was shaken into the bucket and it was a week before I got the last of the gunge out of the clothing. Life rolled gently on in tune with the movement of the ship. There were long lazy days in the sun, where only the occasional sound of the sea broke the perfect silence, and the gentle tropical breeze sent the welcome smell of food from the galley wafting throughout the ship.

Reaching the Cape Verde Islands we anchored off St Vincente to take 400 tons of bunkers on board. The Agent said that it had not rained there for five years, an observation borne out by the rocky and barren appearance of the shore. Swarms of bum-boats arrived with bananas, coconuts and souvenirs and there were calls from the young lads on the boats for us to throw coins into the water for them to dive for. As we passed Madeira fresh orders were received, changing our destination from Bremen to Hamburg. The weather deteriorated and there was an SOS from a Panamanian freighter 80 miles distant, to which the rescue tug *Dexterous* was proceeding. We discharged our cargo at Hamburg relatively swiftly, but found time to look around the town before sailing for Hull, berthing once more in King George Dock. It had truly been a round trip, ending within yards of where it started, and I signed off at the Shipping Office in Posterngate on the 14th of August 1948, some fifteen weeks after signing on there.

5: HENGENVARALINEN

It was good to be home again and to see familiar faces; during the trip to South America Sheila had become engaged, otherwise everything was much the same. After some late night record sessions, lunchtimes in town and visits to cinemas, I signed on the *Kalev* at the Shipping Office in Hull. As with the *Grainton,* she flew the Red Ensign, but the crew this time was a mixture of Estonians and Latvians, my only compatriots being Alf the cook, Eric the steward and George the galley-boy. The *Kalev* was old and fairly small. The wireless cabin had been built, as an afterthought by the look of it, on the after-casing above the engine room, between the port and starboard lifeboats. The wireless gear was mostly standard Marconi but the main transmitter was pre-war Finnish. On the bulkhead was a red and yellow metal sign with the word HENGENVARALINEN in large letters and a drawing of a bolt of lightening alongside it, so I thought I'd better watch my step here until I'd sorted out all the electrics and power generators. Needless to say there was not a manual or layout diagram in sight.

On the last day of August we sailed for Skelleftea in northern Sweden, breezing across the North Sea and into the Kiel Canal. The scenery along the canal banks was quite beautiful and was enhanced by interesting bridges that crossed the canal. The pilots who took us through the canal were offering to barter goods of all kinds; life was still very difficult for everyone and would continue so for many years to come, people having to sell their possessions in order to buy food and clothing. All over Europe there were huge numbers of refugees on the move; released from prison camps or from slave labour, swelling the mass of people already made homeless by the bombing and fighting. Virtually all were hungry, ill-clad, in poor health, with few possessions and no homes to return to; the Allied occupation forces had a massive job on their hands to deal with the situation. As we passed along the waterway, the pilots managed to sell their goods to the crew; being a point of contact with the outside world, they were doubtless an important cog in the wheels of the local economy.

The weather was fine as we headed north into the Gulf of Bothnia and we made just under ten knots, which was good going for us. There must have been mixed emotions amongst the Estonian and Latvian crew members as we passed their homelands. They had escaped the advancing Russian army in the early days of the war by sailing the *Kalev* from Estonia to Britain, where they eventually found themselves on the same side as the Russians, fighting to defeat the Germans; just one of the myriad ironies of war. Some had made their way back to Estonia after the war ended, but most of those who remained on board the *Kalev* had become British citizens, and for many of them the ship was their only home.

Orviken was the small port for Skeleftehamm. Alf and I took the bus into town for a look around, meeting Gunnar, the Manager of the local timber operation. Gunnar and his wife Kerstin invited us to their home for lunch, after which we played cards all afternoon, this being the start of some very happy times which developed into life-long friendships. Alf, Eric, George and I, spent most of our spare time at their house, having some riotously funny parties well into the small hours, before wending our way in the darkness along the narrow wooden jetty back to the ship. We smuggled bottles of spirits ashore as our contribution to the party atmosphere.

Our timber loading was completed at Kage, a short distance away. Gunnar and his cousin arrived there on motorbikes and took me to his home, calling at a café on the way where there was coffee and wondrous cream cakes, the like of which I had not seen since before the war. Loading completed, we set off in gale force winds for the UK, struggling to make three knots; the Baltic, being a shallow sea, becomes choppy very quickly. The cargo of Baltic pine was stowed in the holds with the remainder lashed down on deck, above and around the hatches. Going on deck to bow or stern was hazardous in bad weather, and lifelines were strung out to hold on to. The sea and spray came over the bow and from the beam, soaking the timber, which became heavier on the weather side as time went on, causing us to list alarmingly, and making steering difficult. The voyage to the Kiel Canal, which had taken two days going north, took five days going south. At Kiel we stopped for minor repairs and took on board three refugees, a woman and two young boys, for passage through the canal. Leaving the locks at Brunsbuttel, we anchored in Cuxhaven Roads waiting for the gale to blow itself out. It took its time, and we stayed for three days, in company with thirty other ships, until the weather abated sufficiently to set off across the North Sea.

When we reached Alexandra Dock in Hull, the ship was listing so badly from the soaked timber on deck that the Harbour Master expressed doubts about allowing us through the lock gates. The list was 30 degrees, witness to a very uncomfortable passage indeed. It was some time before we were eventually allowed to proceed through the lock, with the wing of the bridge overhanging the quay and the ship's side only inches from scraping the edge of the dock wall. The week in port followed the usual lines, including a day spent at Whitby and one at Scarborough where we had tea at Gloria's. Dad took me to Accrington to see Hull City win on its famous sandy sloping pitch, thereby establishing a new English League record for the most consecutive wins, (9), at the start of a season. When the team returned to Hull, there were 12,000 people gathered outside the Regal Cinema for an official welcome, at which Raich Carter made a speech from the balcony, but we missed all this, being still on the train coming home.

Mother and father came on board the *Kalev* for lunch with Captain Lepvikmann, who was on good form that day, he could be quite humorous, often unintentionally, and it was a pleasant afternoon as they toured the ship and met the crew. We made another trip to Sweden, this time to Burea near Skelleftehamm, so we were once more able to spend time with Gunnar and Kerstin. In those isolated snow and ice covered latitudes there wasn't much else to do but party. The ship moved along the coast to Mo to complete loading and then to Ornskoldvik, where we received orders to proceed to London. The fog in the Baltic gave way to gales and became a storm as we passed Gotland. Our nightly games of chess in the saloon were abandoned in favour of crib, where there were no pieces to slide off the board.

We berthed in Surrey Docks. A visit to the British Museum was rounded off quite wonderfully by examining the Rosetta Stone; I had just finished reading about its discovery, its place in history, and here it was, almost unbelievably, right in front of me. Foyles was the next stop, a paradise for book lovers; floors and floors of second-hand books. Making a mental note to take sandwiches on my next visit, I left there eventually and trawled through the portfolios in the bookstalls off Tottenham Court Road, buying Morden maps of the North and West Yorkshire Ridings for 30/- each, to join the East Riding one already at home. The following day, after reporting to Marconi's in East Ham, I had lunch with Uncle Les at the Windmill Café in Great Windmill Street, only yards from the Lex Garage where he worked. Soho and its people intrigued me and we spent an interesting afternoon there as the café clientele ebbed and flowed around us. The ship stayed in London for a week before moving up the coast to Immingham to load coal for Copenhagen, and there was time for a couple of days at home before we sailed to Denmark where a few days were spent looking around before we sailed for northern Sweden. With the calmer weather and the onset of winter came the fog. It was a hazardous trip and, with no radar to guide us, we picked our way carefully through the congested sea-lanes as we made our way north up the Baltic.

6: POUISHNOFF

Going alongside at Burea, I took the bus to Skelleftea to meet Kerstin; we exchanged news over coffee and cakes and wandered around the shops before taking the train home to Klemensnas. After dinner we played cards and I stayed overnight with Gunnar and Kerstin, taking the morning train to Skelleftehamm and catching the bus to Burea. The parties at their house often included relatives and friends so my circle of acquaintances grew steadily and there were invitations for meals during the daytime. I did a fair amount of travelling around that area of Sweden, mostly by bus. It was all very enjoyable, the crisp clean air, the trees covered in snow, blue skies and fluffy white clouds.

One night when returning alone to the ship, very late, I was the only passenger aboard the bus when it stopped in the middle of nowhere to pick up a girl of about 18. If hearts could stand still mine did then, she was the Swedish blonde goddess men dream about but never quite get to see, wild and free like the forest she had appeared from. She took no notice of anything around her, just looked out of the window. She had it, she knew she had it, and surely there was a whole world out there for her to conquer. She could have started with me. Instead, she disappeared into the Swedish moonlight a little later; out of my life but seemingly not out of my mind.

After more party nights with Gunnar, Kerstin and friends, the *Kalev* left port laden with pine, which gave off a wonderful smell when it became soaked, and headed for Sharpness in the Bristol Channel. This was another dodgy trip, deceptively fine at first, but the fog soon descended and we had to anchor twice between Brunsbuttel and Kiel. Often we couldn't see the fo'cstle from the bridge, so instead of trying to follow the coastline the Captain decided to head straight down the middle of the North Sea, our penetrating siren a poor substitute for radar. The weather rapidly worsened and we entered the Straits of Dover in the teeth of a southerly gale, with green seas breaking over the bow. The timber on deck had become thoroughly soaked and the list was increasing by the hour. Mercifully, the lashings held firm throughout the buffeting we took in the Channel and the cargo stayed put. The gale was still raging as we passed Land's End and it was a relief to dock at Sharpness and get out of it all.

After a few days at home, and back on board once more, the *Kalev* moved to Roath Docks in the Bristol Channel to load coal, giving time to sample the sights and night life of Bristol. In the middle of December we left for Oporto; the weather was good crossing the Bay of Biscay and Christmas decorations were put up in the saloon, Christmas dinner was eaten whilst off the Portuguese coast, and we berthed at Port Leixoes in time to greet the New Year of 1949. Brass artwork was popular in the small curio shops and two filigree ship models were bought for mother as a change from 'Californian Poppy'. Alf and I spent most evenings in the 61 Club or the Balalaica cafe on the dockside until, cargo discharged, we cleaned ship and moved to the outer harbour to load pit-props. A fortnight was spent in Leixoes, and most days I escaped the noise and dust by taking the tram to Oporto, walking around the town fuelled by cups of coffee.

Two weeks is long enough to be in port, after that things tend to become routine and predictable, so we were glad when sailing orders came to take the pit-props to Newport, a five day trip, from where Alf and I decided to go home for a couple of days. We returned from Hull together but when we reached Newport the ship wasn't ready to sail so we went into Cardiff for the day; the ship leaving in the evening for Bordeaux. It was a pleasant journey down the Bristol Channel, passing Land's End's flashing beam at midnight, making Ushant and then docking at Bordeaux in good time. A few of us established our HQ at the Two Sisters café, which was virtually at the end of the gangway. We also paid the occasional visit to the Queen Mary club further along the quay, and this variation from routine was probably Alf's undoing because he went ashore by himself late one night, seemingly forgot that the ship was opposite the Two Sisters café and not the Queen Mary club, couldn't find the ship in time and we had to sail without him. He obtained passage in another British ship as a DBS, Distressed British Seaman, and turned up a couple of days later in Newport, which was good news for us because the assistant cook, whilst doing his best, was just hopeless. Maritime regulations decreed that there are two crewmembers that a ship may not sail without, a cook and a wireless operator.

From Newport the ship moved to Port Talbot to load coal for Marseilles. We used to say that the *Kalev* was built head to wind, and she bore it out on this trip, making very heavy weather of it. We took a week to cross the Bay of Biscay to Finisterre, struggled past Gibraltar and on past the Balearic Islands, where the weather was unspeakable, across the Gulf of Lions until at long last we gratefully propped ourselves up at the quayside in Marseilles, feeling that we all deserved a pat on the back for our efforts. I went to see Roger Battisano, whose address was listed in the Jazz International Directory, a book that always accompanied me on my travels. Some records were bought from him and many more listened to during the afternoon over sandwiches and coffee.

From Marseilles, with its ultra modern lifestyle, a two-day journey across the Gulf of Lyons took us back to the Iron Age in the shape of La Garrucha, a small Spanish seaside village just south of Alicante. Iron ore is not a seaman's favourite cargo because if anything untoward was to happen the concentrated weight would likely take you straight down, no messing. As we approached the village the blue waters of the Mediterranean lapped gently along the edge of a sandy beach, overlooked by a group of shuttered houses nestling in tiers on the hills beyond; a small curved breakwater ran out a little way from the shore, sheltering a handful of fishing vessels. There was no jetty or harbour suitable for loading so we dropped anchor about 200 yards off the headland opposite some mine workings. It seemed the equivalent of anchoring off Flamborough Head to load chalk.

A boat put out from shore with the local Customs, the Agent, the mine boss and his two teenage daughters. Whilst the ship's business was being sorted out I went along to see whether the girls were alright. They spoke no English, and I very little Spanish, but it seldom matters in these circumstances and I thought things were going rather well until I got a hefty slap across the face from one of them. What prompted this was a mystery, but it was a novel experience and I did behave like a gentleman by not instinctively returning the compliment, the matter passing off amicably. When it was time for them to go ashore we parted with mutual expressions of goodwill, although I thought better of giving her a hug as she left.

Mounds of what looked like brown earth were piled up ashore near the entrance to the mine workings. This was iron ore and was shovelled into small wicker baskets, carried on the workers' shoulders to waiting barges at the water's edge and then rowed out to the ship. A large metal pan was lowered over the ship's side and the contents of the baskets were laboriously emptied into it. When the pan was full it was hauled up, swung across the deck, rested on the hatch combings and the contents tipped into the hold with a tremendous crash and clouds of dust. Estimates amongst the crew to complete the loading ranged from three to six months. It actually took twelve rather long and tedious days, laid at anchor, with nothing to do and nowhere to go. Apparently we were the first ship to visit La Garrucha since the war, Spanish Civil or WW2 not specified. During the calm and sultry hours of the day and through the quiet nights, the sound of the church bells from the village came floating across the water to where we lay at anchor. One day the weather became too rough for the small boats to leave the beach and we had to take shelter behind the headland; another day a boat capsized in the swell, a full load of iron ore being lost and the men having to swim ashore.

Because we were technically still at sea and in coastal waters, a Spanish pilot remained on board at all times. Using his faltering English and my fractured Spanish we got along well, and he told me some interesting facts about the locality. What we had thought was an obelisk, probably connected with the civil war which had raged around the village, was actually a chimney; it stood on the highest point of land overlooking the town and was an exhaust from an underground mine. On the slopes of a mountain to the south a small Moorish village, Majorca, huddled in a cleft in the rock with a stream flowing lazily through it down to the sea.

We were short of just about everything by the time we finished loading so we made for Gibraltar and went alongside for bunkers, water and stores. The battleships *Vanguard* and *Duke of York,* the aircraft carrier *Implacable,* two other carriers, the cruiser Newcastle and three other cruisers plus a score of destroyers crowded the harbour. It was five years since I was last in Gibraltar and with all that assembled hardware it felt like the wartime all over again. We left Gibraltar for Middlesbrough, passing very close to the *Albatross,* a four-masted schooner in full sail, a wonderful sight. Off Lisbon we passed the *Bagdad,* another full-rigged vessel, then through the Bay, the Channel, along the east coast past Flamborough Head, finally reaching Middlesbrough, where there was no berth ready for us and we had to anchor in the river for a couple of days. There was no point in my going home because this was the end of the trip; we were due to sign off the Ship's Articles in Middlesbrough, sign on for the next voyage and then go round to Immingham. Alf disappeared once more, but this time at least we could go ashore for fish and chips until he re-appeared.

A week in Middlesbrough was overkill. The furnaces of the steel mills cast a picturesque red glow in the sky at night, but that, and the novelty of going back and forth across the Transporter Bridge, soon wore off. The one bright spot was a piano recital on the Saturday afternoon in the Town Hall, a Chopin recital by Pouishnoff. His appearance was what one would associate with a Polish pianist, shoulder-length white hair, dinner jacket, bow tie, slightly stooped, distinguished. The shafts of sunlight that forced their way through the dusty windows fell upon the assembly, which barely struggled into double figures. Goodness knows what the number would have been if Middlesbrough had been at home; probably the whole lot of us, plus pianist, would have been at Ayresome Park watching the match.

Pouishnoff beamed at us from the front of the hall, then, with a few words, motioned us to the seats nearest the piano. In the manner of English audiences when faced with large empty spaces, we were sitting as far away from each other as possible. We shuffled to the front couple of rows and sat together, close to the piano, like disciples at the feet of the Master. From then on he had us all in the palm of his hand, it was just this wonderful man, playing for a group of friends some of the most beautiful piano music I'd ever heard. Between the pieces he talked to us, about the music, about Chopin, about Poland a little, then he would be off again into a magical world, taking us with him. It was an enriching interlude for the soul, seldom given an outing amongst the workaday life of coal and ships.

7: CADIZ AND MUSIC HALLS

We left that same night for Immingham to load coal and I went across on the ferry from New Holland to spend a couple of days at home. By then, much to everyone's relief, Alf had found his way back to the ship and managed to heave his large genial frame on board before we sailed one gloomy evening for Spain. It was foggy in the Channel and there were SOS calls on 500kc/s. Quite often birds alight on ships, sometimes disorientated by fog or when exhausted in the middle of an ocean migration. A small bird with a long beak settled on board, making its home in the wireless room until the fog lifted, before going on its way. It also seemed to be glad that Alf was back because it ate some food, whereas birds often don't eat in these circumstances. We passed Cape Finisterre and were breezing down the coast past Lisbon, when a flock of birds with white breasts, red and black faces and black wings settled in the wireless room overnight. Some of them found a corner to huddle in, but a couple roosted on the aerial leads before they flew off the next morning. Listening to morse signals with a chorus of chirrups in the background was a novelty, but needed more than usual concentration.

Berthing at Cadiz, half a dozen of us went ashore to reconnoitre, pronouncing it an intriguing place in which to spend a few days. The shore gang worked round the clock so there wasn't much sleep to be had on board, consequently anyone who wasn't directly involved with working cargo spent as much time as possible ashore. There were lots of cafés with tables outside so we set up HQ at a cafe in the central park and anyone who went ashore at any hour of the day or night made for this rendezvous before moving on. Alf and I took two girls to see the film Burlesque at the town's best cinema; one good point about the spread of Hollywood's influence was that wherever you went, there were English-speaking movies, dubbed in the local language. I came to know Cadiz well, enjoyed walking alone through its shadowy squares and narrow streets, often late at night or early in the morning when it was silent, peaceful, and the atmosphere of the city draped itself around you. In some places you wouldn't feel at all like that, but Cadiz was as warm and friendly as the night air.

Clubbing together, we bought a Communal Lottery ticket, winning 100 pesetas, which quickly vanished in a communal celebration. The cathedral was built about the time of Spain's colonial expansion and the Captain and I went to explore the building. We climbed up the steps inside one of the twin bell-towers and had a marvellous view of the town and out to sea. We wondered if we could have been standing in the footsteps of Villeneuve himself, looking out over Napoleon's massed French and Spanish fleets in the harbour and to the waters beyond, where Nelson awaited him in the *Victory*. Unfortunately the bells started to ring only a few feet away, deafening us and interrupting our soliloquy, bringing us sharply back to the 20th century as we retreated hastily down the winding stone steps to investigate the catacombs, where it was considerably quieter.

It was April and the Levant was blowing strongly, so walking through the narrow walled streets of the old town became a test of strength, not only for us but also for the 'Processiones' preparing for the Good Friday weekend festivities. These were something we hadn't experienced before and we joined in the carnival atmosphere, fuelled by generous helpings of Muscatel. After a week of round-the-clock noise and dirt on the ship, most of us had established base camps ashore and the café tables in the Park now included camp-followers with accommodation. Scouts went down to the dock periodically to check on any likely departure, but otherwise we continued to live happy and untroubled lives ashore in the sunshine.

Discharging completed, we made the short trip from Cadiz to Huelva, staying for a couple of days anchored in the river whilst waiting for a berth alongside. The sounds of music and gaiety drifted over the water, so it looked as though the locals were making the most of the holiday in this flamenco corner of Spain. When we did get alongside, a group of us went to a café where there was flamenco dancing and I lapped it all up, admiring people who can let their hair down and really enjoy themselves as Latin peoples do. The Captain took me with him in a small boat across the Rio Tinto to the Convent la Rabida, from where Columbus sailed in 1492; we saw the room and the table where he laid out his charts and spent his last hours on Spanish soil before setting sail in the *Santa Maria* into the unknown.

In Huelva we completed the loading of 2500 tons of pyrite, a mineral containing sulphuric acid, so it was said. Remembering the rule, 'always add acid to water and never water to acid', we hoped that the hatch covers wouldn't leak if we encountered bad weather, otherwise the resultant fumes could see us all off like a modern day *Marie Celeste*. Once out to sea the weather was perfect and a procession of large vessels passed us, including the *Stratheden* and the *Worcestershire*. It took us a week to reach Ipswich, where I saw Aldershot lose at Portman Road on the same day that the Tigers beat Stockport 6-1 and were assured of promotion from Division 3 North. The ship moved from Ipswich to Immingham to load coal, and a couple of days were spent at home, the time being extended by boiler trouble on board.

Loaded down to the Plimsoll line, we set off outward bound

for Cadiz once more. This pleased the whole ship, because we had all put down roots and felt at home there. Shortly after leaving the Humber we passed the *Hendonhall* inward bound with Geoff on board, so we narrowly missed seeing each other after eight months away; we had kept in touch on our 6mc/s schedules every day for the last week or so and it was disappointing to miss each other by a few hours. Discharging at Cadiz took five days during which our appreciation of Spanish wines increased as did our circle of friends. We left for Casablanca to load 2500 tons of phosphates and there was time to relax at café tables in the sunshine before taking a walk around the Casbah looking for Ingrid Bergman; but without any luck. Leaving Casablanca, we set off for a 'British port' orders to follow later. Eventually, a message came through Land's End Radio for us to discharge cargo in Ipswich once more.

This Ipswich visit was an improvement on the previous one. Our first night in port was a Friday and the programme at the Hippodrome theatre was 'The Palace of Varieties', an old-time Music Hall show featuring Margaret Lawford. After the show I made my way backstage to introduce myself. The following afternoon Margaret came back with me to the *Kalev* where she had a tour around the ship and met the crew. We talked about theatres and life on the road whilst Eric organised tea in my cabin, after which she left by taxi to be at the theatre in time for the first house at 6pm. The Mate and Eric wanted to see the show so they accompanied me to the theatre. We saw the first performance from the Stalls before going backstage to Margaret's dressing room, remaining backstage throughout the second house, meeting Ernest Longstaffe and other members of the cast. This was another world and I loved it, the music, the lights, the bustle, the smell of greasepaint. We went for drinks with the cast to a nearby pub after the show, later escorting Margaret back to her lodgings by taxi; it was Saturday night and the show was moving on to pastures new the following day.

8: CRICKET IN MOROCCO

After discharging the phosphates in Ipswich we moved up to Immingham and, after levering Alf free of the nearest bar counter, we crossed the Humber on one of the old paddle steamers, *Lincoln Castle* or *Tattershall Castle,* to spend a few days at home.

I was fortunate to see Len Hutton batting all one day at the

Circle, making 146 not out. The *Kalev* meanwhile had filled up with coal so Alf and I returned by ferry to New Holland, caught the train to Immingham and sailed on a peaceful evening for Cadiz. A few days later Hutton made 101 and Compton 103 batting for England at Headingley against New Zealand, helped by Alf, Eric and I cheering them on in the wireless room.

Normal service was resumed at Cadiz, where my female companion, Solle, was waiting on the quayside to meet the ship when we docked; she possessed better shipping-movement intelligence than Lloyds of London. So it was back to bottles of wine in the sunshine and revelry by night. There was a fiesta taking place, 'Corpus Christi', very colourful, with processions through the streets and the city celebrating the event far into the night. After a week in Cadiz we left for Safi in French Morocco to load gypsum. Safi was a small town with a fairly modern main street surrounded by older sun-baked buildings, their plaster peeling off under the hot sun. Mosques with minarets pointed skyward, but they, like the shops on the waterfront and the small houses on the outskirts, all seemed asleep amidst the heat haze. The water tasted terrible; flat, slightly salty, it spoilt our tea and coffee. We sat on the beach and watched the fishermen landing their early morning catches of sardines, buying some to take back on board for Alf to fry for supper.

We took our 2,500 tons of gypsum off to Port Talbot, still following the cricket, where Compton with 116 and Bailey with a stubborn 93 saved the day. Trevor Bailey, now there was a man who knew how to defend his wicket, often bored you stiff to watch him mind, but he knew how to occupy the crease. B&B was provided for a baby petrel overnight in the ship's aviary, (sometimes known as the wireless room), and it flew away happily the next morning leaving me to clean up after it. We arrived in Port Talbot on a Sunday; deadly, with not even a cinema open, it reminded me of Scottish Sundays in wartime so I went home.

Hezikiah Tebbs, alias 'Hezzie', was also in Hull and came round for tea; we had not met up for some time. Hezzie was Nigerian and had been one of those studying at the Tech. in 1942, he had seemed lonely and I had taken him home for meals, after which the family 'adopted' him and he visited my parents whenever he was in Hull, calling them 'mother' and 'father'. He wrote letters to them asking for pairs of socks and stuff and whether mother could travel to see him in Liverpool or other ports up and down the country. The relationship had long since served its original purpose but was still ambling on and seemed destined to turn into one of those long drawn-out affairs that had passed its sell-by date. Hezzie had left the sea and was now well established ashore and doing nicely, but still looked on the family as his own, came round for meals and signed his letters 'son'. Eventually it all became lost in the sands of time, as these things often do.

A week later I returned to Wales, only to find that we were still discharging cargo in a very desultory fashion. Our berth was next to a local holiday beach and games of cricket were organised with a bat and ball borrowed from the Agent. When rain stopped play we repaired to the Jersey Bay Hotel, near the beach at Margam. Some engine-room repairs had materialised in my absence which would prolong our stay in port, also there was work to be done installing a new receiver and putting up a fresh set of aerials ready for a new transmitter, expected later. That taken care of I went home again, via London, where most of the day was spent in the Science Museum. At home for a second week, there was cricket on the school field, snooker with dad, and days out with Geoff who had left deep-sea and was now on trawlers sailing out of Grimsby. We went across on the ferry to see him off on the *Esturian*.

Back in Port Talbot, some mail was awaiting at the Agents. To while away the time at sea I had joined a Seafarers Correspondence Course in astronomy, run from an address in Cambridge. Long spells in the solitude of the ocean may turn seamen into amateur philosophers, the nearness and intensity of the night sky drawing you closer to a world of mystery. However, too much technical detail can obscure wonder, and I didn't get very far with the course, content just to stand and stare. The repairs finished, we made for Partington in the Manchester Ship Canal to load coal, picking up the pilot off Anglesey and anchoring in the Mersey, waiting for the tide before proceeding up the Canal. Once alongside, I was off sharpish before the coal dust blanketed everything, catching a bus to Manchester, visiting a news theatre and the Belle Vue Amusement Park. Returning aboard, everything was dark, ill-lit and covered in coal dust, so I had to pick my way along the gangway and alleyways very carefully to avoid getting coated with dirt and grime.

Next morning we left for Melilla in Spanish Morocco, anchoring off the harbour entrance until a berth became available. For ten or more years after the war the oceans of the world were swarming with ships of all types, from liners, cargo ships and oil tankers to trawlers and river traffic, so it was not unusual to wait your turn for a berth. Having arrived off Melilla at midnight, four of us played cards until dawn, fortified by the red wine brought out to us by the local entrepreneurs, laughed a lot and went to bed after breakfast. The next night we wined and dined ashore. On our last day in port the Captain and I, together with members of the crew, paid a visit to the cemetery to lay wreaths on the grave of a British airman whose plane had crashed near Melilla during the war. The airman was the son of a Director of Pelton's, the shipping company who operated the *Kalev;* we had carried a wreath on board from his father, and the crew subscribed to lay a second wreath. Some photographs were taken of the grave and its surroundings to take back to the family. From Melilla we moved to Oran to load esparto grass. Alf, Eric and I spent a happy few days there, practically living ashore at the cafés, bars and other entertainments, which seemed little altered since 1943. Oran entranced me with its 'Casablanca', atmosphere, full of character and bubbling with life.

Walking around the narrow back streets of Oran, past an ancient Moorish building with barred windows, a number of women waved from one of the windows. I waved back at them, half expecting to be whisked off for breaching the rules of the Casbah. My steps quickened just in case someone on a white horse came galloping along to ask me if I wanted to be a eunuch. The esparto grass came aboard in bales, and when the holds were full the grass was stowed on deck, the smell of new-mown hay filling the ship all the way home. Eric and I spent most of our time in Oran at the Villa Rose bar or the Coq d'Or cafe, where we drank lemonade laced with some unidentified spice, admired the scenery and also the bronze statuettes behind the bar. At a loose end one morning I went aboard the tanker *Deepdale H* to help the Operator, who lived in Paull Lighthouse near Hull, fix his Auto Alarm, which was on the blink. When that was sorted out we took a bat and ball and played cricket on the quayside, explaining all about the game to Lydia and Lily, our girlfriends, as we went along. Efforts to clarify middle stump, long leg and maiden overs, although bringing forth peals of laughter, advanced the cause of cricket in North Africa not one jot, although there were incidental benefits.

Whilst the ship was being readied for sea, I was busy going back and forth between my cabin, the wireless room and the bridge, when I noticed a movement under the canvas cover of the lifeboat outside my cabin. Alerting the mate, we went to investigate. It turned out to be a deserter from the Foreign Legion, a young German who was stowing away in order to escape life in the Legion, which he later described to us cheerfully as, 'No gutt'. We gave him something to eat and drink and yarned the time away whilst waiting for the Gendarmes. Unfortunately for him we had little choice but to hand him over to the shore authorities; stowaways can be expensive and a lot of trouble for the ship and the owners, consequently, whatever your personal feelings, stowaways have to be put ashore. I was in favour of putting him ashore and saying nothing; maybe he would have better luck next time.

The weather was good as we left Oran for London and we had a pleasant aromatic week's trip before docking at Gravesend. City's match with Leicester was broadcast, Carter and Burbanks scoring in a 2-1 win and as Yorkshire also beat Glamorgan to become joint League Champions it was good news all round. After drawing some money from Marconi's in East Ham my next stop was Collins Music Hall, one of the last of the old-style theatres, which had a bar at the back of the stalls from where you could watch the show with a pint in your hand. Catching the train at King's Cross for home, I shared a compartment with two Gambian Chiefs in national dress and had a long and interesting conversation with Phillip Mickman, who had swum the Channel a few days previously. His photo had been all over the front pages as a result and that was how I recognised him. He said he had found the Channel very wet.

It was early September, City were now in Division 2 and there was just time to watch them beat Blackburn in front of 40,000 people at Boothferry Park before a telegram recalled me to the ship. Hastening back to London, it turned out to be a false alarm and we didn't sail for another few days. The ship had moved from Gravesend in my absence and was discharging cargo in Surrey Commercial Docks, so local commuting was now much easier. My aunt and uncle were living in Wandsworth and evenings were spent with them, daytimes being given over to Foyles bookshop, sightseeing and lunching with uncle Les in Soho. Evening theatre visits included the revue 'Latin Quarter' at the London Casino and 'Sauce Tartare' at the Cambridge Theatre with Jessie Matthews, Claude Hulbert and, in the chorus, a young Audrey Hepburn. After watching Brentford lose to Leicester at Griffin Park I settled for the evening at the London Jazz Club where Humphrey Lyttelton's band was holding forth. As usual, the joint was jumping, 'trad jazz' was in its golden era, yet still remained primarily the province of the returned Forces and the younger element, who were having a struggle to convince the BBC that it merited equal coverage with Victor Silvester and his Ballroom Orchestra. It seemed an uphill task to get anything new recognised by society; but maybe that's what youth is for.

9: URGENT XXX

The *Kalev* moved from the Thames up to Hull to load coal. Mam and dad plus Geoff and his girlfriend met us at the lock gates towards midnight, coming on board for coffee before going home, some of us to sleep, others to play records until breakfast time. All-night record sessions were the norm, my parents' hospitality seeming unlimited, though doubtless their tolerance was often stretched. A couple of days later mother came down to Albert Dock to see us off when we sailed on the evening tide for Malaga. The Channel was busy, with Cunard liners off Southampton, the *Stirling Castle* and *Edinburgh Castle* followed by the *Andes* and the *Queen Elizabeth,* which passed close by our stern, towering over us. There were so many wonderful vessels in those days, the great liners, the ships of the South American Saint Line, the Cape vessels and the P&O liners amongst them, and their classically graceful lines added beauty to the world's oceans.

We discharged 800 tons of coal in Malaga over a couple of days before moving to Almeria to off-load the balance of 1600 tons. Both ports were gently sleeping in the sun, attractive, unspoilt Spanish fishing villages, little suspecting what lay round the corner. In the market place I bought a caged bird, released it, then wondered if that was the right thing to have done, whether its freedom would last long enough for it to learn the necessary survival skills. We sailed to Djidjelli in Algeria to load iron ore for Middlesbrough; this was similar to loading iron ore at La Garrucha but was quicker as we were alongside a quay. Shortly after leaving Djidjelli, a green bird became waterlogged in the gash bucket, (the receptacle outside the galley for food waste waiting to be thrown overboard). It had seemingly decided to cut out the middle man and gone straight to the food source, only to get itself gunged up in the process and was now unable to fly. I took it to the wireless room, bathed it in a bucket of soap and water and dried it in the warmth from the galley stove, but sadly it didn't survive.

Calling at Gibraltar for coal, water and supplies, I went ashore for old times' sake, to post letters, buy nylons for my female acquaintances and visit the recently established 'Flying Angel' Club on the trawler quay. Along the Portuguese coast the *Himalaya* passed us, going south on her maiden voyage to Australia. At Middlesbrough all the crew trooped down to the Shipping Office and went through the routine of signing off the Ships Articles for this trip and signing on for the next trip. This procedure included stamping the seaman's Discharge Book, which all merchant seamen must possess in order to sign on. The book is authorised by the Mercantile Marine Office of the Registrar-General of Shipping and Seamen at Cardiff, shows the ship's name, tonnage, the type of voyage, the dates of the seaman's engagement and discharge, his rank or rating and a report of character.

Attached to my Discharge Book is a 'Certificate of Proficiency, Merchant Navy A/A Gunnery Course' stamped at the D.E.M.S. Training Centre, Hull, on the 21st May 1943. Two bitterly cold days were spent with George at HMS *Galatea,* the naval base at Earl's Yard near Alexandra Dock on Hedon Road, where we took guns apart, put them together again and fired them over the Humber. This activity resulted in a Certificate verifying that Jack Close had 'completed the Merchant Navy A/A Gunnery Course and is qualified in the firing, cleaning and oiling of Hotchkiss and Marlin guns'. Also in the Discharge Book is a 'Naval Active Service' postcard dated 12th July 1944, sent home whilst on the *Eminent.* This was the only correspondence that you were allowed to send during the Invasion to let your family know that you were, 'quite well, sick, wounded', (strike out as appropriate). Threats accompanied its completion: 'NOTHING is to be written on this side except the date and signature of the sender. If anything else is added the postcard cannot be forwarded'. It must have seemed an eternity to those waiting for news of loved ones, because no mail at all was allowed out of 'the box', the area of southern England inside which the build-up of men and material for D-Day was taking place. The whole of the south coast had been sealed off for weeks before the 6th June, and remained so for some time thereafter, with neither people nor mail allowed across the boundaries. One of the many amazing things about the invasion was that this huge, huge, operation was kept secret. They knew we were coming but they didn't know where and they didn't know when; until we arrived on their doorstep.

Meanwhile, after signing on the *Kalev* for another voyage, I went to Ayresome Park to watch Middlesbrough draw with Arsenal. A taxi had been ordered to be outside the ground for halfway through the second half, to take me to the station in time to catch the Hull train for the last night of Hull Fair. After a couple of days at home I rejoined *Kalev* in Middlesbrough to take her round to Sunderland to load coal. There was time for a day out in Newcastle before we left for Barcelona, just as the weather began to worsen.

In the Dover Straits, within the space of 24 hours, there were three distress calls, a man-overboard alert and a vessel which had struck a mine. There were large numbers of minefields laid during the war by both sides, not all of them were charted, and not all had since been cleared. In bad weather the mines broke loose from their moorings and floated to the surface, where there was very little chance of seeing them in the choppy seas, and even less of avoiding them. There was also an XXX signal out for the Falmouth lifeboat, which was itself in difficulties. The XXX signal is one step below that of an SOS and denotes a dangerous or urgent situation. Our own problems abounded; we had been heading into the storm off Ushant for 24 hours, and even with engines full ahead were only just holding our own, sometimes being blown backwards. Birds were blown onto the ship and stunned, one exhausted small bird slept in my cabin for a day until the weather abated and then flew off, seemingly none the worse for its experience. The liner *Chitral* swept past us at speed, grand enough to be untroubled by anything as paltry as a raging sea.

In Barcelona we played soccer on the quayside until the ball was run over, when we played chess instead. The usual exploratory walk was made around the old port and the town centre, moving briskly past the Sagrada Familia, until eventually my feet gave up. We completed discharging and headed for Nemours in Algeria, where the first thing I saw ashore was an Arab on a white horse, followed by a group of veiled women on foot. This white horse and its retinue was one of many seen during the day, seeming to be the regular mode of transport for men. Nemours boasted a single cinema which opened once a week, and some of us paid it a visit, watching a French film with no subtitles and not making much of it. The Arab audience didn't seem to make much of it either judging by the amount of chattering that went on throughout the film, all but drowning out the soundtrack. As there seemed little else happening in this isolated community, perhaps the weekly cinema was more a social occasion than a visual spectacle. It was Armistice Day, no loading took place and we left Nemours for Bristol later than expected, decks piled high with esparto grass, destined to become high quality writing paper, almost like parchment. We bunkered at Gibraltar on the way and had an uneventful trip to England, only to find ourselves unable to dock because of fog, having to anchor off the mouth of the Avon until morning. In Bristol a couple of us visited the Mauritania pub, with its long bar made of wood from the old passenger liner, before going home for a few days.

From Bristol, discharging completed, the ship crossed to Swansea and spent five days loading coal; cinemas and pubs filling in this damp and depressing period until we sailed, covered in coal dust, for Antwerp. The fog in the Channel soon gave way before strong winds and by the time we needed the Antwerp pilot none was available, a gale was blowing and it was too dangerous for the pilot launch to come across to us. In company with a score of other ships we cruised up and down, eventually obtaining a pilot from Zeebrugge late the following day, to take us to our berth in the Leopold Dock at Antwerp. We spent two days discharging coal before moving to another berth to take on yet more coal. It seemed as though we were just shunting coal all around Europe, but of course there was coal and there was coal, different types for different jobs. South Wales coal was good quality steam coal, whereas our present cargo was Ruhr coal and as fine as sand. It was obviously a desirable commodity in Rouen, for that was where it was destined. The weather was still bad, we were delayed leaving Antwerp and missed the tide to enter port when we reached Rouen; to make matters worse it started snowing hard as we swung at anchor.

10: POLITICS AND JAZZ IN THE PARK

As soon as we docked I caught the train from Rouen to Paris, setting out from the Gare St. Lazaire on foot to see the sights, being duly impressed and also, by the end of the day, duly footsore. The day out cost me $4.00 and was totally free of coal dust. Included in my itinerary was Rodin's 'The Thinker', but it was boarded up when it finally hove into view and I felt mildly cheated, having gone out of my way to track it down, charting a route on the Metro especially to see it. And it wasn't until after retirement, when researching the affairs of the d'Andilly family, that it became evident I had also missed the portraits of d'Arnauld d'Andilly and Robert Arnauld d'Andilly whilst wandering around the Louvre.

We left Rouen for Swansea to load coal. After a bleak few days in South Wales we set off for Amsterdam, collecting the pilot at Ijmuiden on Christmas morning, eating our Christmas dinner whilst moving up the canal and going alongside at teatime on Christmas Day 1949. A couple of days were spent wandering around Amsterdam whilst the coal was discharged, then another couple of days wandering about Rotterdam whilst we loaded yet more coal, this time for Caen.

Thinking things over, although the *Kalev* was a happy ship and it looked as though similar voyages could have gone on for some time, I felt that I'd had enough of transporting coal around Europe, and needed a change of scenery. Radar was being progressively installed on merchant vessels, and it seemed as though combining a radar course with living at home for a few months would be just the job. The Technical College enrolled me for the next course, commencing in mid-January 1950; Geoff was also in favour of a working holiday so we went back to college.

In the meantime the *Kalev* had arrived at Ouistreham. On my last visit there our ships were shelling the town whilst we were trying to build our harbour nearby and much of the Mulberry Harbour material was still visible offshore. One of the threats to our shipping had been the low flying bombs that the Germans sent across the anchorages and we judged at the time that they came from the Ouistreham area. War damage was still evident around the canal entrance, also in Caen itself which had been at the core of the fighting during the Allied advance into Normandy. We stayed a short time in Caen before going across to England, where I left the *Kalev* at Blyth early in January 1950.

For the next three months there were radar lectures during the day, with records and girlfriends in the evenings and football on Saturdays. Geoff and I had our favourite resting places but we also had a subsidiary agenda, which entailed visiting those hostelries threatened with demolition in the Charles Street and Wincolmlee area. Bomb sites scarred the city landscape and the clearance of large areas was either active or pending. We visited the Central Hotel, the Tivoli, Star of the West, the Station Hotel tucked away in its own little square, the Criterion and the Society

Tavern, the latter known to seamen the world over. Mention Hull in a bar in Saigon or Panama and everyone knew the Society Tavern, although it was more often called 'Freddy's' after its landlord, Freddy Nunn.

Dan was at home, working at the Hawthorn Garage further down the Avenue, next to the Salvation Army and the Chalk Lane Working Men's Club. George was also at home, learning the job at Fretwell's, the family printing business. Not many people possessed a car but George had one that went with the business and we made full use of it, touring the lanes and by-ways of the East Riding, calling at quiet country inns and enjoying the fact that the four of us were together again for the first time in many a long day. Deciding one hazy afternoon that we needed a photograph, three of us went to Jerome's in Whitefriargate where I took the opportunity to date Eileen the receptionist, who, at 18, had just volunteered for the ATS; interrupting my relationship with Audrey to fit this in. There were no such thing as seat belts and it was a lot of fun cramming six or more people into the five seats in George's car as we visited 'Nellies', the Ferguson Fawcett, Pipe and Glass and others places of refreshment further afield.

Freddy Randall's band came to the Fulford Ballroom and groups of us went to listen to one of Britain's under-rated trad bands. Dan was playing rugby for Hessle RUFC and we all enthusiastically supported him at the frequently held club's socials at the Marquis of Granby or Darley's Arms. Studying took up two or three evenings a week; a group of us went on the train to Leeds to hear Mr R. D. Smith give the Faraday Lecture on Radar and the class also examined the radar installations on the ferries *Tattershall Castle* and *Lincoln Castle,* the two paddle-steamers that ran a regular schedule across the foggy Humber from Victoria Pier to the jetty at New Holland. Eileen Joyce gave a Chopin recital at the Queen's Hall and a crowd of us went to a pantomime at the Tivoli, but I thought nothing to it and spent the latter part of the evening in the Sandringham, (oh yes he did).

Lester and Judy were still in the flat in Pearson Park and we regularly climbed the stairs to this comfortable little eyrie to play records and talk politics; or perhaps more accurately to argue politics, because Lester, Judy and I were Labour and Geoff and some others were Tory, although party loyalties were liable to switch temporarily during the evening. In those exhilarating optimistic days after the war, people would spend time discussing politics, social issues and the whole new better Britain that seemed just around the corner. However it wasn't long before somebody put on a record and the evenings passed contentedly until some departed to walk home and others bedded down on the settee or on the floor. The flat looked out over the trees and the pond towards a similar flat at the other side of the park, to be occupied some few years later by another jazz fan, Philip Larkin. April came, the exam with it, and in due course my Certificate of Maintenance of Radar Equipment on Merchant Ships, No.322, arrived from the Ministry of Transport. Geoff also passed the exam, and the next two months drifted by lazily for both of us as spring gave way to a glorious summer and it became difficult to contemplate stirring from a very agreeable lifestyle. Sessions at the snooker hall were punctuated by regular games of tennis at West Park and record evenings at friends' houses.

Word reached me that the Kalev was in Immingham; I took the ferry across and spent the day on board, pleased to be amongst friends, reminiscing about the good times we'd had ashore, also some of the hard times at sea that we had been through together. It was like a family reunion, because for many of them the Kalev was their home. They wanted to know what had become of Margaret and were pleased to hear that she was doing very well, her name being mentioned often in the theatre news, her picture appearing in the newspapers, and later on the front page of Tit-Bits, and Reveille, ('The Forces Newspaper', now gone civilian.) On the strength of the visit I sent Margaret some flowers and a note telling of the visit to the *Kalev* and of the interest of the crew in her career.

Not everyone had passed the Radar Exam and a few of us went to the college a couple of afternoons a week to help with the re-sits. Ye Olde White Harte was the focal point for any friends who were in town across lunchtime and we frequently had lunch there in the nook by the fire. There was a stag's head over the chimney-piece and George invariably stuck a lighted cigarette in its mouth until Josie became fed up with us and threatened to bar us. After lunch we visited the News Theatre, which operated in the Tivoli theatre, unless the snooker room at YOWH had a table vacant in the tiny billiard room across the passage, when we stayed there past closing time.

We walked everywhere in those days, and a walk to the town and back from Geoff's house in Calvert Lane was a regular journey, as were evening walks to Hessle or Kirkella and back. Most people were fit and energetic, and if you weren't walking you were cycling. Back home and in bed, the sturdy gun-metal grey 1155 valve set was tuned to 'Midnight in Munchen', the jazz programme from AFN, with its theme tune, 'Pompton Turnpike', by Charlie Barnet's orchestra. I took a girl called Pat to the Boulevard, at her request, to see Hull beat Marseilles 9-0 but don't recollect any further progress, so maybe I was ditched for not showing enough enthusiasm, (for the game). Colin Matheson, our Chief R/O at Campbeltown, had married a WREN whilst stationed there and they had since returned to Hull, Colin setting up a radio servicing business near the docks at Marfleet. George and I went to see them and spent an afternoon reminiscing about Campbeltown days and people. Time passed happily in that lovely summer, until it became apparent that a decisive move had to be made.

11: A TENTATIVE FOOT ASHORE

An advertisement for technicians to work in their Cambridge laboratories had been placed in the local paper by Pye Limited. Talking it over with Geoff, we tossed for it, I lost, and without much enthusiasm posted off an application. We could both see the possibilities opening up in the fledgling television industry and thought that we should investigate. I travelled to Cambridge for an interview, got the job and fixed up some digs in Montague Road. Pye had just won the contract to supply equipment to the newly opened BBC Lime Grove TV studios and my job was on the shop floor in their Television Transmitter and Photo-Camera Department. The hours were from 8-12.30 and 1.30-6pm for 2/5d an hour and I didn't think much to it. However, as I'd gone to all the trouble to get there it deserved my best shot, but by the second morning of getting up at seven o'clock I was fed up. The job itself was routine, interpreting wiring diagrams and turning the result into a mass of intelligible circuitry inside a television camera. A canteen was available, but my lunchtimes were spent in a characterful old pub with a pint and sandwiches. Walking back to the digs in the evening along the riverbank was the best part of the day; fresh air and freedom. It had been plain that I wasn't cut out for a shore job when the possibility of taking over the post office loomed darkly on the horizon; shore jobs seemed a non-starter then and Pye's only served to confirm it.

For three weeks I enjoyed the life of Cambridge outside of work, visiting theatres, cinemas and old pubs, spending one evening at Tony Short's house in Victoria Road, playing records, listening to him playing the piano and fending off his dog. Tony played the piano in pubs, which was where we met. He did get to record a couple of sides for Decca, but a harsh critic reviewing the record said he sounded like Teddy Wilson with a whip behind him and he didn't make many more records after that. But stay, don't scoff, how many of us get that far in life to leave something behind, even if it's only a poorly received jazz record.

Pye's had a stable of cricket teams and my first game was with their 3rd team against Marshall's on Jesus Green, scoring 8 out of 36, which was sufficient to see me promoted to the 2nd team for the next game, an evening fixture on Parker's Piece, also against a Marshall's eleven. Although down to open our innings, the other team batted first, the light became too bad to continue and the match was abandoned before I even took guard. Solitary meditative walks along the backs, and sampling the local brews in riverside pubs in the summer evenings were a real pleasure, and memories of those evenings remain with me still. There was a jazz fan in Humberstone Road, and a couple of evenings were spent at his house, listening to records and talking until all hours. Some quality cricket was watched on Parker's Piece most evenings, and there was a fair on Midsummer Common, but it was time to leave Cambridge with its picturesque riverbanks, gentle pubs and bicycles, and go home.

The train wended its long, slow way through the flat countryside to March, where, during the war, the WVS never failed to provide cups of tea on trays at each carriage window when trains stopped at the station. The trains were crammed so full that you lost your place if you left the carriage. Memories out of nowhere were conjured up on that sunny June afternoon with the birds singing, the meadows stretching to the horizon and the platform deserted, where once there had been such an urgent hustle and bustle of khaki and blue and cups of tea and sandwiches. This was what we had fought for those few years ago, so that there wouldn't be a German sentry at the end of the platform, only pieces of unattended luggage baking in the sunshine.

Once back home there was an easy routine to settle into, tennis with Geoff in the mornings, lunches in town, evenings playing records, visits to jazz clubs, continuing work on a model ship and cycling to cinemas on the edge of town. Operators were still scarce, firms paying good money, and Geoff and I travelled to

Edinburgh in a car borrowed from his dad, staying overnight at the Imperial Hotel, the next morning going to Salveson's of Leith to enquire about jobs with their whaling fleet. The money was even better than deep-sea but, after making a few enquiries, neither of us can have fancied it because, although we could have been taken on their books, nothing came of it. However we made the most of the trip, stopping at old coaching inns we came across, in York, Thirsk, Newcastle, Berwick, Coldstream and Dalkeith.

Yorkshire came to the Circle for a three-day county match and the whole period was spent at the ground, lazing in the sunshine. George came with me to visit some wartime shipmates on the *Reward* when she came into Albert Dock, one of them being Lt. Cdr. Hunter who had been Captain on the *Eminent*. A weekend was spent at the Palm Court Hotel in Scarborough with George and Joyce, Geoff and Pat. A brass plate outside the hotel entrance advised that there was a dance instructor on the premises, the plate containing the words 'Cassini, Cert.'. This phrase was thereafter absorbed into our vocabulary, not only to indicate dance steps of a high standard, but to indicate excellence in any sphere whatsoever.

The Shipping Museum at the entrance to Pickering Park was a small rectangular building, a treasure trove for children and grown-ups alike. Large marine skeletons hung from the ceiling, strange objects in glass cases, carved ships' figureheads, narwhal tusks, old prints, skeletons of fish, flags and wonderful ship models abounded. All manner of intriguing things relating to the sea had their home there. It smelt slightly musty, of ropes and tar, was wholly absorbing, exciting and stimulating to the imagination, creating a world of adventure and a thirst for knowledge. Another museum of character, that in Albion Street which Tom Shepherd had made his pride and joy, was destroyed by the Germans in 1941. Frequent visits were made to the Shipping Museum, locking my bike up outside and browsing around its fascinating and stimulating world. Sadly missed, both of them, on so many counts.

Dan and Bunty moved into the family house in Newington Street, Geoff went off to Bear Island on one of Northern's trawlers and I met Jean accidentally in the town, a little while before she was about to be married. We went home, where mother made us coffee and the three of us had lots to talk over. My life was still sea-going and Jean and I had drifted apart, our friendship being renewed a lifetime later when these pages came to be written.

12: NORTHERN LIGHTS

Why I went back on trawlers is something of a mystery. Having left the *Kalev* in order to see more of the world, there wasn't going to be anything fresh to see up in the Arctic; and it can't have been for the money, because equal or better money, and an easier life, was to be had on merchant ships. Large numbers of distant water trawlers sailed out of both Hull and Grimsby, but Operators didn't boil livers out of Grimsby so I decided to cross the river and give it a go from there. It would mean shortening an already brief time at home between trips, because not only would there be tide times to work around but also the travelling time from Grimsby to Hull and back again, inconvenient train times and ferry sailings, plus a taxi journey at both ends. A number of last minute ferry-jumps, platform dashes and quayside leaps lay ahead, but luckily I always made it to the North Wall in Grimsby in time to clamber aboard before we sailed.

The owner of the firm I sailed with, Croft Baker, was a collector of old English clocks; he currently had four vessels in the fleet, some of which were named after English clockmakers, the *Daniel Quare,* the *Edward East,* the *Glen Kidston* and the latest addition, the *Thomas Tompion,* the latter practically straight from the builder's yard. The *Thomas Tompion* was registered GY126, built at Beverley by Cook, Welton & Gemmell, was 171 feet long and 590 tons gross with a crew of about 20. In the wireless room was a Marconi Trans-Arctic transmitter/receiver, a Marconi 993 receiver and the workhorse CR300 receiver, little changed from the wartime B28 and CR100 receivers, at that time standard equipment on most British deep-sea rescue tugs. There was also a Marconi 'Lodestone' D/F and a Cossor radar. Her skipper was J Arthur Whittleton, a large genial man who was to play a major part in setting up the Grimsby Fishing Museum many years later. The chief engineer was from St. George's Road in Hull, we shared taxis and travelled to and from Grimsby together each trip.

My first voyage in the *Thomas Tompion* was to Iceland in the middle of August 1950. Subsequent trips were to Iceland or the White Sea, with occasional forays along the north Russian coast and to the north of Bear Island, all of them following the same routine, only differing in that you never knew what your catch was going to be or what the weather would be like. There were only rudimentary weather forecasts and these were broadcast in Icelandic/Norwegian from the local radio stations. Knowledge of the weather was all-important and you quickly learnt a few key words like the Norwegian: Kuling = gale, Sterk = strong, Minkenin = fining away, plus the points of the compass, and the forecast areas, from Sletnes in the north, through Fruholmen, Torsvag, Andanes, Sulen and Kraknes down to Slotteroy in the south. Locating the right station at the right time and on the right frequency wasn't easy, because most of them were small stations with weak signals. Reception was also hampered by fjords, headlands, static and an aerial acting as an independent direction finder as the ship rolled about.

Iceland was worse as regards scrabbling around for weather information. And weather really did matter on that NW corner of Iceland, where the Arctic storms came thundering down the Denmark Strait without any warning. The Icelanders had no weather stations to the north of them, so any forecasts they were able to give their ships were probably by guess and by God. The most reliable source of weather conditions was another trawler. In the unlikely event that you knew the location of one you could ask what the weather was like with her, but this was hit and miss, and seldom could you contact a ship in the location you were interested in when you needed to. On our first trip to Iceland we took a deckhand into Seydisfjord for medical attention; he had fallen down the fish room hatch, was pretty badly injured and we had to leave him behind. Depending on where we were fishing would determine whether we could pick him up again; if we made our last haul on the other side of Iceland he would have to wait in Seydisfjord and come home on the next ship that called there.

An average haul of fish could be anything from 20 to 60 baskets for a tow of maybe $1\frac{1}{2}$ hours, if you were lucky. Sometimes there was no fish to speak of, or what did come up in the net was rubbish and not saleable. However, that was better than having the belly of the net damaged by hauling aboard a massive dugong, as we did once, or having it ripped out on some sea-floor obstruction and coming up standing. That meant laying-to, mending the net and losing fishing time or, if the damage to the trawl was too bad to mend quickly, changing the whole set of gear over and trawling from the other side of the ship, usually the port side. Fishing would continue from the port side until the starboard gear had been mended. Whichever way, it meant that fishing time was lost, and the damaged net still had to be mended. If the men had been on a freezing deck gutting fish and hauling in heavy gear for the past 18 hours or more, were due for a doss down but instead had to stand on a heaving deck deluged with sleet, working on the net with fingers so numb with cold that they could hardly feel them; well they must have wondered what the hell they were doing there.

But it was always Christmas for the seagulls. If the haul was rubbish and was swilled through the scuppers they ate it, if the haul was good and the guts were swilled through the scuppers they ate that. It was quite a sight to see flocks of gannets, (wild ducks or wilocks as they were called) diving at speed into the water. Early in the year the cod gathered along the Norwegian coast to spawn and huge quantities of fish could be trawled. This was known as 'swagging' and also happened regularly off Bear Island. There was a plentiful supply of fish for years after the war and certain areas became the focus for trawlers of all sizes and nationalities, often being referred to as 'fish shops'. Everyone fished and fished until they were full up and could turn for home. Some nights, the arc lights that lit up the decks where ships lay gutting would show to the horizon, a cluster of bright dots beneath the dark sky. And the Northern Lights putting on a free show. Well maybe fishing wasn't such a bad game after all.

Every trip was a fresh adventure, never knowing whether it would turn out to be a success or a disaster. Would it be a trip with the fish room full, cod liver oil overflowing the tanks, a buoyant market and a beaming trawler owner waiting on the quayside? Or would it be a half-full ship coming in on the night tide with only a watchman to take your lines, slipping off home before anyone noticed you'd docked. The Skipper and the Mate were the only two on board who depended entirely for their settling on a share of the catch, the crew were on wages, plus a small share of the catch, poundage, and a share of the liver money. Cod, haddock and flatfish were the premium catches, plus the occasional halibut if you were lucky; the best fish were shelved, placed individually on wooden shelving in the fish room with ice distributed carefully over them so as not to crush or damage the skin. These would be the fish displayed on the wet fishmongers' slabs, or shipped off in boxes to Billingsgate in London for distribution to the best hotels. The proletariat fish were unceremoniously thrown into the hold, had shovelfuls of ice dumped on top of them and ended up in the neighbourhood fish and chip shops. And of these shops there was a multitude, there being at least four within easy walking distance of home.

What the catch sold for on the market determined how much was the 'settling', the money you took home. This usually worked out to be an average weekly shore wage, but seemed greater because you received it in a lump sum and only had 48 hours ashore in which to spend it, catching up with life. The clubs and pubs along Hessle Road, like Dee Street Club, Subway Club, St. Andrews Club and the Star and Garter (only ever known as Rayner's) were popular calls and always busy. It was easy to judge trawlermen wrongly if you didn't know them. They did get drunk, often; and they did fight, sometimes, but they were vital, they laughed a lot and were very generous. They were alive, brave, mad and happy all at the same time. People on Hessle Road understood them and that was all that mattered, because that was their world and they seldom strayed far from it. The fishing industry was eventually sacrificed to national politics, and with its demise came the demolition of the smoke-houses and the streets along Hessle Road, the close-knit community being scattered amongst estates and high-rise flats on the outskirts of the city where the sense of community was virtually nil, the city losing much of its character in the process.

Wireless Operators came from all parts the city, and many from outside the Hull area, so any rendezvous needed to be central and near to the Marconi and ROU offices; the Wheatsheaf pub in Jameson Street conveniently filled the bill. In addition to meeting up with other Operators, debts were settled through the medium of 'the slate', kept by the proprietor behind the bar. Debts and bets, created in the form of pints of beer during fishing trips, were dutifully paid for in cash by the Operator when his ship docked, and were noted on the slate by the proprietor. When the beneficiary trawler docked, the Sparks would go to the bar, collect his dues in the form of pints and the landlord would wipe the slate clean.

There were between 400-500 deep water and middle-water trawlers sailing out of the Humber alone, plus swarms of German, Russian and Icelandic vessels, all fishing to within three miles of the Icelandic and Norwegian coastlines, so at times there were large gatherings of trawlers in those northern waters. Some ships hitched up their loudhailers to music from the wireless room's spare receiver and relayed it to the men working on deck. At night, the source of the music could often be traced by the vessel's arc lights, but sometimes the music came floating out of the darkness, seemingly from nowhere. Operators kept watch until well after midnight, when wireless traffic and Skipper to Skipper yarns petered out and they had the air to themselves to swap yarns, play music, or recite their own poetry. I remember 'Norman' being particularly entertaining with his poetry and caustic observations.

Over this whole trawling period it was remarkable how Geoff and I coincided in landing times, sailing in company and seeing each other regularly; it could hardly have worked out better if we had arranged it ourselves. He was sailing with Northern Trawlers, also out of Grimsby and even when in mid June the *Tompion* ran onto a sandbank in the Humber just as we were coming in to land, and there was an extended time ashore whilst her hull was examined, Geoff's ship came in on the next tide and went on the slip for repairs.

13: LITNA STORMS AND CODE BOOKS

Graeme Bell's Australian Jazz Band was touring the UK and Geoff, Dan and I went to see them when they came to Withernsea, ten of us cramming into the back of a small van for a hilariously uncomfortable trip. Geoff and I played tennis at West Park every morning for the fortnight that our ships were being repaired, then sailed to Iceland within 24 hours of each other.

Apart from one overnight stay in Reykjavik, where there had been time for a look around, the only places that I set foot ashore in Iceland were the tiny fishing havens in the NW fjords. These were settlements of wooden huts huddled against the rock face, with the occasional small store, a medical surgery, boat sheds and fuel tanks. Equivalent ports in Norway, like Harstad and Tromso, were larger and had shops and many more facilities. Between the north of Scotland and the Vestmannaeyjar Islands there is a hole in the ocean bed, if you can find it, wherein large shrimps abound, and netting some of these provides a culinary treat. The skipper knew the right place and we brought up basketfuls of shrimps, cooking and eating them straight away, putting a smile on everyone's face. The Vestmannaeyjar Islands afforded us a haven from the elements more than once, but seeking its shelter could be a hazardous operation. There was no anchorage where you could drop the hook and swing round it, the water being too deep. An ominous dark rock face rose sheer out of the water to the north and you tucked up under its lee, skating the fine line between being driven against the rock face or drifting too far away from it and having to battle the rough seas forcing their way into the refuge from the open ocean.

It was July in the arctic and the sun was busy never setting. In the outside world England beat South Africa by 9 wickets with Len Hutton making 98 not out, and Randy Turpin took the World Middleweight title from Sugar Ray Robinson. Contentment reigned aboard the *Tompion* as we ran off in good weather and shot the gear for the first haul of a new trip. Our euphoria was short lived. We pulled aboard a decent haul of five bags but unfortunately it was of the wrong colour, red. There is nothing wrong with red fish, it tastes fine, but the Great British Public didn't like the colour and wouldn't buy it, so we let the sea reclaim its own, moving on to find some white fish acceptable to the GBP. As the net sweeps along, hopefully it fills up with fish; when the engine is stopped and towing ceases, the ship loses way and the trawl floats to the surface where it streams out long and narrow. The net is hauled aboard and a rope is passed around it at intervals to divide it into sections. These sections are called bags and, as one bag holds about 60 baskets, our five bags of reds would have been a very acceptable 300 baskets, had they been but pearly white.

The gulls were forever squabbling over the remains of fish or offal and would perch next to the men in the pounds, often snatching at the entrails whilst the fish were still being gutted. They stalked about the ship and settled on any available vantage point. Those that could find no spot for themselves ousted those who had, and there was a constant racket going on as they circled around the ship. After being gutted, the fish were washed with hoses to clean them, then passed down the hatch to the fish room for storage. About this time, 1951, fish-washing machines were being fitted aboard vessels and these performed the task more quickly and efficiently.

Underwater cameras were also thought to be imminent. Luddites grudgingly approved of these innovations whilst muttering that things would never be the same again. Let's hope not, if some of the stories I'd heard about the old days were true, when keel-hauling was talked about and working conditions were made more severe than need be by some Skippers. Anything that made working conditions better for the men on deck surely had to be good news.

Daylight was shortening now and we were going through the

Norwegian fjords almost every trip, which was idyllic. Wireless watch was kept on R/T (voice), and the loud-speaker was switched through to the bridge so that anyone could listen, relieving me from having to stay in the wireless room. The scenery in the northern fjords in winter is magnificent, snow and ice covering the towering sides of the mountains down to the water's edge. One night we were proceeding through the twists and turns of the fjords when we made out a strange light some way ahead, glimpsed and then eclipsed by headlands. As it came nearer we heard snatches of music but were no wiser as to what it was, except that the lights now seemed to be floating in mid-air. We were only a few ships' lengths away before we realised that it was a Christmas tree adorned with fairy lights, perched on top of the mast of a pilot vessel which was proceeding at a leisurely pace through the fjord. We exchanged Christmas greetings as the two ships passed close to each other and the last we heard of her was the sound of carols floating back across the water in the darkness.

The weather on that particular trip, once we had put our nose outside the shelter of the land, was dreadful, and we spent more time laid or dodging than we did fishing. The glass was staying down and no one was happy, everyone saying they were going to sign off after this trip and look for a shore job. The *Boston Seafire* was dodging near to us when her bridge was stove in by a massive wave; a graphic picture of her damaged bridge appeared in the Hull Daily Mail, taken when she came into port. Although caught in the same storm, we escaped without serious damage. Ice was forming on our superstructure and rigging as we were preparing to shoot the trawl off the Russian coast, and it was a continuous job to chip at it to keep it under control. It was uphill all the way on that trip and we pulled very little fish aboard.

Trawlers and deep sea rescue tugs are the most perfectly designed of any working ships, combining perfect lines with total practicality of purpose. But maybe I'm biased. Now that the war had ended and all such restrictions were lifted I took a camera to sea, once helping a deckhand, John Gittens, by shooting footage with his 8mm camera from the bridge; some of the bad-weather footage appearing in his documentary, 'Out with the Tide'.

The winter wore on and we continued our Norwegian trips. On one occasion when we were homeward bound through the fjords between Honningsvag and Lodingen, the snow came down so thick and heavy that it settled on the water around the ship. When the gentle turbulence created by our propeller had settled, the snow surface re-formed astern, giving us the strange sensation of moving yet standing still at the same time. Seaward of the landmass that was presently sheltering us, the weather forecaster was telling us that there was a litna storm blowing, which meant about force 10 or 11. It was a Tuesday, and we had hoped to catch the tide for Saturday morning's market, but the weather was so foul when we poked our head out of the fjords that all hope of that rapidly disappeared. This was not good news for the owners or for us because the next market would be Monday, which meant that the fish would remain on board over the weekend.

The atrocious weather made it impossible to carry out the odd jobs that I was saddled with on the way home, such as the bond bills. Every seaman was allocated an allowance of duty free spirits and cigarettes each trip and it was my job to distribute these, making a note of who got what, handing this note over to the office so that the necessary amount could be deducted from each individual's settling. Neither could the wireless room receive its usual clean-up; it was always in a mess at the end of a trip because during the time on the fishing grounds everyone's efforts were focused on the sole reason for our existence, catching fish, and such details as keeping the wireless room tidy went by the board. Now the squaring up wasn't getting done either because it was impossible to stay upright long enough to do it. We were being struck by huge waves in an unrelenting assault of boiling angry water. Being thrown about continuously in a confined space for days on end is taken for granted as part of the scenery in small ships, but sometimes it goes over the top. We eased down to three knots, there was no point in rushing about when it became obvious we weren't going to make the market, so we tried to make life a little easier for ourselves. The Skipper described this particular storm on page 79 of his book, 'Wooden Ships and Iron Men', by Arthur Whittleton, and when the Mate said that he had 'never seen solid water like that' in his life, the Skipper replied 'Yes, you only see one like that once in a lifetime'. The book also describes the black frost that we encountered off Varanger Fjord, between Norway and Russia, when we eventually had to turn back because of the danger of capsizing due to the weight of ice forming.

We docked on the Saturday afternoon, Geoff's ship followed us in the next morning, having been through the same dreadful weather conditions as ourselves. The Hull Jazz Club had moved again, this time to 121 Beverley Road, and Geoff joined me there on the Sunday evening, sleeping the sleep of the exhausted when we reached home. Skipper Whittleton went on a RNR course and a relief skipper took over the *Tompion* for a couple of trips. But first she had to go on the slip, which extended our time in port. It was during this period that Charlie Sleeth, the relief Skipper, took me home for a beer and played some records of Erna Sack, a German soprano who had been a favourite of Hitler. I had not previously heard of her, but afterwards bought some 78s and became a fan of hers, which may be due in part to the unusual way that I discovered her music. Introduced to opera by a tough Grimsby trawler Skipper - not every day of the week.

In the desolate waters towards the top of the world you experienced some strange radio reception. Although Russian, Norwegian, Swedish and Icelandic stations predominated, you also heard Canadian, American and Japanese stations coming in strongly for a time before fading away, like ghosts drifting across the ice. One time we were fishing in company with the *Vizalma,* well off the Russian coast, when she brought up a mine in her trawl. She managed to keep it away from her side and towed it out to deeper water before dumping it; there was a thunderous explosion as the mine struck the seabed and we felt the shock waves through our hull. The world's oceans were still full of mines, many floating loose, waiting to be scooped up in trawls.

The American Forces had opened a radio station in Iceland at their radar base at Keflavik Airway, so that was a step in the right direction. A step in the wrong direction was the extension of the fishing exclusion zone by Norway and Iceland from 3 miles to 4 miles. This cut out many inshore grounds like Breidi, Utscalar, the Horns, Lion and Thollack, which had been fished for generations. Some of these fishing grounds were named after locations, others for the appearance of the land. When you got two pillars of rock lined up to look like a pair of horns and the fathometer showed 30 fathoms then hey presto, you were in the right place to catch fish. Or the wrong place if the fish had remembered an urgent appointment elsewhere.

Each Skipper had his own store of knowledge, which he hugged close to his chest. It was often garnered over years of experience, so he didn't spread it about and let all the young upstarts benefit from his hard-won knowledge. However, over the years he would have formed fishing friendships with other skippers, passing on tips if he found a shoal of fish large enough for two ships to benefit. The only problem was how to let your mate know the location of the fish without letting every trawler within a hundred mile radius know as well.

Thinking along these lines, I devised a Code which was printed at George's works. It consisted of an eight-page booklet with a thin cardboard cover. The pages listed all the words and phrases commonly used on the air such as compass points, geographical locations, numbers, letters, distance, fathoms and weather conditions and also had a number of blank spaces for personal entries; in short everything but the kitchen sink. Loose inside the cover were gummed strips numbered from 1-1,000. All you had to do was cut the strip of numbers at any point and then stick the strip alongside the tabular list of the words and phrases. Starting at a random point, you continued sticking the numbered strips in sequence in the book until you got back to where you started. Simple. Make an identical numbered copy, give it to your friend, and you had a private code to which only you and he held the key. On air you passed him a few numbers, and he knew from his copy that you were fishing four miles west of Andanes, the weather was good and you were getting loads of cod so why not steam over and fill your boots? It would not have kept Bletchley Park up all night, but was more than adequate for trawling purposes. We sold six. I was a genius and unrecognised in my own time; concluding that old habits die hard and that trawler skippers were no different from anyone else. So the radio waves continued to carry thinly veiled hints from one ship to another as to where the fish was thick and plentiful, and these hints, decipherable by well-experienced listening ears, continued to result in 'fish shops' being set up all over the Arctic. I sulked.

14: PANLIBHONCO

The familiar urge to seek new horizons arrived once more. Someone up there must have sympathised with me because, at home between trips, I was stricken with German measles. First of all there was the responsibility to the ship to be dealt with. Urgent phone calls and telegrams to Grimsby sorted that out and the *Thomas Tompion* sailed only an hour late, with an Operator sent over from Hull. So much for the ship, now what about me.

I was tired, 24 trips in 20 months was enough, and now there was a couple of weeks to think things over whilst the doctor issued me with regular sick notes. When the ship returned to port I went over to Grimsby to collect my gear that was still on board, said goodbye to any shipmates to be found on board or in the nearest pub, and officially signed off the *Thomas Tompion* on the 23rd of April 1952. The International Ballet Company was at the New Theatre so I went almost every night for the next week, also there was tennis with George, visits to the cinema and playing cricket for Norman Milner's XI in the Fish Dock League. That year our first match was against Hull City Supporters Club and my contribution of 25 not out, was my only decent score all season. I enjoyed my time with the lads of Milners that summer; our home pitch was on Costello playing fields and included the use of a rickety wooden pavilion. In the hope of fulfilling the promise of the first match I had purchased a pair of white flannels, but this self-promotion was frowned upon by God who brought me to heel by sending me a dose of chickenpox. So once again I was cut down in my prime and confined to barracks; building another model ship, the Santa Maria, helped to pass the time.

Cycling around the countryside was freedom personified in that perfect summer, the feeling of space appealing strongly after the confines of small ships. Tennis progressed to doubles, with George and Joyce playing Audrey and me. Neither of the girls could play and the balls flew in all directions, frequently over the park fence onto Anlaby Road, and more time was spent laughing than playing. Audrey and I went for cycle rides, stopping off at favourite country inns in the evening sunshine. A cricket fixture was played at Brandesburton Hall, where a superb tea was laid on for us and we won by one run with the last man in. Audrey became our unofficial team mascot as she always came to support us, including when we hired a bus to take the team and a few supporters to play an away match at Scunthorpe. We lost, but made up for it by having a lively sing-song in a pub at Thorne on the way home. The return fixture against the Hull City Supporters Club came along and I made 14, this seemed to be the only club I was any good against, except for 23 against Coal Exporters.

Dad and a friend from the days when they both worked at Sissons, a paint firm in Bankside, played billiards regularly each Wednesday night, and Dan joined me in playing them occasionally. There were a few billiard halls dotted around the city and the one they currently favoured was at the rear of the Rialto/National cinema next to Stepney Station. Their pre-war venue, Sloans in Jameson Street, had been bombed during the war. I visited both grandmas at least once a week; both of them now living alone. Most Saturday afternoons dad and I watched

Yorkshire League cricket with Hull CC at The Circle. When Yorkshire came for their regular three day county match we were down there early with friends, eager to secure a seat on the wooden benches which ran round the boundary fence, staying all day from eleven until the close of play at six o'clock. Hutton, Sutcliffe, Watson, Lowson, Lester, Yardley, Close and Wardle were all in the same team and those were the days when, if Yorkshire was not winning the Championship on a regular basis, there were mutterings in the pubs all over the county. The favourite radio show in our house at this time was Bedtime with Braden, a successor to Breakfast with Braden, a sharp comedy show with Canadian Bernard Braden and his wife June Kelly. Other shows regularly listened to were the incomparable Goon Show and Round the Horn.

Audrey and I continued our cycle rides to the coast at Hilston where we lay on the beach all day and dallied in secluded country lanes on the way home. One day as we lay in a field off Priory Road we saw smoke rising from an old gatepost nearby. It was broad daylight, we both watched it over a lengthy period and it was very intriguing. Just this plume of smoke coming out of the middle of a gatepost. Years later I read an explanation of this phenomenon, which seemed eminently and scientifically plausible, but it didn't explain the eerie sensation it engendered at the time. August broke fine and hot; Geoff broke off his engagement to Pat and I broke off with Audrey. With things breaking up in all directions we discussed our next move over a liquid lunch. I finished my ship model, played another couple of games of cricket, went into the ROU office in Percy Street and found myself a ship. If I had known what lay ahead of me I would not have bothered. Meantime, it was all rushing around getting my gear together for the forthcoming voyage and bidding everyone farewell.

The ROU looked after the normal union activities between employees and employers, Marconi and Siemens being the two major employers of radio officers, and also acted as intermediary when officers went freelance on foreign vessels. There were now increasing numbers of foreign-flag ships around, mostly Greek owned, sailing under the so-called flags of convenience: Panama, Liberia, Honduras and Costa Rica ('PANLIBHONCO' vessels). By registering their vessels under these flags, the owners evaded the heavy taxation levied on British merchant ships and also crewed their vessels at cheaper rates. It was to avoid any deterioration in wages or conditions that the ROU acted as go-between, offering contract facilities between the R/O, Union and the shipping company. The wages on foreign flag ships were much higher than those offered by Marconi but they lacked long-term social and pension benefits, so I continued to pay my own half of contributions into the Merchant Navy Officers Pension Fund, also paying stamps to safeguard Social Benefits.

In addition to the flags of convenience vessels there were the national-flag ships which also required Operators, and it was under the Norwegian flag that I first sailed as a freelance. The Union representative had said to me, when we were settling the contract, to look out for anything unusual on board, because the previous Operator had disappeared in mid-ocean, 'in mysterious circumstances'. I didn't take much notice of this conversation at the time, being preoccupied with the last minute haste of getting on board before sailing, but was to wish I had given it a little more thought.

15: VIKINGS, HURRICANES AND COLD STEEL

The ship that I joined was the *Fido*, pronounced 'Fedo', the name being steeped in Nordic mythology, so they told me. She was registered in Kristiansund, Norway, was about the same size and age as the *Kalev* and was laid alongside at Grimsby, where I signed on at the end of August 1952 shortly before she moved round to the London river. We passed the liners *Stratheden*, *Himalaya* and *Strathnaver* laying in Tilbury docks, as we made our way to the working part of the Thames, tying up to Enderby's Wharf just above the Blackwall Tunnel. There we commenced loading 40 miles of submarine telephone cable, due to be laid across the entrance to the St. Lawrence River in Canada. Loading it was a specialised job; the 40 miles of cable, in its many layers, was being manufactured in one continuous length in the factory and loaded straight into our hold. The operation involved lots of people in the factory all working continuously to a tight schedule for a number of hours. The finished cable appeared out of a small aperture in the wall of the factory, was fed gently over rollers across the quay and into our hold where it was coiled, gradually tapering to the top.

The cargo, as these things go, was a light one of seventy tons. However, the weight was not evenly distributed throughout the ship as, for example, coal would have been. Instead, the entire cargo was contained in the one hold, forward of the bridge, with ballast aft to counter it, and bore similar loading characteristics to the iron-ore cargo that we had carried on the *Kalev*. The whole business did not inspire confidence, and no one was looking forward to crossing the North Atlantic at this time of year in what was, in effect, an unbalanced light ship. While all this was going on I was finding my way to the Agent's in Houndsditch, then to the Norwegian Consul to sign on the Ships Articles, on the way being given a medical and jabbed against smallpox for good measure. After a meal in the West End, we sailed at six that evening.

Going down the Channel the weather was good, and everything seemed fine until we were halfway across the Atlantic when the wind dropped away and wisps of fog appeared. Radio reports told of a hurricane centred between Bermuda and Cape Hatteras and a tanker being driven ashore near Charleston. The centre of the storm was moving northwards. Our weather was mostly clear and sunny with a calm sea and we were making seven knots, eight when the blood went to her head. Next morning however, I felt distinctly uneasy, the weather reports showed that the hurricane was now moving steadily northeast, directly towards us. At seven knots we couldn't get out of its way, and the wind kept on increasing. We ploughed on doggedly through gale force winds and then spent many hours driving through the circular wall of the storm proper. Finally, entering the eye of the hurricane, the cacophony and the mountainous seas that had surrounded us for the last couple of days, stopped dead, just as if someone had pulled the plug from a loudspeaker. The hurricane force winds, heavy seas and swells dropped away, leaving the sea calm and blue with flecks of white foam around the edges. It was like opening a door, on one side of which everything was chaos, whilst on the other side all was peaceful and calm. Driftwood, some dead birds and other flotsam floated on the surface. Everything around us was dull and grey, yet above us the sky was blue with shafts of sunlight, a few seabirds circled high above, outlined against the bright sky. It was eerily quiet. The ship had stopped behaving like a mad thing and we were all looking at each other as if to say, 'What the hell was that all about?'

The Captain knew exactly what it was all about, for the past 48 hours he had not slept, charting our course in conjunction with any weather reports that I could give him, continuously turning her head into the ever increasing spiral of wind and the boiling seas. Now becalmed in the eye of the hurricane, we had the brief time that it took the storm centre to sweep forward before the wall of wind and water would hit us and we had to go through it all again. The deck lashings that had come adrift were mended, the cook made sandwiches and we had the hot drinks that we'd missed for the last couple of days. I called up Halifax Radio and gave them the barometric pressure and our estimated position as 125 miles NE of Cape Race. The situation was now reversed, previously they had told us about the storm, now we were telling them about it. At first hand. Our information would help pinpoint the storm centre for the shore stations, other vessels and the meteorological services who were tracking it. And then we waited.

The weather reports from the American and Canadian coast stations that I was monitoring indicated that the storm had a radius of 500 miles from its centre, with the winds around the centre estimated at a minimum of 120 knots and that the whole weather system was travelling NW at 35 knots. The wind, tearing round in its circular pattern, made me think of the sheer sides of the Wall of Death at Hull Fair and as 'the wall' approached us the howling and screeching commenced afresh, though there was nothing to be seen except greyness all around. Then the wall of wind and water hit us and we hung on. Believe me we hung on. The ship was squared up so that she was nose to wind; any other direction and we should have been rolled over. She was a gallant old girl and just dug her bows into the shrieking mass of wind and water and hung in there, ourselves with her. Mountainous seas were breaking on deck from all quarters, often from above us, and it needed two seamen at the wheel to hold course. At first we headed straight into the wall, then gradually altered course to counter the spinning wall of water, turning so that we were always head to wind.

With an estimated 500 mile radius, and we virtually its hostage, the storm held us in its grip for the best part of another day before it fell away sufficiently for us to attempt steering our way out of trouble. There must have been some periods when everyone thought that we weren't going to make it, but nobody said as much. I recall elation and fear and then feeling drained when it was all over. The ship and the Captain came out of it with flying colours. Pointing in the wrong direction and miles off course we may have been, but we had come through it. We sorted ourselves out and prepared to resume the voyage.

A couple of nights later, asleep in my bunk, the trusty sixth sense wakened me. There was a young seaman in the cabin wearing a red woollen hat with a bobble on the top. I looked at him, neither of us spoke, he left, and I went to sleep again. In the morning it was difficult to convince myself that it wasn't a dream, and I would probably have thought no more about it, except for what happened the following night. My cabin was long and narrow, with a porthole at one end and a door at the other that opened onto an alleyway opposite the galley; the door was always left on the hook at night to let air through. Around daybreak the infallible sixth sense wakened me once again. I had been lying face to bulkhead and sensed that there was someone in the cabin. Without making any sudden movement I turned over, to find the galley boy standing about an arms length away from my bunk clutching a large butcher's knife in his hand, frozen in the act of moving quietly towards me. I said, 'Morning, is it time to get up?' as casually as I could, and slowly made to get my legs over the side of the bunk ready to stand up. He reacted automatically, moving back to give me room. As I continued moving slowly, he turned and left the cabin, not having spoken a single word.

There were three British firemen aboard, the rest of the crew being Norwegian. Unobtrusively I sought out one of the firemen to see whether he could help me make sense of it all. He couldn't, but told me that one night when he had been working alone in the bunkers he had felt a tap on his shoulder. He was in an open area with nowhere for anyone to hide, yet when he looked round there was no one to be seen. He also said that on the following watch two of the firemen had been together in the bunker when they heard one of the wheelbarrows being wheeled along, but saw nothing moving nor any other person down there. Together they searched the bunkers but found nothing. Talking to both the firemen later, they confirmed the story and also said that about eighteen months previously, before they joined the ship, an Arab trimmer was said to have knifed himself before jumping overboard.

The snippet of conversation in the Union office came floating back to me. Unexplained disappearance of previous Operator at sea, butcher's knives before breakfast, and now ghostly goings on in the bunkers. People knifing themselves and then throwing themselves overboard; surely you don't knife yourself before you jump, more likely someone knifes you and then you get pushed? Was the ship possessed by demons? Had the hurricane disorientated somebody who was susceptible to high winds and electrical storms? These thoughts and many others occupied me, stuck in mid-ocean and surrounded by nutters. Heigh-ho. I decided to watch my back, kept my cabin door locked and, for good measure, slept with a long bladed screwdriver under my pillow.

Surely this burst of extra curricular high jinks would die down, peter out, whatever? But it was not to be; a couple of nights later I heard the cook and the bosun talking in the coal bunkers in the middle of the night. My cabin was directly above the bunkers and there was no question that there were voices and that I recognised those voices. What was the cook doing in the coal bunker in the middle of the night, or the bosun for that matter? Both of them were well out of their respective territories, and outside any possible watch periods. 'Curiouser and curiouser', as Alice would have said. And what about these characters from Nordic mythology, did their spirits demand human sacrifices even if they inhabited a steel framework? I began to look at the Vikings in a different light, made a mental note that the whole ship was probably mad and locked my door every night from then on.

Next day we anchored off Halifax, Nova Scotia. It was my 27th birthday, I drew $25, grabbed a lift ashore in the Agent's launch and went for a walk, encountering my first parking meter and also Lana Turner, but not, unfortunately, in the flesh. Hank Williams' music followed me down the sidewalk as I passed the open doors of the rows of music shops and I began to feel reassured that everything was normal after all, and that I wasn't living in some nightmarish dreamworld. The ship moved from Western Union's wharf, where we had delivered the submarine cable, to take on bunkers plus the first consignment of our timber cargo for the return trip to England. The weather was good when we left Halifax, bound for Country Harbour some 80 miles to the north, which turned out to be more a logging camp than a location, and we anchored about five miles upstream in a narrow inlet, surrounded by floating logs. The logs were cut in the forest, rolled down the hillsides into the water, rounded up by small motor boats, towed to the side of the ship, winched aboard and loaded into the hold; a slow process. The township of Country Harbour was a few miles inland and some of the crew went to the big weekly event, a Square Dance, on Saturday night.

The weather was perfect so I took a rowing boat into the middle of the inlet, laid down in the afternoon sunshine and let the boat drift, enjoying the peace and solitude, the smell of pine-wood, the scenery and the apparent freedom from evil spirits and hurricanes. We completed our part-loading and moved to Sydney on Cape Breton Island to take on logs and bunkers, but not before a Polish trimmer had skinned out. The police caught him and brought him back on board, but you felt that he was only awaiting another opportunity to jump ship. Sydney impressed me on a walk-about, seeming to be a very pleasant town. We left before dawn for Ridham Docks in the UK and were not far out to sea when it was discovered that one of the English trimmers had jumped ship just before we sailed. Never a dull moment.

We had logs in the holds and more stacked high on deck fore and aft, so we set off hoping there would be no heavy seas or torrential rain, otherwise we should end up doing the last part of the trip walking on the bulkheads. We were abeam of Cape Race when Halifax Radio put out a hurricane warning. The Captain decided to take shelter in St. Johns, Newfoundland and await events. Once bitten, twice shy, you don't mess with hurricanes. When we arrived in St. Johns, the harbour was full of Portuguese fishing schooners and looked just like a painting from a previous century. The small stores along the main street were all playing country music. We were there for three days, during which time another of the English firemen jumped ship before we sailed. There was something about this ship that made people want to get off it and I knew just how they felt.

The voyage home was uneventful. The *Queen Elizabeth* passed quite close to us, heading for New York, and looked every inch a Queen. The trip should have taken ten days but took half as long again due to rough weather. We anchored off Sheerness a few hundred yards from an American ship wrecked on a sandbank, which, the pilot casually informed us, had been there since the wartime and contained 8,000 tons of ammunition and bombs. Half its cargo had been removed safely but they couldn't get the remainder out without the risk of the whole ship exploding and taking much of the Thames estuary with it, so they left her there, high and dry on the sandbank. We lay at anchor all night trying not to be too concerned about our close proximity to thousands of tons of unstable explosives, and were relieved when a tug arrived the next morning to tow us to Ridham Dock. The next day was a Saturday so I watched Spurs at White Hart Lane and then immersed myself in the normality of London for a few days before we moved up the coast to Grimsby, where I paid off.

You bet your sweet life I did.

16: THE LEANING TOWER AND A WATER JET

During a couple of weeks at home I went to Leeds to see a performance by the Sadler's Wells Ballet in the afternoon, and to the City Varieties Theatre in the evening for 'That Paris Feeling', an otherwise unremarkable touring revue except for Valerie Walsh, who took various parts in the sketches and also had her own speciality spot called Singing and Teasing. Going backstage after the show led, a couple of days later, to lunch with Valerie in the Turks Head, a visit to a cinema and coffee at Jaconelli's before returning to the theatre, where I watched the first performance from the front of the house and spent the second house backstage. It was good to be amongst theatre people again, amid the hustle and bustle and the smell of greasepaint. I met the cast and became friendly with Sonny Farrer, who sang old-tyme music hall songs; he and others were interested to know about my voyages and sea-going life, seeming to find my world as fascinating as I found theirs. Valerie and I met again a few weeks later when the show was in Doncaster; had lunch at the Elephant Hotel, saw an afternoon film and returned to the Grand Theatre in time for the early evening performance. Going home on the last train we ran into fog, and by the time the train reached Hull it was so dense that the trolley buses had been taken off the road, no taxis ventured forth, and a two mile walk home awaited me.

Humphrey Lyttelton and his band came to the City Hall and the following night I saw the inimitable Frank Randle at the Palace. After a month waiting for a ship one eventually turned up and I crossed to Immingham to sign on the *Leonardia,* a Swedish vessel due to sail for Livorno in Italy with a cargo of coal. My salary was 700 Swedish krona per month. The crew included four British, a couple of Austrians, two Maltese, a North African, an Estonian, a Dutchman and a Frenchman, the remainder being Swedish.

We set off down the coast in bad weather. In common with many vessels of the time, we were not yet fitted with radar and, to compound matters, an aircraft had flown into the aerials of GNF, the coast station at North Foreland. As a consequence we had no weather forecasts or vital navigational information to help us through the crowded straits of Dover, and with the seas breaking green over our bows and a gale raging I wondered why I hadn't stayed at home. However, one consolation was the food; excellent at sea and a superb smorgasbord when in port. With bad weather most of the way the voyage from Immingham to Italy took a fortnight, battling our way down the Channel, across the Bay of Biscay, past Gibraltar and across to Corsica before limping into Livorno. I went ashore to reconnoitre and the following day a few of us caught the bus to Pisa, where we had a meal at a café preparatory to climbing up the Leaning Tower, a strange sensation. There were no outer rails or ropes to hold on to, so you kept close to the centre column where there was a rope, in places. When the continuous winding slope seemed to be taking you upward there was a sensation of falling forward, even though your legs told you that you were walking uphill. It was even more unsettling coming down.

Diary note from December 1952: 'The Chief Engineer, (6'2", 15 stone), has twice threatened to kill the Mate, who was sacked from his position as a senior pilot in Sweden for drinking, (still drinking). The Mate, (Swedish), regularly threatens to kill the 2nd Mate, (Estonian), and the 3rd Mate, (British), argues violently with both of them'. The 3rd Mate had clambered aboard at the last minute as we were going through the lockpit at Immingham and also seemed to have a drink problem. Previous experience of Scandinavians and drink had led me to the conclusion that the two didn't always mix well, so none of this surprised me. A few days into the trip the Chief Engineer refused to sit down for meals if the Mate was present; never a day passed without an argument going on somewhere and the atmosphere on board could best be described as fraught. We left Livorno, empty ship, for Djijelli in North Africa to load iron ore for Antwerp. The town had expanded a little since my last visit, but there was still nothing to do ashore. The 3rd Mate brought a bottle of Vermouth on board, sleep was eluding us both so we shared it and played cards in his cabin until six in the morning, then went for a walk round the dusty streets, watching the town waking up to another sunny Mediterranean day.

Everyone was pleased to leave Djijelli even though it blew a gale all the way to Gibraltar, where we put in for water, stores and bunkers and for the crew to top-up with Anisette. This seemed to be the usual procedure after arriving in port, spirits were either smuggled on board or hauled up from bumboats. Steering what may have been an unsteady course, we crossed the Bay of Biscay on Christmas Day in a SW gale, everybody celebrating in fine style and the ship, for all I knew, looking after itself. It may not have been quite like that, because I'm sure the Captain could have been relied upon, but there were raisable doubts about some of the others.

In Scandinavia many people celebrated Christmas Eve as a holiday, the children being given their presents at seven in the evening; on board ship there were many varieties of cold meats, a large ham, dried fish, cold rice pudding with cinnamon and bottles of beer and spirits in the saloon. When we arrived in Antwerp I went ashore to see the doctor about my stomach, which had been giving me trouble for some little time. The resultant prescription had to be made up, so I walked around Antwerp for a couple of hours until it was ready. We finished discharging and pushed off for Bremen, arriving there during the morning of New Year's Day 1953.

Two uneventful days were spent in Bremen loading coal for Gavle in Sweden; on leaving, we passed the *United States* laid alongside at Bremerhaven, then traversed the Kiel Canal and entered the southern Baltic. But this was not the mild sunny Baltic I was accustomed to, it was January and ice was floating all around us. We reduced speed, sometimes to dead slow. The ice sounded like thunder as it scraped along the ship's sides and we travelled for about fifty miles in this fashion, before picking up the pilot at midnight off Gavle. Another visit to the doctor's resulted in more tablets plus the generous offer of a stomach pump, (declined). Gavle was frozen in and the Baltic to the north was ice bound. A week alongside gave plenty of time for walks, also the consumption of far too many Swedish pastries and cups of coffee. Eventually, cargo discharged, the voyage was officially completed and I signed off Articles at the Shipping Office in Gavle, bidding farewell to the *Leonardia* with few regrets. With time on my hands before needing to be at the railway station, I went to see an ice hockey game before catching the night sleeper to Gothenburg, arriving there early next morning.

My parents had friends in Gothenburg, made on a trip they had taken on the *Volo,* one of Ellerman Wilson's ships, a year or so before. After locating their apartment block and having breakfast with them, they showed me around the city, ending up at a large Amusement Park, and it was midnight before I reached my bed in the Royal Hotel. The next couple of days were spent exploring Gothenburg whilst waiting for the *Saga* to arrive. A trim little vessel, the *Saga* could accommodate 375 passengers but only about a hundred were taking passage on this voyage. A rude awakening awaited me when taking a shower in the cubicle in my cabin. Faced with an assortment of piping, flexible nozzles and taps, I selected a lever at random and received an enthusiastic jet of icy water in my groin. It's not the sort of thing you forget in a hurry. Showers with handsets were still something of a novelty in 1953 and I was still feeling lively when we boarded the boat train at Tilbury for St. Pancras.

There was some radio business to sort out with the ROU in East Ham, after which I had tea at Valerie's house, and in the evening we went to the Duke of York Theatre to see Kay Hammond in 'Happy Marriage', afterwards going back to her house. Her dad had been on the books of Arsenal in the 1930s so a lot of family conversation was about football, and next day we watched Spurs play Sheffield Wednesday before having tea at a small restaurant in Drury Lane and going to the Phoenix Theatre to see Alfred Lunt and Lynne Fontaine; a show which didn't set Val alight as she preferred the music hall. Back home, her mother cooked everyone a meal at two in the morning and then helped her make a dress for an audition at the Hollywood club in Marble Arch, Valerie phoning me when I got home a couple of days later to say that she had got the cabaret job and had also landed a TV audition. All this was really good news because she was set on a show business career and looked to be off to a flying start.

17: AMERICA CALLS

After three weeks at home, enjoying nights out with Dan and George, a priority telegram came from the ROU office in Newcastle offering me a Liberian ship, berthed in Newcastle and ready to load coal for Italy. I accepted with fingers crossed, later signing the contract in the ROU office at £58 per month. It was snowing hard that evening when Dan, George and I went to the Three Tuns for a farewell drink. The next morning it was still snowing heavily on arrival in Newcastle, but by then the good ship *Milly* had moved to West Hartlepool and had commenced loading, so the day was spent in Newcastle in preference to going on board and getting covered in coal dust. We left the following day for Savona, the voyage being made at our full speed of 8 knots flat out, and by the time we reached the Mediterranean everyone was wearing sunglasses and sunbathing on deck. Better than snow in Hartlepool by some distance.

We stayed a few days in Savona before leaving in ballast for Sousse in Tunisia to load part cargo of esparto grass. The atmosphere seemed very relaxed in Sousse, but after investigating what the town had to offer and finding little of interest, I tried my hand at cargo tallying. The esparto grass came aboard in bundles of five bales at a time, was swung out over the hold and lowered into the depths, accompanied by gestures, shouts and a few oaths from the tally-man stationed on deck. Most of the Arabs working the cargo appeared to be stoned on hashish. They informed me that the word for up was 'abra' and left me to my own devices. With a lot of arm waving and some vocal encouragement to the workers below, about 500 bales were tallied during the afternoon before we sailed to Sfax in Tunisia to complete loading. In Sfax I did more tallying, restricting my going ashore to the evening when it was much cooler. Surprisingly the cafés closed about eight in the evening, leaving only a couple of cinemas open showing French and Italian films. The weather was freshening when we left Sfax for Scotland and after going through a few days of driving rain we developed quite a list. Off Gibraltar, three aircraft carriers with their destroyer escorts passed us close to, the sun broke through the clouds and an owl tried unsuccessfully to nest in the grass. We reached Granton, the trip had been about six weeks and I paid off with £79, travelling part of the way home on the LNER's regular main line service, the North Briton, from Waverley to Kings Cross.

A few days later I took a train to Leicester where Valerie's show was appearing at the Palace Theatre, booking myself in at The George. We had lunch at the Hare and Pheasant and after the evening show I went backstage, seeing old faces and yarning about the trip and their adventures on the road. Next morning we walked through Abbey Park and talked over lunch at the White Hart before she left for the theatre and I caught the train home.

Geoff, still on trawlers, was home between trips so we accompanied George to Powolneys, the Imperial, and the Empress, enjoying each other's company, the real ales and the atmosphere of the pubs of the day. Visits and phone calls were made to the ROU; no ships seemed to be in the offing so I cycled all over town, visiting friends, spending time with both grandmas, playing snooker with Dan and going to the cinema most afternoons, but it wasn't long before I felt restless.

'Paree for Me' had meantime returned from touring and was again playing at the City Varieties in Leeds. Geoff was still at home, so we talked his dad into loaning us a car for the day and set off for Leeds, watching the second house from the stalls and going backstage afterwards. The three of us came back to Hull in the car, Geoff acting as chauffeur, and after stopping in York for some chips, arrived home well after midnight. The five of us stayed up talking until Geoff had to go home to collect his sea gear because he was sailing on the morning tide. Val slept in my bed, I slept on the settee, and after lunch she caught the train to Leeds for the first show.

A local firm of ships chandlers rang home whilst I was having an afternoon at the pictures. Dad told them which film I had intended seeing, and a message was flashed on the screen at the Tower cinema asking me to phone them as soon as possible. It was unusual to be contacted through such a source so I rang the firm to find out what it was all about. A shipping firm appeared to be using them as a go-between, offering me a ship on a private contract. I wasn't willing to enter into such an agreement because, once a ship has sailed, the owners can do as they wish, and I had no desire to be paid off in roubles in Vladivostok and have to find my own way home.

I took the train to Sheffield to watch City beat Sheffield United 2-0 and become League Champions. The cricket season was beginning and the Australians were touring, so I took the train to London and put up at a hotel in King's Cross, the next morning going to Lords to watch MCC v Australia from the Tavern. A routine phone call to the ROU in Hull revealed that a ship seemed to be imminent, and sure enough, on returning home a bunch of telegrams awaited, all of them asking me to contact everybody in all directions immediately if not sooner. Marvellous, you stick around at home for ages with nothing happening and then as soon as you fancy a quiet day's cricket at Lords the whole world wants you. But this time it proved worth the wait. The *Fana* was a Norwegian ship en route for New York, where the wireless operator was leaving the vessel. A replacement was needed and the ROU were arranging to fly me out there. I started packing ten minutes ago.

A busy period followed; catching a train before eight the next morning for Newcastle I went to the ROU, the Agents, signed on at the Shipping Office and was taken to the Norge hotel in Osborne Road by the Agent. Next came the medical, then back to the ROU, on to Jeromes for a passport photo, back to the Agents, then to the Union office and finally to the Norwegian Consul. A taxi whisked me from there to the station to catch the early evening train to Edinburgh and on to Glasgow, arriving at midnight, booking in at the St. Enoch's Hotel and sleeping like a log.

Next morning I collected my passport from the Post Office, took a taxi to obtain a visa from the American Consul, then made my way to Quarrybrae Avenue to have lunch with Marjorie and her daughter, Ellie. The flight was scheduled for early the following morning so the three of us went to her parents for the evening, after tea gathering attentively round the latest TV set, a free-standing rectangular box about four foot high with a small black and white screen near the top. After spending the night at Moraine Avenue, Mr Clark drove me to St. Enoch's Station to board the coach for Prestwick Airport, some airhostesses being the only other passengers. After clearing Customs, our small group walked out to the plane waiting on the tarmac, climbed the steps, watched as they were wheeled away, and left almost immediately on the Pan American Clipper 'Fidelity' for New York. A couple of Martinis were brought along even before the seat-belt sign was switched on, and lunch was served just after take-off. This was the life and no mistake. It was the week of the Queen's Coronation and the plane had many empty seats, because all the passenger traffic was coming into the UK and the planes were returning to the States virtually empty. I had a row of seats and a couple of airhostesses all to myself and received the best of attention all the way over.

18: NEW YORK, NEW YORK

We landed at Boston for refuelling prior to the short hop to New York, landing at Idlewild as it was getting dark. The ship's agent met me in his car at the airport and we sped along the Belt Parkway to Brooklyn, reaching the Norwegian Seamen's House in Hansen Place before midnight. As we came into the city that night, the lights of New York's skyline were spectacular, contrasting markedly with the greyness left behind in England; anticipation and excitement began to take over, even though there was probably a ship full of Vikings at the end of it all. Throughout the early '50s England was very drab, with the scars of the bombing still evident, rebuilding took priority, most commodities were scarce and anything saleable that we manufactured, from shoelaces to merchant ships, went for export to pay our way in the post-war world. Food also remained scarce, 'austerity' was the watchword and it would be another few years before rationing ended. There wasn't much money around either and holidays tended to be taken at home, in digs at the seaside, a chalet at a Butlin's Holiday Camp, a tent or a caravan, in the days before mass tourism crept over the horizon.

It is a common-place observation that travel broadens the mind, but it can only do so if you have an open mind to start with and let your experiences in; if you go abroad and take your bigotry with you, then travel won't do you much good. As Peter Ustinov observed, 'On any journey there is always more to learn than there can possibly be to teach'. Exotic restaurants serving continental and eastern dishes were available at home only if you searched for them, though probably not many outside Soho. And you could hear foreign music, but only by searching the short waves. As for sex, oh dear, it was all a bit seedy and full of guilt in England. Coming back home seemed akin to revisiting the Dark Ages. Spirits only lifted when the last rope was cast off and the ship pointed down river to the sea, to fresh horizons and fresh experiences. Many things have changed since then, foreign foods are available only a few yards from home, the world's music is available at the touch of a button, and you are even allowed to have fun with sex. But hold on to it all tightly for it wasn't always so and there may be someone planning, even now, to stop it or tax it. Now read on.

The *Fana* wasn't anywhere near arriving in New York so I prepared to enjoy myself; there were four more days at the hostel, plus a further ten days whilst we were loading cargo to look forward to. In that fortnight I walked all over Manhattan, and some days, upon returning to my room at night, my socks were stuck to my feet with dried blood. Whichever port or town I found myself in I wanted to get the feel of the place, learn about the people, the food, the transport, the sights, everything; and you can't do better than walking the streets, riding the subway, the buses, the trams, reading the papers, eating the local food and listening to the music. New York was a challenge though; despite street, subway and elevated-rail maps, I.R.T. schedules, bus timetables and other aids to navigation, I sometimes found myself well away from where I thought I was heading. A good place to rest tired feet and eat hamburgers was the concourse in Grand Central where the sun streamed in through the high windows and it was almost like being in church, except that everyone was rushing to board trains.

One morning, needing to visit the Agents in Broad Street, I took the subway as far as Wall Street. This was the place, you could smell the money as soon as you turned the corner. From Broad Street I went along the Avenue of the Americas to 42nd Street, afterwards making my way to Rockefeller Centre to set up a bank account against a rainy day. Tired by then, the subway took me to a movie house in Flatbush Avenue before returning to the hostel. The following morning saw me down at the pier at the foot of 21st Street to meet the *Fana*. She was late in berthing, so time was passed in the Seamen's Union House at 20th and 4th, boarding her when she came alongside late in the afternoon. There can be a feeling of mild apprehension when meeting new shipmates, especially after the recent bunches of weirdo's I had sailed with, but first impressions seemed favourable.

During my stay at the Norwegian Seaman's Hostel I had taken a tumble on the stairs. It was a twelve-storey block and my room was on the top floor, which meant taking the lift as far as it went and then walking up the remaining stairs to my room. The light switches in the stairwell were the type that stayed on for a limited time before switching themselves off and, suddenly plunged into darkness, I tripped and hurt my back. The next day it began to stiffen up and I worried about possible spinal damage, so later that evening I went down to the foyer to enquire about doctors.

The nearest Surgery was some ten minutes walk along the deserted streets of the dock area of Brooklyn; it was ill lit and gloomy as I wended my way there. At 111 Montague Street was the practice of Ernest F. Lampell M.D., the doctor in attendance being Dr. Hause. The waiting room with its net curtains and hard seated cane chairs brought to mind scenes from black and white movies. Dr. Hause examined me and said that I was lucky, if the injury had been an inch or so lower it might have involved the base of the spine, which could have had serious consequences. Naturally relieved, it was only then I realised that I had very little money with me. Back home maybe the NHS to the rescue but not in Brooklyn. All I had was a £1 note, which I knew from experience would be as useful around there as a dose of the pox. I left the name of the ship's agent to whom he could send the bill.

The ship had now docked and the Agent helped me transfer my gear on board. The *Fana* moved out from the wharf, anchoring in Upper New York Bay to await a vacant loading bay. The new *Mauritania* passed by us, very close to. Our anchorage was directly in the path of the Bay Ridge Ferry, which plied between Brooklyn and Staten Island, and after a day or two at anchor regular commuters began waving to us as the ferry went past. Eventually we moved to a berth at Pier B in the Erie Basin, Brooklyn, where we commenced loading general cargo, including a quantity of shiny new Hudson 'Jet' motorcars, very swish and streamlined. Going ashore, I located the office of the licensing authority and obtained a new Radio Safety Certificate for the ship, then blew $3 on a sightseeing bus tour which took in 5th Avenue, Grant's Tomb, Central Park, Broadway, Times Square and the Empire State Building. My own perambulations took me to 'Lindeys' in Times Square where I absorbed the real life 'Mindy's' of Damon Runyon; it was like living the dream.

Walking around the area 42nd to 52nd Street was to discover one small jazz club after another, their music spilling out over the sidewalk. This was a wonderful time to be in New York, jazz was healthy and taking tentative steps around yet another corner, this time towards be-bop. Jimmy McPartland and his band, with Freddie Washington and Shad Collins, were holding court at Child's 'Paramount' in Times Square. Having made myself known as a jazz fan from England, during the intermission the band came across to my table, and over a few beers we talked about jazz in general and England in particular. Here was I, talking to Jimmy McPartland, the man who had played alongside Glenn Miller and Benny Goodman in the '20s and taken over the trumpet chair from Bix Beiderbecke in the 1924 Wolverines. And here was he, pushing his trumpet across the table to me whilst he went to freshen up for the next session, saying, 'Look after that till I get back, Jack'. That trumpet was guarded like the Crown Jewels until he got back. Shad Collins asked me for a favourite tune, the band rendering a spirited Riverboat Shuffle, which they enjoyed playing as much as I enjoyed listening.

One evening, wandering along 42nd Street amongst the small clubs that abounded there I almost got myself heaved out of one jazz-cum-strip joint. When I entered, there were some customers gathered at the bar at the back of the room and the rest of the floor space was filled with tables and chairs, all of them unoccupied. As the big attraction, in more ways than one, Tempest Storm, was about to perform down at the front of the auditorium, I sauntered down and sat at one of the tables towards the front. There was just Tempest and me for a while until I felt a presence at my side. A large gentleman in a tuxedo bent over and said something to the effect that there was an extra charge for seating, had I paid, and would I like a drink. I could imagine the price of both these items and didn't have much money anyway so I sat tight, trying to look like a mobster whom it was best not to mess with. The waiter hovered about, both of us unsure of the next move and watched with interest by the group at the bar. Figuring that the best course of action was to walk out looking as if I'd been offended, I did just that and got away with it.

Dan and I were both fond of American popular literature and were familiar with Runyons' Broadway characters of the 1940s, often incorporating their unique prose into our conversation. Spanish John, Harry the Horse, Good Time Charlie and the rest of that eccentric mob were a part of our lives and vocabularies. So much so, that when my feet touched Broadway everything seemed familiar, surrounded by people I felt at ease with, and this probably helped me when frequenting bars, ignoring the house rules and having to leave early just ahead of the bouncer and the bums rush.

19: REVOLUTIONS AND RIVERBOATS

The *Fana* was a modern cargo ship with cabins for a couple of passengers. Unfortunately just before we left New York one presented herself, complete with a ticket for the round trip. Passengers on board cargo ships are mostly bad news. At meal times officers have to don uniform instead of the casual gear usually worn at sea, the captain feels the strain of being polite all the time and everyone has to shave, stop swearing and look a little less scruffy than usual. We set off for Charleston, South Carolina where we loaded general cargo and more cars. I went to the cinema and also bought half a dozen Arrow shirts; usually buying in bulk if I like something, much to the dismay of family members. Passing the Bahamas, San Salvador and Cuba the weather was perfect and the music that flooded in from the radio stations as we passed by was the final touch to our idyllic surroundings. There was only one drawback and that was the passenger, who, the only woman on a ship full of sailors, was exhibiting all the symptoms of a nymphomaniac but without the necessary attributes for the role. She thus presented a problem throughout the voyage and slightly clouded what otherwise was a very pleasant trip.

At Barranquilla, on the Caribbean coast of Colombia, we

discharged part of our cargo and took a thousand bags of coffee on board. It was quiet in the afternoon as I walked around the town centre, there were one or two rounds of gunfire close by, but so what, this was South America. Most of the shops were closed, which I put down to the sultry afternoon, all the bars were open and doing a healthy trade judging by the buzz of conversation and the blaring radios. It looked like market day and smelt like it; fish, meat and bread, all with free flies attached, were on sale. The pavements were cracked and grubby and it all looked just as a South American town should look at siesta time on a hot afternoon. Returning on board I was told that a revolution had been taking place in the town whilst I was wandering around, that the President had been arrested, thrown into jail and the Vice President had taken over. Apparently it had been tried before and this time was a fairly peaceful coup, as these things go in Colombia. As we left Barranquilla the sea was like glass, shoals of flying fish surrounded the ship, working up a speed sufficient to skim and then fly some twenty feet or more before plopping back into the water.

We arrived at Cristobal Colon at the entrance to the Panama Canal and went alongside. Walking around, it seemed not dissimilar to Bermuda, peacefully tropical and picturesque. Going ashore that same evening however, Cristobal was a very different proposition, being transformed into a shanty town, with bars and cabarets throwing their coloured beams of light on to the streets and Latin rhythms pounding from every doorway. In between the exuberant cabarets on the main street there were dark and mysterious alleyways down which you would not want to venture. It was a sailors' town, every pleasure there for the taking and every danger awaiting the unwary. I settled in at the Saratoga Club where the surroundings seemed fairly safe by local standards, staying there all evening.

Early light saw us passing through the locks into the Gatun Lake. The next set of locks brought another passenger, a pretty girl of about 20, travelling alone and going with us to Buenaventura. Now she should have been a nymphomaniac but wasn't. Disenchanted by the injustices of life, we continued through the Miraflores Locks and out into the Pacific. The passage through the Panama Canal must be one of the most interesting eight hour trips you could wish for, and could have been even more interesting with a bit of luck.

A day's run along the Pacific coast of Colombia found us

anchoring in Buenaventura Bay awaiting daybreak. In the morning we proceeded slowly up river to Buenaventura, only to find a dozen ships already alongside and many more at anchor awaiting their turn, so we dropped anchor and joined the queue. Dense jungle covered the opposite riverbank, broken only by a gathering of grass huts, from where an occasional canoe brought people across the river to work on the quayside. Exotic it may have been, but we soon tired of it as there was nothing else to see except endless jungle. We lay at anchor, suffering the oppressive heat and humidity for three days which seemed like three weeks, so I helped paint the lifeboat to pass the time. The sun set at teatime, the insects came out and we sweated the nights away.

The Captain took me ashore in the launch to the Agent's office on the quayside. Cargo was being worked on two or three of the ships alongside, but progress appeared to be slow. A small pusher seaplane regularly landed and took off very close to the ship and watching this was our only excitement. Eventually we secured a berth, went alongside, discharged our cargo and commenced loading coffee for Jacksonville, Florida. Most of my time was spent listening to the Test Match on the BBC World Service, England drawing with Australia, Hutton making 145. Those were the days when the World Service virtually united the Commonwealth, every Briton abroad listened to the World Service, the strains of 'Lilibulero' being used to locate and tune in the news broadcasts from the many stations crowding the short wave bands.

One thing that was not united was the dockside scene below us, where chaos appeared to be a way of life, though at a South-American tempo. There was little space between the warehouses and the edge of the quay and all activity had to be conducted in the narrow space available. A small railway engine, British circa 1850, clanked up and down the length of the quay day and night, pulling a few decrepit wagons behind it. When the engine needed to transfer from one narrow-gauge line to another there was widespread confusion, men with iron bars appeared from nowhere and by dint of much honest Colombian exertion, and probably not a few Colombian oaths, inserted the iron bars in amongst the rails and forcibly moved the points over. This operation took about twenty minutes, during which time the driver and any others not engaged in the proceedings drank coffee, read the paper, shot dice or stood around and whistled at the girls.

There were women on the quay, some bringing meals in little

tin pots to their men-folk, others walking up and down with baskets of pastries on their head or carrying receptacles full of lemonade. The latter items had to be purchased and, as nobody seemed to have any money, there was a great deal of talking, cajoling, and laughter whilst pockets were turned out. This activity went on all day to the detriment of the cargo-loading. Occasionally a man appeared in a large clapped-out car who, by his manner appeared to be the Big Boss, and he would remonstrate with the workers who were partaking of refreshments or reading the Wall Street Journal in the firm's time. These admonishments had little effect and after a while he would go away again, body language radiating defeat. Dinnertime arrived and everyone knocked off. Or if it wasn't a mealtime then it would have started to rain, resulting in a scramble to pull the tarpaulins over the hatches. This was followed by a general exodus from the holds, where the trimmers had been enjoying a siesta, in order to find the nearest shelter suitable for a card school. A couple of hours after the rain had ceased the workers emerged, looked up hopefully at the sky for signs of further rain before reluctantly resuming work.

Coffee laden, we set off for the Canal but had to anchor off Panama until a Pilot became available, later spending a few hours in Gatun Lake waiting to go through the locks. The Pilot told me that they handled about 15 ships daily in both directions. We left Cristobal in a cloud of flying fish, a US Navy dirigible had a look at us between Cuba and Key West and a group of turtles tried to outpace us off Daytona Beach. We reached Jacksonville unscathed by these encounters and I went ashore for a walk whilst the coffee was off-loaded. After discharging was completed we moved from the town quay to the Standard Oil jetty to take on bunkers, before setting off, light ship, for Chandler in Gaspe County, Quebec Province, Canada. Strong head winds reduced our speed from 13 knots to 4 and saw us virtually at a standstill off Cape Hatteras. The *Queen Elizabeth* passed us bound for New York. The wind had dropped by the time we arrived off the coast of Nova Scotia, a thick fog descended and we had to crawl along the Cape Breton shoreline into the Gulf of St. Lawrence and across to Chandler.

At Chandler we loaded bales of paper. The shore gangs worked through the night which meant that we had little sleep with the winches screeching away, people shouting all the time and the continuous tramp of feet on the metal deck above our heads. Ashore, there were a few shops and a couple of drug stores with soda fountains. It was all very healthy, smelling of pine forests and fresh air, a lovely little place if you were about to retire and wanted a quiet life, otherwise not much going on. The pilot who took us alongside was going on 80 and had formerly been the town's mayor. Anyone familiar with Stephen Leacock and Mariposa would immediately recognise Chandler; Mariposa is an enchanting place, and to be carried along with Leacock's gentle humour into its world is a journey to enjoy.

Before we left Canada a storm passed overhead one night; there was a great deal of buzzing in the wireless room as the aerials picked up the lightning and passed the charge through the radio room to earth, or in our case to the sea. Ships' aerials are always earthed in port or when not in use and I wondered how many volts passed through the ship that night. We put out to sea in bad weather, which turned to fog soon after we left Nova Scotia, heading for Cape Race on the tip of Newfoundland. The fog dispersed, the weather brightened and we had a perfect crossing to Sheerness, where we anchored before moving up to Rochester to discharge cargo.

The Captain asked me to take half a dozen seamen to Lancaster Gate and oversee their paying-off at the Norwegian Consul, giving me a four-figure sum in cash with which to do so. Duties discharged, I stayed overnight at the Great Northern Hotel and the following day wended my way with the crowds to The Oval to watch Peter May make 135 and Laker and Bedser bowling to Reg Simpson. London was at its most beguiling and my stay at the hotel was extended for a few days, watching cricket, visiting the Science Museum and dining at the Koh-i-Nor. I returned to Rochester in time for the completion of discharging and the official end of the voyage, paying off there in early August 1953.

A day or two later the Yorkshire Pullman took me home from King's Cross; Geoff was at home so the four of us were together once more. Although regularly keeping in touch with the ROU about another ship, a few weeks passed in which nothing eventuated so Geoff suggested a holiday. We motored down to London, staying at the Premier Hotel in Russell Square, visiting nightclubs and having dinner at midnight in the Mapleton Hotel. We watched Australia make 275 at The Oval before spending the evening at Humphrey Lyttelton's Club and having a meal at Chez Auguste in Old Compton Street. The following morning saw us seeking culture in the British Museum, also spending more time than was necessary for research purposes in the Cheshire Cheese. Late in the afternoon we staggered up the steps to the Whispering Gallery in St. Paul's, all the while wishing we hadn't taken quite so much ale on board across lunchtime. After a day of intellectually stimulating experiences we retired to the Windmill, then went to the Palladium to see Kay Starr, to Macks Jazz Club and, finally to dinner in Soho. Exhausted, and unable to keep up this punishing schedule, we left for home next day.

Towards the end of August, Dan, Geoff and I went on a Riverboat Shuffle from the Victoria Pier, the music provided by Bob Wallis's Port of Hull Jazz Band and the Wool City Jazz Band from Bradford. The vessel was the paddle-steamer *Tattershall Castle,* complete with running bar and buffet, and she wended her way up river awash with jazz fans drinking steadily in the drizzle. A week later a Finnish ship was offered to me on a direct contract by a local firm, but was declined. With things quiet on the shipping front it seemed a good time for me to learn to drive. We had never had a car in the family but dad was now earning just enough to contemplate buying one, so a course of driving lessons was embarked upon with Cammish's of Massey Street. The last time dad had been in charge of a motor vehicle was in the army during the latter stages of the 1914-18 war, followed by a period of driving a lorry on the fish dock in the early 1920s, but apparently his licence still held good and the authorities were willing to let him loose on Britain's roads without a further test. The car, a second-hand Ford Prefect, was given a family outing to Whitby and Robin Hood's Bay, from which everyone returned highly chuffed at the new horizons opening up.

My parents had the use of a caravan at Tunstall, so odd days and weekends were spent there. It was on the cliff top, near to steps cut out of the clay which led down to the beach. In the evenings it was beautiful, tranquil, often with not a soul in sight for miles along the sands in both directions and there was only the ripple of the water on the shingle for company. It was just the place to wind down, but for reasons unknown I was winding up, headaches and stomach pains plagued me most days without obvious cause.

At a loose end, I took to writing to the local paper about the dismal lack of night life in the city, that it was now six years since the war had ended and it was time that, as the Continent was coming alive, so should we. Hostile replies ensued, all of them upholding the city's current state of gloom and despondency. I engaged, writing further letters saying that there was nowhere to go and nothing to do, and calling the place a ghost town after 10pm when the last trolley-bus hared off down the road to the depot. Letters poured in telling me that some people had to sleep and get up to go to God-fearing legitimate jobs in the morning, early. I responded, saying that I had also worked hard, often 18 hours a day, and didn't see why people shouldn't be able to enjoy themselves after ten at night if they wanted to. If they could do it on the Continent then why couldn't we? It was all very well, it passed the time, but it didn't get me a ship, and in the meantime my stomach pains were becoming worse.

Margaret was now getting ever more publicity in the papers. Valerie was having her photo and articles in the newspapers too, although her best period lay ahead when she played a comedy stripper in the stage version of 'Gypsy', then Calamity Jane in Betty Grable's London stage show 'Belle Starr', and was Mike Reid's cockney girlfriend in the TV series 'Yus, My Dear'. For a girl who had polio when she was eight and took up dancing to help regain the use of her legs, she had earned everything that was coming her way and I was pleased for her. Just before we lost touch I had given her my 'Saint' books, a shared enthusiasm, and I liked to think of her reading them in a dressing room somewhere whilst waiting to go on stage.

By contrast, all the wrong things were coming my way. Towards the end of September I was examined at the Hull Royal Infirmary by Dr. Groves, who diagnosed, 'query peptic ulcer' and sent me to Bannens and Hernon, a medical practice on Beverley Road, for a stomach X-Ray. The plates from Bannens revealed no ulcer, but did highlight a small suspicious area at one side of the duodenum so I was referred to a surgeon, Mr Blackburne. Following a visit to his consulting room in Albion Street I found myself heading to Sutton Annexe for an operation.

20: NURSE FRITH

It would be an understatement to say that this episode changed my life. The first time I saw Nurse Eileen Frith was on the James Reckitt male surgical ward at Sutton Annexe, where she was rushing up and down the 30-bed ward holding mysterious objects under linen covers. I was sitting up in bed, apprehensive about the forthcoming operation and generally feeling sorry for myself, but

Mam & Dad, Marjorie & Bill
Glasgow 1947

Sugar Loaf Mountain,
Rio de Janeiro

The *Grainton's*
spark transmitter

s.s. Grainton,
Rio de Janeiro 1948

St. Stephen, under Grimsby registry

s.s. Kalev, loading esparto grass in North Africa, 1948

Loading iron ore in Spain

Alf, Ken, Eric and George

Thomas Tompion, under Hull registry

s.s. Fido, Cape Breton, Nova Scotia 1952

s.s. Fana, Jacksonville, USA 1953

Valerie, Abbey Park, Leicester
1953

Staff Nurse Eileen Frith
1954

with Dan at Hawthorne Avenue

Dad and the Ford Prefect

s.s. Gannet, Muroran, Japan 1954

Eileen and I at Tunstall
1954

s.s. Gannet in Vietnam,
proceeding up river to Campha

with Antonios Papadimas, 1954

Wedding Day 1955,
Trafalgar Street
Church

Captain George & friends outside
the New Kobe Hotel, Japan 1956

'Modified' Henry

s.s. Golden Eagle, Kobe 1956

Eileen & Raffe
at 265 Beverley Road, 1958

Mam & Eileen on
s.s. Golden Eagle at Southampton

s.s. Manhattan in Argentina, 1958

Geoff & Eileen, Scarborough 1958

Eileen & Raffe

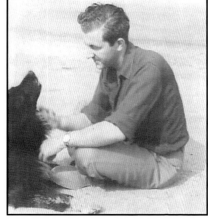

Beach picnic with Raffe at Tunstall, Summer 1958

my heart was having none of this self-pity and had embarked on a different tack altogether. The first time we actually exchanged words was in the ward bathroom when she was preparing me for the operating theatre. She was so lovely I would have done anything for her. She had a length of rubber tubing in her hand and said to me, 'Swallow this, and don't be sick, I haven't time'. What? Talk about love at first sight. Who could resist such blandishments, such words of love and passion? I went to theatre with my head in a whirl, returning minus a duodenal diverticulum, and an appendix for good measure.

Two weeks in hospital passed, and a couple of days after being discharged I rang the Nurses' Home at Sutton, (an ex-directory number obtained by dubious methods), and asked to speak to Nurse Frith. Consternation. Regulations were extremely strict concerning nurses receiving phone calls from ex-patients and I had to persevere before eventually managing to talk to her. Even then it was far from plain sailing. After being rebuffed a couple of times I managed to arrange a date, pleading my case as a convalescent in desperate need of after-care. We met in the town and I was told, quite definitely, that we had nothing in common. We met again two days later, our meetings being fitted in around her duties. When Eileen was on night duty and needed to sleep in the daytime, meetings were difficult to arrange, so things jogged along but did not prosper. I wooed her with jazz records, but she preferred the classics. I explained what a wonderful team Hull City was, but to no avail. My parents loved her; I loved her, but still no go. To paraphrase Dorothy Parker: 'The sun's gone dim, the moon's gone black; I loved her, but she didn't love back'.

My stomach was still playing up and yet more X-rays were taken. Eileen had a couple of days off and we took the car to Bridlington, Flamborough, Danes Dyke, went for long walks on the sands and to the end of Filey Brigg, where we were very nearly cut off by the tide, and crammed a lot into a little time. There were days when she had to attend lectures in the late afternoon and I took her to and from these in the car. My mystery ailment persisted, and with no definite diagnosis it seemed to be all in the mind, although the pain in my stomach seemed anything but imaginary. And the ache in my heart certainly wasn't. Suddenly, there seemed all too many emotions to cope with.

Amidst all this I failed my driving test. It wasn't my fault, honest. Our Ford Prefect was used for the test, but had been poorly maintained by the person entrusted to service it, and the test was failed on 'starting correctly'. It subsequently transpired that the juddering start which we had always attributed to dad's bad driving, was actually due to the fact that one of the four bolts holding the engine to the chassis had dropped out at some stage. Thus, the engine wanted to move forward but the chassis wanted to stay where it was; a game of shuddering stop-start ensuing when the car moved off.

But there were things other than driving tests to worry about; a Dr. Malton in Coltman Street was consulted about my stomach pains, the vagus nerve figuring largely in our discussions, and a course of white pills was embarked upon. Some of my time at sea was spent making model ships, and the Golden Hind had been brought home to finish off, a soothing occupation to take up at this time. I was also watching Hull City, never a soothing occupation at any time. Humphrey Lyttelton and his band with Neva Raphello came to the City Hall, but small group jazz in concert halls is out of its element, flourishing best in small, intimate, slightly down-market clubs where the atmosphere transmits itself between musician and audience, setting feet tapping and building up a shared experience. A little alcohol helps too. And you don't get that ambience in a large hall, which is better suited to big bands with large reed sections and banks of brass. And they belong in dance halls anyway.

Eileen and I travelled to York by car, illegally, as I was still without a driving licence, (Eileen all unaware). After exploring the Minster and climbing the Tower we visited the Castle Museum, ate beans on toast in the café and walked through its Old Street, rejoicing in the word 'Apothecary'. Back home we played records and talked, after which I walked Eileen the three miles to her home in Rose Street and it was well after midnight as I made my way home through the quiet streets, walking on air. Vic Damone's version of 'On the Street Where You Live' became imbued with nostalgic significance, as inconsequential things do when you're in love.

Dan and George were still available for nights out and Geoff returned periodically from arctic waters, so life went on much as before, except that there was no longer any rush to find a ship; love had complicated the plot. We continued to explore the East Riding countryside on Eileen's days off, walking on sandy beaches accompanied by Eileen's dog, Raffe, the most loveable dog I've ever known. A black and white border collie of great personality and vitality, his tail rewarded you every time you spoke to him. He loved to tear along the deserted beaches on our days out, and turned somersaults at the sight of the car if he thought he was going somewhere with us. Also, it seemed a good start, having the family dog on my side. Apparently I was the only person outside the family he was friendly towards and Eileen's elder sister Kathleen viewed this as significant.

By now Eileen had been lured to Boothferry Park and we sat in the West Stand while I explained the offside rule to her. Excursions were made to the caravan at Tunstall so that the offside rule could be discussed in greater detail and it is surprising how long this can take. Some days at the caravan the whole of the coastline and the miles of sandy beach that stretched to the horizon were totally deserted. As it was late November and bloody cold this was not surprising. The beach was freshly washed by the tide especially for us, lending itself to illustrating the offside trap in the sand, but all to no avail. Despite being regularly informed that our relationship wouldn't work out, I pressed on, and had made some progress when the time came to go back to sea, although I don't think she understood the offside rule any better than I did. Word had reached me from the ROU about a Greek ship, presently in France, that needed an Operator. Eileen saw me off to London on the train the next day; I booked a room at the Great Northern Hotel and fell asleep wondering what the future held for us.

The following morning contracts were signed at the ROU Offices, a visit was made to the ship-owners, Goulandris Brothers in St. Mary Axe, and a taxi took me to the travel department of Marshall and Snelgrove to collect my ticket for the journey to France. Catching the boat-train to Southampton I left towards midnight on the *Normannia* for Le Havre, finding an agreeable travelling companion in the person of the London correspondent of the 'New York Herald Tribune'. He had been on D-Day, covering it for his newspaper, so there was no shortage of things to talk about until we docked in Le Havre as dawn was breaking. A taxi took me to the Agents' office, but it was not yet open for business so time was spent in the warmth of 'Le Commerce' bistro next door, drinking numerous cups of black coffee until the Agent arrived. The Captain, George Mandarakis, took me to sign on the Ships Articles, then to the Hotel Roubaix to lodge with others of the crew until the ship was ready to receive us. She had started life as the 4412 ton American Liberty Ship *George G Meade,* one of the 2,000 Liberty Ships built during the war. She first saw service in October 1942 and on the 9th March 1943, whilst on a voyage from Bahia to the States, had been torpedoed in the Atlantic by U510 and towed into Paramaribo for repairs. At the end of the war she became the French vessel *Rouen,* and was now being taken over once again and re-named.

21: RED EGGS AT MIDNIGHT

When Goulandris took over the *Rouen* they named her *Gannet,* registering her in Monrovia, Liberia, along with many of their other vessels also named after birds. The funnel was painted in the blue and yellow colours of the company. There were six officers and a couple of dozen Greek seamen staying at the hotel, where the routine was breakfast at 0900, on board by 1000 working and checking on the gear, back to the hotel for lunch at 1300, return to the ship and then dinner at the hotel at 1900. A group of us usually went for a walk after the meal, with occasional expeditions into town by ramshackle buses or single-decker electric trolley buses. On the other side of the dock were the liners *Liberte* and *Ile de France* and we walked round to see these magnificent vessels up close. The weather was cold but I was busy dashing around on ship's business and hadn't much time to notice it. The meal in the evening was the high point of the day, bottles of red wine and crusty bread sticks awaited us when we returned from the ship and these kept us going until the main course arrived.

In the week before Christmas 1953, all 32 crewmen transferred themselves and their gear from the hotel to the *Gannet.* My first job was to walk round the docks looking for a British ship from which to beg borrow or steal a chart to take us as far as Dakar, and also a Brown's Nautical Almanac. These essential items had been sent to us from London, along with that important little red book for merchant vessels, The Ships Captains Medical Guide, but had not arrived; I didn't reckon that the Captain of the *Ile de France* would have a spare copy so I gave her a miss. I had no luck at the first attempt as there were no other British ships nearby, but our departure was delayed and the missing items turned up before we sailed. There was still a lot of work to be done in the wireless room, particularly on the batteries which were almost dry. These had to be topped up with distilled water before being brought up to the required specific gravity by the addition of sulphuric acid from a carboy, stored in the battery room.

We left Le Havre in ballast for South America, first stop Dakar in French West Africa for bunkers. By the time we passed through the Canary Islands the ship had settled comfortably into sea routine, all was peaceful and there were two eggs for breakfast, a promising start. We spent half a day fuelling in Dakar which gave time for a look around, but there wasn't much of interest and I was back on board well before we set course for the River Plate. One drawback about a Liberty ship's radio room was the ventilation, adequate in cooler climes but unsuitable for the tropics. There was only one small porthole on the port side, so if there was no breeze coming from that side, tough luck. In the tropics it was usually well over ninety degrees inside the wireless room and the breeze created by our 12 knots hardly stirred the air inside the cabin. There were wind-scoops that fitted into the portholes to catch the wind and direct it inside, these helped a little but mostly you just sweated it out, the fans only circulating the stifling air around the cabin.

Crossing longitude 30`W the wireless Time Zones changed and there were five watches that day instead of the usual four. As we rolled further south we received orders from Buenos Aires Radio to proceed to Necochea as our first loading port; when we reached there we found its small harbour crammed full of shipping. All ships' documents are in English and, being the obvious candidate, the Captain took me ashore with him to help with the ship's papers. This was fine by me as it meant getting off the ship before anyone else and swanning around in offices, lunching ashore at the ship's expense and travelling everywhere by taxi.

Peron still held power in Argentina, Evita had died only recently and was still deeply mourned by the people. Sunday was the big family day and the townspeople walked or drove down to look at the ships, sometimes being invited on board for a look around. There were many ships in the harbour but only half a dozen were actively working cargo, so we considered ourselves lucky to get away with only a week's wait for a berth under one of the grain silos. Adjacent to the dock was a beach, where we spent our time lazing about or playing football. Once work started it took a couple of days to load our part-cargo of barley, after which we left for Bahia Blanca, only to find yet more shipping waiting for berths alongside the grain quay.

After passing the time walking around Bahia Blanca every day for several days we completed loading the barley, plus a quantity of bagged rye, and left for Rotterdam, expecting to make about ten knots in good weather. There was no excuse for not writing home and I'd done that regularly every week since 1943; it was much simpler now because there was no need to leave the folks back home wondering how and where you were. During the war we found a way round the secrecy problem by purchasing two identical small atlases, leaving one at home and taking the other to sea. My letters home would contain three numbers somewhere in the letter; the first was the index page, the second the column and the third the line reading down the column. It was rough and ready but it worked well throughout the war, although any censors must have marvelled at some of the cricket scores that were quoted. There was no need for such subterfuge now, but there was double the correspondence, one home and one to Eileen. Letters home dealt with the same topics as they always had done, places, ports, departures and arrivals. But the letters to Eileen, oh dear me! Things were at a crucial stage in our relationship; I knew that I wanted to marry her but she wasn't sure about it. She was a Christian; I wasn't; we seemed at opposite ends of the spectrum.

Eileen was ten when her father died in 1942 from an illness related to his 1914-18 war service, her mother becoming the sole breadwinner for herself and three young children. The infrequent, unskilled work she obtained brought in wages insufficient to pay the rent, feed and clothe the family and their possessions were gradually sold off to survive, her mother often going without food in order to feed the children; there was no Social Security, unemployment benefit or health service to fall back on. Eileen's Elementary School education was interrupted by the war, being spread over five different schools where the level of education was inadequate, as many teachers were serving in the forces. Together with her elder sister Kathleen and younger brother David, she was evacuated to Wilsford, a small village in Lincolnshire, where two teachers struggled to cope with 40 pupils aged between 5 and 16. Although eligible and eager for further education, Eileen had to leave school at 14 to earn money for the household, working as a clerk at Wm. Field's bakery. She joined Trafalgar Street church, became a Christian and acquired an 'extended family'; this experience changed her life. Feeling that nursing was her vocation she was accepted for three years nurse training in 1951. Later, the Hull Daily Mail, reporting on the 1954 Hull Royal Infirmary Prize-Giving, quoted the Senior Nursing Tutor as saying, 'I have never presented so many prizes to one student'; she received a Silver Medal, Bronze Medal, Medical prize, Anatomy prize, Practical Nursing Prize and a prize for the best All-round Practical Nurse. Eileen intended to further her nursing career, possibly becoming a missionary and, as a State Registered Nurse, her life was before her, achievement and fulfilment. Then along comes this character with his chat-up line about offside rules, threatening to disrupt it all.

We were writing lengthy letters to each other, and what a difficult and confused correspondence it turned out to be. Forget telephones, e-mail, mobile phones, internet, think steam post. I would send a letter from South America and, at the same time, receive mail from Eileen written weeks earlier; neither letter answered recent questions posed by the other, and another exchange of letters would follow, endeavouring to clarify matters already discussed. Letters followed the ship halfway round the world, crossing with more recent letters, and so it went on for the next twelve months. Eileen talked to God. I blamed the Government. Things were bound to get better I told myself.

The good ship *Gannet* steamed on through the South Atlantic, oblivious to human foibles. In the middle of the ocean we saw a six foot snake swimming along, black with yellow stripes, obviously a City supporter. Caribbean and American radio stations flooded into the wireless room once more as we passed through the doldrums. Between watches I laid on the hatch sun-bathing, cooled by the breeze and the occasional spray thrown over the bows and wondered why everybody didn't go to sea. We called at Dakar for bunkers and mail and learnt that our owners were officially the Bahia Salinas Navara Company of Panama, even though we were crewed by Greeks, owned by Greeks, chartered to a French shipping company and registered in Liberia. We arrived in Rotterdam. Like Hull, it had taken a real pasting during the war but had picked itself up, largely rid itself of its bomb damage and in a few short years had become a thriving port city. Quantities of pastries were devoured over the fortnight that we stayed there, and letters from home arrived regularly by hand of the Sparks on the *Melrose Abbey* when that vessel made her scheduled crossing from Hull every 48 hours. Each day the Captain took me with him on his travels around Rotterdam by taxi, on ship's business, shopping and eating out, so it was all very pleasant.

All good things have to end, and we left one beautiful spring evening in ballast for Newport News, Hampton Roads, Virginia. Shortly after leaving Rotterdam the messboy threw the radar wiring diagrams overboard whilst cleaning the radio room. Wiring diagrams are the life blood of the wireless room and indispensable if anything goes wrong with the gear whilst at sea. Operators had used and cared for these through war, changes of flags and different owners, and the culprit came nearer than he realised to following them overboard. At lunch that day we were served octopus, and that did nothing to improve matters, although things were to get better. Norfolk, Virginia was a sailors' town, a US Navy sailors' town. Its life centred round the dockyard, where we were berthed amongst cruisers and destroyers, it teemed with uniforms, had an air of urgent activity throughout the 24 hours and was my kind of town. In the mornings there was shopping, and in the afternoons walks around the parts of the town not covered in the morning. At night, there were numerous burlesque theatres, bars and cabarets to investigate and it was well after midnight when I got back on board. This routine went on for a week whilst we loaded coal, but was not long enough for me, and I was still operating at maximum revs, when we put to sea, bound for Japan.

The ship was covered in coal dust and we went through the usual hosing down routine before leaving it to the freshening wind to finish the job. The breeze blew all vestiges of the shore away too, for there are few things more satisfying than to feel the gentle lift of a ship as she greets the sea once again, her natural partner. It's like witnessing an intimate reunion, with you as a privileged onlooker. Sure, there can be bad days at sea, but there are far more good days, and on those good days there is no more wonderful place to be than on a tramp steamer, free of the land, heading for who knows what new adventures over the horizon.

A *Missouri* class battleship overtook us and a dirigible lazed overhead, reminiscent of a wartime barrage balloon. We passed San Salvador, Haiti and Cuba, with the weather still calm, the sea blue, the radio stations playing Caribbean rhythms all day and half the night. We went alongside at Cristobal to take on bunkers and a few of us went ashore to the Broadway and the Copacabana cabarets, returning aboard in the small hours, though well in time to join the early morning convoy through the first lock. The shore activity on the locks of the Panama Canal is a continual source of interest, with 'mules', a motorised engine on rails, pulling us along as they moved up the gentle slopes on the side of the lock, the lock itself filling up meanwhile, the ship rising with it. I spent the whole eight hour trip on deck, enjoying the tropical scenery and the occasional flock of brightly coloured birds that flew overhead. The day warmed quickly as we made our way through the canal, the bare deck becoming hot enough to feel through the soles of your shoes. Leaving Balboa in the early afternoon we greeted the sunny Pacific and set course for Honolulu.

Was it not in Panama that Cortez stood silent upon his peak in Darien as he gazed at the Pacific; and were we not sailing over submerged long lost cities of gold? Maybe not, but we should have been, it all felt romantic enough. Even the flying fish were larger than life and in greater shoals than ever before. Sometimes life grants you magic days, maybe not often enough, but you remember them when they happen along. The sea was like glass and our bow hardly disturbed the surface as it cut through the water. The ship's log streamed out aft, making scarcely a ripple as it measured our progress across this vast stretch of ocean, and everyone settled down for a peaceful three weeks of ocean voyaging. A flock of birds joined us, roosting on the main mast cross-tree and looking much as birds do when perching on telegraph wires. They disappeared in the daytime but returned to us every evening to roost on the mast, grab a night's sleep and a free ride.

Good Friday was not observed on board but Easter Sunday was marked by the omission of certain foods. On the Friday following Good Friday we had shrimps, bread and Anisette. The next day there was soup at midnight and we collected our red eggs, the ship's bell was rung and rockets were sent up, complete with small parachutes. The Captain had checked with me beforehand to see whether there were any ships in the vicinity and I told him that we seemed to have the whole Pacific Ocean to ourselves.

We steamed on, consuming our 25 tons of fuel per day and began picking up a dozen or so Hawaiian radio stations from a great distance, loud and clear. In those latitudes there was no radio interference from mainland stations to contend with, though the ever present static crowded in as evening approached. Land showed as a dot on the radar from 80 miles away and we made Honolulu a little less than three weeks after leaving Panama. The best part of a day was spent refuelling, taking water and stores on board, so this gave plenty of time to explore. It was about this time, April 1954, when 78rpm records were being replaced by LPs, and the record shops in Honolulu were selling off records cheaply so I bought a dozen. Quantities of iced pineapple juice sustained me on my perambulations, viewing Diamond Head in the distance and walking along Waikiki Beach with its pounding ocean surf and surf-boarders. The weather was perfect and it all looked just like the movies.

The second leg of our voyage to Japan was expected to take a little over a fortnight. We crossed the International Date Line on the day that Roger Bannister became the first man to run the 4 minute mile, Dien Bien Phu fell in the war in Vietnam and a telegram arrived from our Japanese Agents, Dodwell & Co., giving our destination as Muroran in Hokkaido. The next day, typhoon Elsie was reported moving north from the Philippines, gale warnings came from Japan and a storm warning was issued from Kodiak, Alaska, so it looked as though our Pacific idyll was over and that normal service was about to resume. The temperature became noticeably cooler each day and we encountered banks of thick fog approaching the coast of northern Japan. At Muroran we berthed near a large steelworks. The mail came aboard, including a notification from the Agents of a change to our future sailing orders. We had expected to go from Muroran to Canada and then home to Europe, but were now to slot in an extra trip back from Canada to Japan before returning to Europe. This meant even more weeks and months before Eileen and I would see each other, and this came at a crucial point in our relationship. It was not the best news in the world.

22: THE INSCRUTABLE EAST

Disheartened at the news of an additional voyage, I was just about to turn in when Antonias Papadimas, the dapper 3rd Engineer, poked his head round the cabin door and said, 'Come on, five minutes to the dock gate and one beer before we go to bed'. We set off in the semi-darkness and after stumbling over pipelines and other obstacles for an hour we reached the dock gate. According to the sign on a small railway station that we passed, the area was called Winashi. After walking along ill-lit dusty streets for some time, we came across a couple of narrow streets which appeared to be the centre of social activity. There were lanterns swinging from shop fronts, tiny bells tinkling on curtains and people shuffling along in nightshirts, wearing little round hats perched above inscrutable yellow faces. The air smelt of fumes from the steel mill, incense and alcohol. The dirt roadway had no definable edges and, where the pathways should have been, there was an open drain covered by wooden boards, most of which were missing, the pungent odour blending with the smell of chemicals from the steel works. Ah, the aroma of the mysterious East. Pulling aside a tinkling curtain we entered one of the dives, sat at a table and ordered a couple of beers. The place was noisy, full of chatter and reeking with smoke. The old boy sitting next to me seemed to be high on something and kept chuckling away, all the while scoffing green seaweed from a bowl with the aid of chopsticks. Most of the others were doing likewise though some were smoking pipes which gave off a strong smell and clouds of smoke. We stayed for half an hour before walking back along the dirt road towards the bright lights, the noise of the steel works and the ship.

Ian Fleming wrote 'All my life I have been interested in adventure and, abroad, I have enjoyed the frisson of leaving the wide, well-lit streets and venturing up back alleys in search of the hidden pulse of town'. It would have been enjoyable playing Boswell to his Johnson.

A photographer had snapped the *Gannet* as we came into port. The next day she came on board selling the photographs, also taking photographs of individual crew members which she incorporated onto a postcard of the ship. These were very good and I bought a couple to send home to remind people what I looked like. Many questionable people come aboard ships in port to sell things, but seldom so many characters as in Muroran. There were people to cut hair, sole and heel shoes, sell you souvenirs, toothpaste, lighters, direct you to shops and all manner of entertainments and activities, including the local brothel, (licensed), press your suit, paint your portrait and probably your toe-nails as well, you name it, it was there for the asking. They took over the table in the saloon, also the spare cabin and laid out their wares until the ship looked like Paddy's Market. In addition to this commercial activity the cargo was being worked on a 24 hour basis with all its attendant clatter, so there was coal dust and chaos everywhere. The ship didn't seem to belong to us anymore and the peaceful Pacific of a few days ago was but a distant memory.

The Captain wanted to have a kimono made for his wife, and now that we were to make another trip back to Muroran, this became feasible. The cutting and sewing of a quality kimono is not a rushed job and may take weeks rather than days to complete. I thought it would be nice to have one made for Eileen also, so we spent a lot of time in the kimono shop, calling there every day on our trips ashore and being entertained by pretty Japanese girls who giggled at everything we said. Captain George, six foot plus and built like a Sumo wrestler, fascinated them and they dissolved into fits of laughter every time he said anything at all. They plied us with green tea and bits of seaweed, amongst other things, during our frequent visits.

Language difficulty always confronts seamen, wherever they go it's different. Buying goods in small shops can be an interesting experience, although ordering a beer is usually very easy anywhere in the world, so you carry bits of different languages around, enough to make yourself understood wherever you may be. On the *Gannet* I had been co-opted into giving English lessons to a handful of the crew once or twice a week, this was not easy because it had to be done through the medium of pidgin Spanish, which the majority understood.

George and I went into a small tearoom next to the kimono shop, full of lanterns and bonsai trees, language difficulty at maximum +10. We wanted tea and cakes. Nobody understood anybody, but the usual pointing and sign language got us our tea and cakes and everything was going along fine until George decided that he wanted an ice cream. None was on view that we could see, but two ladies at a nearby table were enjoying some, so, all other means having failed, George gestured politely towards them and the waitress understood our wishes. Not so. A little later a girl came along bearing two ices on a tray, swept past us, deposited the ices on the ladies' table and pointed towards us with a smirk. Two surprised ladies whispered to each other behind their fans before slowly rising from their seats and bowing towards our table. By this time the situation was way past retrieving. We got up and bowed back to them. Shortly afterwards we paid the bill and made our exit, accompanied by smiles from the other customers, still minus our ice creams.

Having discharged our 10,500 tons of coal, we left Hokkaido in ballast for Seattle. For the first few hours I was on the bridge continuously, watching the dots on the radar screen that showed a sea thronged with fishing boats. We threaded our way slowly and carefully through them all night, in the cold and the fog. The weather steadily deteriorated as we ploughed along south of the Aleutians, the forecasts were continuously bad, rapidly worsening, and I thought to myself, 'Not again'. On the 27th of May, the wind had increased to storm force and we were battling our way through mountainous seas and swell. We broke through into the eye of the storm at 49.58N, 179.18E. Whilst we sailed through the calm in the centre, everyone tried to catch a quick nap or grab a bite to eat before we had to go through it all again. We crashed through the storm wall again and then, in the middle of the blackest, windiest, wildest night you wanted to imagine, somewhere on the outer edge of the storm centre, one of the steel wire stays that supported the radar platform snapped and the loose end wrapped itself around the radar Scanner.

Fuses blew in all directions. I shut the equipment down and took stock of the situation. There was nothing for it but to climb up to the radar platform, try to unravel the wire and free the Scanner. The rain was pelting down and the ship was rolling heavily from side to side, but we needed a radar picture and we needed it immediately because the storm was blowing us towards the shore and repairs couldn't wait for better weather. With jobs like this, coats or oilskins get in the way, so I donned trousers, shirt and sandshoes and psyched myself up. The metal rungs on the radar mast rose about 20ft to a small platform, which was itself about level with the top of the ship's masts. I climbed up the thin radar mast, struggling to hold on to the rungs in the gale whilst bracing myself against the violent lurching movements of the ship. Once on the platform, soaked through and cold in the bitter wind and rain, it was the traditional sailor's situation, one hand for yourself and one for the ship. Luckily, a first look at the Scanner showed it to be undamaged. With one arm crooked round the central stanchion and working with my free hand, I disengaged the wire and secured it out of harm's way. The ship was still thrashing about and rolling heavily so most of the time I was out over the water, first one side and then the other. The rain continued to fall in sheets and the wind did its best to blow me out to sea, so by the time it was all over my hands were frozen and I was shivering with cold, but we had a picture of the scattered islands of the Aleutians on the screen once more, and that was all that mattered.

The journey through the Straits into Puget Sound was truly scenic, vast sweeps of pine forest covered the mountains down to the water's edge, where lay sandy coves, small beaches, and an occasional hamlet trying to hide away from civilisation. Above and beyond were snow-capped mountains with streams glinting in the sunlight. The gentle breeze from the land brought the smell of the forests, and between the sunshine and showers came the rainbows, vivid in colour and clarity, so near that they reached the ship's side.

We rounded a headland as dusk was falling and there was Seattle, its waterfront streets and buildings coming alive with twinkling lights. We longed to get ashore but couldn't do so until we had dealt with the Customs, Immigration, Doctor, Agent, Port Authority, Stevedores - the list seemed endless, and it was the morning of the following day before we set foot ashore. It was a couple of miles to the centre of Seattle and I walked happily along through the suburbs, gazing around and taking everything in like a tourist. The whole day was spent in Seattle, walking around the centre, stopping only to refuel with hot-dogs and coffee until dusk brought another dimension to the city and it was long after midnight when I got back aboard.

The Captain's brother and his wife came down to the ship; they had left their home island of Andros many years previously and had not seen George since then. Seattle is a great town and our stay there was very enjoyable. We left for Port Angeles where we dropped the American pilot, then steamed for a couple of hours to Victoria on Vancouver Island to pick up the Canadian pilot, who took us to Nanaimo in British Columbia, dropping anchor a few hundred yards offshore. The opportunity to catch some fish was not to be missed so we all put a line over the side. There were red fish in profusion but not much else, it mattered not whether you had a proper rod and line or just threw a piece of string and a hook overboard, everyone caught the same amount of fish.

From Nanaimo we sailed north for 24 hours to Texada Island to load iron-ore. This was a very pretty island with one small township called Vanada and lots of deserted beaches strewn with driftwood. A few of us walked up the trail to the mining camp, a distance of about four miles. As we walked along the rough roads through the forest we noted the signs, 'Beware Cougars', so we kept a good look out for bears, cougars and deer but saw nothing in the way of wildlife. The pine forests smelt wonderful in the rain and sunshine. When the ship returned to Nanaimo George took me for a meal at a Greek restaurant, where the proprietor was another long lost friend of his. Later the same day we moved out, dropped the pilot off Victoria, and left for Japan loaded down with iron ore. Apart from a brief stoppage for tube repairs down below, the trip was pleasant, uneventful, and made even more enjoyable by helping George consume the mountain of Greek sweet-cakes heaped on him in Seattle.

23: FOOTPADS AND INJECTIONS

Eileen and I were still engaged in heavily emotional correspondence, not helped by being half a world apart, and now there were concerns about finance. My lifestyle was that I went to sea, earned money and saved a good percentage of it to see me over whilst sitting exams or staying ashore between ships. The last period ashore had been lengthened by my operation and the subsequent recovery period, so funds were lower at a time when they needed to be higher. My desire to be ashore with Eileen was at odds with the need to go to sea and earn more money. Improvements were gradually being made in seamen's working conditions, it was acknowledged that we worked a 24 hour 7 day week and we now received a supplement for Sundays at sea; it didn't amount to much, but in the context of saving up, every little helped. Letters home included cuttings from magazines or newspapers, one being about a native tribe in the New Hebrides, I sent it to Eileen saying that the New Hebrides sounded like a remarkable and fascinating place.

Radio working in these latitudes proved unusual. For traffic from the States it was often best to work KFS Palo Alto, near San Francisco, with him on MW and the ship on 12mc/s SW. This was unusual, as both ship and shore invariably worked the same wavebands, either MW or SW. In the UK all Coast Stations operated through the auspices of the PMG, but in the States the operators ranged from the US Coastguard and the US Navy to commercial firms like Radio Marine, Globe Radio and McKay Radio. Geoff was still on trawlers; we each had a 6m/cs plug-in crystal, bought from Fanthorpe's in Hepworth's Arcade just after the war when surplus radio gear flooded the market; these particular crystals were from aircraft transmitters, probably Lancaster bombers. We arranged a schedule for a certain time each day to contact each other, wherever we were in the world. We didn't always manage to get through, but more often than not we did and it provided us with a bit of fun. Presently I was at the top of the Pacific and Geoff was at the top of the Atlantic, so we weren't that far apart, and with the clear conditions free of static we made some good W/T (Morse) contacts before transferring to R/T (voice). We said, only half in fun, that these yarns were helped by the radio waves skidding over the ice. The regulations covering the use of wireless frequencies were pretty lax for a few years after the war, so what we were doing was probably illegal; it was all regularised later by the introduction of international frequency allocations.

Whichever country we were passing, the local radio station was tuned in between watches and music played over the loudspeaker in the wireless room, so there were always some of the off-watch crew sitting on the deck outside the porthole, listening to the music. On some ships there was a built-in receiver and loudspeaker system in the crew's mess-room, but where this facility didn't exist, the Operator often fixed up some Heath Robinson arrangement instead; you couldn't do it on the *Gannet* because yards of open deck intervened. With my musical tastes stretching from one end of the spectrum to the other, the chance to hear so many different types of music was another bonus of going to sea. There were also some gems to be heard along the way, like the Japanese announcer introducing the record 'Lady in Bed' which turned out to be 'Lady in Red', (the original), proving something of an anti-climax.

We took our iron ore across the Pacific and berthed once again in Muroran. More coffee and cakes, more visits to the kimono shop, more seaweed, more giggles. One day on our wanderings we walked into a Geisha House, mistaking it for a tea-house, or anyway that's what George said. There was a Japanese Customs Officer living on board whilst we were in port, this being one of the Port Regulations. He occupied the spare cabin next to mine on the bridge deck and seemed to read, eat and sleep, with no call whatsoever on his services. Japanese vessels the same size as us carried a crew of 50 and 3 R/Os, compared to our crew of 30 and a single R/O. Amongst the shore gang were women, working the winches and trimming the cargo.

Loading was progressing fairly swiftly and, as is usual on the last night in port, most of the crew went ashore for a farewell pint or whatever, and Antonias persuaded me to accompany him on a wander about. We imbibed a couple of beers in a local bar before wending our way back to the ship, and were making a short-cut through an unlit alleyway between two brightly-lit main streets when, halfway along the alley, the hairs on the back of neck syndrome kicked in. I turned around just in time to see a small figure with an upraised arm and bottle attached, aiming to land it on the back of my head. It was quiet in the street and he had made no sound coming up behind us. I looked at his face in the dim light and invited him to go away, in the first phrase that sprang to mind.

There was an instant of suspended menace before he melted away into the darkness as silently as he had come, and we continued our way towards the safety of the bright lights and the main street.

Antonias and I often talked about religion and philosophy, in our cabins or on the bridge; we watched the night sky together and fathomed out the origins of life to our mutual satisfaction. He had once spent a year alone on a small Greek island, his only book being the Bible, and was quite an unusual character to find on a ship. During this trip I was the only one on board whom he would allow to give him a prescribed course of penicillin injections. I have a horror of all things medical, and giving a week-long, twice daily course of injections in somebody's behind was the last thing I needed. But we were in the middle of the ocean, someone had to do it and I drew the short straw. Both of us found the whole thing hilarious for some reason. Maybe it was the type of laughter that takes over when something is a bit serious and you have to find the humorous side to help deal with it. Antonias told me about Theofilos Kairis, a philosopher hanged on Andros in the middle of the 19th Century whose body was burnt by the Church. His writings are kept under lock and key on the island and the government will not allow them to be examined; they have remained unseen since his death, together with a room containing preserved animals. One wondered what he knew that the authorities didn't want the people to know.

We crossed the date line once more, the days merged into one another and time meant nothing, except in the wireless room and on the bridge where we had to keep touch with reality. Every day at noon the time signal was taken from Rugby LW radio station in the UK to check the accuracy of the ship's chronometer. This allowed the Captain to verify the ship's noon position, which he took by sextant and duly entered in the ship's Log Book. Whilst George was on the wing of the bridge adjusting the sextant I was in the chart room leaning over the chronometer balanced in its wooden box waiting for his signal. When he shouted, 'etimos', (get ready), followed seconds later by, 'poop', (whatever that meant), I noted down the exact time shown on the chronometer, enabling him to carry out the calculations to fix the ship's position and make any necessary adjustment to our course.

During the two-hour wireless periods, all ships maintained a continuous watch on a common frequency, 500 kc/s. Contact was made by morse with other ships or coastal stations on this calling frequency, after which the two stations moved to a working frequency in order to leave 500 kc/s clear. Twice every hour, at 15 minutes and 45 minutes past the hour, all traffic on 500 kc/s ceased for three minutes so that any faint distress signals could be heard. At fixed times, all coastal and international shore stations broadcast traffic lists of ships' four-letter call-signs in alphabetical order, the ship then calling the station on one of its working frequencies to obtain its message. Weather reports and navigation warnings were also sent at fixed times by coast stations and these were monitored and passed to the bridge. In addition to the PMG 'Handbook for Radio Operators' all ships carried an 'International List of Coast Stations' which gave the information necessary to communicate with any coast station anywhere in the world. All shore stations were given a 3 letter call sign and all ships a 4 letter call sign. There was also a 'List of Special Services Stations', which included D/F stations.

The sighting of whales was a common occurrence. On this trip we passed so close to a pod of half a dozen of them that we could hear the sound they made when blowing water into the air and, had the wind been in the right direction, we should have had a free shower. We reached Vancouver, spending the best part of a week discharging cargo and moving from berth to berth. Canada seemed much like the States but slightly more reserved, the States being more 'wide-open' and easy-going. Our last berth in Vancouver was close to the entertainment district and was far too convenient for the likes of me, who practically lived ashore when the ship was in port. One stage show that I saw featured a floating piano. Don't ask.

We passed Stanley Park and sailed beneath the Lion's Gate Bridge on our way from Vancouver to Britannia Beach to load pyrite, a type of iron-ore that looked like cement. It was very heavy and a small bulldozer was continuously at work in the hold, levelling it off. Ashore were the mine workings and a solitary store, offshore a few fishing boats bobbed about at anchor. In 1921, heavy rain had breached the dam above the little town, washing its buildings into the sea with the loss of fifty lives. From Britannia Beach we crossed to Nanaimo to load timber, before returning to Vancouver. Our next port was New Westminster, typical of many of the small townships in the area with its wide main street and forested backdrop of snow-capped mountains. There was the usual mix of small shops with canopies over the sidewalk, at least one cinema and yet more Greek cafes for George to lure me into and stuff me full of cakes. We returned to

Nanaimo for a couple of days, loading cargo before moving the short distance to Port Alberni. It was all very beautiful, the grandeur of the snow-covered mountains, the endless forests bathed in sunshine, the blue skies with an occasional white cloud, the blue waters and invigorating air.

24: LUMBERJACKS AND FORESTS

Port Alberni had knocked off for the weekend when we got there so nothing would take place with the cargo until Monday. The weather was perfect, not a cloud in the sky, so three of us hired a boat with an inboard motor for $1 an hour and set off to explore the coastline, picnicking where we fancied and trying our hand at catching fish. As the *Gannet* moved about the area between ports we had noticed the many small whirlpools created by currents running out from rivers and narrow passages between islands, so we kept our little boat near to the shore and clear of them. In the evening the ship chandler took a few of us in his car to the Stamp River Falls, which looked to be a typical salmon river as it roared along through a thickly wooded rocky gorge. Signs at the roadside read 'Live Cougars' and 'Deer on Roadway', but we saw neither. On the way back to Port Alberni we made a call at a drug store for milk shakes before travelling along the Alberni Highway to Cameron Lake, stopping by the lakeside to eat peaches, grapes and cherries whilst the sun sank behind the mountains and the surface of the lake went dark. The drive back took us through McMillan Park and we were on board by midnight.

The *Cormorant,* another of the Company's ships, was on a similar trip to ours and we kept meeting up with her in these small ports, so there was a lot of coming and going, singing of Greek songs, and sounds of revelry by night. When we were ready to leave Port Alberni it was discovered that one of our crew was missing. After phoning around he was located in the local hospital, but apparently no one there could understand what he was trying to tell them, so the Mate took me to the hospital to help with the interpreting. Situations like this where there is a mild panic and you tear around in taxis, working against the clock, expense no object, were always a welcome diversion. We sorted it all out and sailed, almost on schedule, for Port Tahsis. There wasn't much wrong with the seaman concerned and they flew him back by seaplane to rejoin us at Port Tahsis a couple of days later.

Seaplanes were the usual mode of transport in those isolated places and our Agent made his visits to the ship in this manner. It was a joy to watch the plane coming in low over the water and see the spray flying as the floats touched the surface. In the primeval silence you could hear the plane's engine from some distance, and there was usually an audience leaning over the ship's rail by the time the plane came skimming over the water, coming to rest near the ship. Port Tahsis was a one-mill town with the whole population of six hundred being employed by the timber mill, logging, sorting, treating, stacking and loading. There were no roads or even trails out of the township as it was hemmed in on all sides by mountains; it lay at the head of an inlet and the only way in and out was by boat or seaplane. Weather permitting there were two planes a day, morning and afternoon. Low cloud accumulated in the inlets where the mountains were high, but more often the snow on the mountaintops could be seen, sparkling in the sunlight until the last rays disappeared. In the late evenings you could hear many different animal calls which continued into the silence of the night. What a contrast to the clanging of winches, the sound of chains being dragged along the deck and the banging of iron upon iron that was our usual fare when trying to sleep in port.

When we had arrived in Port Tahsis, the Customs Officer, Immigration Officer and Health Officer had boarded us to deal with these various matters, but this didn't take long as they were all combined in the form of Sid. I was dealing with the ship's paperwork as usual and after we had finished Sid invited me to his house for a meal. His wife was called Betty, they had three children, two kittens and a dog. The housing was supplied by the Company and reminded me of similar timber houses in Sweden. Sid's wife and children had only arrived seven months previously but he had been there for nine months prior to that, waiting for a suitable house for the family to move into. They told me about the cougars in the area, one of which had only recently carried off their neighbour's dog, and less than three months before that, a cougar had attacked a woman as she walked the short distance between neighbouring houses. Mountain lions had seldom attacked people or small animals in the past, but as logging camps spread across the countryside men gradually killed off the deer, the cougar's natural food, and the hungry cougars turned to attacking cats, dogs and even humans, who happened to stray into their territory.

Cougar attacks mostly took place late at night, and it was late at night when we were sitting around in Sid and Betty's house, quite some distance up a lonely track and well away from the ship. Consequently, it was a relief when Sid said that he would get his torch and the dog and accompany me back to the ship. It was a dark unlit lonely road, with the mountainside, undergrowth and the noise of a waterfall on one side and bushes, (ideal cover for an enterprising cougar it seemed to me), crowding in on the other. I was talking to Sid in a high-pitched voice as we walked along, my mind in overdrive imagining mountain lions leaping out from both sides of the road at once, and it took some little time to calm down sufficiently for sleep, once back on board.

The amenities provided for its workers by the timber company included a coffee shop and a small cinema, which showed films twice a week, admission 60c. The films were all quite old, but it was an event, and a few of us went along one evening, sitting amongst the lumberjacks and loggers on wooden benches, watching some black and white epic, the name of which escapes me now, as it probably did even then. There was also a barber, who conducted business for a couple of hours on four nights of the week in a storage shed. We borrowed a small boat and paddled along the shore and round the headlands looking for oysters, of which we found but few. Pulling the boat onto the beach we scrambled amongst the bushes and wild flowers inland a little way, but the only wildlife we came across was birds and squirrels.

The weather was fair when we left for the UK with 50,000 planks of Douglas fir stowed high over the hatch level, so we hoped that it would be a calm trip without bad weather, otherwise we should have a really splendid list by the time we reached England. Putting into San Pedro for bunkers, I was gifted a cord necktie from the Pilot, with whom I had been having a long and interesting conversation, as he took us through the channels into port. The passage down the Californian and Mexican coast was uneventful, but as we approached the canal we really copped for it, with strong winds and lashing rain. Panama was reached at two in the morning and we anchored off until Customs came aboard at first light, then passed through the locks at Balboa at breakfast time. Sheets of rain swept us through the Gatun Lake, reaching Cristobal at teatime and going alongside in a tropical downpour. Establishing myself in the Olympia Bar, just across the street from our berth, I stayed there until we sailed at midnight, the rain continuing to bucket down, thunderstorms, lightning, cloudbursts, the lot. The US battleship *Missouri* passed us in the gloom, making for the canal; she was the vessel on whose deck the Japanese signed the surrender document which finally ended the Second World War. Hurricane Carole was sweeping through the Caribbean before turning herself into Hurricane Dolly, and we felt that the sooner we got out of the area the better.

Gradually we pulled out of the storm belt, headed east across the Atlantic and entered the NE trades, carrying only a slight list. The sea was calm, affording the opportunity to put up a new set of aerials, a job best done at sea when the deck is clear, but this time there was the deck cargo to contend with. The bosun and crew laid the lengths of aerial wire along the deck between the masts, draping them up and over the deck cargo as they went. I measured the down leads, made allowance for the varying height of the deck cargo, shackled on the insulators, calculated that the array would be the right length when hoisted into place, crossed my fingers and hoped I'd got the figures right. All went well and the job took a little over a day.

The trip to Gravesend was uneventful, and we anchored there before moving to a discharge berth in the Surrey Commercial Docks. The Yorkshire Pullman took me home from King's Cross and I treated myself to a 1st Class trip behind one of the LNER's streamliners, all shiny green livery and alive with steam and smoke. Eileen arrived before midnight; it was wonderful to feel her in my arms once more and we talked through the night, leaving after breakfast for Rose Street. In the days that followed we spent time at the caravan by the sea, walked along the beach once again, talked through the months of crossed and confusing correspondence until, all too soon, it was time to return to London and the *Gannet*. The next few days were spent attending to wireless matters, in between visits to the Maritime Museum at Greenwich, the Granville pub in Fulham to meet friends and watching Charlton lose to Sunderland. Two seamen who spoke no English asked me to show them around London one day, so I took them by tube and bus to St. Paul's, the Science Museum, Piccadilly Circus, Trafalgar Square, the Windmill, and for a meal in Soho at the Tyrol Restaurant, as being a representative tour in the time available.

The *Gannet* left the Thames for Hull, where we spent the next three weeks in King George Dock. This was propitious but no more than I felt we deserved after all the emotional anguish of the past months. Eileen and I were able, at long last, to talk through important matters at length and sort ourselves out. Captain George was escorted into town, fitted with a suit at Lipman and Silver's then taken home to meet my parents and have dinner. He was also taken to Bridlington in the car, whose springs never quite recovered from the experience. Many of the crew came home for meals at different times; mam and dad went on board for a meal and were taken around the ship by Captain George. Eileen piloted Captain George on shopping trips and Dan and George also went on board the *Gannet*. Eileen and I went to the coast by car, walking along the deserted sands whilst Raffe turned double somersaults and shook seawater all over us. After a trip to Castle Howard we called at Riccall to see Duckie who had returned home after Cambridge and Ghana; his health wasn't too good but he was his usual jovial self, delighted to meet Eileen, and there was a lot to talk about. Meanwhile, time at home was passing all too quickly and the *Gannet* moved across river to Immingham where she languished for a couple of days awaiting fresh orders. We were being chartered for six months by her previous owners, the French line Compagnie Messageries Maritime, to go to the Far East.

25: ARTIFICIAL WHALES

The *Gannet* left England for Dunkerque in mid-October 1954. On arrival we went alongside but nothing much happened for over a week, which seemed expensive at £366 per day charter hire. Some French charts had been left on board and George pointed out that they showed Paris as zero degrees longitude, and not Greenwich, as did the rest of the world. 'Vive la France'. A lot of interesting-looking boxes also came aboard, including half a dozen cases of wine for the French supercargo, taking passage with us as the representative of CMM. The supercargo occupied the cabin next to mine, so hopes were raised that some of the plonk would find its way into my cabin in the interests of entente cordiale. A doctor came aboard and injected everyone in sight against cholera, and me against smallpox as well because my previous jab was about to run out. This particular doctor was very enthusiastic with the needle and would probably have injected the ship's cat if it had been around at the time. At the end of October we left Dunkerque for Algiers, the weather was turning chilly and the wind freshening up for the winter, so it seemed the ideal time to leave Europe behind and seek the sun once more.

George had decided that the ship's hull would look smarter painted a silvery grey rather than the black which we had inherited. As a prelude to this he had orchestrated a chipping campaign to remove the years of accumulated rust from the deck, and a symphony of chipping hammers enveloped the ship. We had presently reached the red-leading undercoat stage and everything smelt of paint. The Supercargo came down to breakfast every day and went round the saloon table shaking hands. I hoped that we wouldn't reach the cheek-kissing stage, as had happened to me soon after I first went abroad, and had caught me off guard. But not so much off guard as occurred once inside the Arctic Circle. In those cold regions the concept of domestic hospitality can be all-embracing, and hopefully my actions were those of a gentleman when such hospitality was offered me.

The Supercargo had been listening to the French radio and told us there was rioting in Algiers, shooting in the streets, people were being killed and the troops had been called in to restore order. We were due there the following morning so this was a little unsettling. We spent two days alongside in Algiers and, although there was some tension, the troops must have sorted the situation out swiftly because we didn't experience any trouble. On both days, time was spent ashore with the Captain and the Agent on ship's business, our excursions being fortified by meals at sidewalk cafes. It was pleasing to be back in Algiers, my previous visit in 1943 had also taken place in a tense atmosphere, but this time it was possible to walk the streets and mingle with the crowds without looking over your shoulder. But Algiers was Algiers, always a tinderbox, and many people openly sported revolvers on the streets.

Back out at sea, heading for Marseilles, the blue Mediterranean, cloudless skies and warm gentle breezes blew away the troubled world of Algerian street life. Navigation notices continued to warn of drifting mine sightings and other problems. One of my favourite notices was one sent out by Land's End Radio, 'Artificial whale approximately 65 feet long lost by film company reported adrift vicinity of Strumble Head and is possible hazard to navigation'. Suppose you could say that. Better than a mine though. These sort of things generally invoke trains of thought and I imagined some old man in a beach hut, employed as a night watchman to guard this monstrosity, being carpeted by the boss and asked to explain why he had let go of the string.

As we left Algiers, I made contact with Geoff, whose ship was just off Suez; he had given up trawlers and gone deep-sea some months previously. The mail that we had received in Algiers included photographs, taken when the ship was recently in Hull, and these were distributed amongst the crew, much to their delight. The *Gannet* rolled gently on towards Marseilles whilst I settled to a fresh chapter of the marathon correspondence with Eileen, presently focussing on whether to emigrate to Canada.

The French coastline loomed through the morning mist, sandy grey jagged cliffs with the odd clump of green vegetation adorning its slopes. A railway running over a viaduct travelled the full length of the seaward side of the range before disappearing into the distance. The dock area of Marseilles is a tough locality, dotted with bars and small cafés set in poorly lit streets. As you walked from the old port area towards the town centre, along the Rue Canbierre, through Jolliette Square and down the Rue de la Republique, the bars gradually gave way to shops and offices. On Sundays the old port lay peaceful, with its fleet of fishing smacks and pleasure boats bedecked with flags and notices advertising harbour or river trips. Along the Canbierre were many cinemas, at least one of them open through the 24 hours. Near the Travel Bureau was the British and American Bar situated on one corner of a square, where the outdoor black market flourished on my last visit. It seemed quieter now, but foreign monies still exchanged hands at favourable rates, the usual merchandise of a dubious nature was in evidence and you felt that a murder could be arranged, if you had the necessary money. Behind the square lay the Opera House, flanked by shady bars and hotels; beyond that was the open market, a riot of colour and smells, with a book-stall at every corner to hinder my progress. The boulevards were lined with trees and the benches bedecked with lovers. What better country to be in love than France.

The radar had gone seriously haywire on the way over from Algiers and during our stay in Marseilles the French technicians spent some days sorting it out. The Captain knew many of the local Greek community and took me to lots of Greek bars and cafes, filling me up with Ouzo every night except one. That night I went to the Opera House to see 'Lohengrin', with Regine Crespin singing the part of Elsa, experiencing an embarrassing moment for my trouble. I had arrived in the Opera House at the last minute, gently awash with Ouzo, just as the curtain was going up and with the auditorium blanketed in Wagnerian darkness. The usherette took my ticket, showed me to my row, flashed the torch along it, handed me my ticket stub and a programme and waited expectantly. Alone in a strange land, beset on all sides by unfamiliar customs, there was only a split second to decide what to do in order to avoid keeping a row of French opera-goers standing up, waiting for me to pass along to my seat. It seemed reasonable to assume that, as the usherette was still hovering nearby, she was either entitled to a tip or wanted money for the programme, possibly both. Delving into a pocketful of unfamiliar coins, I grabbed one and put it in her hand in the darkness before moving down the row. Nicely settled in my seat, I became aware of a rustling sound. The rustling reached the lady in the next seat who turned to me and, without a word, gave me a 10 cent coin. With any luck it would have been a franc, five franc, a ten-franc piece but no, it had to be the most insignificant coin of all. Sometimes fate is not kind to you, but there's nothing you can do about it. Maybe I should have stayed with George and his friends in safe hands on the ouzo circuit.

Our cargo included 10 motor cars, 2,000 barrels of Algerian wine and a motor-launch, the latter secured on the after-deck. Also on deck were several hundred carboys of acid and carbon tetrachloride, stowed in the open because of the danger of fumes escaping in confined spaces. In the holds were bags of flour, sacks of parcel mail, drainpipes, roofing, rolls of newsprint and packing cases of all shapes and sizes. Most of the cargo was for Saigon in Indo China. We left Marseilles in good weather, and at midnight passed Stromboli, glowing ominously in the night sky.

Passing through the Straits of Messina, we arrived at Port Said just ahead of the dawn. A small amount of cargo and mail came on board and we traded with the bum-boats whilst workmen fixed a large searchlight on to the bow, ready for the trip through the Canal. It was a beautiful soft golden morning and reading the letters from Eileen I felt at peace with the world. Sleep was out of the question, I had been on deck as dawn broke, had watched the lights of the town fading before the sunrise and was now wide awake. Small boats glided over the water as they moved from ship to ship trying to stir up interest in their wares; wicker baskets were hoisted up with the goods and money sent down the same way, all this accompanied by shouting and gesticulating. I bought a pair of camel-skin sandals, a camel-skin photograph album and a camel-skin wallet, wondering what would happen when they ran out of camels. Camel-skin smells when your feet get hot so buy wallets not sandals.

The Suez Canal seems symbolically to separate east and west; even your thoughts adjust to different expectations. In his book, Surgeons Log, Johnston Abraham, on his first trip to sea, wrote 'for the first time I smelt the indescribable smell of the East, the smell of every inhabited place beyond Suez, the smell of foetid narrow streets, of teeming populations, of temples and joss-sticks, of tropical suns beating upon rotten vegetation.... at times when you're back home, a nostalgia starts an unrest in your blood, sends you down to the docks to watch the great ships outward bound... and envy those leaning over the rails'. Any merchant who found a rope hanging over the ship's side clambered aboard, setting up shop on one of the hatches until chased off. A 17-jewel watch offered me for £5 soon dropped to £4 and then £3. As the price went ever lower, the vendor revealed that he had a wife and seventy-five children, his house was falling down and his grandmother had dry-rot. So I bought the watch and, like everyone else on board, never left a porthole that was not screwed down, or a door that was not locked, until we left the other end of the canal.

By noon seven ships had assembled, sufficient to make up a south-bound convoy, and we set off in single file through the canal. The terrain of flat sandy scrubland gave way to the desert, stretching for miles on either side, occasionally graced by small settlements on the canal banks that brought to mind scenes your imagination creates from the Bible. Twice during the trip we had to moor to the bank to allow the north-bound convoy to pass us in the narrow waterway. As dusk fell the searchlight on our bow was switched on, illuminating the small waves that gently lapped the canal bank and showing up the stern of the vessel ahead. The whole convoy system operated continuously through the 24 hours. We anchored in the lake off Ismalia for a few hours before moving on to Suez, discharging a small part of our cargo before setting off down the Gulf of Suez and into the Red Sea.

The land was rocky on both sides, gradually flattening out into a red sandy desert, with mountains glimpsed in the distance. Reception on medium wave was blotted out by static as we sweltered under the molten sun, only the 12mc/s and 16mc/s bands coming through loud and clear. Just before leaving Suez we had taken on board four tons of benzene. What with the benzene and the acid containers, which between them covered nearly all the available deck space, we devoutly hoped that we wouldn't be struck by lightening. Krakatoa eat your heart out.

Indo China had been a trouble spot for some time. The communists in the north were threatening the south of the country, where the Americans were propping up the French government in Saigon. The government was a colonial administration just about on its last legs and it looked as though the Americans had backed a loser. There had been a long drawn out battle at Dien-Bien-Phu where French and American troops were encircled, eventually over-run, and that seemed to have been the symbolic end of hostilities. The colourful French Indo-China of my schooldays was in the throes of change, and the sooner we got there the better.

We called at Djibouti to take on bunkers and cargo and toured the town in a jeep with the Agent, drinking numerous small cups of strong coffee at each stop. Leaving the Red Sea, we entered the Gulf of Aden then the Arabian Sea, where the weather was good and sunbathing was the order of the day. Taking the Admiralty Pilot Vol.1 from the bridge I laid out on the hatch, reading about the native boats that put out from shore in this area, feigning distress in the sea lanes and causing ships to stop and offer them assistance. Once on board, the men spin yarns about being blown out to sea, begging and stealing anything they can, all their stories are false, and an instance is known of a Captain and seamen being attacked and killed by these pirates. Another odd warning for the collection, this time from Columbo Radio who broadcast the following Navigational Warning to Shipping: 'ss Bharatyal passed a huge dead body of an elephant in position 0940N, 7607E'. You couldn't make some of these up. The most interesting Navigation and Meteorological Advices were those received from the U.S. concerning patches of discoloured water reported by ships, unusual current movements revealed by bottle messages, and many other strange and unexplained mysteries of the oceans.

The owners advised us that the Charterers had exercised their option to make the voyage into a round-trip, and that we should be returning to Europe after Vietnam, with possibly further charters thereafter. This was good news; although it could mean more separation in the immediate future it would help raise the money we needed in order to get married. Foreign-flag ships were becoming harder to come by as more and more R/Os were going freelance, and I had been ashore many weeks before joining the *Gannet*. Having finally landed one of these ships it behoved me to stay as long as possible; the money was twice that of a British ship, and it was cash we needed now.

On St. Nikolaos Day, the seventh of December, we had fritters and brandy for breakfast, St. Nikolaos being the patron saint of seamen. Every night there was a perfectly formed ring of cloud round the moon and, with no light pollution in the middle of the ocean, the Milky Way and individual stars stood out clearly, their colours sparkling even more intensely when viewed through powerful binoculars. Conversations, philosophical or otherwise, help to pass the lonely night watches at sea and I would sometimes go on the bridge after my last watch, to talk with the men on watch or just borrow the binoculars and sit alone under the night sky wondering what we are supposed to be doing here, specks of stardust adrift in a cosmic ocean. We were now approaching land, about ten miles south of Ceylon and encountering hot and humid land-based weather as we made for the Malacca Straits.

At Singapore we anchored off until dawn, going alongside the oil terminal at Pulam Buko to take on bunkers. Cousin Geoff was doing his National Service in Singapore and had been alerted by letter ahead of time. Going ashore in the Agent's launch, I phoned him and we met outside The Arcade, spending a couple of hours sightseeing, then going to a Services club for a game of table tennis before it was time to return on board. Geoff came with me in the launch and, as we had a little time before sailing, we put this to good use in my cabin with wine and cigars. Last seen, he was disappearing happily but unsteadily down the rope ladder to the waiting launch shouting 'Merry Christmas' and 'Up the Tigers'.

Leaving Singapore for Saigon, we arrived off Cap St. Jacques at the entrance to the Mekong Delta and anchored in Coconut Bay to await the Pilot. It was the week before Christmas 1954. With the Pilot on board we moved up river to the Lazarete anchorage, staying there for a few days so that the local mosquitoes could size us up and the large flying cockroaches could use us for target practice. A number of Russian ships passed us, taking released Vietminh prisoners back to Haiphong in North Vietnam, wooden huts having been erected on the decks of the ships to provide accommodation for them. George said that if you burn sugar it keeps the mosquitoes away at night; but if you stay awake all night burning sugar when do you sleep? Chess was popular; the supercargo was good, and he, Antonias, George and I made up the usual contestants. After Chess, Crib was the next most popular pastime, apart from the perennial Newmarket. We moved up river, commenced discharging cargo and this was our first chance to go ashore.

26: SAIGON MEMORIES

Everything about Saigon fascinated me. The smell of flowers and incense, the busy street scenes, the temples, the architecture, the grace of the women, even the name, all spelt romance. French colonial decadence, books remembered, films recalled, and here it was, laid out before me like all the travelogues and film sets I'd ever seen, just waiting to step into. Only this was real, this was the Orient, with all its promise of excitement and adventure.

The Rue Catinat in Saigon has been called the most beautiful street in the Orient. Selecting a table in the open lounge of the Continental Palace Hotel, I prepared to watch the world go by. The rickshaws weaved their way through the crowded street, Eurasian girls in their elegant national dress glided by, arguably the most beautiful girls in the world. The large ceiling fans distributed the warm air gently and impartially throughout the lounge. Sitting in the rattan chair under the canopy that stretched out over the pavement, ice-cold beer on the table beside me, Somerset Maugham, Hemingway, Graham Greene writing about his Quiet American, were all there at my elbow. Drama, intrigue, colonial architecture, beautiful women; all the ingredients for my fantasy were in place. I was happy. This was where I belonged.

I belonged there until the money ran out. After that I walked the streets and the boulevards, mingling with the crowds, taking everything in, the time passing quickly until late in the evening, when it was time to go back on board. Berths alongside were at a premium, the port was full of ships and we were moved to a buoy in the middle of the river to await a discharge berth alongside. The barges that transported goods up and down the river, and the sampans that carried people and smaller loads, all had a pair of eyes painted on their bow. Even should the boat be filthy and its sails ragged, there was always a freshly painted pair of eyes to help it on its journey.

Ships laden with military hardware continued to pass by. A French aircraft carrier, with planes scattered across its deck, edged so close to us that the overhanging flight deck came within touching distance of the wing of our bridge. A houseboat-cum-fishing-boat had attached itself to our mooring rope and a dozen or more people were busy gutting and cleaning fish on its deck all day long. It seemed to be the local mother-ship, because fishing-boats from up and down the river were constantly dumping their catches on its deck, so we lived with the fish smells, flies, heat and mosquitoes pretty well round the clock. In the daytime the birds, dragonflies and butterflies were truly beautiful, but the horrors that came by night were altogether different. Some of the insects were over six inches long, fat and ugly and crawled about aimlessly after they'd landed. They had chubby, hairy white thighs and were beyond a joke. The Praying Mantis was intriguing, its drastic mating habits an apposite comment on life. Fascinating, the human-like movements they made as their head turned to follow your every move. They came aboard in swarms, invading the cabins, and all our meals were eaten under the surveillance of scores of swivelling heads on stalks.

Christmas and New Year came and went whilst we languished in the middle of the Mekong River. George ordered the stages over the side, and chipping and painting became the order of the day. Stages are wooden cradles that can be lowered over the ship's side on the end of ropes for the crew to stand in and chip away rust, or paint the hull. However, more often than not a stage consisted simply of a plank with a rope around each end, and these could be a bit hazardous to stand on, especially in a crowded river. The port was crammed so full of ships, people, military personnel, refugees from the north, goods and military hardware, that it seemed at bursting point. Everyone leaving North Vietnam under the cease-fire agreement had to be evacuated within a matter of weeks, hence the bustle and the pressure on Saigon as this mass of people and material poured south, down the river and into the port.

During the month that we stayed in Saigon, I walked around the streets almost every day, often all day, bought fruit and trinkets in the Cholon Market, ate all manner of food from the street stalls, visited the cinemas and admired the flower stalls that adorned every street corner. I rode in the bicycle rickshaws, bought sandalwood soap, quantities of colourful postage stamps, a conical Chinese straw hat and a set of hand-painted Vietnamese scenes on silk. Much of the time was spent just sitting at sidewalk café tables, absorbing the faded beauty of the city, watching the passing parade. The atmosphere of empirical colonialism was slowly dying, suspense and apprehension taking its place. It was an exciting month but a sad one; immense changes were taking place and I felt lucky to have captured my Saigon dream before it vanished forever.

My parting memory of Saigon should have been something romantic, but in fact was of the Rue Catinat with myriads of shiny bottle tops embedded in the tarmac, glinting like jewels in the sunlight. It was the 23rd January 1955 when we made our way down the Mekong river, past the chunky wooden houseboats with their dogs and roosters and washing hanging out to dry, past the huddles of thatched dwellings on the riverbank, the palm trees at the water's edge, past the rice fields with their bent figures, and so out to sea. It was good to feel a sea breeze again as we turned northward, making for Tourane/Da Nang. The navigation lights along the coast had been extinguished in 1950 and had not yet been reinstated, even though the war had been over for six months, so we kept to a course that took us well away from the rugged coastline. When we arrived in Tourane there were no Pilots available and everyone was holidaying for the Chinese New Year, so we dropped anchor in the bay and resigned ourselves to waiting. Lighters put out from shore late the next day, moored alongside us and women climbed aboard to work the cargo. The discharging was slow work and took three days, during which we played chess on deck and watched the local fishermen in their coracles setting their fishing lines close to the ship. We left Tourane empty, going north to Haiphong, the port for Hanoi.

Haiphong is in the Gulf of Tongking, to reach it we had sailed from South Vietnam to a still-hostile communist North Vietnam and were feeling just a little apprehensive. The pilot took us up river, passing through rugged scenery shrouded in mist and drizzle, which complemented the sombre beauty of the surroundings. It took three hours to reach our berth and as soon as we were alongside George and I went ashore to the Agent's. The wharf was busy with ships loading all types of cargo, but the centre of Haiphong was quiet and the few shops that remained open were doing little business. Everyone who wanted to get out of North Vietnam had already left for Saigon and all that was left behind on the dockside were crates and vehicles waiting to be shipped out. In the town centre the gardens and plazas were full of army tents and there were numerous compounds surrounded by barbed wire where prisoners must have been assembled for transportation to the south. All was silent and deserted.

The R/O from an American ship, the *Coddington,* came aboard the *Gannet*, and we entertained each other for the five days of our stay in Haiphong, yarning, exchanging books and walking through the almost deserted streets. We visited the few local cafés and bars that were still open, but were often the only people there. Four or five ships left for Saigon, laden with crates and trucks. We loaded some military equipment on deck and then sailed for Campha, going back down river and proceeding cautiously along the craggy shoreline out to sea.

Thick fog descended as we made our way north along the rugged coastline and we had to anchor twice, close inshore. The journey took six hours from Haiphong to Campha and would have been extremely hazardous without radar; even with it, the trip was scary. Our siren was continuously in use as we crept along in poor visibility, its sound echoing back to us in the fog. We reached the Pilot Station a little before midnight, still in thick fog, dropped anchor and laid for the night and most of the next day. The atmosphere was dank and still, quiet as the grave, foggy and gloomy. Eventually the Pilot came aboard and we moved off, passing through the Norway Islands before anchoring again. Some hours later, when the fog had thinned to a mist, we were able to continue and it became clear why we were stopping and starting so often. Crags and stumps of islands rose sheer out of the placid waters, their sides covered in vegetation with wisps of fog clinging to them. Irregular in shape, they were dotted all around us and for three hours the pilot steered a meandering course between these sinister looking islands, often coming very close to them. Passing one tiny island, we were near enough to make out gun-emplacements cut into the side of the rock, the vegetation that hung over the ports camouflaging the guns that pointed straight down the channel through which we had just come.

27: CAMPHA AND TIGERS

At the end of a long and tortuous journey up river, the reason for our trip came into view, a huge open-cast coalmine. It was very impressive and you could see why a country at war would want to protect it. The Agent took a party of us on a tour of the mine workings by car and told us about it. The mine had been opened in 1886 and since 1946 had yielded over a million tons of coal a year, and would continue to do so for another dozen years at least. 80,000 people worked there, the whole area was solid coal, the face being worked by the 10-ton grabs as we watched was over 500 feet high. Tigers and leopards occasionally visited the outlying workings and the Agent told us that, 'Bits of dead bodies', were picked up from time to time on these lonely roads that skirted the workings. We were well inland, not far from the

Chinese border, in communist territory, on a deserted road sheltering hungry tigers and I began to feel a long way from country pubs, hot-dogs and all that I held dear.

We finished loading after midnight, moved away from the quay in the darkness and crossed over the bar to anchor and await daylight. As dawn broke, the wisps of early morning fog that clung to the islands began to lift, and we set off through the meandering channel between the islands on our way back to the sea, heading for Tourane. Once free of the land the weather was good and we turned south to follow the coastline for the next few hours.

There was tragic news on the World Service; the Hull trawlers *Roderigo* and *Lorella* had foundered near the Denmark Strait. They had been caught in a storm in the same area and in the same manner that we had on the *St. Stephen.* With no chance to run for shelter they had turned to face the onslaught, but eventually their luck ran out as the storm continued unabated and they had been forced to edge further and further northward. Once they began icing up, the increasing weight of ice on the deck and superstructure had eventually taken both ships under with all their crew. George Hobson was the operator on the *Lorella;* we had been good friends since studying together at the wireless college in 1942 and had met up often since then. A really nice lad, the last time we met was a couple of years previously when he had moved into a new house with his wife and baby. We were the same age, and it bore witness to just how tenuous is our hold on life.

Berthed at Tourane, we took some fifty pieces of army equipment on deck, tractors, trailers, lorries, landing craft supplies and general hardware, the vast majority of it American. The loading was supervised by German soldiers from the French Foreign Legion. About 80% of the Legion soldiers were German and paid £18 a month; the Officers were all French. After the cargo was lashed down, an international deputation from the Armistice Commission came on board to check that everything was to their satisfaction and we set off, expecting to take the equipment to North Africa and the coal to a French port, yet to be advised.

The trip down the China Sea to Singapore was tinged with the anticipation of receiving lots of mail. We had been moving around in the war's aftermath, and surmised that the owners had decided against sending mail to us in Haiphong due to the volatile situation, and were sending it to Singapore to await our arrival.

We weren't disappointed, the ship received masses of mail, and our brief time at Pulam Buko was devoted to writing hurried replies before we sailed again. For some little time I had been experiencing pains in my chest, and felt that it would be wise to seek medical attention in Singapore before facing another couple of weeks at sea. The Agent took me ashore in the launch and by taxi to the surgery, where the doctor was a White Russian, very direct and likeable. He dispensed with mod-cons like stethoscopes, put his ear to my sweaty chest, chatted a while in broken English, pronounced me deficient in calcium and sent me on my way with some tablets and lots of guttural joviality.

Passing down the Malacca Straits under blue skies, we settled into seaboard routine once more, preparatory to the two-week trip to Aden. The outside air temperature was 110F and in the wireless room 94F. The idea of emigrating to Canada after I left the sea was still in the forefront of our planning. For economic reasons it would probably mean my going to live there whilst studying for the necessary wireless qualifications, with Eileen joining me later, the aim being to obtain work on one of the Canadian coast stations so that we could be together. The dust was blown off Dowsett and studying recommenced. At least I studied when it was possible, between frequent interruptions by George, who most times simply wanted to sit down in the wireless room to have a yarn. It can be lonely at the top sometimes.

The anti-insect routine had been intensified over the past few weeks and supplies of Sheltox and Dieldrin for our pump-sprays were running low. We were not pestered by mosquitoes and other small flying insects when out at sea, but the resident cockroaches remained a constant menace, regarding the ship as their home and viewing everyone else as interlopers with whom they grudgingly shared space, food and sometimes beds. The Supercargo had left us in Singapore and the cockroaches had gone into mourning. Throughout his stay aboard he had enjoyed all manner of nibbles in his cabin, like cheese, biscuits and sweets and, whether he knew it or not, had shared these with the residents. Now that he had departed for the bon-vivant lifestyle ashore, the cockroaches were distraught. The supply of French goodies had suddenly and inexplicably dried up and they were no longer able to enjoy the lifestyle to which they had become accustomed. Patrols were sent out to find other sources of the good life, and, as the wireless room was next door, I copped the lot. Emergency measures were called for. Waiting until their search parties had congregated inside my cabin, I closed the portholes, sealed the vents, pumped the room full of insecticides and retired immediately. All that remained was to sweep up the corpses. Naturally it wasn't the end of the matter because Son of Cockroach appeared later to carry on the dynasty, but it helped.

Our port of discharge orders had been confirmed as Algiers for off-loading the military cargo, but there was no word on where the coal was going. It was a while since some of us had had a haircut so the cook volunteered to do the honours. A box was set up on the hatch in the sunshine, the cook brought an apron, comb, scissors and plenty of enthusiasm but little finesse. George went first whilst we all looked on with interest. The result was quite acceptable so many of us followed George into the chair over the next couple of days. We were coming within range of the Greek radio stations as we moved into the Red Sea and I found myself spending a couple of hours after my last evening watch, tuning around the dial to find some news and music to entertain the listeners clustered by the wireless room doorway. The signal from the Athens short wave station was very weak and the small radio sets in the crew's quarters were not yet able to pick up any Greek stations, so the ship's more powerful equipment and large aerial array was put to good use on their behalf.

We anchored off Port Tewfik in Suez Bay to await a convoy through the canal, which was very busy. Some of the crew were leaving the ship at Port Said to return home to Greece and were being replaced. Antonias was one of those leaving; after fifteen months we had become good friends, and our last night was spent on deck talking and drinking ouzo as the ship glided through the canal. Fresh water and stores came on board in Port Said, accompanied by the familiar hurry to get everything done as quickly as possible. There were all the ship's papers for me to sort out, plus the laborious one-finger typing of half a dozen carbon copies of the crew list needed at every port; this in addition to reading, assimilating and replying to my own mail. And then we were on our way to Algiers at daybreak, eyelids propped open with matchsticks.

The weather was good with us, but news unfolded on the radio that told a different story up ahead. There had been an SOS from a Greek trawler caught in bad weather in the Gulf of Taranto and the liner Stratheden had sent a boat manned by seven British seamen to assist her. They had rescued eleven of the trawler's crew and were returning to the Stratheden when their boat capsized in the rough seas, all eighteen men on board being drowned.

Algiers was as fascinating as ever. Discharging didn't take long as it was all deck cargo, slung by our own derricks and lowered into barges tied alongside, but everything ahead was still confused. Which port or ports were we going to, how long would we be staying there, were we having any repairs done; if so, where and how extensive, what of the next voyage, where to and for how long? What combination of these events would allow time to see Eileen? Everything revolved around her. We received orders to proceed to St. Nazaire, still with everything up in the air.

28: ENGAGED AND PARTED

The first morning in St. Nazaire saw me up with the lark, catching the first available train to Nantes and on to Paris, arriving at Monmartre by lunchtime. Normally there would have been no time to think about going home whilst the ship was discharging cargo on the continent. However, this time we were scheduled for a spell in dry-dock in St. Nazaire after finishing cargo; and anyway there were things on my mind. There was a special BEA flight scheduled to take the Welsh rugby team back from a match in Paris the previous day, and a seat was found for me on the plane. The flight left in the late evening, giving time for a walk around Paris in the afternoon before getting to Le Bourget Airport in time to catch the flight to London, arriving at Heathrow about ten that night. Taking a taxi to King's Cross I phoned Eileen at Lambeth Hospital, where she was doing her Part 1 Midwifery training and starving to death in the process. It was just before midnight when I left London, arriving home at five in the morning.

After a couple of busy days I caught the morning train, and Eileen, having just come off night duty, met me at King's Cross. A taxi took us to the Premier Hotel where we booked two rooms. SUCCESS! At three o'clock that afternoon I asked Eileen Frith SRN, earning £9 per month, yet again if she would marry me, and at last she said, 'Yes'. After reassuring her that I wasn't after her money, I said that I didn't know what the future held for us but whatever it was it wouldn't be boring. The following morning, before she could change her mind, we walked into the West End where she chose the ring at the Goldsmiths and Silversmiths jewellers at the corner of Oxford Street and Regent Street. Back at the hotel I fitted the ring on the finger of the most beautiful girl in the whole world. Afterwards we listened to the radio, England beating Scotland 7-2, and in the evening went to the Royal Festival Hall where Andre Kostelanetz was conducting a Tchaikowsky concert, concluding the day with dinner at Chez Auguste.

The next day we wandered around London, hand in hand, me on clouds seven, eight, nine and ten, and in the evening took a taxi to Lambeth Hospital where Eileen was due on night duty. The parting outside the hospital was awful. Months and months apart, then meeting, the proposal, the engagement, a surge of happiness and now everything deflated, all within 48 hours. Eileen had her duties to help her cope, for me there was a solitary journey by the night ferry from Victoria Station back to France. The sleeper was comfortable enough but I slept little, and was still feeling sorry for myself over breakfast as the train pulled into the Gare du Nord at nine in the morning. Depositing my bags at the Monmartre station I walked around Paris, the city of lovers, alone, until it was time to catch the train to St. Nazaire. The *Gannet* was in dry-dock, and with everything shut down, she was cold, cheerless, practically deserted and it seemed a fitting end to the day.

The charter period had ended and the *Gannet* was being returned to her owners so there was a deal of paperwork to help George with. The routine wireless inspection was carried out successfully and a new Certificate issued, also a new lifeboat transmitter had been delivered. A couple of days later we came out of dry-dock and sailed in ballast for Casablanca, on our way to the Far East. A pile of literature had arrived from Canada about wireless schools and, after studying this, Toronto looked favourite, but it seemed we should need at least £1,700, which we didn't have.

When we reached Casablanca there was trouble in the town. The Captain and I went ashore to the Agents but didn't stay long and once back on board he cancelled all shore leave after 8pm as a precaution. We loaded 10,000 tons of phosphate for Japan and, with all doors and portholes tightly closed against the swirling phosphate dust, were virtually prisoners in our cabins whilst the loading took place. The cabins became unbearable in the heat and it was a relief to put to sea when loading finished the next morning. As compensation, we had a placid weeklong trip to Port Said through a sparkling calm blue Mediterranean.

At Easter there was the celebration party at midnight

culminating in the red egg ceremony, when last year's red egg was thrown overboard and a new one took its place. My egg was hung by a piece of string from the main aerial switchboard in the wireless room and I wondered if its talismanic properties would manifest themselves in the year ahead. As we approached Malta, a flock of small white-breasted blue birds took over the ship, flying up and down the alleyways, through open doors and portholes, twittering away like canaries. Some flew into the wireless room, had a look at the red egg and flew out again, except for one who stayed to let me tickle its chest before flying off.

George told me that there was a 32,000 super tanker building in Japan, also a 12,000-ton cargo ship building in Sunderland, Goulandris wanted him to take the cargo ship and he asked me to go with him. We passed the *Himalaya* close up off Port Said at midnight. The Agent brought the mail aboard shortly after we anchored and everyone stayed up reading and replying to it, ready to post our letters at the other end of the canal. We passed the *Devonshire* en route and heard that the *Empire Fowey,* homeward bound from Hong Kong with 1600 troops on board, had gone aground in the canal, causing an obstruction. Fortunately we had just passed the blockage point when this happened, and continued our passage unhindered into the Red Sea, where sea-watches were set once more. The early morning watches in the tropics are free of static unless there is a storm around, but as noon approaches, the static increases on MW until by teatime it becomes one long snap, crackle and pop. You have to turn down the volume control as far as possible whilst still trying to hear morse signals through it all. It is so bad by the evening that only stations close to hand can be heard. The *Canton* and the *Neptunia* passed us as we made our way south.

Going alongside in Djibouti we got a lift in the ship-chandler's jeep to a café, afterwards looking around the shops, which were few and uninteresting. I went aboard an Italian ship to see the R/O, then onto a Costa Rican vessel where there was a British R/O. Greek owners operated 800 ships world-wide, only a quarter of which were registered in Greece, the remainder sailing under flags of convenience. The tax savings under these flags of convenience were very considerable to the owners, and they were not the only ones to benefit. Over 9,000 Greek seamen manned these ships and together they sent some £500,000 back to their families, and thus into the Greek economy, every month.

Off Socotra we enjoyed the usual dolphin escort, about twenty arriving to show us the way, leaping gracefully across our bows before plopping back into the water, in what appeared to be sheer enjoyment. During the night, flying fish landed on deck, attracted by our deck lights. They were silver, about a foot long, and when cooked for breakfast had a pleasant and distinctive, taste. Nearing Singapore we saw an eel-like creature flipping along on the surface, twisting and turning as it went, barely touching the water before skimming along for another hundred-yard spurt.

Once again at Pulam Buko, we took on bunkers. Attempts to contact cousin Geoff this time were unsuccessful; there was some trouble ashore, so he was probably involved with that, if not actually causing it. We left Singapore for Japan to the news that the Chinese Nationalists were mining the Formosa Straits and the islands nearby. The *Gannet* presently looked like a mobile sunset, covered in red lead, which was not an appropriate colour when passing Formosa. There had been the sound of chipping hammers every day for the past year or more and we all hoped that the noise and effort was going to prove worthwhile in the end. A waterspout appeared in the distance and a couple of USN flying-boats flew low over us off the coast of Formosa, probably checking our course. We passed Bataan, the scene of desperate fighting not so many years previously. When we reached the Japanese coast we proceeded by swept-channel buoys to a point off Kobe before traversing another swept channel to reach our berth in Osaka.

29: THE BIRTH OF A STORM

Going ashore in Osaka with the Captain, his wife and the Chief Engineer, I found myself pushed to the fore whenever we needed directions or information. My Japanese was no better than any of the others, but there you go. We took taxis everywhere because we hadn't a hope of negotiating the public transport. In most foreign countries you can make out enough words to navigate, but not in Japan. Aboard our taxi, which we had hired for the day, it was hilarious at times. Once, wishing to see a famous pagoda and all communication attempts having failed, I tried the driver with the visual approach, giving gentle, downward, sweeping movements of the hands indicating the layers of a pagoda, whereupon his face lit up with comprehension and we rushed off at great speed to the nearest brothel. We did eventually get to see the pagoda and were back on board by midnight, a great day being had by all.

The Captain and his wife spent most of the following day shopping in Osaka but, with Canada in view, it was imperative to save as much as possible, so I opted out of the shopping expedition, going instead for a walk on my own along Shinsaibashi, one of the main pedestrianised streets. Here the shops were busy all day, joined by the bars which came to life in the evening, their neon signs illuminating the sky as well as the streets. It was all very colourful and made you wonder why similar activities were so drab back home; perhaps you had to lose a war to qualify for the good times.

We dined in a swanky restaurant, at the entrance to which was an arched stone bridge over a stream. Lit by lanterns, the pathway led to a stone garden with tiny streams meandering through it; seating ourselves at a table overlooking a narrow river we watched the hustle and bustle in the shopping streets below. Then, when the hot towels were brought round, we launched into a meal the like of which none of us had eaten in months; the Captain paying. There was still more shopping to be done, after which, tired and submerged in packages, we took a taxi to the Metro Cabaret, where we had the best table in the house on the edge of the dance floor.

The Metro claimed to be the fourth largest cabaret in the world and there seemed no reason to disbelieve them. The gently curved velvet settee that encircled our table was opulent and a work of art in itself. A 25/- ticket entitled you to a girl companion of your choice from lots of lovely creatures, all marvellously gowned, a meal, a drink and all tips taken care of. I hadn't seen so many pretty girls in one place at one time for ages and felt like advancing on all fronts, but it didn't seem the time or the place. Anyway, I was engaged to the most beautiful girl in the world; though it didn't help that she was half the world away. What might the words of the song have been, 'When I'm not near the girl I love, I love the girl I'm near'. Think pure thoughts I told myself, and engaged George in conversation about mineral futures and the price of wheat in Saskatchewan, subjects dear to his heart and always good for a boring half-hour. The wine flowed, the cabaret was excellent and apart from the Captain, who was accompanied by his wife, we each had our girl table companion to engage in innocent conversational fun with, and it all made for a very enjoyable evening.

When the cabaret party got back on board, past midnight, the Captain and his wife busied themselves unwrapping packages and holding forth about the day's activities to the less fortunate who had not been ashore; all this at the top of the vocal range and continuing into the early hours. None of us understood the Mysterious East any better after our day out, but money talks in any language, sometimes very loudly. It wasn't talking very loudly to the dockers working in our holds however; they earned 300 Yen, about six shillings, for a day's work, about the same as a decent cup of coffee in the fashionable part of town.

It took 48 hours to sail from Osaka to Yokohama, the weather was perfect and we had a picture postcard view of snow-capped Fujiyama, Japan's sacred mountain, passing it about forty miles distant. In Yokohama there was the usual trail around in the morning to the Agent's, the Ship Chandlers and other concerned parties, the afternoon was spent in the Isezaki Street shopping area and we were back on board by teatime. The next day there was more shopping, sightseeing and a slap-up meal at the Seven Star restaurant.

The following day the Captain, his wife, the Chief Engineer and I travelled from Yokohama to Tokyo by taxi, the best part of an hour's journey. We visited the Liberian Consul before going to the offices of Dodwell and Company, the Ship's Agent, who sent us all our telegrams in the Pacific area. Poor innocent Dodwell, if they'd only known how their name was taken in vain when we received their cables ordering us to different ports, to do extra trips, or giving us other information we felt we could do without. I would take the message up to the bridge and hand it to George, who would read it, snort, and say, 'Plenty bastard Dodwell', after which I'm sure he felt a lot better. Business at the Agents completed, we went sightseeing, first to the Emperor's Palace then walked up and down the Ginza, the main shopping street. Wherever we went, George was the centre of polite attention, being very large, and dwarfing everyone around him. Feet complaining, we dropped anchor at the Shirobasha Coffee House, paying a worker's daily wage for a cup of coffee.

The party wanted to visit the Zoo but I demurred; when you've seen one ostrich you've seen the lot and seeing animals kept in captivity disturbs me. Instead, I stayed in town and took photographs of the gaudy neon signs that were springing to life as dusk crept over the city, enjoying the freedom of walking through a strange city alone, not knowing anyone, nor the language, or even what the signs meant. Late in the evening I caught the train from Tokyo to Yokohama and had a beer in a dockside cabaret whilst waiting for the ferry to the ship.

We left Yokohama in ballast for Canada. The weather was misty, but cleared up when we were free of the land. As our curving course took us further north, it became colder and the fog came down, persisting until we reached Vancouver, where the *Orsova* preceded us down the channel to the docks. We had been carrying some dirty cargoes lately so the holds needed cleaning thoroughly before we could load our grain cargo. After dusting and washing down, wooden posts were fastened round the perimeter of the holds which were then lined out with strong paper. Our berth was in the middle of town at Evans Coleman Evans wharf, which was very convenient; too convenient for someone trying to save money. But it cost nothing to walk and I was good at that; also the cinemas were cheap and passed the time agreeably. Cleansing completed, we were moved to the Pool Elevator, miles out of town, to spend a few days loading bulk wheat. During previous visits to British Columbia I had become friendly with Bill Corson, the local Marconi inspector, who was originally from Hull. On one of his free days he collected me in his Ford Zephyr for a drive round Stanley Park, English Bay and other tourist spots. We sailed from Vancouver on a beautiful June day, bound for South Africa with a full cargo of wheat.

In Greece, or anyway in the Greek islands, where the majority of our crewmen came from, when a girl gets married she must possess a house as her dowry. I made a note to tell Eileen about this. On an annual salary of £108 I reckoned she should qualify for a sizeable mortgage.

Reaching San Pedro after an uneventful coastal voyage, we took on bunkers and left for Balboa. The weather was becoming warmer day by day as we trekked south down the coast and I felt sorry for those on board who worked in sweltering conditions, like the cook and the men in the engine room, the latter seeming to get thinner each time they came on deck for some fresh air. On the 6th July 1955 in position 14.50N, 98.08W all was calm when I turned in around midnight; it was hot, but not unduly so. By 0400 the sea began to run heavy and the wind suddenly went from zero to 55 knots. There had been no weather warnings from the San Francisco Weather Bureau, on which I had been keeping watch, so we decided to send off an OBS, a weather observation, to the nearest coastal radio station. During the day we received requests from shore for further OBS and it was apparent that we had the dubious honour of being the first to observe the formation of a new storm centre. A few hours later the first of a series of 'Tropical Storm Warnings' was issued by the US Weather Bureau at San Francisco for 'Posn. 15.08N 107W at 081200Z moving WSW'. Having moved on by then, we were experiencing thunderstorms and heavy rain but no longer the active storm conditions. We passed a large group of turtles going nowhere fast, they had just a small part of their shell showing above the water, raising their heads now and then to breathe and to check that the road ahead was free of traffic.

A few days later we entered the locks at the Panama end of the Canal and fresh water for the boiler was taken from the Gatun Lake as we passed through it. After a few hours ashore we left Cristobal late that night for Trinidad, and there followed five lazy Caribbean days enjoying the music from the West Indian radio stations on our way to Port of Spain. We anchored in the bay and I took the first available launch to shore, but after walking the streets for a while, Port of Spain didn't seem to have much going for it, not in the daytime anyway. We left for South Africa, discharge port to be notified later.

30: DEVIL'S ISLAND AND APARTHEID

The Apprentice was well educated, his English was good and we sometimes got together to create a pool of sanity when things on board got us down. Writing to Eileen also helped to get things off my chest. It was vital for me to stay on board as long as possible in order to save the money we needed, but it was becoming harder by the day. One of our firemen was sick and we radioed New York Medico for advice. They replied that, from the symptoms described in our wire, he was probably suffering from heat exhaustion, the treatment they prescribed being a saltwater drink four times daily. I took salt tablets in the tropics and worked above decks, so the diagnosis and treatment made sense. We passed near to a small island, Fernando de Noronha, about 4S 33W, known as the Brazilian 'Devil's Island'. It looked lonely and forbidding, a dot in the vastness of the ocean, baking under the shimmering equatorial sun.

In the middle of the South Atlantic I struck up a conversation on the key with Sam, the Canadian R/O of a Liberian ship, the *Marcell*. In the lonely stretches of the ocean where there aren't many other ships about, you sometimes heard a ship's morse signals becoming louder as two vessels made to pass each other, often out of sight. In this case we were following the same course, the *Marcell* being about a hundred miles astern of us. Operators often called each other up on 500kc/s and then transferred to a working frequency, either W/T or R/T, exchanging TR's and news about their voyage, or simply to gossip. Sam had called me up, having heard my signals and call-sign, which on the *Gannet* was ELIN, saying that his fiancée was called Eileen, so that got us off to a good start and I took the opportunity to quiz him about radio operating in Canada. What I learnt was depressing. He told me about the conditions, rates of pay, expenses, lay-offs, cost of living, the fact that no families were allowed on the weather stations up north, (where the pay was very good and where I had hoped to recoup some of our setting-up expenses), also it was much more costly to sit for wireless certificates than anticipated. Suddenly the whole idea of Canada seemed much less practicable.

Passing through Latitude 07.34W, the *Gannet* had completed circumnavigating the globe going east to west since leaving Casablanca on the 13th April, 115 days previously. Orders were received advising that our destination was to be Port Elizabeth. We were abeam of Walvis Bay, where George said that the swells were amongst the largest in the world, sometimes up to 30ft. high; they were presently making life pretty uncomfortable for us and we were spending as much time bouncing off the bulkheads as walking upright, using muscles we never realised we had, and becoming sore in every limb. The weather was much colder and we were slowed down by the Agulhas Current as it swept westward round the Cape from the Indian Ocean.

Port Elizabeth was very busy, the *City of Exeter, Warwick Castle* and the *City of Hull* were alongside and we were directed to a buoy to await a vacant berth; frustrating when you've been at sea for a month and were looking forward to reading mail from home. Our eventual berth at the quay was alongside the Port Radio station and shortly after we docked, Alf Townsend, the R/O in charge of the station, came on board. We got on famously and most of my spare time over the next three weeks was spent with Alf in the control room, occasionally running the station for periods on my own. It was all good fun; an unusual and enjoyable interlude. The station was on the top floor of a tower at the end of the quay, commanding views along the coast, out to sea, over the docks, the town and for miles inland. With the powerful radio equipment available you could hear the 'Voice of America' station in northern Luzon on medium wave, half a world away.

A diver was called to clear our discharge valve which had become blocked. We watched him getting togged up, his helmet screwed into place, pipes, pumping gear readied and men standing by the equipment. I had positioned myself ready to take a thoughtfully composed picture of him descending the ladder when he suddenly jumped over the side instead. The cargo discharge was slow, shovelling the grain into bags and manhandling them on to the quayside was a lengthy business; also, work stopped at teatime. But at least we had a good night's sleep for a change. The *Stirling Castle* and *Capetown Castle* arrived in port, with their sleek hulls and classic lines; poetry afloat. The pace of life was leisurely in Port Elizabeth and we found ourselves slowing down as well. Visits to the cinema, or the 'bioscope', as it was known locally, became more frequent, except on Sundays when they too embraced the general lassitude and closed their doors. There was segregation in the cinemas as everywhere else, from buses to toilets to beaches.

Upon arrival in port we had each been handed a leaflet headed 'Advice to Visiting Seamen' issued by The National Advisory Council for the Welfare of Merchant Seamen in Union Ports. The leaflet listed 9 items, including:

2. Premises, particularly in the Coloured and Indian quarters to which touts, pimps, or taxi-drivers, hansom-cabs and ricksha's may take you for liquor or women are to be avoided; you are liable to be drugged, assaulted and robbed at these places.

(a good start, this).

3. (This one in CAPITALS).

SEXUAL INTERCOURSE BETWEEN WHITES AND NON-WHITES IS A SERIOUS CRIMINAL OFFENCE IN SOUTH AFRICA AND IS PUNISHABLE BY UP TO FIVE YEARS IMPRISONMENT WITHOUT THE OPTION OF A FINE. MARRIAGE BETWEEN WHITE AND NON-WHITES IS PROHIBITED BY LAW.

7. It is illegal to smoke Opium or Dagga. Heavy penalties for handling, smoking, supplying, possession of narcotics, (etc etc).

8. The consumption of Liquor in the streets, in cabs or in public squares or buildings is a punishable offence.

The Liberian ship with the Canadian R/O was passing Port Elizabeth on her way to Lorenco Marques and Alf gave me the OK to contact him and identify myself. Sam must have wondered what on earth I was doing, first on the *Gannet* and then a week later apparently operating a Port Radio Station. Coincidence

Department: the *Fana* had also been in Port Elizabeth, quite recently too by the look of the fresh paint on the quay wall near to us. Ships' names and dates are often found on dock-walls, left by their crew whilst painting ship; the marine equivalent of 'Kilroy was here'.

The Captain received a letter from the owners which was to prove significant. They were now offering him the plum job of taking over the super-tanker presently building in Japan. This would mean him leaving the *Gannet* at the end of the trip, taking home leave until December then leaving Greece to join the new ship. Having previously mentioned this to me, George wanted to know if I would go with him. Apart from anything else, the pay would be £90 per month, tax free, another attraction of the flags of convenience. At this time the pay on British ships was about £40 a month, (£35 at Coast Stations, both taxable), so £90 a month tax free and all found was appreciably more than was available elsewhere. And this opportunity arrived just as the Canadian venture had turned sour; it was time to write an even longer letter than usual to Eileen explaining these recent developments.

A message from Alf: 'a very nice girl' had asked him if he knew 'a nice, white, English Radio Officer' who would appreciate her company to dances, cinemas, days out etc. whilst in port. This opportunity was turned down because I couldn't get Eileen out of my mind. Dan, George, and Geoff would never have recognised this as the action of the reprobate they had come to know over the years; ('reprobate' being their word not mine). Reflecting afterwards, perhaps this could have been my entry into South African society, though with my luck it could all have gone wrong, with me ending up on Robben Island next to Mr Mandela.

At the end of the wharf there was a Campanile, erected to the memory of the first British settlers in 1870. There were 200 steps to the top, a superb vantage point for photography, but a bit noisy because of the bell which tolled every quarter hour. Alf took me for a drive into the surrounding countryside, passing some shanty towns and stopping frequently to allow groups of monkeys to cross the road in their own time. We visited a Kafir village, then called at ZSQ, the main Coast Station, to have a look around and meet the Operators, ending the day at Alf's house for a meal. Back on board, orders had been received to proceed to Durban to load grain.

During the trip to Durban, all the talk with Captain George was about the new ship, and having thought it through, I agreed to go with him. He said it was a large vessel, with two Operators, and that I would be in charge. However, having sailed on 2 and 3-Operator ships previously I preferred sailing on my own, though the work and responsibility was obviously greater, and George agreed to put this proposal to the owners, who later gave it their approval.

31: A MARRIAGE HAS BEEN ARRANGED

Captain George invited Eileen and me to spend part of our honeymoon with his family on the island of Andros in the Ciclades. It all seemed too good to be true, not only in the broader picture but the minor aspects too. At a time of currency control, when travellers were only allowed to take £100 out of the country, we should be able to transfer abroad whatever money we wished, and have our path smoothed generally. George also promised to have my original salary increased. It was the top job in the company for both Captain and R/O so George said we ought to be well paid, and I agreed with him wholeheartedly.

Durban was very pleasant; reputedly the most British of the South African ports even down to the double-decker trolley-buses, the buildings were traditional, the streets clean and the beaches delightful. The cinemas, however, had an annoying practice of halting the feature film halfway through in order to show twenty minutes of adverts, thus encouraging the audience into the foyer to consume ice cream. We stayed alongside the grain elevator at Maydon Wharf for a week, loading 9,500 tons of maize for Europe, calling at Capetown on the way for bunkers.

Before leaving Port Elizabeth we had been honoured by the arrival of a cat. We expected she would go ashore in Durban, but instead she roamed all over the ship and those of us who were cat-wise reckoned she was looking for a nest. Apparently I was responsible for her coming aboard, though unwittingly. There was an Italian ship close by our berth in Port Elizabeth and I had been aboard her, swapping stamps with the R/O, and had noticed a cat roaming around. She was affectionate, I had stroked her and she had followed me off the ship onto the quay. She took a lot of persuading to return on board, but eventually trotted back up the gangway; or so I thought. The Apprentice told me later that he had seen her follow me along the quay and onto the *Gannet*. A suitable box was procured from the storeroom and she settled in a corner of the wireless room happily enough. There were orders put in for four kittens, if and when. She accompanied us to Durban, and then to Capetown, obligingly presenting us with four kittens on the way, all of which were spoilt rotten.

George had written to the owners confirming that he wanted me on the new ship, showing me the letter that he had sent to the Directors. It was written in glowing terms and he said to me, 'I don't write even for my own brother as good as I speak Mr Goulandris about you'. If only everyone was as perceptive as George. We stayed a day in Capetown, long enough to get my walking boots on and see everything there was to see; it was my 30th birthday so a day out in Capetown had to suffice as a celebration. The captain-to-be of the *Gannet* came on board; he was accompanying us to Europe where he would take over the ship when George left. He was the brother of Eugena, George's wife, and was a very likeable man. During the war he had been torpedoed off Capetown and then settled ashore but now wanted to get back to sea.

On the voyage north, the chipping and red-leading had given way to oiling, and the decks were being regularly swabbed with fish oil. This was not good news in the tropics; the whole ship smelt of fish, but after a few days the burning sun scorched the oil off the deck and serious painting began. Crossing the equator, the kittens opened their eyes. The mother went all the way down into the engine room to the bilges when nature called, and it was really cute to see her trotting down the metal companion-ways, later bounding back up to return to her kittens. I had been in the habit of supplying her with milk by surreptitious raids on the pantry during my night watches, but one night she and her family disappeared. It was a long way down from the wireless room to the galley, and even further down to the bilges, so it was not surprising that she had 'done a moonlight', taking her family with her. She had decided that the Penthouse of Her Dreams lay in the darkness beneath the bunk in the donkeyman's cabin, more convenient for the bilges and directly opposite the galley where the cook was a soft touch. Cats take life as they find it and get on with it, they don't waste time complaining, if the scenery is better elsewhere they up anchor and go.

We pulled into Dakar once again for bunkers then passed through the Canaries between Gran Canaria and Fuerteventura. We received a telegram advising our discharge port as Rotterdam. England would have suited me much better because I was signing-off and had all my baggage to lug around with me. Ships' destinations are often notified to them by radio quite late in the voyage because of the price of their cargo, wheat/coal/whatever. If the cargo is fetching £19 a ton in Swansea and £20 a ton in Rotterdam, all else being equal you go to Rotterdam.

On the 9th of October we were abeam the Isle of Wight, some 50 miles south of Winchester where Eileen was taking her Part 2 Midwifery training. When we arrived at Maashaven, Mr John Goulandris came on board to meet his two captains and to sort out company business. He told me that there was a job for life with the company if I wanted it. We got on extremely well and were in touch for many years after I left the firm. The new R/O arrived and was shown over the gear, a luxury seldom achieved for myself. Often you take over a ship at the last minute, or when the previous Operator has already left, everything in chaos and no one to explain anything. And if you are particularly unlucky you get to take over a ship where the previous Sparks had disappeared overboard anyway.

The following day, farewells were said to the crew on the *Gannet* before boarding the *Bury* with my bags, eager to get home. Sailing was delayed so the time was spent yarning with the R/O and the captain until we left. The *Bury* could carry about 200 passengers on her regular Hull-Rotterdam schedule but had only a handful of people aboard this trip. The weather was rough, ten of us had dinner that evening, but nobody at all joined me for breakfast. Dad met me at Humber Dock and Eileen came home from Winchester the following day; she had worked a month's notice and was to complete her midwifery training in Hull after we were married.

A hectic month followed. There were many late nights and for a break we went to London for a couple of days, choosing Eileen's wedding ring from the Goldsmiths and Silversmiths in Regent Street. We saw Joan Sutherland in 'Carmen' at Covent Garden and had a meal at Chez Auguste. Eileen came with me to see Humphrey Lyttelton and his band at the City Hall and I joined other regulars at the Black Boy in the High Street for a 'Last Worthington Ceremony' on the day that they stopped serving draft Worthington at the pub, the 5th November 1955. Not many people know that. I watched City, played snooker, listened to records, saw Dan and George frequently, walked a lot and talked a lot. Dan was to be Best Man at the wedding and my bachelor night was spent at 'Ye Olde White Harte' in Silver Street, with Dan, George and Reg White of the ROU, Geoff being half a world away somewhere. The wedding was arranged to take place at Eileen's church at Trafalgar Street, the Reception being held in the church hall. We organised the honeymoon travel with Thomas Cook, everything being completed within the six weeks available.

Wedding day, 19th November 1955. At the ceremony I was nervous, Eileen was adorable and I wanted to be alone with her but had to wait. I remember making a hesitant speech at the cake and wine reception in the church hall but almost everything else was hazy. We left on the late afternoon train to King's Cross, sharing a 1st Class compartment with another honeymoon couple, finally coming to rest at the Strand Palace hotel in London and were on our own at last.

32: MULE TRAIN IN ANDROS

The following morning we left Victoria Station for Folkestone on the Southern Railway's 'Golden Arrow' boat train to Calais. We had dinner on the train and reached Paris in the late evening, to be met at the station by a Cook's representative and taken by taxi to the Hotel Universe and Portugal. Three days were spent in Paris doing the things lovers and tourists do and seeing the sights, from the Notre Dame to a table at the Lido nightclub and ascending the Eiffel Tower. We left Paris at seven one evening on the Rome Express, dining in the restaurant car, followed by a blissful night in our sleeping compartment. Passing along the coastline of the Italian Riviera the next morning the weather was perfect, the sunshine and the blue Mediterranean like a picture postcard; reaching Rome we took a taxi to the Hotel Villa Loudovici.

During the next three days we saw the sights of Rome by day and again at night, threw coins into the Trevi fountain, visited nightclubs, the Coliseum and the Catacombs along the Appian Way. The feeling of history is very tangible in Rome, we were alone when we visited the Forum and many other sites and were grateful for the solitude; it can be difficult to get a sense of anything much except statistics if you're with a group. But it was now late November, tourists were thin on the ground and the only company we had that evening, or needed, were the feral cats whose home it was.

Thomas Cook's representative took us from the hotel to Rome station to catch the train to Brindisi. Needing something to eat for the journey, we bought a couple of chicken dinners and a bottle of wine from the trolley that was being wheeled up and down the platform, laying out this feast on the small semi-circular collapsible table beneath the carriage window. It goes without saying that what a collapsible table does best is to collapse, and it did this shortly afterwards, taking our meal with it, so we spent the next few hours admiring the scenery on empty stomachs.

We boarded the *George Potamianus* in Brindisi at eleven that night and sailed for Greece in calm waters. The ship called at Corfu the following day and we had a tour of the island before setting off for the Gulf of Corinth. Next morning it was still dark at half past five as we walked about the deck, enjoying the passage through the Corinth Canal. The scenery was quite dramatic in the moonlight as the ship moved between the sheer rock sides with little room to spare. Piraeus was reached after breakfast and we took a taxi to the Acropole Palace hotel in the centre of Athens, spending the next few days visiting the Acropolis, Parthenon, Temple of Zeus, Theatre of Dionysos and seeing the Parthenon by moonlight. We counterbalanced all this culture by exploring Athens' nightlife, and at one of the cabarets we were both taken with a trio of local singers and bought some of their records to take home.

The vessel *Despina* took us from Piraeus to Andros, where Captain George lived. Visitors to the island were few. There was no wharf on our side of the island and George met us in a rowing boat into which, watched with great interest by passengers and crew alike, we packed ourselves and our suitcases, leaving about half-an-inch of freeboard. It was a couple of hundred yards to the shore, where a vintage taxi was waiting to take us along the winding roads to the village of Stenies, perched on the hillside overlooking a blue Aegean Sea sparkling in the sunlight. We walked up the path to the house, our cases following by mule.

In this idyllic setting we stayed for ten days, getting up in the mornings when we felt like it, and lazing the days away. There was a beach below the house, reached through groves of tangerines, oranges and pomegranates. George's house was on the outskirts of the village and he walked me down the rough road to Louis' coffee shop to introduce me to some of his friends. The coffee shop, on its tree lined terrace overlooking the sea, was bathed in the late afternoon sunshine and seemed to be sleeping its way through the day. It was plainly a man's world, the few tables in the shade of the trees were peopled by the village elders, the peace broken only by an occasional rush of conversation, or the need to order more tiny cups of black coffee.

306

The church of Santa Valvara was only open once a year and we joined the villagers on their annual pilgrimage. Following the service there was a straggling procession through the village, a few of us walking up the hillside to Ipikia, where we had lunch with one of George's friends before returning to Stenies. The monastery of St. Nikolaos was about three miles distant and George took us there one day, riding on mules over the rough track. The mountain top was shrouded in mist but we came out of it and picked our way down the other side. Religion plays a prominent part in island life and, following our visit to the monastery, the next morning we went to the church of Santa George. After the church service we were invited to several houses, drinking wine and eating sweet-cakes in celebration of St. Nikolaos day. This was a very happy occasion and we needed a long sleep in the afternoon. The same evening we walked along a rough path to visit a captain's house for a meal of many courses, and several bottles of wine. The return home, full of goodwill towards everyone and led by George waving a storm lantern, was made along the uneven path and accompanied by a lot of stumbling and laughter.

Valmas, a seaman from the *Gannet*, took us down to the beach one evening, crossing over a broken bridge which led to a wartime German encampment on a hill overlooking the bay. We had meals at the homes of other crew members of the *Gannet*, who were on leave before accompanying George to the new ship. Yianni was one of these; his mother was presently quite ill and Eileen went to visit her. One evening we accompanied George and his family to dinner at a nearby Captain's house, where the food and wine, as always, was bountiful. An abiding memory was the circular dinner table, which had a hole in the centre and was covered by a thick blanket, touching the floor and fitting around the diners' legs. Beneath the table was a charcoal fire, keeping the dishes in the centre, and our legs under the table, beautifully warm. It was just what was needed on a brisk November night.

A midnight service was being held at the monastery on the mountain and we rode there on mules in single file, ascending the rough winding track, following the lantern ahead as best we could in the darkness. A Greek monastery service is very colourful, with the incense, the play of the candles on the stone walls, the rich fabric of the priest's robes and the chanting of the packed congregation taking part in the traditional Greek Orthodox ceremony, all contributing to the atmosphere. The culmination of the proceedings saw everyone filing down the aisle to the front and kneeling to kiss the prized and revered finger bone of St. Nikolaos. We made our way home down the mountainside by lantern light on the backs of the mules, lurching from side to side. At the mountain top was a spring which has never ceased to flow, supplying water for the families of the village and the village wash house, a stone open-air natural basin where the women socialised whilst dashing the family laundry against the weathered stone slabs.

We left Stenies for the town of Andros in an ancient taxi, our luggage following by mule. In Andros we said our goodbyes to George and his family over coffee then boarded the bus for Batsi, joining villagers and crates of vociferous poultry for the journey. The bus was old and battered and we embarked on the journey with some trepidation. A peaceful night was spent at the Ayra hotel in Batsi where our room overlooked the quayside, awakening in the early morning to the sounds of the fishing boats going about their business in the harbour below. The ferry-boat *Karystos* took us to Rafina on the mainland, from where we went by bus to Athens and by taxi to the Hotel Thessaloniki. A last look around the shops, visits to nightclubs, and the next morning we went through seemingly endless formalities before boarding the *Achilleus* for Brindisi and Venice.

Leaving the *Achilleus* in Venice, we went by gondola to San Marc, then along the Grand Canal to the Hotel Regina. The weather had turned very cold, it was approaching Christmas and our walk after dinner was brief, but seeing the Canal in the moonlight provided a romantic ending to the day. The next morning we joined a tour and then spent a couple of days on our own, exploring Venice, feeding the pigeons in the Square, travelling by gondola and walking by the Grand Canal.

Our itinerary included a short stop-over in Milan where we had intended to visit 'la Scala', but our luck was out, when we reached Milan it was Monday and the Opera House was closed, so there was more time to look around the town and the Arcade. Our hotel was in the square opposite the cathedral, truly a striking building. Also striking was its clock, which chimed every quarter hour and kept us awake half the night. A Vickers 'Viscount' took us from Malpensa airport to London and the warmth of the Strand Palace hotel, from where we only ventured as far as the Adelphi theatre to see Shirley Bassey and Al Read in the revue, 'Such Is Life'. The next morning there was ship's business to attend to in

33: KOBE AND THE GOLDEN EAGLE

Arriving home, there was a lot to catch up on with family and friends. City spoiled the festive season by losing to Liverpool 2-1 in the last minute, but Raffe came to the rescue; we took him for a walk from Rose Street to the Pier and back again and his tail didn't stop wagging once over the four miles. Christmas was divided between the two houses, and at the New Year 1956 we went to Anlaby Common, meeting my cousins John and Paul Toffolo and their girlfriends. The weather was particularly gloomy throughout January with thick fog and snow showers so Raffe didn't get as many walks as he would have liked. But Eileen and I were together, that was all that mattered, and there would be no more late-night lonely walks home. Towards the end of the month Eileen started work as a relief District Nurse until the second part of her midwifery training commenced. City drew 5-5 against Blackpool, the second half being played under floodlights, a big deal at the time.

February announced its arrival with the heaviest snowfall since the harsh winter of 1947, the snow being measured in feet rather than inches, roads were blocked, villages cut off and services disrupted. On Eileen's day off we stayed in bed until the afternoon. Snow enhances the countryside but doesn't do much for the city and Raffe thought little to it either. We went to the New Theatre to see 'Manon Lescaut' and 'Don Giovanni'. A letter arrived from London regarding the new ship and asked me to have a cholera vaccination. The snow came thick and fast all day and every day, traffic was badly affected in the city, roads in the countryside remained blocked, cars had to be dug out, helicopters dropped food and medicines to isolated farms and snowploughs operated on the railways. Eileen gave up making her district nursing visits by cycle, going everywhere on foot like the rest of the city.

A hectic couple of days saw Eileen and me preparing to leave for London in the third week of that cold bleak February. We stayed at one of a row of typical London B&B's, contracted by the owners, where the crew of the new ship was assembling. It wasn't much of a hotel, the weather was miserable, we were dreading the forthcoming parting and it was not a happy time. We said goodbye at King's Cross on the 26th February 1956, one of the most depressing days of my life. We had clung together the previous night, not wanting to go to sleep, talking, whispering, anything to stretch out the last few hours together. But it all came to an end on a cold platform on a Sunday morning after a last cup of tea in the station buffet. All that was missing was Rachmaninoff's 2nd Piano Concerto.

Eileen returned home on the train and I boarded the British Airways plane 'Arcturus' at London Airport, leaving at noon for Frankfurt and the first stage of the long trip to Japan. It was still snowing gently as we took off; a fitting departure. Rome was twinkling with evening lights as we came in to land and this only served to rub salt into the wound. It was warmer on the ground at Beirut and even warmer at Bahrain, where it was now Monday. Our next stop was Karachi and then Calcutta, where it had just crawled into Tuesday. By the time we landed at Rangoon it was hot and humid, and we couldn't wait to get out of the sweltering terminal building and back into our air-conditioned cocoon.

Flying into Hong Kong's Kai Tak Airport for the first time was quite an experience. The plane flew low over the city for much longer than I had expected, until suddenly a large rock face appeared, almost dead ahead. At the last moment the plane veered to the right and the runway opened up before us. We were to stay overnight in Hong Kong, so passengers and crew were installed at the International Hotel. I set off to see as much as possible of Hong Kong before we left the next morning. The Star ferry from Kowloon to Hong Kong seemed a good starting point, and when I was footsore in Hong Kong I caught the ferry back and got footsore in Kowloon. The 'fragrant harbour', though something of a misnomer, is one of the great harbours of the world, the streets a never-ending kaleidoscope of colour and activity around the clock.

Next morning we boarded the hotel bus to the airport and took off, flying low over the water at the end of the runway. We landed at Okinawa for re-fuelling and, on US Army orders, had to make the approach to the island with the window blinds drawn; they were opened whilst we were on the ground but closed again when we were cleared for take-off. The chief cabin attendant had been a chief steward and shipmate during the war so we had a lot to talk about when he found time away from his cabin duties.

We landed at Haneida, Tokyo's International Airport, at teatime on Wednesday, some four days after leaving London. The Agent met me at the airport, driving to the Hotel Tokyo and installing me in a magnificent suite, the like of which I had not seen outside of a Hollywood movie. A phone call to room service produced steak, ice-cream and coffee and was followed by a luxurious bath before testing the king-sized bed. Flight exhaustion caught up with me and approaching noon the next day I was still asleep. I rallied quickly however and after breakfasting in the room set off on foot to sort out Tokyo, walking around the Ginza area all afternoon, returning to the hotel in time to be collected by a taxi and taken to Tokyo Station to board the over-night train to Kobe. The swish and impeccably clean train, a bullet train or close relative, left at eight o'clock and was due to reach Kobe early the next morning. Not being able to sleep sitting up, the night was spent drinking coffee and watching the lights of the towns and villages flash past in the darkness. On arrival in Kobe the Ship's Agent met me at the station and whisked me off to the Oriental Hotel, at that time rated the tenth best hotel in the world, according to the brochure. After being shown to my room, handed a boiler suit and hard hat, I was given a note asking me to take breakfast and be in the lobby within the hour, ready to go down to the docks.

Garbed in boiler suit and tin helmet I felt like an Air Raid Warden. But however strange I may have looked, it was nothing compared to the sight of George; it must have needed two Japanese-sized boiler suits stitched together to cater for his king-size frame. He had been in Kobe for some days and was very pleased to see me, phoning my room at the hotel even before my bags were unpacked. He was like a dog with two tails over his new charge and had every right to be, she was a beautiful ship, a real super-tanker of the day at 32,000 tons. Everything was new and smelt of hot metal and paint; there would be no chipping or fish oil here. And she had been given the perfect name, *Golden Eagle*. We were on board all the day, I was busy trying to make sense of the wireless room and its gear in between accompanying George on his inspection trips all over the ship and having things pointed out to me. At five o'clock we left the shipyard for the hotel where dinner was at seven and I just managed to do it justice before falling asleep.

In the month that I lived in Kobe the routine didn't vary a great deal. After breakfast at the hotel we were down to the shipyard by nine, working on board until noon when lunch was taken in the canteen of the shipbuilders, Mitsubishi Heavy Industries. Work continued in the afternoon until we returned to the hotel by taxi at five, with time for a shower and a drink before dinner at seven. The cuisine, the room, everything was first class, indeed luxurious; particularly enjoyable were the breakfasts, where strawberries and cream preceded the bacon and eggs, the strawberries being flown in daily from Israel. My shore wages were £20/16/- a week, plus Yen 29050 (£29/-/-) living expenses, making around £50 a week. This was a sizeable sum at the time, particularly as it was tax-free and all the hotel expenses were paid for by the Company. An occasional letter was written to Eileen on the back of a menu from the opulent dining room, to show her I wasn't kidding about the food; all letters were written from my room overlooking Osaka Bay.

The day arrived when we could take the *Golden Eagle* out into the bay on preliminary sea trials. The ship was swarming with dockyard staff, plus whatever crew had arrived to date, and there seemed to be hundreds of people still beavering away in every corner of the vessel. An aircraft flew overhead taking photographs of the ship, whilst George and I were standing on the monkey island, one of these being reproduced in the Mitsubishi company newspaper together with an article in Japanese entitled, '*Golden Eagle* meets the Spring Sea'.

Technicians were wiring up the radio gear and I would have liked answers to questions from time to time, but their English didn't stretch to explaining the more complicated parts of the installation, so I took the manuals back to the hotel each evening, trying to relate the diagrams to what I had observed earlier in the day. Further sea trials took place almost daily and when these commenced in earnest the Yard didn't mess about. We were called at five in the morning, had an early breakfast, then taken by taxi to the shipyard and by launch to the anchorage. The trials commenced at seven in the morning and continued non-stop until ten at night, after which the launch brought us ashore, leaving just enough time for a shower, dinner, and a couple of hours in bed before it started all over again at five the next morning. After a week of this we were all knackered, and after one particularly long and hectic day, when we were all on our knees, we came ashore towards midnight looking forward to bed, only to find that a banquet had been arranged for us at the Grill Tampey in the town. We were taken by taxi directly from the ship, boiler suits and all, to a private room in which kimonoed girls plied us with saki and fed us with sukiyaki and other tasty dishes, but we really would have preferred to have gone to bed.

None of us was adapting particularly well to this increasing tempo; leisurely breakfasts and back to the hotel by late afternoon was more our style. However, I had reckoned without George, who was also feeling the strain in all quarters. One day he announced that he needed time at the hotel to catch up with his correspondence and wanted me to assist him. By ten in the morning we were all done, George went out shopping whilst I stayed in my room writing letters, and in the afternoon we both went shopping in Kobe. The centre of Kobe had modern buildings and good road surfaces, but near the dock area there were lots of narrow side streets with uneven pavements, lopsided wooden telegraph poles, long sticks with lanterns hanging from them, little bonsai gardens at the entrance to tea houses, miniature stone gardens, cherry blossom trees, Japanese writing and colourful neon signs everywhere. And of course, Japanese people in abundance, all of them polite and inscrutable.

Life on the streets in Japan was a noisy affair, the trams and buses used their sirens continuously and loudspeakers blared from every street corner. Shops advertised their wares to passers-by, cinemas bombarded the sidewalks with their soundtracks as well as ringing bells for long periods before each performance. At night the colourful neon signs would surely have made any Japanese city visible from neighbouring galaxies.

George took me with him on ever more shopping trips as he sought out goods for his new house, being built in Andros. He left me to flannel through the negotiations with counter assistants, and after a few days my Yorkshire accent took on a Japanese inflection, the shop girls dissolving into giggles when addressed, or indeed on any pretext whatsoever. There were frequent meetings in the offices ashore; many of these I had to attend even though most of the discussions had no bearing on wireless matters. However one day there was an unusually large conference in the works office, and the next day we brought the Golden Eagle into harbour to tie up to the buoys. Forty more officers and crew had arrived and were housed in a large hostel especially built for incoming ships' crews by the Mitsubishi company. The officers' accommodation was six to a room but the late arrivals demurred at this, indicating that they wanted something better, so I was detailed to visit a short-list of hotels in the neighbourhood to find something more suitable. The New Kobe Hotel was chosen as being satisfactory, and not only were the new arrivals moved in there, but we stalwarts from the

Oriental as well. Bang went the five star luxury, the air-lifted strawberries and the delightful little Japanese girl in the morning saying, 'Half past seven please', on the hotel phone.

The New Kobe Hotel opened off the street and was in traditional Japanese style with sliding bamboo doors, mats for sleeping and an array of slippers in the entrance to change into when we came in off the street. Japanese prints adorned the walls and bonsai trees were dotted around. The family who ran the hotel brought in temporary beds, did their best to adapt the oriental menu to western tastes and made us very comfortable for the rest of our stay. The dockyard canteen food was good and, as the hotel was some little distance from the shipyard, we took most of our midday meals there. Workmen were busy painting the cabins and as we couldn't go aboard until they had finished, a few days were spent wandering round Kobe in small groups, sampling the local brews, shopping, sight-seeing, visiting cinemas and invariably ending up in the Morocco night club, which the ship had adopted as its shore base.

Excursions with George that were particularly appreciated were to the Ship Chandler's to order provisions for the ship. The vast aromatic warehouse was a treasure trove of comestibles; all manner of foodstuffs in boxes were piled against the walls and there were assorted meats and cheeses in abundance. George would cut off a slice of salami or a hunk of cheese, hand it to me, taste some himself and ask my opinion. As this went on all afternoon we didn't want much to eat by the time we arrived back at the hotel. Through the grapevine we heard that the *Gannet* had broken down and was presently laid up in Norfolk, Virginia, for two months worth of repairs. Two months stuck in Norfolk, Virginia would have suited me fine at the moment because the pace in Kobe had become little short of exhausting. The work in the wireless room had been completed, but in my opinion was not up to specification so, on behalf of the owners, I refused to accept it. There was a temporary impasse, but if I didn't sign for it the ship didn't sail, and as the Chief Engineer wasn't ready to sign for his engine-room either, it looked as though there would be further delay.

34: PAGODAS AND GEISHA GIRLS

Genghis Khan is not my cup of tea but, not having been to a cinema for a while and wishing to see a decent film, I consulted the English-speaking daughter of the people running the hotel and together we perused the local paper looking for likely films, but found only one in English, 'The Conqueror', about the life of Mr Khan. Not my first choice of entertainment viewing, but any port etc., so I wended my way through the narrow streets to the cinema, which turned out to be on the third floor of a large building adjoining the Sannomiya railway station. Every time a train came into the station the place shook, every time a whistle blew or a train departed we heard it, and it occurred to me that they should make a hole in the wall and let the train passengers look in for free because we all seemed to be part of one big happy family. Ceiling lights were left on in the cinema during the film and these were bright enough to read a newspaper by. The film didn't appeal; the only remembered bit was when Genghis Khan takes his wife to a feast, she scoffs at the dancing girls, and he says to her, 'Despise not the dancers if you do not have the talent'. It was dark and raining heavily as I left the cinema, everyone had parasols except me and I was becoming soaked as I picked my way through the pools and the mud, avoiding the edges of paving stones sticking up like the sea defences on a Normandy invasion beach, steering clear of the open drains that ran alongside the footpath, coming to the better roads, and eventually reaching the hotel, drenched. So much for oriental cinemas. And the sweets they sold in the foyer were insipid. Signed: Disgruntled, East Yorkshire.

At the Mission to Seamen, which was almost next door to our hotel, I picked up a leaflet on Osaka, the twin town of Kobe; it seemed an attractive city, so on my next free day I took the train to Osaka to have a look around the centre and visit the White Heron Castle, a well known pagoda. After walking around for a while, browsing in the shops and stopping to refuel in a restaurant, I took a taxi to Castle Park, showing the driver a leaflet with the photograph of the Castle on the front in order to prevent any misunderstanding. The pagoda did indeed live up to expectations, being aesthetically beautiful and worth the effort made to see it.

George was badly in need of help. I dug him out from under a pile of papers and we worked together until two in the morning, at which time he put through his regular nightly trunk call to the London office, (£15 for 3 minutes). He made another long call at 0400, after which it was hardly worth while going to bed as we had to be up at five for yet another trial, this time the Owner's Sea Trial. This particular trial was a significant one, when we could at last began to feel that the *Golden Eagle* belonged to us and not to the dockyard. Spares had arrived for the ship and the job of checking them off fell to me; some of my radio manuals were missing but luckily a nearby vessel had a copy of the Admiralty edition of D/F Stations, and some time was spent copying out details of those stations that we might need to use on our maiden voyage; enough to see us through until we could get our own copy of the book in Europe. There were lots of odd jobs still to take care of, all of them interesting, and some enjoyable, particularly the visits to the ship chandler's.

The Apprentice from the *Gannet* had been promoted to 2nd Officer on the *Golden Eagle*, and was able to take some of the clerical jobs off my shoulders. He was a bright lad and would be a sensible companion if we had the chance to go ashore, although, by the nature of the job, shore time looked like being a scarce commodity in the months ahead. Eileen and I were in full flow again with letters, about us, things for our home, (wherever, whenever), what job I would do ashore, (the biggest problem), our finances, (stretched but improving), but mainly about how much we missed each other.

The Yard invited all the officers to the launching ceremony for the cargo ship Arizona Maru. It was raining heavily as we assembled in the shadow of the steel hull that towered above us and we looked like getting thoroughly soaked, until a bus drew up bearing the dignitaries who were to perform the launching ceremony. A flunkey alighted from the bus with an armful of umbrellas, leant them near the door of the bus and began handing them out one by one to those disembarking. Choosing my moment, I carefully removed a couple of the umbrellas and thereafter we watched the ceremony in relative comfort. Clouds of balloons were released amidst music cheering and speeches, then the chocks were knocked away and the ship started to slide down the slipway as we stood almost beneath her. This was the only time I attended a launching for real and it was an impressive experience.

Another cinema showing occasional English or American films had been discovered, the Asaki, which was screening 'Richard the Third', with Olivier and Gielgud. It was a pleasant surprise to find a quality film like this in the neighbourhood so I went along and thoroughly enjoyed it. We were all quite happy in our hotel and were trying some of the Japanese food, eating with chopsticks, becoming addicted to saki and listening to Japanese

316

popular music on the radio. But it all had to end sometime, and around the end of March we left the hotel and went to live on board ship. The Chief Engineer signed for the Engine Room, I signed for the Wireless Room and George put his neck on the block and signed for the whole ship. The *Golden Eagle* was ours at last.

The traditional party was given by the Mitsubishi Company to celebrate the handing over of the ship. It was held at a splendid restaurant, the food was excellent, the setting lavish and Geisha girls danced to music played on the Koto, which has a very evocative sound. The Geisha dancing seemed repetitive and continued all the evening, between courses. During one of the lengthy dances, I whispered to George that it might be an improvement if the girl took her kimono off, an unworthy remark but one which amused him greatly. We ate with chopsticks and used the same plates for all the courses, which kept on coming and coming, as did the saki. George made a speech, half of Mitsubishi Heavy Industries made a speech and everyone was toasted, from Mitsubishi, Goulandris, the *Golden Eagle*, its captain, its crew, the United Nations, Mothers Day, and I proposed a toast to Hull City which was responded to in Japanese by those still standing. On and on it went at a merry pace until we were all practically asleep, but still the saki flowed, the girls danced on and the revelry continued until the early hours, when we were all poured into taxis and escorted safely but unsteadily back to the ship.

The night before we were due to leave, oil was being pumped aboard when a large quantity of it went through a pipe that wasn't there. The deck flooded with oil and there was general panic and confusion everywhere so I went to bed. Typhoon Sarah had made her appearance east of Manila; but that was a problem for another day. In Kobe our weather was all sunshine, blue skies and white clouds as we left port one day in early April to the sounds of the dockyard workers cheering, martial music amplified through a loudhailer from the shore, boats with hoses spraying water in the air and a plane circling above us. We set course for Singapore, some hours late on the day and one month behind schedule, but at last we were free of the shore, the ship had her first taste of freedom and everyone set about acclimatising themselves.

We were sailing in ballast and expecting to roll a bit if the weather took a turn for the worse. None of us had any experience of what a tanker felt like to sail in, empty or full, so it was a case of see how we go. Luckily, Sarah had blown herself out before we reached the waters off Indonesia and we passed through the Luzon Strait into the South China Sea with calm seas and blue skies.

There were three Japanese technicians on board; two were leaving us at Singapore with the other remaining on the ship for a year. Wireless traffic was heavy, and due to the time difference between Europe and the Far East, continued night and day, so I was on watch almost continuously, sleeping in short spells when it became feasible. This hectic period extended over some weeks whilst messages flew back and forth to Goulandris and Mitsubishi in English, and sometimes to Mitsubishi in Japanese, concerning every last detail of the vessel's problems and performance. Most of the wireless stationery that had been ordered had not arrived on board before sailing, so I made up a Log Book from writing pads. There was a navigation warning, (TTT), 'British tug Bustler towing Panamanian Semiramisire position 0400Z 16.21N 117.23E course 045 speed 7 knots. Lights on tow extinguished - Master.' This would be the same H.M.R.T. *Bustler* now plying her peaceful trade as a commercial vessel in the South China Sea. My first ship, the *Allegiance,* also under commercial owners, was later to founder in a typhoon in these waters.

The voyage from Kobe to Singapore gave time for everyone to get the feel of the ship and to see how she handled. On the radar there was a Differentiator Unit for use in rain, this proved its worth when helping us find our way through the Straits into Singapore at four o'clock one morning. It was pitch black and bucketing down, with visibility so bad that we could hardly see the bow and we brought her in by radar alone with me standing by the screen relaying information to George who joined me for a look before deciding on changes to our course. We berthed once more at Pulam Buko.

Having written to cousin Geoff ahead of time from Kobe I went ashore in the launch to meet him in the Agents office. We made our way to the Britannia Club then to a Services Club for a game of snooker, after which Geoff showed me around Singapore until it was evening and time to return aboard. Waiting in the darkness at the Jardine Steps for the small launch back to the ship, time was passing, the launch was late, the wind was steadily increasing and the water in the harbour rapidly became too choppy for comfort. The lengthy trip to Pulam Buko was made with spray and waves coming over the sides of the boat and I arrived on board an hour later, soaking wet.

35: THE ARRIVAL OF HENRY

George and I were overwhelmed by the volume of work still requiring our attention and commiserated with each other, agreeing that we should both be at home with our wives if it wasn't for the fact that we needed the money, he for his new house, me for starting married life. After pointing out to George that we ought to be grateful to have the opportunity of earning the money we needed, he cheered up a bit and we drank to that. George said that if I needed to stay at sea another two years to get enough money to settle down, I should really stay three years to, 'Fix good all everything'. This, and other George-isms, became part of our family vocabulary. I said pebbles to staying three years, they will be carrying me off to the funny farm before then. The *Golden Eagle* could discharge oil at the rate of 4,000 tons per hour, invariably at the end of a jetty and miles from anywhere, so it didn't say much for any relaxing shore time in the foreseeable future.

Making my way along the catwalk to breakfast the next morning, there was the familiar panorama of white clouds tinged with gold low on the horizon, a clear blue sky above and flying fish skimming over the water. Life suddenly seemed a whole lot better, as if you'd been away somewhere and returned to find everything just as you left it, as it always was, as it always would be. The catwalk was an exposed metal-grid with handrails, about ten feet above the deck, which provided access to the bow from the accommodation and bridge amidships, and from midships to aft. As the wireless room was amidships and the saloon was aft, there were regular daily excursions when going for meals, and mad dashes were often made along the catwalk if the seas were crashing over the side and threatening to drench you en route.

The next stop was Bahrein for bunkers, before going further up the Persian Gulf to load oil at Umm Said where we moored between two large buoys, on one of which were the ends of various pipelines. We pulled these pipelines on board and had telephone communication through one, fresh water through another and our crude oil cargo through another, the latter coming aboard at the rate of 2,400 tons an hour. When loading was completed, we opened the doors and portholes which had been shut against the unpleasant smell of crude oil and the millions of flies, then moved from the buoys to the anchorage to await high tide.

The passage out of the Persian Gulf, through the Gulf of Oman and into the Arabian Sea, was our first experience of handling the ship with a full cargo and George seemed happy with her. Passing through the Suez Canal on the night convoy meant my being on watch until we left the Great Bitter Lake. We took on more crew in Port Said, bringing our total compliment to 49. I had contacted Geoff on 6m/s a few days before we reached the canal, and collected some wireless stationery that he had left with our Ships Agent in Port Said when his ship passed through the canal a few days ahead of us. We berthed at Le Havre, staying longer than usual and, as there wasn't much to do, I walked around the dockside photographing the ships, including the liners *Antilles, America, Ile de France* and the *Maasdam*. We left for the Persian Gulf once more, passing Geoff's ship off the Channel Islands, and I had a long conversation with him on the phone. Going south through the Canal we passed an Italian ship with a deck cargo of camels, which struck me as odd. Bandar Mashur was advised as our loading port.

When we reached Bandar Mashur the temperature was 117°F in the wireless room and 124°F on deck. Everyone was suffering in the scorching heat. The galley was shut down during loading and we had hard boiled eggs for lunch. Visibility was nil due to the sand blowing off the desert, not that it mattered because there was nothing to see except miles of jetty, pipelines, storage tanks and desert in every direction. Sandstorms frequently halted the loading process and at such times there was nowhere to escape to except the cabins, which were already like ovens. If you ventured on deck, the metal under your feet baked your shoes and the wind and sand stung your flesh. When the ship eventually moved off and the portholes and doors were opened to allow the breeze in, you also welcomed in the mosquitoes and other insects that followed the sandstorm. The temperature in the wireless room was steady at 105° after we left the jetty and caught a faint breeze over the open water.

We reached the Suez Canal in mid-June 1956, the pilot told us that it had been 110° the previous week, with many people dying of the heat and collapsing in the streets. Our route to Lavera, a tanker terminal in southern France, took us through the Straits of Messina and the Straits of Monifacio. We discharged our cargo at Lavera over a 24-hour period and took on 15,000 tons of seawater as ballast. There was time for a meal at the Central Hotel in Lavera with George, but there was nothing ashore worth investigating. We left for Port Said, staying alongside for a couple of days to paint the hull before transiting the canal; when we reached the Gulf the temperature was 116° as we proceeded north to Umm Said. Loading took 8 hours and we set off back down the Gulf, the Red Sea and through the canal to Le Havre, passing the *Queen Mary* and the *Gannet* soon after we left the Mediterranean to head north. The *Queen Mary* ignored us, but I called up my old ship and was pleasantly surprised when the R/O turned out to be Reg. Dolby, a friend from our days together at wireless school.

I was rapidly becoming bored with tankers. Gone were the lengthy stays in port, gone the idle hours at sidewalk cafes, gone the visits to raunchy cabarets, gone most of the things that made life worthwhile. But the money was good and we needed that, so I got my head down, wrote ever lengthier letters to Eileen, listened to every ball of every Test Match and read a lot.

When we reached Le Havre, George took me to the Hotel Roubaix, having a meal there for old time's sake, even sitting at the same table. It was exactly as we remembered it from two and a half years back, when we were waiting to join the *Gannet.* Orders came for the *Golden Eagle* to have some repairs carried out. Now that sounded interesting, but where? We left Le Havre in ballast for Ras Tannurah to collect another load of oil. As we sailed along the Mediterranean President Nasser was making noises about seizing the Suez Canal, and all manner of frantic British/French/American negotiations were taking place as we neared Port Said. On arrival everything appeared normal and we passed through the canal without incident, carrying lots of free-loading storks, cranes and flamingos which had landed on deck.

Great news, letters came aboard advising that our repairs were to be carried out in America. Down the Red Sea we went, the whole ship in a much happier frame of mind, through the Gulf of Aden and on to Ras Tannurah where we filled up and set off for Philadelphia to discharge cargo and have our repairs carried out. It seemed that we were going to the American east coast for a routine overhaul under guarantee. Aside from the fact that everybody needs oil, I wondered why we were going to Philadelphia instead of somewhere nearer home, surmising that because the *Golden Eagle* was a large ship there would not be many dry docks in Europe capable of accommodating her. I was only partly right.

For some time now I had sought permission from the owners to have Eileen on board for a trip, but established procedure was that only Captains and Chief Engineers were granted this privilege. George had endorsed my request and the owners were quite amenable to Eileen coming aboard; their difficulty was in creating a precedent. There had been unhappy experiences with women on ships in times past, complaining in general and telling the cook how to bake bread etc. However, permission had now come through and this was wonderful news; it meant that we should see each other earlier than expected, also a period together would help me to continue aboard that bit longer than might otherwise be the case. Should Eileen come with us it would be as a fully-fledged crew member, being signed on as an Assistant Stewardess at 1/- a month. Wherever this girl goes, riches follow.

Meantime we were having the cabins painted. The oil vapour that pervades the atmosphere on tankers leaves a light oily coating on the bulkheads, so George had ordered an extra crew member, a painter, to join us at Suez; he immediately busied himself washing the alleyways and cabins, then painting them. This could be a job for life, like the Forth Bridge. Some oil cargoes do not smell very strongly but others were quite pungent, particularly that from Umm Said.

Different oils need to be discharged at different temperatures. Our current cargo required an 86F discharge, so for three days prior to making port the cargo was slowly brought to the required temperature, whilst we prayed for cross winds to blow the resulting smell from the cargo ventilators away from the ship. A head wind down the length of the vessel into the saloon could put everyone off breakfast. After discharge of cargo the tanks had to be cleaned, and this was done by a machine spraying hot water being lowered into the tank. Occasionally, men had to go down into the tanks to rectify a problem with the machine and had to be hurriedly winched up again when the fumes threatened to overcome them.

The previous time we transited the canal we had taken on seven crewmen to replace men returned to Greece as being unsatisfactory, including the Chief Engineer, who was not playing according to the rules. On most ships the Captain and the Chief Engineer meet over the equivalent of a pink gin every morning at eleven in the Captain's cabin, discussing day to day problems and generally oiling the wheels on board. However, this wasn't happening, and George was seldom sure how much fuel or water remained, what repairs were pending, and so on. As this was plainly an unsatisfactory situation he felt little option but to make a change over. There can be a traditional rivalry between deck and engine room on any ship, perhaps stemming from early years of training. Deck officers spend their early years in classrooms or at sea learning their trade, whereas engineers spend most of their apprenticeship in engineering works, factories or brass foundries. In the latter the influences of unions and works committees are often strong, and by the time the engineer goes to sea his formative years will have differed in many ways from that of the deck officer. This seldom matters at sea as everybody has their own job to do and gets on with it. Where differences do arise, they would probably have arisen anyway because of the personalities involved, rather than any deck/engine-room rivalry.

A recent arrival on board was Heinrich Schwarze, Electrician, thin, sandy haired, 44, married, a German with a permanently worried expression. He had joined us direct from one of the company's passenger vessels where crew standards were high, and it was taking him a while to come to terms with life aboard the *Golden Eagle*. His English was good and it wasn't long before he began to share his troubles with me. He was not finding matters in the engine room up to his standard and he was also dismayed at the general domestic life aboard. Despite reassuring him that he would become used to it, he seemed doubtful, and often came into the radio room to engage in what he termed 'normal conversation'. These discussions were of benefit to me as well, because much of my shipboard conversation was conducted in broken English or pidgin, and after a while I began to doubt my ability to construct a coherent sentence in English. We discussed world affairs, as well as events aboard ship, and our talks acted as a mutual safety valve.

36: BROADWAY AND A NEW STEWARDESS

Arriving in Delaware Bay we proceeded up river to Westville, New Jersey, to discharge cargo. On the way we passed the US Navy mothball fleet, including the battleships *South Dakota* and *California,* half a dozen aircraft-carriers, numerous destroyers and the old Tennessee and Olympus from the Philippines campaign. Once alongside, there were Immigration formalities to go through, including the issue of shore permits. Seventeen of the crew were refused permits to go ashore, nevertheless one deserter succeeded in slipping through the net before we left.

It cost $5 for a taxi to Philadelphia but shore time was precious and there was no time to waste. The walk around the town centre didn't excite, although it was pleasant just to be amongst familiar things again and to recharge my batteries. After seeing the Liberty Bell and Independence Hall, a large beef and onion sandwich with a glass of milk kept me going until my feet eventually gave out and I came to rest in a burlesque theatre, probably not one of Minsky's because the show was pretty poor. The burlesque theatre in America paralleled our music halls and was also feeling the pinch due to the emergence of television. The big name artistes had deserted the stage for the clubs, where the money was better and they had a decent dressing room instead of being sandwiched between the hot water pipes underneath the stage. For a big city like Philadelphia there didn't seem to be much going on, or perhaps I was in the wrong part of it; a taxi took me back to the ship around midnight.

We spent the day at anchor in a foggy Delaware River, moving off next morning for New York. The fog had blown away during the night and by the time we poked our head out, the wind had increased to a howling gale, the waves boiling green with anger as far as the eye could see; storms at sea can be very exhilarating. We picked up the New York Pilot at the Ambrose Light Vessel some 24 hours later, passing close by the Statue of Liberty on our way to the yard of the Bethlehem Steel Company in Hoboken, New Jersey. We berthed at breakfast time and an hour later I was boarding a bus that took me through the Lincoln Tunnel to the 41st Street Bus Terminal on Manhattan. Ah, New York, New York; it was good to be back. I walked along Broadway, 8th Avenue, 5th Avenue, Times Square, 42nd Street, the West Side, went into a cinema to rest tired feet, ate my way through yards of hotdogs and watched the steam rising from the manhole covers, enjoying the rhythm and sounds of this most vibrant of cities. New York gave me that comfortable feeling of being amongst things familiar and unchanged. Tired from walking all day, I bought some papers and magazines from a news stand and made my way back to the ship.

There was no clue as to our length of stay in dry dock, so I went ashore again the next day, travelling by tube and bus to explore Newark, New Jersey. A whole day was spent exploring it but I was not much the wiser. There were impressions of great activity and industrial might but little else of note and relaxation was eventually sought in Minsky's Theatre, which was showing a film as well as a stage show. There was still no word about sailing so I went ashore again the following day, this time to Jersey City. It seemed similar to Newark, and even though there was nothing special about either city, they both possessed that vibrancy that, for me, epitomised America and it felt good just being part of it.

We left New York for Curacao, having stayed much longer than expected, bequeathing the city five deserters as a parting gift. In turn, New York sent us on our way with a faulty main steam line from which the packing blew out shortly after we left harbour. *Golden Eagle* 1, New York 1. It took the Chief six hours to fix the steam line, he was not a happy man and neither was George. We set off afresh for the Dutch West Indies, our personal black cloud hovering above us. Off the Florida coast, the skies blue, the sun hot and tempers gradually cooling, another packing blew out, this time damaging the main steam pipe in two places. We bobbed about on the ocean whilst the Chief and his minions cursed down below, many Greek swear words echoed round the stilled and quiet ship; most of them were new to me and not for sensitive ears. George, meantime, had been overhauling the ship's medical supplies, recently topped up in port, and asked me, 'Do you please think Mrs Eileen can do fix well the medicine chest when she come?' There were dozens of bottles and boxes on hand, George didn't know what most of them were for, nor did anyone else, and I steered clear of it all in case I got landed with more injections.

At Curacao we went alongside in Caracas Bay, miles from anywhere. George took me with him in a taxi to the Agents in Willemstad, travelling across the pontoon bridge that joins the two parts of the town. An expensive lunch was enjoyed at the Americano hotel and, after taking on board a full cargo of oil, we left for Argentina, taking nearly a fortnight to reach the River Plate. Off Montevideo a small tanker came alongside and took off 7,500 tons of cargo, reducing our draught so that we could proceed further up river. At Recalada Roads a stop was made to take a pilot on board and to discharge yet more cargo. Apparently we were one of the largest tankers to reach that far up the River Plate and the authorities were not accustomed to dealing with vessels of our size and draught.

It was spring in the Argentine, the weather was cold under a clear blue sky and a weak sun; I was more accustomed to it being sunny and warm in the grain season and felt cheated. Berthed at the oil terminal, the Agent brought lots of mail on board and said that there was trouble ashore; so nothing new there then. But you could still hear more quality opera and classical music from the radio stations in the River Plate than anywhere else I knew and I was happy to listen to music all day long, not caring about going ashore. The terminal was a long way from the centre of Buenos Aires, almost in the countryside and there were horses grazing in the fields by the oil jetty. A horde of local entrepreneurs descended upon the ship, most of them Greeks who had been kicked out of Greece during the Civil War for being communists. Going to a fascist country to make a living seemed to be doing things the hard way, but maybe they had friends in Argentina and few other options. The ship was quiet, George and wife having gone ashore, so I took the opportunity to reply to letters and post them before we left as the next leg of our trip was going to be a long one. Eileen's big news was that she had passed her Part 2 Midwifery Exam, was now a State Certified Midwife, Eileen Close S.R.N., S.C.M., and was to take a post at Sutton H.R.I. as a theatre staff nurse until she joined the *Golden Eagle*.

We left Argentina in ballast and, after successfully dodging Tristan da Cunha and other chunks of rock in the South Atlantic, sighted the coast of South Africa ten uneventful days later. Having painted the wireless room I started on the cabin during the voyage, taking advantage of the cool weather, the paint smell dissipating quickly in the stiff breezes off the Cape of Good Hope. I had a long yarn with Alf as we passed Port Elizabeth, taking the opportunity to give him Eileen's address, so that he could write her saying we had passed by and all was well. The weather, Agulhaus Current et al, conspired to slow us down off Durban where we started rolling badly and were only making half speed. We took on 5,000 tons of seawater to increase the ballast and minimise the shuddering as her bow went under, depositing torrents of green water on deck in the process. Many years later I saw a TV documentary about the unusually large number of ships lost off the Durban coast, where apparently these mountainous waves can occur but cannot be foreseen. Now they tell me. There must be times in life when you go around blissfully unaware of the potential dangers around you.

There were two more peaceful weeks at sea before we reached the Persian Gulf, ready to commence loading at Mena al Ahmadi. It might have been peaceful on board but was not so ashore, where the on-going tension between Israel and Egypt had finally erupted, the Admiralty advising all shipping to avoid the Suez Canal. Meanwhile Britain, France, the USA and Russia were busy vetoing each other's Resolutions in the United Nations. Matters went from bad to worse when President Nasser scuttled a number of ships in the Suez Canal, completely blocking it. Israel destroyed 100 Russian planes on the ground in the Sinai Desert, British and French planes bombed airfields and Israeli ground troops took 15,000 Egyptian prisoners. In the midst of this turmoil on our doorstep, Henry and I decided to let them all get on with it and went ashore to the canteen on the jetty. However, the atmosphere there also smelt of trouble, we could feel the waves of hostility all around us.

At seven the next morning, an hour before we were due to cast off, British and French paratroopers landed near the Suez Canal. And so, on Guy Fawkes Day 1956, we left Mena al Ahmadi with a full cargo of crude oil and few regrets, heading for the open sea and the Continent. With the Canal now closed to us we faced a long haul round the Cape of Good Hope, and would not learn our discharge port until nearing Gibraltar.

Four days later we crossed the equator, and six days after that Alf was giving me all the latest news from home as we passed Port Elizabeth. He had written to Eileen as promised and had received a reply from her, which he read out over the air. At full speed, with a freshening wind behind us and a following current of nearly 3 knots, the ship was charging along at 17 knots. Orders came through Gibraltar Radio for us to discharge in Rotterdam, and how slowly the days seemed to pass from then on. We docked in Rotterdam at 0600 on Thursday the 6th of December 1956 and Eileen, having had a choppy passage across the North Sea on the *Melrose Abbey,* followed by a scary night in a local hotel behind a barricaded door, came on board at breakfast time. At noon we had lunch at the Beure restaurant and spent the rest of the day walking around the town centre, talking, talking, talking. What a relief not to have to put everything down on paper anymore. It was hard to believe Eileen was really there, that I could reach out and touch her. She was signed on the Ships Articles of the *Golden Eagle*, and duly appeared on the crew list as a Stewardess, earning 1/- per month, her arrival having increased the crew number to 50. We should have left Rotterdam the following day but some minor repairs were dragging on; any delay was welcomed by me if not by George. Next day I made wireless contact with Geoff, whose ship was in mid-Atlantic; he was greatly surprised to hear Eileen's voice on the radio-telephone.

When we reached the Canary Islands there were lots of tankers already there, waiting for berths alongside. Since Egypt had filled the Canal full of scrap iron almost every ship had seen its route altered; some ports were crammed with shipping whilst others, particularly in the Mediterranean, were left with deserted wharves, feeling unloved and unwanted. We cruised around the bay all night, it being too deep for us to anchor, berthing the next morning at Santa Cruz, Tenerife. Eileen and I went ashore, walking around until teatime when we sailed for the Gulf. The permission for Eileen's voyage had originally been envisaged as from a European port to the Persian Gulf via the Suez Canal and returning the same way, about a six week trip. However, the Canal was now blocked and the trip doubled in length as a result because we had to round the Cape to get to the Gulf, returning the same way. And that could take three months. Wonderful!

The wireless room was spacious, about fifteen feet by ten feet. There were portholes on two sides and it was light and airy. The two main transmitters stood along one side of the room and a bench with morse-keys, receivers, Auto-Alarm and subsidiary equipment was opposite the door. Another bench with cupboards for spares was opposite the transmitters. Immediately inside the wireless room, to the left, a door led off to the good-sized living quarters. There was a shower and toilet unit, a bunk that was much wider and longer than any on my previous ships, a good sized wardrobe, a desk with drawers underneath, and a settee. Two portholes gave plenty of light and it was a very pleasant cabin. There were wall fans in both rooms in addition to the punkah-louvre system which ran throughout the accommodation. The Captain's suite was the only other living quarters on the same deck, it adjoined the wireless room and was directly below the bridge. The companionway to the bridge was immediately adjoining because access to the bridge had to be quick and convenient for both of us. In bad weather I was usually up and down the companionway, dividing my time between the wireless room and the bridge, where the radar and the D/F were located.

37: FLYING FISH FOR BREAKFAST

It was all new to Eileen and she was loving it. After a couple of weeks it was as if she'd been at sea all her life. The cabin was our first home, up to now all we'd had was a bedroom in our parents' houses, a tent, or a hotel room; the only thing we needed to make it perfect was Raffe. The new Chief Engineer took Eileen on a tour of the engine room, which was spacious and airy compared to those on cargo ships. I would not have liked to work in any engine room and was glad that my quest to be taken on as an engineering apprentice all those years ago had been unsuccessful. We crossed the Equator, Eileen for the first time, receiving a Captain's Certificate signed by George on behalf of King Neptune. At 1118 on the 23rd December 1956 the sun was exactly overhead in position 2355S 0908E, and on Christmas Day we were off Capetown with Table Mountain clearly visible, blue skies and sunshine following us all the way. George and Eugenia, Henry and Mr Matsubara the Japanese Supercargo, came to our cabin in the morning for drinks and Christmas cake.

Henry was chuffed at having another person to talk to, often dropping into the wireless room between jobs to talk to Eileen. When we had time between watches Henry and I had played chess; now he was able to have matches with Eileen during my watch periods and they both enjoyed the diversion, in the cabin, or on deck when the weather was good. On deck you could make your move and then gaze out to sea, lost in thought, until it was your turn once more; by which time your brilliant plan to effect checkmate in one move had evaporated like the morning haze on the horizon.

The Greek New Year celebrations on board were something else. New Year's Eve was taken up playing cards until 'Santa Vasilios' arrived, at which point there was a lot of noise and shouting, followed by a joining of hands and dancing round the saloon until three in the morning when everybody turned in, exhausted. Having experienced this on the *Gannet* and also with Eileen in Stenies at other celebrations, we were well primed. No crockery was broken this time however as we felt that the owners would not have appreciated the gesture. We passed Comoro Island and crossed the line once more. King Neptune, in the large form of Captain George, was busy with his ceremonies, and Eileen, who had settled into shipboard life as to the manner born, gave me a haircut to mark the occasion. The weather turned cooler; our orders were changed and instead of Mena we were to take on bunkers at Bahrain, then load cargo at Umm Said and take it to Aden; following this we were to return to the Gulf. All this was splendid, the weather remained relatively cool and the longer the trip lasted the better.

In Bahrain a Sheffield type cruiser and two American destroyers lay offshore, visible evidence of the recent skirmish around the canal. We moved up the Gulf to Umm Said to discharge our remaining ballast and take on a cargo of their Best Smelly from the Iraq Petroleum Company of Al Quatar, becoming so fully laden that we had to wait for high water to move away from the berth. Back home Eden gave way to McMillan as Prime Minister. Of more importance were Eileen's vital statistics of $35^1/_2$-$22^3/_4$-$35^1/_2$". These were checked every day and entered in a separate logbook which I assured her was an essential part of the ship's records.

At Aden we went ashore in the early morning to the French Café, then to the Crescent Shopping Centre to help George purchase stores at the ship-chandlers. From there we took a taxi to The Crater to visit the Queen of Sheba's wells. Everything shut down between noon and three in the afternoon for a siesta so we returned to the town for lunch, encountering Henry, who was strolling around the shops taking, 'sanity time', as he put it. In the evening he joined us for a meal at a café before taking the 20-mile taxi ride back to the ship, being more fortunate than the Chief Engineer, who was held to ransom by his taxi-driver.

The first 25,000 tons or so of cargo is usually quickly discharged but the remainder is more difficult to extract, and this was the case with oil from Umm Said. In Little Aden, Eileen, Henry and I spent some time in the Seamen's Club at the end of the jetty, went for dusty walks, or just sat on the rocks and watched tiny coloured fishes darting around our ankles in the rock pools. After four days we left Aden to return to Mena al Ahmadi, where we took on a full cargo of crude oil and set off to, 'Land's End for orders'.

A few days out into the Arabian Sea we had flying fish for breakfast and felt that life had resumed normal service. It indeed had, as a couple of days later a cyclone formed in the Mozambique Channel too close for comfort, and the weather began to turn nasty. The person most pleased about this was Eileen, who found the heavy seas, the rolling of the ship and the green seas crashing over the bows an exhilarating and exciting new experience. We were coming up to Durban, where the freak waves turned up unannounced, the mountainous seas continued for some days, rendering the decks off-limits and the catwalk dangerous to negotiate. We would both get waterproofed and huddle under the lea of the bulkhead door, making a dash for it when we felt lucky; it was too far to expect reaching the other end without getting at least one wave over us, we just hoped it wouldn't be too drastic when we were caught.

Contact was made once more with Alf as we neared Port Elizabeth. George called a boat drill, and as we passed Bird Island there were huge numbers of albatross, (sailors souls in limbo), many on the ground and others flying around the island looking for a vacant parking space. When we reached calmer weather I took the aerials down over a period of a week, cleaning and greasing the shackles, helped by the Bosun and the crew to put them up again. Geoff had now left the sea and joined a radio firm in Edmonton; all a bit hush-hush but apparently connected with the installation of the early-warning radar shield then being built across the north of Canada. We were escorted by a large shoal of dolphins as we moved through tropical waters and it was a pleasure to watch them enjoying themselves, ducking and weaving just ahead of our bow, then showing off with bursts of speed and leaping out of the water.

All thoughts of blue skies and dolphins were banished as we picked up the Nab Pilot in thick fog off the Isle of Wight early one morning. This was England as it ever was. The night had seen me up and down to the bridge and standing by the radar, until we handed over the ship to the Pilot at 0300. At 0400 we ran on to a mud bank. At 0600 we floated off and at 0900 went alongside, still in thick fog. So this was Fawley, oil port for Southampton. Not a great introduction. Radar and radiomen came aboard to check over the gear, which had developed faults and needed spares. They were busy in the wireless room all morning so my time was divided between helping them and getting George's port papers ready. All without any sleep in the last 24 hours. Three Company Directors, together with their wives, came on board to see the ship and have a look round so it was mid-afternoon before Eileen and I managed to get ashore.

Catching a taxi to Southampton, we only just made it to the Central Station in time to meet mother who arrived on the five o'clock train. We installed her in the Polygon hotel and the three of us went to a restaurant in Commercial Road before taking her back to the hotel, whilst Eileen and I caught a launch from the Town Quay back to the ship. The following morning we met her off the launch from Southampton and brought her aboard the *Golden Eagle* for a grand tour of the ship, the wireless room explained, had lunch on board and afternoon tea with George and

Eugena. In the early evening she and Eileen caught the launch to Southampton on their way back home and I returned, depressed, to the ship and a lonely bunk. It had truly been a wonderful three months, but now it was back to business. We left at midnight for Tenerife and then the Gulf.

Everyone on board was upset at Eileen's departure. Eugenia, George's wife, had a weep and forgot to hand over some Greek pastries that she had made especially for her. These were delicious, mostly honey and nuts and guaranteed to double your weight in 10 days or your money back, so perhaps it was just as well they weren't handed over. The Chief Engineer's daughter, Litsa, was also on board, and she and Eileen had conducted conversations of a sort over the past few weeks. The Chief came into the wireless room for a yarn and to say how sorry Litsa was to see Eileen leave, because they had become good friends.

38: BREAKDOWNS AND DUSTSTORMS

Henry was a real character; he regularly came to me for solace and understanding, finding the wireless room a sanctuary of sorts where he could regain his sanity. Chess usually calmed him down but his play of late had become increasingly erratic and he seldom won. Most times he simply needed a sympathetic ear whilst he poured out details of the latest example of incompetence perpetrated in the engine room. Without somebody to listen to him and make the appropriate noises he would surely have spontaneously combusted. There were so many items that he found unsatisfactory that he took the only course open to a conscientious practitioner, he modified them to his own high standard. As he was always talking about modifying something or other he was referred to by Eileen and me as 'Modified Henry'. When mother came down to Southampton she had brought with her some of her famous currant buns, or 'fat-rascals' as locally known, and had given some to Henry, which he greatly enjoyed. These were the same buns that I took with me each trip when on trawlers, where they proved so popular with everyone on board that, apart from those kept back for myself, a full cake-tin of them were eaten before we had even left the river.

At Tenerife we collected 2,000 tons of bunkers and went on our merry way into the realms of the sun and the flying fish. There was the regular conversation with Alf as we passed Port Elizabeth and, almost a month to the day since leaving Southampton, we were back in the Gulf. There was more boiler trouble, with one of them having to be shut down; the High Pressure system operated at 800-900'C, so it took a few hours for it to cool down before repairs could begin. About the time the ship's one year guarantee ran out the fun started, a three-inch crack appeared in a pipe that was expected to last the ship's lifetime. Once it had been repaired, the boiler was being brought slowly up to pressure again when the joints in the main auxiliary steam line blew out, the packing having proved inadequate. As there was no bypass line, which would have enabled the engine to continue working whilst repairs were carried out, everything had to be shut down once more. After the steam line had been repaired it took another four hours before we could re-start the main engine.

We stayed in Mena al Ahmadi for 24 hours, loading for the Continent. Shortly after leaving we were in trouble again and had to stop for six hours whilst repairs were carried out; two days later we broke down again and limped along at half speed for 36 hours. Tempers on board were becoming a little frayed, as they probably were in London when our string of telegrams hit the fan. Henry wasn't much in evidence so I assumed that he was down below modifying everything in sight. Eileen's trip proved to have been perfectly timed, as the Suez Canal became fully operational on the 8th April 1957 for the first time since it was blocked five months previously.

I worked out that my average time ashore on the *Golden Eagle* in the previous 13 months was seven hours per month. How much longer could this go on; money was important, but so was my sanity; how long before I started modifying all the wireless gear? The weather was bad and it took us a fortnight to go from Mena to abeam of Durban. We were heading into a strong southerly gale most of the time, but even then, a fortnight was a bit much. In conversation with Alf as we passed Port Elizabeth he wished us well but couldn't promise any better weather up ahead.

Good Friday arrived and there was brandy with breakfast. At midnight we had soup and red eggs after which everyone sat around looking at each other until someone started singing, voices wavering and out of tune. Henry and Mr Matsubara excused themselves and went to bed. Collecting my new red egg, I threw last year's egg as far out to sea as possible and followed their example. Late one evening the comet Arent-Roland passed us, low on the horizon, but despite our obvious earthly importance it appeared not to notice us, so we ignored it in turn, all except

Henry who wanted to get hold of it and modify it.

We docked in Rotterdam after a month at sea, everyone's nerves stretched to breaking point for one reason or another. On cargo ships you could anticipate a few days in port to unwind and recharge your batteries, but with tankers it was all rush to turn the ship around as quickly as possible and we were in and out in a matter of hours, still all tensed up. This time however, due partly to our trail of engine breakdowns, we were to have some worthwhile repairs done and, moreover, done in England. What better conclusion to a trip? This was more like it, and just in time to prevent mass suicide. After discharging cargo and taking on ballast for the short trip across the North Sea, we left Rotterdam for the Tyne. The first stop was the tanker- cleaning depot at North Shields, where Eileen met the ship and proceeded with us to the repair yard. We took a taxi to Newcastle, having a meal at Baimbridge's before catching the evening train home.

Eileen was now working at the Victoria Nursing Home in Westbourne Avenue but managed time off for us to be together. Dan and George were both at home and Raffe had all the walks he could cope with. We borrowed the car for a day out at Kirkham Abbey and had a meal on the way back at Stamford Bridge. Updating took place at the ROU, where Reg was still in charge. Some nights when Eileen came off duty she joined George, Dan, Reg and me at the Royal Station Hotel about ten thirty before we caught the last No.9 bus home along Anlaby Road. The town was still intent on shutting down and getting everybody into bed well before midnight with their cups of cocoa. Would it ever catch up with the rest of the world, I wondered.

The *Golden Eagle* was in Brigham and Cowan's dry dock on the Tyne and daily phone calls to the Agents kept me up to date on the progress of the repairs. Life on board ships in dry dock is miserable, lots of noise, cables everywhere, workmen everywhere, you can't wash or use the toilets and have to go ashore for these and most other needs, so it's best to stay as far away as possible if you can. The call to arms came eventually and we all squeezed into the car and headed for South Shields. Dad had a conducted tour of the ship. There were further engine problems which resulted in yet another day's delay, so Eileen stayed on board for the night whilst the rest of the party returned home. Next day we came out of dry dock and things aboard returned to normal; Eileen had a day in Newcastle before leaving Central Station to return home.

The *Golden Eagle* left South Shields in the late evening but only got as far as the harbour entrance before there was yet more trouble in the engine-room. We anchored and called for tugs, but it was too late to get any and we had to stay at anchor for the night. The morning saw us return alongside, with the Rotor being taken ashore for examination. There was no information as to the probable length of time it would take to repair; it seemed to be one of those jobs that could be completed any minute or it might be next week. This meant that no one could leave the ship for more than a couple of hours at a time.

One evening I took Henry to a dockside pub in South Shields but the environment made him nervous, so we left after one beer and caught a bus to the Marine Grotto in Marsden, descending in the lift to the beach level bar carved out of the cliff face. Henry had calmed down by then and seemed happier there, so we stayed for the rest of the evening. Day followed day, the Rotor was off, then it was on, then it was off, more changes than a stripper but not as interesting. Buses took me to Newcastle, North Shields, South Shields, anywhere in search of decent films to pass the time; the most satisfying part of the excursions was the fish and chips eaten out of newspaper on the way back to the ship.

After four days of living on the edge, when I could have been at home if I'd only known how long the repairs were going to take, I took the bus to Sunderland for the day. Mail began arriving from home. This was ridiculous; months and months of oceanic separation and now exchanging letters with my wife, a hundred miles down the road. On the fifth day it came to pass that we sailed in the evening, in ballast, for the Persian Gulf. It was a beautiful spring evening, sunny and clear with a light breeze and we had an hour's trial off the coast before proceeding southwards on our lawful occasions. England were all out for 186 and the West Indies replied with 474, so everything normal there. Nine days later we reached Port Said, where it was difficult to tell what all the recent fuss had been about. The two statues that had stood at the entrance to the Canal had disappeared and there were a couple of wrecks in shallow water, but that was all there was to see at that end of the Canal. Our convoy went through at night, so I was on watch anyway and not able to see very much, but things appeared to be settling back into their normal routine.

There was a dust storm in the Gulf of Oman and the radar proved its worth, guiding us round obstacles in nil visibility. We picked up the Pilot at Khor Musa, called at Bandar Shahpur to collect the port doctor at two in the morning, and arrived at Bandar Mashur for loading; destination Aden. The blowers were turned off in the Gulf because all they did was blow sand into the cabins, and the heart sank a little when the rushing sound of the forced air gradually faded away into silence. The ship seemed lifeless without the sound and the feel of the air circulating, and it always gave you a lift when it was switched on again as the ship moved out to sea. The blower system had other uses too, it masked noises and provided a reassuring background hum which, combined with the rhythmic sound of the engines, was soothing and lulled you to sleep. So much so, that at home it was difficult to stay asleep because it was too quiet and you became conscious of the smallest sounds. Every home should have a punkah-louvre system.

Henry was gradually sinking into despair. For months he had been railing at the grease-monkeys who regularly painted over his wires and cables, switch boxes, handles, instruments, virtually anything that didn't move. But ultimately he had to admit defeat and was only waiting until his time was up so that he could go home on leave, or to a sanatorium, whichever came first. He saw more of what went on below than I did and thought that the spate of stoppages on the previous trip was due to inadequate repairs and maintenance; if the first repair had been dealt with correctly those that followed may have been avoided. Word had it that the owners were now trying to recruit German engineers and crew for some of their vessels.

The urgent matter of balancing our finances against how much longer I could cope with the heat and the restrictive lifestyle of tankers without losing my marbles, had become the main subject of our letters. The thought of coming ashore to an England where everything seemed dirty, cramped, run-down, short of food and gave up the will to live at ten every night, depressed me. I'd found a bigger, more interesting, world and didn't want to go back, certainly for a while. We were within sight of our target of £2,000, some of it conveniently located in the Royal Bank of Canada in Vancouver, and some in the East River Savings Bank in New York. We had thought about living in Canada but it hadn't worked out; only a return to Hawthorne Avenue seemed to lie ahead. The money we had saved would provide a deposit on a house and the shop would provide a steady living, but was that it; the end of the line?

39: TROUBLE AT t'MILL

We were on our way to Little Aden when Henry flipped. Careless damage done to his electrical motors in the engine room had seen him lay down the law. Why should he work two days down there in 110 degrees stifling heat to repair damage caused by someone else's ineptitude. Let it wait for the next port to be repaired. A new Henry was emerging, one tempered in the fires of frustration and despair. But it had all taken its toll on him, as it was doing with me. His chess was distinctly shaky and he now fell into the simplest opening traps. His appetite was suffering, and he smoked less than usual, when theoretically he should have been smoking more than usual. It was all very worrying.

The boilers were in need of servicing and conjecture was rife as to where this would take place. The situation was more complicated than it seemed. The European shipping firms were in a stew about all the foreign flagships running around under their flags of convenience, avoiding taxes and making life harder for the companies who had to pay tax. The shipping firms couldn't do much about it directly, but they could bring pressure to bear on the major shipyards that they patronised, saying, 'Look, if you repair these flags of convenience ships we will withdraw our considerable custom from your yards'. So most of the larger shipyards were now closed to us, leaving only the smaller yards for our repairs.

George was a marked man. The ship had been fined £1,640 for being overloaded by 1640 tons in Fawley the previous February, and he now had to report to the authorities at each port we visited in order to confirm that the vessel was not currently overloaded. A news item, together with a photo of George, had appeared on television, the matter also being covered on the radio. Fame and notoriety at last, and we knew nothing of it.

We were not the only ones in trouble. The volume of an XXX message from a ship very close to us in the Gulf nearly blew me out of my chair. She was calling Abadan Radio and addressed the message to the 'Commander British Warships Abadan: Anticipate crew mutiny shortly position very serious request immediate assistance: Master'. Nothing further was heard until the following day, when the BBC World Service reported that the ship had been boarded by the crew of a British frigate and was presently under escort on her way to Mena, six of the Chinese crew being arrested and the remainder placed under surveillance.

The cricket improved; Peter May made 285 not out and Colin Cowdrey 154, their 411 partnership being the highest ever in an English Test. Henry had got a grip on himself, his appetite had returned and he was once more smoking like a chimney. The weather was good and nothing had blown up in the engine room for 24 hours. George pointed out a passage from the Red Sea Pilot: 'The southern part of the Red Sea is amongst the hottest places on earth,' and who would disagree. It was 90F at breakfast and by lunchtime you could fry eggs and bacon on the deck, should you be sufficiently deranged to want to try. Some of us toyed with the idea, that's how bad things were.

We arrived at Little Aden tanker terminal, but this time sans Eileen. In the evening I went across the jetty to see the operator of the BP tanker *British Fidelity,* who knew me even before I introduced myself. Some of their crew had apparently met Henry wandering aimlessly around Aden during the day; he had told them all about the stressful situation aboard the *Golden Eagle*, about Eileen's trip and lots more, and they had invited us both over for the evening. A great time was had by all, especially Henry, who arrived shortly after me. Lots of banter and songs, the beer flowed generously and it all reminded me of the days when it was possible to sail on normal ships, doing normal things. We left the party at midnight, loaded down with a carton of English beer, a bottle of gin, a bottle of lime juice, fifty pocket books and dozens of magazines. The *British Fidelity* was a happy ship, with kind people aboard and Henry and I talked about them long afterwards.

One of our seamen was over the side on a stage painting the hull, when he suffered heat-stroke and had to be taken to hospital. George received orders that we were to go from Aden to the Persian Gulf and then return to Aden. No one thought anything to this idea. Five of the crew had been to the doctors with heat-stroke already that morning whilst the remainder seemed to have something heat-related wrong with them. And June was just the start of the silly season. The reason given for our additional trip back to the Gulf was that the Canal had silted up, due to lack of dredging over the previous six months, and our draft was too deep to allow us to carry a full load through the Canal back to Europe. We wanted BP, our charterers, to pay us for the trip fully loaded or not, pointing out that it was hardly our fault that we couldn't carry a full load through the Canal; indeed we should very much have liked to do so. It didn't sound to us like a convincing argument at the time, and BP didn't think much to it either, replying in effect: 'Tough, get yourselves on a shuttle to Aden from the Gulf, where you are able to carry a full load, and earn your keep'. It took four days to discharge our cargo in Aden, it was as gassy as the stuff from Umm Said, the fumes coating every surface with a black film of oil. The oil was discharged at 100 degrees F as this was the lowest daytime outdoor temperature.

We left Little Aden in ballast for Mena al Ahmadi. When we arrived in Mena, Henry accompanied me for a walk along the quay to have a glass of lemonade in the canteen's recreation room, alcoholic drinks being taboo. Also in the canteen was an obstreperous wireless operator from a British tanker, with whom I fell into conversation about wages on British ships compared to those on freelance ships. He said that with his salary, plus pension contributions, plus whatever, he would beat me in the long run. I didn't like him and he didn't like me, the tone of the conversation, and probably the body language, made Henry nervous and when he heard the words, 'beat me', he became quite alarmed and dragged me out of the canteen and back on board. Even though I tried to explain to him the colloquialisms inherent in the English language, he was still in a state of some agitation when we left port.

Mena was at this time the largest crude-oil loading terminal in the world, a fact confirmed by the appearance in the next berth of the *Sinclair Petrolore, 57,000 tons*. Still, we had been the biggest, or one of the biggest tankers in our day. We arrived back in Aden just as a sandstorm blew up. This broke the mooring rope of the ship next to us and also activated our own siren, which moaned continuously for the hours that the storm lasted. It also caused a ship at anchor to drag herself half a mile out to sea. Luckily we were being blown against the jetty and not away from it. With the light turning an unearthly colour due to the flying sand, the siren moaning away, people rushing hither and yon securing anything moveable and shouting orders to others, who couldn't hear what they were saying anyway, the wind howling and shrieking, it was nevertheless exciting in the sense of complete chaos descending where all had been peace and calm only moments before. The storm lasted for some three or four hours, about half an hour at its peak, and cooled the air wonderfully.

From Aden we went to Mena, only to be told by B.P. that we had to do yet another trip back to Aden. Henry and I said to George that if the ship continued on these trips back and forth from Aden to the Gulf then the next trip the ship would require a new R/O and a new Electrician, because we had both had enough. All this unrest on the way back to Aden was amplified when the Chief Officer announced that he also wanted to leave. This was followed shortly afterwards by three of the Engineers wanting to sign off. A cable came from London offering the whole crew a 25% pay increase until we left the Gulf for a European destination. As there was no move towards replacing any crew members we were stuck with the situation, bonus or no bonus. The Chief Engineer would doubtless have liked a few words with London too; he was carted off to hospital that very morning with heat exhaustion.

Some of the crew had bought canaries in cages and the accommodation resounded to bird song. One of the birds was in a cage in the saloon, the only air-conditioned part of the ship, and each mealtime I gave him/her some bread. Whenever it saw me, but no-one else, it set up a frenzy of chirping and hopping about until it had been fed, after which I could get my own meal in peace. Discharging was completed; the Chief Engineer was still in hospital undergoing a week's rest plus treatment, and George took me with him into Aden to phone London on the radio link and give them the latest glad tidings. In the event he couldn't get through because the fading and static were too heavy and, as there was no direct cable link to fall back on, we had to give it up. Ships are not allowed to use their transmitters whilst in port, otherwise we could have got a message through ourselves on short wave.

The boilers were found to contain a significant percentage of salt water where there should only have been pure distilled water. We finished discharging and moved out to anchor whilst this problem was sorted out, the 2nd Engineer taking charge of the engine room in the absence of the Chief. Our sister ship the *Opportunity* was also in Aden and similar problems existed aboard her.

Word came that further shuttle trips had been cancelled because the canal had now been dredged sufficiently to allow deep-water passage. This was good news indeed and it looked as if we should take on cargo at Bandar Mashur, then proceed to Land's End for orders. George went ashore by ship's boat the next day and upon his return the boat could not be raised inboard. After we had got George safely aboard by rope ladder, the boat had to remain alongside all night. Upon inspection the following morning, it appeared that the pulleys for the boat lowering gear were made of iron and had become seized up with rust. The deck fittings were also of iron and not brass or steel, so there was conjecture as to how long these would last.

A Superintendent Engineer arrived by air from Piraeus; when he had assessed the situation and sent his report to London, work commenced on the boilers. After 12 more days sweating it out in Aden we left for Bandar Mashur, leaving the Chief Engineer behind, still in hospital. Stopping at Khor Musa on the way in order to clean the tanks, we took on cargo at Bandar Mashur and headed for the Suez Canal, bound for Europe. We transited the Canal with the night convoy, the searchlight on the bow showing up the canal banks, the dwellings, the vegetation, a few people and restless animals, as we glided silently along. Some of the crew left the ship at Port Said to return to Greece and their replacements came aboard including, to my pleasant surprise, Antonias Papadimas. We hadn't met since the *Gannet*, our Japanese bottle incident, and the mid-ocean injections. He berated me for not looking him up in Athens on our honeymoon, but I detailed all our unavailing efforts to find him and was forgiven. A letter came from Eileen about her new-found wanderlust and desire to travel; I wanted that for her too, but only if we could travel together. Orders were received via Lands End Radio to proceed to Fawley, George's Nemesis, to discharge cargo, and then cross to Rotterdam for repairs.

40: THE CORNFIELDS OF SUMMER

The *Golden Eagle* docked at Fawley in the late evening. Eileen had travelled all day by train from Hull and then caught the launch from Southampton across the water to Fawley, arriving an hour after we berthed. She had experienced a somewhat alarming crossing, having to be locked in the boat's small cabin by the skipper for her own protection against the unwanted attentions of some of the passengers. We stayed up talking until four in the morning, surrounded by oily bulkheads and enveloped in the fragrance of crude oil. Shipboard life may not be everyone's cup of tea; on tankers anyway.

The Marconi technicians came aboard early next morning to carry out work on the radar and were still busy at teatime. Eileen and I took the ferry across to Southampton where we walked around and, after dinner, caught the same launch as Henry back to Fawley. There was so much that Henry wanted to tell Eileen about events since they last met that it was scarcely possible for me to get a word in edgeways. Discharging completed, we set off for Rotterdam with Eileen on board. At long last we had been able to have a proper conversation, instead of exchanging letters, and had decided that this was to be my last trip on the *Golden Eagle*. The wind was gale force off the Hook of Holland and we dodged from early light till mid-afternoon before the Pilot was able to scramble up our rope ladder and get aboard. We proceeded slowly up the canal and moored to buoys near the shipyard. Eileen helped pack my gear and we went ashore to arrange tickets for the sailing of the *Melrose Abbey* to Hull.

It was the end of August 1957 when I signed off the *Golden Eagle* in Rotterdam, 18 months almost to the day after joining her in Japan. Henry came ashore with us on the last evening for a farewell dinner at the Old Dutch Restaurant in Rotterdam. It was a landmark meal, there was a lot to talk about, the good times and the bad times shared, and now the parting of the ways. The following morning Eileen and I said goodbye to George, Henry and everybody on board, caught the Autobus to Schiedam and the train to Rotterdam, where we passed the time shopping until boarding the *Melrose Abbey* for her evening sailing. It was a quiet voyage across the North Sea and we berthed at Alexandra Dock jetty in Hull at ten the next morning. The strain of the past months gradually slipped away, the determination to keep going, when all I really wanted after the first few months had been to sign off and go home, was not needed any more, but it had taken its toll and I felt drained. Luckily for me I knew the therapy needed to bring me back to life, it came in a trim little package not much over sixty inches high. Raffe did his bit too and he received more than his usual quota of walks over the next few days. Eileen was still working at the VNH, so our time together had to be fitted in around her duties. Raffe wasn't working anywhere and looked upon me as his personal property and walk-provider. We bought some furniture, a Welsh Dresser, four wheel-back dining chairs and two fireside chairs; even though there was nowhere to put them we felt that it was a positive step towards having a home of our own one day, meantime they went into storage.

Wanting to get away on our own, we arranged a week's holiday in the Lake District. The family car was prepared and we set off, via Aysgarth Falls, to a farmhouse near the head of the lake at Bassenthwaite where we spent a wonderful week, wandering down lanes, discovering country inns, rowing on the lake and visiting the falls. We also climbed Skiddaw in everyday footwear, but visibility was obscured by mist when we reached the summit and we scrambled down with difficulty through thick pine forests and bracken, discovering some enchanted red-spotted mushrooms on the way. The food at the farm was good, we slept like logs every night in an enormous feather-bed and it was all exactly what was needed.

Back home, more records were bought at Gough & Davy, after listening to them in one of the cubicles that lined the walls downstairs. There was a lady in charge of the record department called Miss Allenby who was sweetness itself; a friend since the early war days when she would search at length through catalogues to locate a particular record I wanted. As the war took over our lives and supplies of everything except bombs dried up, the record business virtually ground to a halt but I always called into the shop to see her when home from sea. A phone call came from Henry and a letter from Goulandris about joining another ship. I phoned Mr John Goulandris and settled for the *Manhattan,* due to reach Europe in a couple of week's time.

Meantime, we were making trips in the car all over the East Riding on Eileen's days off, taking Raffe with us when we could. I was still driving on a Provisional Licence as there never seemed enough time to complete a set of lessons and take the test anyway. An outing to the North Landing at Flamborough was a huge success as far as Raffe was concerned and he spent the time rushing in and out of the cave pools getting thoroughly wet, returning to shake water all over us then repeating the process until exhaustion set in. It felt good to be on a cycle again and there were trips all over town during the daytime, calling on people and meeting friends. We cycled to Anlaby, picked brambles near Tranby Croft, went on to Swanland and Waudby Green, picnicked at Raywell near a hay-stack and lay in a hay field all afternoon before cycling to Ferriby foreshore and walking along the riverbank. You may go to the ends of the earth, see wondrous things, but it's being together, taking Raffe to Flamborough and picnicking in corn fields on a summer's day that you remember best when you're back at sea.

We went by car to Gainsborough to see Dan, who was working in a garage there, staying overnight. A day out in York was otherwise as far as we got, because it was time to leave home and join the *Manhattan* in Germany. At the end of September I left for London, going from King's Cross to Liverpool Street, registering my luggage for it to go by rail direct to Kiel. By the look of the complex journey ahead, the numerous changes en route and the number of pieces of baggage, registering my luggage appeared to be the best solution. The rest of the day was spent at the Goulandris office in the City fixing up the contract, and I left London at teatime on the boat train, boarding the *Arnhem* at Harwich at ten o'clock that night.

The ship arrived at the Hook of Holland after breakfast and I took a taxi to the railway station, catching the Scandinavian Express to Rotterdam Nord, then through flat marshy lands as the early morning mists were rising from the dykes. The sun was still casting long shadows across the landscape as the train called at Utrecht, then Amersfoort, Deventer, Bentheim, Osnabruch, Bremen and Hamburg, where we changed for Neumunster. There, we changed again, this time for Kiel, arriving there at teatime. The low-lying countryside we had passed through was similar to that at home, but the houses were mostly of wood with large sloping roofs.

At Kiel, all attempts to retrieve my luggage from the clutches of the Station Kommandant proved fruitless, the release process being efficiently Teutonic and unyielding. They had a point, because registered luggage apparently could not be released under 24 hours from the time of its arrival at destination. Unfortunately, nobody had thought fit to inform me of that salient fact when the luggage was checked in at Liverpool Street. The Agents had arranged for me to stay at the Hotel Slabig in Kiel, together with an Apprentice Engineer who was also joining the ship. When checking in, the hotel staff had seemed very unfriendly, so I went to bed after dinner, tired, concerned about my luggage and, for good measure, with a chair wedged under the door handle. The *Manhattan* was due to pass through the Kiel Canal the following day, but would my luggage appear in time? I wasn't keen to do a two-month round-trip to South America in the clothes I stood up in, but neither did I want to delay the ship by waiting for my luggage to be released by the railway authorities.

The following morning I walked around Kiel before returning to the hotel for lunch, phoning the Agents to see how the luggage situation was progressing. Stalemate appeared to be the answer so time was spent in the hotel lobby waiting for something positive to happen. Eventually the Agent arrived and together we went to the railway station where the luggage was finally handed over. We loaded it into the car and drove to a landing stage on the Kiel

Canal, where it was a relief to climb on board the *Manhattan* later that evening. As usual, there was no Operator to take over from, to tell me where anything was, about any peculiarities of the wireless gear, what the crew and the food were like or conditions aboard.

Bunkers were taken at Ostermoor and we left Brunsbuttel the following afternoon for Dakar. There was a force 8 gale blowing in the Channel and the ship was rolling and pitching alarmingly, just what I needed after the parting from Eileen and the hassle with the luggage. The weather slowly improved; a carrier pigeon called to see us abeam the Channel Islands, carrying a message in Spanish from 'Zozo' dated the previous day. We fed and watered it, put a note in its clip giving the ship's name, position, date and time but it declined to take off and stayed with us for a couple of days before eventually deciding to leave. Perhaps it was catching a lift on the way to its destination, or perhaps the Greek food had disorientated it and it actually had no idea where it was, or maybe it liked Greek food and wanted to be adopted; it flew off without telling us.

41: A SHIP FULL OF WOMEN

My first impression of the *Manhattan* was that she had been given her name out of cynicism; the only part of Manhattan she could possibly have related to was the Bowery, (flashbacks of black and white films, Leo Gorcy, the 'Dead End Kids', rotting wharves). She was a Canadian vessel from the middle war years and looked as though she had been worked to death; a typical tramp steamer. The radio gear was fairly new but had not been well looked after, so a clean-up was needed. The cabin was also grubby so the Mess Boy was commandeered, and together we cleaned everything before spraying it with Lysol. The wireless room was aft of the bridge and chartroom, with my cabin two decks below, off the main port side alleyway. The flag was Liberian, she had been Greek-crewed for seven months and prior to that had been the British registered *Tridale,* also owned by Goulandris, before being registered overseas.

Careworn, and with most of the stuffing knocked out of her, she would be expensive to run and could only be an economic proposition when markets were good and freight rates high; which was not the case at the time. Freight rates were down and ships continued to be laid up across the world. If the Company was forced to lay up some of its fleet in order to economise, the *Manhattan* would surely be amongst the first to go to the wall. However, as October/November was the early grain season in Argentina there would always be a job for ships like the *Manhattan*, though there wouldn't be much profit margin after deducting her running costs. The steadily lengthening list of R/Os awaiting ships at the ROU highlighted the fact that I was lucky to be in a ship at all, thanks probably to the stock of Brownie points built up with the company.

The crew members were different from the last ship, quiet for the most part, there was little shouting and conversations were held at normal levels. The 2nd Officer had arrived a few days previously; apparently they had sent him to join the *Golden Eagle* in Rotterdam but he didn't fancy the idea when he got aboard her, and chose to join the *Manhattan* instead. Meantime it was back to letter writing; the partings became worse each time and, whatever lay ahead, we could not go on like this.

During his evening watch on the bridge, I had long conversations with Vasili, the Chief Officer, about classical music, theology and current affairs. This was something not on the menu over the past couple of years and was unnerving, my brain unaccustomed to being exercised in this fashion. The Captain seemed bright and jovial, he had only recently joined the ship but had already instigated a thorough clean up. The Merchant Navy Programme on the BBC reported that there was a quarter of a million tons of British shipping laid up in UK harbours, so the outlook was gloomy indeed and it seemed that any decision about when to come ashore was likely to be taken out of my hands. Just before we reached Dakar some tubes blew down below and we steamed along on two boilers whilst repairs were carried out. On this ship it was possible to ask for tea with lemon, and get it; this indeed was civilised living. After eighteen months on tankers it seemed strange to see men smoking on deck once again.

Vasili went to the doctor's in Dakar about a pain in his leg, returning with some tablets and a ten-day course of injections. There was never any doubt who was going to cop for this. Vasili himself was the nominated Medical Officer on board and so it had to be someone else. He said that all the engineers would treat the needle like a pneumatic drill, you don't ask the Captain in normal circumstances and everybody else was chicken, so he hoped I would do it because I was, 'sensitive and would have a gentle touch'. So each day for the next ten days it was puncture time, with each injection having to be done twice because the dose was large and our only syringe was small.

We ambled along at nine knots in the general direction of Argentina, entered the River Plate one gentle evening, anchored off the Recalada Pilot Vessel, a converted naval vessel from the turn of the century, and waited for the tide. Pilot aboard, we proceeded up river towards Intercession, colliding with a tanker, the *Esso Campana,* on the way. The channel was narrow, the tanker was empty and high out of the water; we were fully loaded and not easy to manoeuvre in a narrow seaway. I was on the bridge at the time, realised that a collision was inevitable and retreated to the chartroom to brace myself in a corner to await events, only too aware of the imminent possibilities. Our bow bounced off her quarter, the two vessels slid close by each other and choice language was exchanged between the two Pilots. Luckily for everyone concerned we escaped with only a badly scored hull and some scraped paintwork. At Intercession we anchored to await high tide before proceeding to Buenos Aires.

It seemed likely that we should be in Buenos Aires for some time so there was no rush to go ashore. The workers who came aboard said that this particular dock was a dangerous place to return to your ship alone, especially at night. But all docks are potentially hazardous, it goes with the territory, and even quaysides that look innocent enough in the daytime can look sinister at night, ill-lit, with dark shadows everywhere and mountain lions with knives ready to leap out at any moment.

A bus service passed the dock gate; for 60c, providing you were willing to stand packed like sardines for twenty minutes, you could reach the centre of Buenos Aires quickly and cheaply; a taxi could cost fifty times as much. Returning from town one day, standing the whole way on the crowded bus with odds and ends of shopping for myself and others, the ship had moved a mile up the quay. Hot and tired, feet aching and fed up, I trundled along the quay, carrying my parcels and looking for the *Manhattan* amongst the crowd of ships. Eventually she hove into view some hundred yards out from the quay, stuck on a mud bank and with two tugs trying to pull her off. After a brief shouted conversation with the Captain on the bridge and Vasili on the bow, the only sensible thing to do was sit at a table outside the nearest bar that afforded a view of the proceedings, and wait. Climbing aboard some hours later, even more tired and fed up, I went straight to bed.

The Chief's wife had a gold bracelet and a ring stolen from her cabin whilst we were in port. Worst of all for thieving was Port Said, where you couldn't leave anything lying around; portholes had to be secured and cabin doors locked at all times. Even when in your cabin, you needed to keep half an eye on open portholes for a hand, or a stick with a hook on the end, coming through. Sailors' tales abounded, including that of one seaman who became so browned off with the ever-clutching hand coming through his porthole that he slashed the next one off at the wrist with a butcher's knife. Correspondence arrived from Eileen about leaving home and finding a flat or a bed-sit; this was all right in principle but I was naturally concerned about her living alone in a flat. The Peronista workmen had started unloading our coal at last, but not very rapidly; they were not in favour of the current government and this was doubtless their way of registering disapproval.

The ship was full of women. We stayed in Argentina long enough for everyone to have acquired a female companion and they were all over the ship. Groups of sailors and their girlfriends went ashore in the evenings to bars or dance halls and it was all very jolly, the Captain and Chief Officer leading by example. Female laughter rang out around the ship day and night, particularly in the evenings after the coal dust had settled and the workers had folded their tents and stolen away.

42: MARZIPAN, TANGOS AND SATCHMO

Two of our ships had recently loaded grain for Italy and both had received orders that they should take on board only sufficient stores to cover the trip to Europe. This looked ominous and it seemed certain that they would be sent to Piraeus for laying-up after discharging their cargo. Argentina was a favoured place for ships to store up on meat for the long term, being of excellent quality, cheap and fresh. Some of the best steaks I have tasted anywhere were in Argentina, and the last time there on the *Golden Eagle* we had stocked up with enough meat for a whole year. The *Manhattan* had not received any orders to limit stores so we hoped this meant we were not being sent to the knacker's yard yet awhile.

Vasili believed that the characteristics of people were related to their star signs. Whilst agreeing with me that the stuff in the newspapers was very questionable, he went on to highlight some of the characteristics of the crew, which proved to be quite near the mark. Vasili was a Water Carrier, my sign is Virgo, the Captain was a Bull, the 2nd mate was a Crab, and we derived innocent amusement from observing how the theory worked in the field. The local shops sold bars of marzipan, whether for baking or as a confection I know not, but they were cheap, and I ate at least one slab every day. It provided something to look forward to, the leisurely stroll ashore, the look of recognition from the shopkeeper, the few words of Spanish exchanged, the light that appeared in his eyes as money was passed over, the protestations of goodwill on both sides, the promise to meet on the morrow and finally, sitting in the sunshine watching the dockside activity whilst savouring the marzipan. All part of life's rich tapestry. A bit sad really but you could do worse.

The shops outside the dock gate were in a run-down suburban area, reached along cracked and uneven pavements. The roads were almost as bad as the pavements, with rivulets of dirty water forming stagnant pools in the gutters. Waste paper and dirt blew into corners, where it stayed until the next high wind whisked it off to some other resting-place. The houses were mostly single-storey buildings, with plaster peeling from the walls and paint fading on the wooden shutters. The neighbourhood shops seemed to have been there since the last century. Outside the photographer's shop, when you stopped to look at the pictures in the frames, Greece mixed with old Argentina stared back at you. Dark faces with old-fashioned moustaches, caught in unlikely poses, looked out with a seriousness that was touching. I wondered, was life that hard in this windswept corner of God's earth, or did they throw away those wide-brimmed hats when they left the camera's searching gaze and go dance the tango somewhere.

The Eden, a dance hall in an old two-storied building, was situated near to the docks. The workmen on the ship had told me about it and how to find it. It was just that, a local dance hall down a back street, where tourists didn't stray and the occasional stranger was unusual, but accepted. The orchestra and the dancing was life itself, the women danced to seduce the men and the men danced like matadors. Some were dressed for the occasion, others more casually, but they all shared a passion for the tango, and the music was the real thing, not westernised or watered down. Around the dance floor was a thickly carpeted balcony with worn red velvet upholstered chairs and settees. Most of the seats were close to the velvet covered balustrade, from where you could lean over to watch the orchestra and the dancers below. However, judging by the muffled laughter that came bubbling out of the shadows behind me, the settees at the back of the balcony were being put to an altogether different use.

The music stayed with me, and although I tried to buy some records that would capture the moment I had no success. Maybe the Argentine companies didn't get as far as back street dancehalls or even stray far from the city centre where the bands were more sophisticated. What B.A. needed was a John Hammond, who took his early tape recorder into the back street bars of America, recording blues artists whom the big labels didn't know existed; without him and a couple more like him, a whole swathe of jazz, and the rock and roll that sprang from it, would not now be on record. Eventually I did lay my hands on three 78s of authentic tango music and managed to get them home without breakage, no mean feat in itself, and they served to bring back memories of an evening spent in a smoky dance hall in Argentina.

Discharging was dragging its heels. Our *Falcon* and *Harrier* left for Europe with expectations of being laid-up on arrival; the outlook was as black as the coal dust that blanketed the ship. There was a temporary lightening of the gloom when Louis Armstrong came to town, and I booked a seat at the Opera House for the evening concert, also reserving a room at the nearby Esmeralda Hotel for the night. After spending the afternoon walking around Buenos Aires, I returned to the hotel in the evening preparatory to going to the theatre. The floor man in attendance showed me to my room and we fell into conversation. He was Polish, spoke good English and had served in the Polish Air Force in England during the war, a very pleasant young man who had seen his homeland destroyed, his family with it and by some mysterious route had ended up halfway across the world. When he left me he routinely enquired whether a senorita would be coming later, and was surprised to hear that I would be returning alone. The performance started at eight o'clock before a packed house; the All Stars backing group were unremarkable except for Ed Hall, a coloured clarinettist of the old school, but by any reckoning it was the chance of a lifetime to see and hear a genuine legend, and was a glimpse of history on a night to remember.

Later the same evening I went to the Theatre Maipo in the middle of town to see a variety show. When it finished at half past one I made my way along the streets, still buzzing with life and lights and noise, to my hotel. It was just like home I reflected, all these people out enjoying themselves at two or three in the morning. The hotel clerk was surprised to see me still alone; hardly anyone returned unaccompanied to their hotel room in Buenos Aires. The hotel was an old colonial style building, with rooms leading off the inner balconies that overlooked a central courtyard with shrubs and a fountain. The rooms were spacious, with high ceilings and windows that opened onto a balcony overlooking the street. A couple of ladies knocked on the door in approved South American hotel fashion, unaware that I was still wrapped in my own world of New Orleans jazz and had no need of theirs. The trams clanked up and down the Via Esmeralda and the sounds of conviviality from the pavement below my balcony drifted up on the soft night air, lulling me to sleep.

Breakfast was at eight, coffee and rolls, the coffee arriving in a cup the size of a soup bowl. Sallying forth onto the Corrientes to buy some necessities from nearby shops, the streets were already becoming hot and I consumed two iced banana fruit juices with cream, (pure heaven), to keep me going whilst waiting for a bus back to the ship. Two Marconi men were busy on board trying to solve the problem with the AA; they had been once but had retired baffled and today was round two. One of them was a Mr Newell, an ex-R/O from Manchester, and during our conversation it transpired that he had also been to Campha, so we formed an exclusive 'Campha Club' on the spot, as neither of us had ever met anyone else who had been there.

We now had a young guard on duty at the top of the gangway, supposedly to prevent smuggling. He was resplendent in sailor type uniform and apparently appointed by the Ministry of Marine. This bright spark brought a girl on board with him and stopped any other women from boarding the ship. There was a boss of a small engineering firm who, whenever he came aboard a ship to carry out repairs, brought his daughter along to keep the Captain company whilst he got on with the work. Nobody thought any of this at all unusual, it was the accepted way of life. The walk to the Post Office was half a mile along a dockyard road, on one side of which was white fencing daubed with slogans such as, 'Vote al Partida Communista'. The communists were trying to capture the leaderless Peron supporters; however the coal tubs that went up and down our holds had PERON painted in large white letters on their sides, and you felt that Eva's shirtless ones were still there,

351

simply biding their time.

After two long weeks discharging, we headed up river to Rosario in Santa Fe Province. The photographer had been and gone, leaving me with another black and white photograph for my rogue's gallery. Rosario is Argentina's biggest inland port and a main outlet for the grain coming out of the Pampas. There were lots of small houses on the riverbank and, being Sunday, there were people in canoes, horses and riders down by the water's edge, families enjoying themselves picnicking and children running about on the grass. Everyone waved to us as we glided past, often only a few yards from the riverbank. It was our second wedding anniversary and we were writing 10 and 12 page letters to each other regularly, two or three times a week when a lengthy stay in port made it possible.

A Dutch cargo-passenger ship, the *Helanus,* lay alongside and we received a visit from the 1st Officer on behalf of the Captain, asking if there were any stamp collectors on board. I gathered together my duplicates and went to meet the Captain. He was an extremely affable man in his fifties and welcomed me into his cabin, which was strewn with stamps spread over every available surface. He had thousands of stamps in albums, and kiloware yet to be sorted lay piled on the settee. Apparently he had only got the bug two years previously but, in his own words, had gone, 'full steam ahead', since then. The Dutch Consul arrived whilst we were busily engaged in stamp talk and he became part of the coterie as we talked about shipping, freight rates, flags of convenience and all manner of topics, over tea and biscuits. Having acquired about 500 new stamps in exchange for half of my duplicates, it was not only a successful stamp afternoon but also a very pleasant interlude in what was becoming a rather threadbare way of life aboard the *Manhattan.*

It was nine years since I last visited Rosario, on the *Grainton,* and here we were, loading grain under the very same silo. There were many ships waiting to load, but all the grain silos were massive and there was a good turn-round, with vessels regularly moving away from the quayside and others taking their place. Nevertheless, the workers were determined to prove a point, starting work at eight in the morning and finishing at five in the evening. As a result of this, Vasili was free from cargo supervising duties after teatime, so we took the bus to town most evenings and walked around, stopping frequently to tank up on milk-shakes. One evening we were both so hungry that we bought a large cake in the town and scoffed half each on the bus back.

Most days I caught a bus to town after breakfast, conducted my business at the Post Office, browsed in the bookshops, the big stores and then rested in an air-cooled cinema across lunchtime. There was no point in wandering the streets between noon and three because it was too hot and nearly everything closed down for a siesta. After the cinema, and the obligatory quota of milkshakes, a taxi took me back to the ship, loaded down with shopping for myself and others. When the heat of the day had subsided, the *Manhattan* took on the German ship next door at five-a-side soccer on the scrubby grass near to the ship, playing until it was too dark to see the ball. Everyone wore a different shirt so it was easy to pass the ball to the wrong side and all the goals were offside anyway. It was good fun as well as good exercise, and sleep came easily on those nights.

The mornings saw me, stiff and with sore insteps, joining other seamen and workmen outside the dock gate waiting for the penny bus which meandered through the suburbs into the middle of town. The vehicle could, at best, be described as ramshackle, but at that price who could complain. Purchases would likely include shoe polish, American magazines and blocks of marzipan. Following a rest in a news cinema there was the daily call at the Post Office and consumption of yet more milk-shakes. Rosario seemed a much pleasanter place than Buenos Aires, the people were polite and smiled readily, in contrast to B.A. where everyone seemed to be rushing about with set expressions. This was not unique to B.A., many large cities have similar characteristics. Although Rio certainly didn't.

A fair amount of time was spent at the cinema, and one day there was such torrential rain that even the newly built cinema that I was in at the time sprang a leak. Some of the roads on the way back to the ship were flooded, and how the people who lived in the shanty towns that our bus passed through coped with it, was hard to imagine. Most of them were standing in the doorways of their wood and corrugated iron huts looking disconsolate. They must have been very poor, their huts were like those on allotments at home and were equally as bad as those seen in South Africa. Minutes later the bus passed through an avenue of jacaranda trees in full flower, a mass of rich purple in the weak sunlight that was now chasing away the rain clouds. It was unsettling to pass from poverty to beauty so rapidly. Returning on board, after a steak in a dockside cafe, I went to Vasili's cabin, drank his beer and disagreed with everything he said. Not that he said anything amiss, the idea was to stir him out of the comfortable state we were slipping into, so that our discussions henceforth would have a sharper edge, but he saw through this cunning ploy and refused to be drawn.

Days turned into weeks with trips into town and writing long letters to Eileen. There were theological and philosophical conversations with Vasili which stimulated my mind in ways not experienced since similar talks with Antonias on the *Gannet.* Gurdjieff, Ouspensky and Kahlil Gibral were all new to me, but these and others were read in order to keep up with Vasili. In self-defence I borrowed a book, 'Introduction to Philosophy', by George Patrick, from the local Seamen's Library. Emboldened by this new-found interest in philosophy I ventured deeper, opening the covers of a book on metaphysics but soon retreated, agreeing with the adage, 'When he who speaks does not know what he is saying, and he who listens comprehends not what he hears, you have surely stumbled upon metaphysics'.

Meantime, we had lost the football in the dock, a heftier than usual Teutonic boot having seen it sail high and handsome into the space between the two ships. This occasioned a full scale rescue operation, with many hands offering help and yet more giving advice. Lengths of rope with buckets tied on the end proved not to be the answer. Eventually a volunteer on a rope ladder lowered over the bow did the trick and the game was resumed, now grown in popularity to about 15-a-side plus 2 enthusiastic dogs.

Sunday came, and with it the familiar cavalcade of families on an afternoon walk in the sunshine, down to the docks to see the ships. Before the war my family and half of Hull did just the same. A trip into the town on the tram, 1d adults, $^1/_2$d for children, then a walk from Carr Lane down Princes Dock Side and Humber Dock Side, with the AHL boats *Bury* or the *Melrose Abbey* alongside, and the town docks full of ships. On to the horse-wash, the two-tiered Victoria Pier and then the walk along the Riverside Quay with its stately clock tower, all the while immersed in the smells and the atmosphere of ships and cargoes with their promise of far-away exotic places. People are much the same the world over, all they want is a job, enough to eat, to be left in peace to raise a family and look at the ships on Sundays; it's the politicians and Captains of Industry who louse it all up.

The quayside matches now saw me playing in goal because I couldn't run fast enough in open play due to the blisters on my feet. It wasn't easy playing in goal, because people took shots from behind the goal as well as from the front. It was a few days since my first game and my body still ached all over, though it was improving, and by the time we eventually sailed I was something like fit. There were shopping trips to town most days, rejoicing in the fact that marzipan was half the price it was in B.A. Grain trips often entail lengthy stays in port, giving time for incoming mail to catch up with the ship, and correspondence was now arriving from Modified Henry and Canadian Geoff along with recently dated letters from Eileen.

43: TRACKING DOWN HENRY

At long last we moved back to Buenos Aires to complete loading, but this time to a berth within the city limits. Law and Order was stricter here than at the previous berth, which was outside the limits. In B.A., any seaman arrested for being drunk and disorderly could find himself spending the night in jail, and early the next morning becoming part of a squad detailed to clean out the public toilets before being allowed back to his ship. Near to our berth a local flying-boat service operated, the flight path passing close to the ship. This was a sight worth seeing and, as it occurred many times a day, we all lined the rail whenever the roar of the engines started up further down the dock, the plane becoming airborne abeam of us about a hundred yards away. The service began before breakfast and continued until dusk.

Current correspondence with Eileen was about the probability of my coming home soon, the search for a flat, our finances, and my lack of job prospects. Everything was coming to a head, not all of it in a satisfactory manner. We had made financial progress since the Japanese days; the wedding, honeymoon, and other bits and pieces had been paid off, but there still remained a long way to go before we could afford to do what we both wanted. Another year at sea would probably be sufficient, but it looked as though that could be snatched away by events outside our control. It was all a bit troubling and I was comfort eating marzipan by the kilo.

If the bus passed any nearer to the ship it would have needed to come up the gangway. You could get from one side of B.A. to the other through the middle of town, for about 3d, so there was every reason to continue exploring the city by bus as well as on foot. Loading was slow because some local trouble had arisen since we were last there, the dock workers had been locked out and the Army was doing the loading. The soldiers were young, fit, and dealt efficiently with the job in hand with little fuss, but it was all sack loading and slow work.

On one of my excursions into town, a leather cup and a set of dice in a shop window caught my eye. Engaging the young girl assistant in my fluent Spanish only drew the usual puzzled expression, until eventually she saw through my sophisticated cosmopolitan demeanour and asked if I was English. It transpired that she was from Manchester and had been in Buenos Aires for seven years, her father having brought the family out when he got a job there. She wasn't enamoured of the people and wished she was back in Manchester. Perhaps if the family had landed in Rosario, instead of Buenos Aires, she may have been happier to stay in Argentina.

Before we sailed, I traded 111 pesos for three US dollars, ahead of the strong rumour that we were going to Poland from Argentina. One $US could be exchanged for 120 Zlotys on the Polish black market according to the seaman's grapevine. The official rate of exchange in Poland was 24 Zlotys to the £, but its street value was about 300 Zlotys to the £. There seemed to be room for fiscal manoeuvre.

We were now well into our fifth week in Argentina and it felt like time to be off. However, no one else expressed any desire to leave, being fixed up with girlfriends and appearing happy to stay in Buenos Aires indefinitely. Doubtless, still single, I would also have been content to stay, but now all that mattered to me was to get home. To add to our woes it rained heavily, the tarpaulins and hatch covers were pulled over the holds until it ceased and much loading time was lost as a consequence. A Danish ship of the Maerske Line lay just ahead of us along the quay and when one of her holds caught fire there was immediate panic, with fire engines everywhere accompanied by the lovely smell of roasting grain for miles around. More storms followed, the Buenos Aires Herald reported trees and telegraph poles being brought down and planes making emergency landings.

Towards the completion of loading I was co-opted into supervising cargo-handling for a few hours; coming to an agreement with the winch-men to ignore my signals if they knew better than I did. When cargo is being loaded and the slings are lowered into the hold, the winch-men lose sight of them at some point, and have to be guided by signals to indicate whether they can continue lowering without endangering the men working down below. Whilst I was in charge the hold was almost full and so the slings were always in view. This interlude brought me 37 Pesos for doing virtually nothing, whilst the main man probably went to the pictures or visited his mistress.

The Sunday before departure Vasili and I were up before seven, made ourselves some cheese sandwiches and caught an early bus to the Retiro. We bought a kilo of tomatoes and a kilo of apricots from a market, then took the electric train to Tigre, about 20 miles distant, a fifty-minute journey. Tigre, a grassy outpost of Buenos Aires was very popular at weekends, with food stalls, scores of rowing boats on the river and a few cabin cruisers moored at the river's edge. We bought milk at a stall, sat on the riverbank and ate our fruit and sandwiches in the morning sunshine. It was still early, but families were already flooding in on trains and buses, attending to their river craft or staking out a picnic place. We walked along the riverbank then sat down to argue about the Bible. After a while Vasili said I was narrow minded; in turn I berated him for having been so dogmatic when the Roman Catholic priest from the Mission to Seamen had recently visited the ship, Vasili having given him such short shrift that the priest had cycled off in a huff. 'Kettle calling the pot black,' I said and then had to explain what the phrase meant. By mid afternoon space on the grass had grown scarcer so we made tracks for home. It was pleasant to have been among trees and flowers and to lie down on the grass for a while.

It was now early December and the sight of a Christmas tree being transported on the roof of a car made me wish for Christmas at home. On our last day before sailing, I had been in the town and in the evening was caught in a heavy downpour. After making use of a nearby shelter for some time, with no sign of the rain easing, I decided to cut my losses and dashed across the road to the bar and restaurant, Revista Varieties. There was an entrance cover charge and judging by the layout and décor it was an up-market establishment, with linen tablecloths and waiters wearing bow-ties hovering around serving drinks. A cabaret was taking place on the small stage in front of me with some chorus girls, a tenor, a sketch which sent everyone except me into hysterics and went on interminably, but then, ah, but then, appeared a girl of 17 or 18 in the minimum of clothing who performed the most sensuous slow mambo I'd ever seen. She was simply a natural and you don't get many of those. Barry Davies once said of Katerina Witt that he would give her 6 out of 6 just for standing there and

I felt the same way about the mambo girl. Anyway, I felt rewarded for my perseverance in not leaving part way through the previous never-ending sketch. It was after two in the morning, it had stopped raining so I caught a bus back to the ship. Imagine, public transport running all night for peoples' convenience, whatever would they think of next?

After six weeks in Buenos Aires we moved across river to Montevideo, took on bunkers and headed out to sea, bound for Dakar. There were the usual eggs and ouzo on Christmas day and half a dozen of the crew, led by Vasili, went around the ship singing carols. Joining in for something to do, I carried a piece of iron on a length of cord and a spanner with which to beat out the rhythm. From time to time I tried to liven things up a bit, but the mambo rhythm foxed the others and had to be abandoned. I wrote a 24-page letter to Eileen on the way to Dakar, where we took on bunkers before setting course for Germany. The weather was very bad crossing the Bay of Biscay, following us through the Channel. The A.A. responded to four distress calls in one off-watch period, in addition to others monitored whilst on watch. We picked up the Sea Pilot at Weser PV at noon, replacing him by a River Pilot off Bremerhaven who took us up river to Brake, where we went alongside at teatime. We were still living day to day regarding the ship's future. The last letter from the owners, received by the Captain at Dakar, had asked him to send his list of stores required for the next voyage by airmail from Dakar, adding, 'If you are not being laid up we will send these stores to Germany'. I'd had enough of living on the edge so I left the Captain to sort it all out and set off to surprise Modified Henry.

The morning train took me through Rodenkirchen and Nordham to Blexen, where I caught the ferry to Bremerhaven. I had written Henry's address on a piece of paper and asked directions of people as I went along. Arriving at the apartment block, his wife Marta opened the door and recognised me immediately from photographs, then Henry appeared behind her and the three of us stood in the doorway of the flat hugging each other and laughing. It was one of my best welcomes in a long time. We had coffee and cake then went to a nearby bar, returning to the flat to watch a variety programme on the proudly displayed black and white television, talked all evening and it was early morning before we bedded down.

In the morning, Henry went off to his job as the Chief Electrician at a fish-processing factory and I spent the day exploring Bremerhaven, returning to the flat at teatime when Henry arrived home from work. It was good to re-live some of the more outrageous moments on the *Golden Eagle*, because he was more relaxed now, back to his normal self and could see the funny side of some of the incidents. On the *Golden Eagle* he had become so highly-strung that another month would have seen him carted off to the funny farm; with me not far behind him.

The devastation caused by the war had left millions of homeless refugees criss-crossing Europe, with little but what they stood up in. What meagre possessions they had, they carried or pushed on a pram or handcart, looking for somewhere to settle and carve out a new life for themselves and their families. At the end of the war Henry and his wife Marta were amongst these refugees. Their home had been in Stettin but they had to leave there with their two little girls, ending up in Bremerhaven penniless, Marta having long since sold her rings and jewellery to buy food. Now they had this warm comfortable little home and it must have seemed like heaven to them. The next day, after we had talked ourselves out over a meal in the flat, they came to the ferry to see me off on my return journey to Brake.

Like me, Henry needed to go to sea to earn money, but didn't want to leave his family. However, jobs were no easier to find ashore in Germany than in England, and the money he earned on the *Golden Eagle* had gone into furnishing the flat. Life ashore was economically very hard for him and just before I left to return to the ship he said to me that if, and only if, we could get a ship together he would go back to sea. However, the shipping situation was worsening, with more and more vessels being laid up, those ships that did put to sea were operating on a tight budget, with wages cut from the Captain downward. Mr John Goulandris sent me a personal letter regretting the reduction in my salary from £95 to £85 a month, mentioning that this figure was substantially higher than others in the company were being paid. But none of it felt right, things were changing and not for the better; even the *Golden Eagle* was laid up in Piraeus along with most of our other ships, and some new ships that the company had on order had been cancelled. These disconcerting thoughts accompanied me to bed, but the sound of the grain being sucked up the chutes that dipped into the holds was very soothing and it was not long before sleep took me out of one world and into another.

The *Manhattan* left Brake for Hamburg in thick fog, but with Pilots on board there was no need for me to be up all night watching the radar screen, as was often the case on short coastal trips. When we berthed at Hamburg the dock was deserted except for ourselves and one other ship. It was a large dock, all the cranes were idle and, by the look of it, the shipping slump had already arrived in Hamburg. Everything was depressing and unsettling, with question marks attached and no answers in sight; I needed to get off the ship for a few hours to clear my head. A ferry service took me to the other side of the dock, and from there I walked to the centre of town, past the main station, through some floral gardens, along a shopping street, around a department store, over a bridge until eventually I came across a lakeside shelter, just right for eating sandwiches. Continuing through the Nieu Stad area into the St. Pauli entertainment area, there was little in the way of neighbourhood cinemas, all such activity seemingly concentrated in one main street. Going into one bar-cum-restaurant I wasn't much enamoured, leaving after one drink to reconnoitre further and coming across the Reeperbahn, which seemed to lack its reputed atmosphere, although it doubtless livened up as the evening wore on. After sampling the beer and entertainment at a couple of bars that could have been the setting for 'Cabaret', I wended my way back to the ship in the gloom and the snow.

Reaching the deserted dock, it was still snowing hard and work on the cargo had become intermittent. A long week had now been spent on a ship in an empty dock in Germany and everything was cold, covered in snow and the future lay under an uncertain grey cloud. A Greek seaman who had been paid off a ship in Hamburg came on board looking for work; he had tried a number of ships without any luck and said he would be happy to work for bed and board only, without any wages. Things were steadily getting worse, and some of the stories that older seamen had told me, about the shipping depression of the 1930s and the hard times of those days seemed all too familiar. It looked as though a repeat scenario was upon us in the 1950s. There was a British Mission to Seamen somewhere ashore, so as an alternative to committing hari-kari, I set off to find it, trudging along the icy pavements looking for the familiar Flying Angel sign. Once located, no one else was there and, after reading some three-day old English newspapers, I had a solitary cup of tea before making my way through the falling snow back to the ship.

360

44: BILLY BUNTER AND THE SECRET POLICE

Snow showers accompanied us as we left Hamburg the next day for Brunnsbuttel, passing through the Kiel Canal in darkness, the cold and snow still persisting. Arriving in Kiel after breakfast, we launched ourselves into the Baltic for the two-day journey to Danzig; or Gdansk if you prefer. The route between the Canal and Danzig was well buoyed and the trip was made through thin sea ice that was continuously forming around us. We reached Danzig at midnight and anchored until four in the morning, going alongside in what looked like a timber basin. There was thick ice in the river and the cylinder barrel of one of the winches cracked during the night due to the bitter cold. After that, we fed steam through the pipes to the winches and left them slowly turning over. There was a mass of timber stacked up ashore, each pile sheltered by sloping boards which gave the impression of rows and rows of houses with snow on their roofs, extending as far as the eye could see.

As nothing seemed likely to happen in the immediate future, the Captain, Vasili and I went ashore the next morning, well wrapped up against the cold. We had to take our passports ashore with us, also an official pass stamped, 'For use in the port, town and harbour area only', so it was plain they didn't want us wandering off. Our passes were checked by a uniformed guard with a rifle and huge snow-boots, who inhabited a sentry-box at the foot of the gangway. This was the Eastern Bloc in the Cold War era, all grim and depressing, the freezing winds and snow adding to the gloom.

We walked through the thick snow for a couple of hundred yards and caught a small ferry across to the far bank of the river, where we trudged through banks of snow to the ship chandlers, Baltona Stores. This emporium appeared to be the only place where you could buy anything. The country seemed very much like our own, 'all goods for export only', period after the war, when anything decent that we made, from woollen goods to merchant ships, had to be sold abroad to raise money for us to live on; 'austerity', being the watchword in Britain for many years. The store was plainly designed as a tourist trap, accepting only British pounds and American dollars. A group of Russian sailors came in whilst we were there, looking at the clothing material, most of which was cheap, tatty and a screaming electric blue colour. The sailors were as diverse a crowd as would be expected from such a vast country, but there was a predominance of Mongol features and high cheekbones. Most of them were sallow complexioned and needed a haircut, but they were well mannered and wandered around the store examining goods and putting them down again, seemingly unsure of what they wanted. One sailor stood out from the others, tall and handsome with a dark moustache, he looked as if he would be more at home in the saddle, or in a Hollywood movie about the Russian Revolution.

From the ship chandlers we caught a rickety old tram for the twenty-minute ride into the centre of the city. In the 1930s Danzig, and the so-called 'Danzig Corridor', had been much in the news as a centre of political dispute. But now it was depressing; street after street lay in ruins and the town centre had been devastated. There were wooden kiosks on street corners selling newspapers, cheap souvenirs, bottles of scent, combs, cigarettes and postcards, but there was little else to buy. The people were poorly clothed, the transport on its last legs and the whole place, in 1958, looked like the rest of Europe had in 1948. The evidence of bombing and destruction was everywhere, the atmosphere oppressive and it was very, very cold, with snow banked on both sides of the street and more preparing to fall from leaden skies.

Poland's suffering didn't end when peace came, she was sacrificed to political expediency by countries that owed her much and should have done better by her. Now, she was still oppressed whilst the rest of Europe was slowly climbing out of the pit into the daylight; nobody laughed, nobody called out to each other, everyone talked quietly as if afraid of being overheard. The Secret Police did not have to be in evidence, the knowledge that they could be just around the corner was sufficient. The people looked tired, the stuffing knocked out of them and with a weight of misery on their shoulders. The history of Poland is one of courage, sadness and betrayal and its people deserved better than the hand they were dealt.

Danzig, city of the middle ages, with its wonderful churches, buildings, libraries, learning, traditions and heritage had once been known as the Queen of the Baltic, but the war put an end to all that. Next to a church, with minarets more reminiscent of Byzantium than northern Europe, were two characterless new buildings, one of which housed the Hotel Monopol. This edifice appeared to contain the only social life in town so we entered, sat down in the foyer and took stock of our finances. We had 30 Zlotys and 6 red-hot US dollars between the three of us. We drew match-stalks; Vasili lost, took the 6 dollars and went back on the streets to do the dirty work. He returned, having negotiated 140 Zlotys for a dollar on the black market, the current official rate being 25 to the dollar. Now, suddenly awash with money, over 800 Zlotys, we ordered coffee, cakes, bottles of wine and prepared to enjoy ourselves.

At seven o'clock the restaurant opened on the floor above us, so we climbed the stairs to investigate. There were tables and chairs set around the walls of a large room, with a small dance floor in the centre and a communist band playing western music for the proletariat. We ordered dinner, which in my case consisted of smoked salmon, potatoes, peas, salad, bread and butter and a bottle of Hungarian white wine. Shortly afterwards I had roast pork, potatoes, salad, black bread and butter and a large beer. This was followed by fruit with whipped cream and coffee and I don't need any comments thank you. We were all too full to move, and simply sat, talked and watched the dancing. None of the women wore make-up, most were drably dressed and didn't appear to have good figures, though it was hard to tell. The men wore heavy boots with their tapered trousers tucked into the tops of them. In the dimly lit room this gave the impression that they were dancing in bicycle clips. We felt it inadvisable to strike up a conversation with anyone, partly because we expected to get the Party line in return anyway, but more because we felt that anyone we spoke to would be looked upon suspiciously by the heavy types dining at nearby tables and be quizzed by them after we had left. And I'm sure they had enough troubles already without being questioned by the Secret Police.

We were aboard by midnight and slept soundly. The whole evening, food and wine included, had cost us one US dollar each, thanks to Vasili's Bureau de Change act down the side street; goodness knows what it would have cost otherwise. We heard of a British wireless operator who had taken a wad of dollars ashore, been picked up by the police and thrown in jail for 24 hours. Prominent notices said that foreign currency could only be exchanged at approved banks, and that changing it anywhere else rendered one liable to severe penalties, (Castration, death optional). It was a good thing that we were all law-abiding people.

Vasili and the rest of the crew did not post mail home to Greece from Poland. Following the Greek Civil War of 1948 many Greek communists fled abroad, and if mail reached an address in Greece from a suspect overseas country, the police could become a little too interested and start asking why the recipients were receiving mail from communist countries, and maybe other awkward questions. There were numerous timber ponds near to the ship, people were ice-skating on them all day long and it was very entertaining to watch the activity from the warmth of my cabin. We had a black and white cat on board that had taken passage with us from Hamburg; mostly he slept in my cabin and drank my evaporated milk. If I was preparing for a wash and he got to the wash basin first, he drank the water coming out of the tap and I had to wait until he had finished.

We were to load coal for South America. Unlike most ports, they did not load us from waiting coal wagons or stockpiles of coal adjacent to the dockside. In Danzig they sent the output from the mine by wagon direct to the ship, tipping it straight into the holds. Accordingly we were dependent upon the speed and continuity of the mine's output; if the coalmine stopped for lunch, we stopped for lunch. There were large chunks of ice floating around in the river and some of these began attaching themselves to the ship's side. Work commenced on trimming the coal in our holds and these were the first signs that loading was approaching completion. Meanwhile I was busy in my cabin buying Polish stamps from unidentified people in long black overcoats and big boots. Stamps were considered to be a form of negotiable currency, consequently dealing in them was illegal and subject to severe penalties, (see above), but I took a chance on it not being a set-up to raise fines and bought some with my hard currency at favourable rates of exchange.

Vasili had a different modus operandi. He had gone ashore to buy clothes, which were cheap if purchased at the black market rate of exchange. We were not allowed to take parcels through the dock gates, so he dressed in the clothes that he had bought. He put on three pairs of trousers, three jackets, two raincoats and a topcoat and looked like Billy Bunter. How he got past the police at the gate I don't know. His success was to prove his undoing however, because the Captain asked him to do the same for him. Some people are like that, if someone else gets a bargain they want in on it, even if they don't need it. Anyway, off trots Vasili ashore the following day, repeats the performance and, what else, was stopped at the dock gate on his way back to the ship and asked to disrobe. It must have had all the elements of a Chaplinesque comedy, Billy Bunter trudging through the snow, stopped by the Police, layer after layer of clothing discarded, the inevitability of retribution dawning. Vasili denied purchasing any of the clothes, saying that his girlfriend ashore had given them to him. He was fined US$40 by a disbelieving regime, a considerable sum. The Captain blamed Vasili for getting caught and offered to pay half the fine. Vasili, who had not wanted to go anyway and had only gone to keep the peace, was fed up. But it was all much in keeping with such things; you get somebody to do your dirty work and then blame them if things go wrong. The Captain tried to rally support for his view that Vasili was fully responsible and should pay the $40, and that he, Captain, was being generous in offering to pay half of it. A couple of boot-lickers supported this view but most mumbled in their beards, and mine was the lone voice that said as he, Captain, was responsible for instigating the operation, he should pay the fine; they ended up paying half each.

45: WINTER STORMS AND A CRACKED DECK

The Port Doctor's routine visit revealed that my smallpox vaccination had run out, and an attractive blonde nurse duly arrived on board to give me a jab. She was quite vivacious and the rest of the crew hurriedly checked up on their medical certificates to spot any omissions. Meanwhile the nurse and I got down to business. I have not had such a laugh over an injection before or since, and all this merriment from behind the closed cabin door gave rise to much speculation, with odd looks being cast in my direction for some time afterwards.

There was another Greek ship close by and some of our crew wanted to go on board to have a yarn, see if they knew anyone, hear any news and gossip from Greece, exchange newspapers and magazines, the usual things. Not here. The sentry of the other ship stopped them from boarding. The sentries even stopped their own Custom Officers and other officials in order to inspect their boarding passes before allowing them on board. They also recorded in a book, everyone who went ashore and the time they returned. Seven o'clock on a bitterly cold snow laden morning; our sentry made quite a picture in the grey light as he stamped around his brazier, the flickering orange flames reflected in the snow around the foot of the gangway. It would have made a good photograph but that would probably have carried a severe penalty, (see above). Also he had a rifle and would doubtless have received Brownie points for using it, so I contented myself by hoping his fire would go out.

News from home was good, Eileen was to rent an unfurnished bed-sit on Beverley Road, which would take my single bed, chest of drawers and the furniture that was in storage. A gas fire and cooker were to be installed after which Eileen could decorate the room and make curtains before moving in; all in her spare time. Other news was dreadful: the Manchester United football team was involved in a plane crash in Munich in the same awful weather covering us in Danzig that day, many players being killed and others injured.

We left Danzig, loaded to the Plimsoll line with coal for South America. Our stop at Ostermoor in the Kiel Canal for bunkers yielded more mail and now Eileen talked of curtains, lino, a Flavel cooker and a Singer sewing machine. We exited the canal, entered the River Elbe at seven that evening and went aground at half past nine. Even with engines full astern, then full ahead, she wouldn't budge. We were high and dry on a mud bank in the middle of the River Elbe and our Pilot couldn't believe it. The *Manhattan* had a 28ft draught and the chart showed 36ft of water where we were aground. Even as we stuck there, ships were steaming past us in all directions. The Pilot said he had been going up and down the river for fifteen years and passed over that spot hundreds of times without mishap. Nevertheless, there we were, stuck. We floated off at midnight and thereafter the bilges and the double-bottom tanks were sounded every half-hour, luckily with no seawater being found in them.

Dropping the Pilot at the Elbe LV we set a southerly course in the face of a force 8 WSW gale and straightaway began shipping water heavily. The weather worsened during the night and early morning, and our speed was down to 3 knots and labouring. Damage was done by the storm to the steam-pipe casing on deck, also to some electrical cables, resulting in a fire in the electrical switchboard on the bridge. The situation looked serious as we struggled along in the teeth of the gale for the next few hours. Throughout the night I was either on the bridge scanning the radar or in the wireless room. The weather was bitterly cold, snowing and sleeting, blowing a gale and worse, but the old girl kept on digging her nose into it and holding her own.

At seven in the morning a 6ft long crack was discovered in the deck plating on the port side, aft of no. 3 derrick post. The crack ran athwart-ships and looked nasty. Water was entering the cross bunker and a cement box was hurriedly constructed in an attempt to seal the crack. The weather was absolutely foul, with sleet, high winds and a rough sea. At noon our position by Direction Finder was 53.35½N, 03.36E; the date, the 10th February 1958. Over a period of years, many unexplained ship disappearances were attributed to metal fatigue or rivet failure. Stress fractures, particularly in icy and bitterly cold conditions, could occur instantaneously, the vessel sinking without even time to send a distress signal. Wartime vessels, hurriedly built, were thought to be particularly prone to these disasters and the *Manhattan* appeared to score maximum points all round. We reported our situation to the owners and received a wire back ordering us into the nearest port, Flushing, for repairs. My last time in Flushing the Germans were outside Antwerp, doodlebugs droned overhead and we were pleased to leave; now here we were, in trouble again, but this time pleased to be there. Going alongside in the repair yard at Flushing at noon, the cracked plate was taken ashore for examination, as was the corresponding plate from the starboard side.

The diagnosis seemed to be that alterations to the ship at some stage in her life had resulted in a small hatch being removed, a steel plate welded on deck in its place, and it was this welding that had fractured. Two new plates were fitted, one on either side of the deck where the original twin hatches had been. Whilst this was going on, the Chief Engineer, his wife and I took the bus into Vlissingen, where many of the people wore Dutch national costume with bonnets, clogs and voluminous black skirts, just as in old Dutch paintings. The only part of Flushing I remembered was the shipyard, whose gantries loomed ever skywards, dominating the town. We left the next morning for Dakar. Whilst in Flushing the cat disappeared, the 2nd Engineer having put it ashore, blaming it for the ship running aground and the crack in the deck. When I asked what he thought he was doing he said that everyone knew cats brought bad luck. I had become fond of the cat and told him he should come into the 20th century and we ended up glaring at each other from a foot apart. However, it was better that the cat lived, because it was not unknown for them to be thrown overboard from Greek ships whenever a scapegoat was needed.

The Captain gave orders for the pantry to be locked from six at night to six the next morning. The only thing in there that affected me was the electric kettle for making drinks when on watch, coming off watch or when on the bridge all night. Annoyed at this petty restriction I stormed into his cabin demanding an explanation. The ensuing exchange was 90% me and 10% him, the outcome being that an electric kettle was presented to me when we called at Dakar, courtesy of the Captain. Shortly after leaving Dakar for South America we discovered a stowaway, a young coloured Portuguese lad, who had escaped detection in the routine check that all ships carry out before leaving port. The Captain, true to form, blamed Vasili for not having discovered the stowaway before we left, and an argument ensued. It wasn't just about stowaways, it was more a clash of personalities. Vasili went about his work like a proper Chief Officer; he did rounds, inspected, delegated work to the Bosun, etc, whereas the Captain preferred a lot of shouting with people rushing aimlessly about.

The number of ships laid up was increasing whilst freight rates were decreasing. Caribbean oil freight rates, 130/- per ton a year previously, had fallen to 13/- per ton. Ships could not possibly trade at these rates, and there was nothing the owners could do except lay their fleets up until the situation improved, whenever that might be. Perhaps somebody, even then, was whispering about containerisation. A statistic heard on the Merchant Navy weekly radio programme was that, of the flags of convenience vessels, 54% were Greek and 40% were American owned.

The real business of the trip had now started, and on the long haul from Senegal to the River Plate there was ample time to pursue our scheme for instant riches. In Danzig we had over-ordered on cigarettes by a sizeable margin. The Captain, Vasili, the Chief Steward and I had noted that cigarettes were cheap in Poland but expensive in Argentina, so we sailed from Danzig, the bond bursting at the seams with American cigarettes, intending to off-load them in Argentina at a huge profit as a buffer against impending redundancy. We had all bought as many cartons as we could afford. On the previous trip it had been arranged with the local mafia that the Chief Steward was to be our contact man in Argentina. All four of us put in the working hours for the project upon which we were now embarking. In wartime, merchant ships carried more crew than in peacetime, plus DEMS gun crews, consequently there were more life-jackets on board than were presently needed. The surplus jackets had been thrown into a locker in the bowels of the ship and forgotten about, until Vasili discovered them. They were standard 'Mae West' issue with blocks of cork sewn into place at intervals round the jacket. These blocks were just the shape and weight of a 200 carton of Camel or

Lucky Strike cigarettes. Need one say more? All that was required was a loosening of the stitching, the extraction of the cork, the substitution of a carton of cigarettes in its place and everything stitched up again. It was finely balanced as to whether our scheme would result in largesse or a spell in a fly-ridden Argentine jail.

Meanwhile, life outside the sewing of life jackets continued as usual, lazy days crossing the South Atlantic at 10 knots, flying fish, sunshine, pleasant breezes, sewing on of buttons, darning of socks, washing hanging out on the line and all was well with the world. Also, wonder of wonders, my complaints to the Captain about the inadequate cleaning of my cabin and the wireless room, had resulted in both mess boys taking the curtains to be washed, the carpets to be beaten, the brass-work polished and everything in sight cleaned and dusted. Although it was very hot, Vasili and I were the only ones to wear shorts. Mine were shop-bought, Vasili's looked like ordinary trousers cut down and, together with a home-made hat cut from sacking, he looked more like a beachcomber than a Chief Officer. The meals had become monotonous, a lump of unappetising meat and a helping of macaroni cropping up regularly. I had bought food ashore and created my own meals on board from time to time; if all else failed a couple of eggs could be boiled in the electric kettle and bread and butter lifted from the pantry. Coffee was my main drink, or tea with lemon, not milk unless it was condensed milk and the tea was strong enough to stand a spoon up in, like trawler tea.

Recent letters from Eileen, collected at Dakar, indicated that the bed-sit had been rented and that our home address was now 265 Beverley Road, above a Doctors' surgery, opposite the swimming baths. It comprised one large room on the first floor with a bay window overlooking the garden at the back. There was an alcove with wash-basin, a walk-in cupboard on the landing, a shared bathroom and an attic for storage. Eileen was doing all the work needed on moving in, like painting and wall-papering, the latter with a colourful design of Dutch tapestry, and here I was, sewing buttons on, darning socks and ironing shirts. A 4-speed Dansette record player had been purchased from Curry's and at last we had somewhere to put our furniture.

The Captain asked me to go through the Charter Party Agreement, looking for unusual clauses or suspicious small print. His English was good, but someone whose first language is English was needed to grapple with this type of document and I had scanned similar papers before, finding such cheerful clauses as, 'Bills of Lading to be paid on sight, ship lost or ship not lost'. It was like reading the heart-warming small print in Life Insurance policies where it says, 'Your earlier death means assured benefits for your family'.

Orders came at last. The first stop was Buenos Aires, to discharge part cargo to lighten our draught, then to Villa Constitucion in Santa Fe Province. There was increasing tension among certain members of the crew as we approached the River Plate. We picked up the Pilot at Recalada at 0230, a wire was sent off at 0300 to let interested parties know our ETA at Intercession and at 0500 we went aground on a mud bank in the middle of the River Plate. This was fast becoming a habit and one that we could well do without. High water came and went, and with it went our hopes of floating off quickly.

Why we became stuck may be worth relating. When at sea the engine uses seawater for cooling and this is taken in through grills near the keel. In rivers, canals or shallow channels, these grills tend to suck in mud as well as water, clogging the system, so they are closed off, grills higher up the ship's side being used instead. This change-over of intake grills had not been made at the appropriate time, and over a period we had been sucking in mud as well as water through the lower grill, gradually causing the whole system to clog up and eventually cease functioning altogether. The engine had been shut down to investigate the cause of the problem, but no one had told the bridge that the main engine was out of action and that, as a consequence, the ship had no steering way. The bridge believed the ship to be still under their control, whereas in fact there was no propeller turning and the only force carrying her forward was her momentum; this gradually diminished until she drifted gently to the side of the dredged channel and hit the mud bank.

The failure by the engine room to inform the bridge that they had no power is about as grave an aberration as can be committed at sea. The repercussions were not known to me, but seemed very bitter, and relations between deck and engine room deteriorated rapidly. As an aside to all this, the friends of Philip Morris and Peter Stuyvesant looked upon the matter from another angle. Lots of people come aboard a vessel after a grounding, poking about in the bowels of the ship to see if she had sprung a leak, and we would much rather they didn't bother. It was really very pleasant stuck in the middle of the river. The Montevideo and Buenos

Aires classical music stations were only a couple of miles away, Mozart and Beethoven filled the wireless room all day between sending wires to all and sundry and receiving swathes of wires back again. The sun was shining, and, apart from Greek oaths and recriminations flying around, it was all very peaceful.

46: FEDORAS IN THE DARKNESS

Amongst the mail that the Agent brought out to us was the official report on the crack in the deck that we had suffered in the North Sea. The report gave the cause of the crack as being the bitterly cold weather that we had experienced in the preceding days. There was apparently no connection between the grounding in the Elbe and the crack, which had appeared shortly afterwards. Meantime, another high tide in the River Plate had come and gone and we were still high and dry. I felt sorry for the Captain because, although neither of the groundings was remotely his fault, a Pilot having charge of the ship on both occasions, the Log Book would show a ship under his command as being aground twice in one voyage. As for me, this was my third or fourth grounding and I was becoming blasé about the whole thing.

At the third high tide we slid off the mud and proceeded to Basin E in the Nieu Port, Buenos Aires, going alongside in the early evening. The Chief Steward went ashore to make his contacts, reporting back that we were to sit tight until after the Customs had been on board the next morning. The Customs inspection passed off without incident and a couple of days later it all happened. We were given a time, later that evening, when the cigarettes, wrapped in newspapers, were to be ready for immediate transfer ashore. We retrieved the cartons from the life-jackets, bundled them into the shapes and sizes required, moved them to a convenient place near the top of the gangway and waited. It was all quiet on the dockside until a black saloon came hurtling out of the darkness and screeched to a halt at the foot of the gangway. Two figures in dark overcoats, their collars turned up and fedoras pulled down over their faces, rushed up the gangway, talked hurriedly with the Chief Steward and mysterious packages changed hands. The four of us and the two fedoras carried the merchandise down the gangway and heaved it into the boot of the car, which sped off towards the dock gate. You got the impression that, although Peron no longer held sway, his followers carried on their way of life as it ever was.

It was all over in less time than it takes to tell. We didn't make much out of it, after the entrepreneurs ashore had handed out pesos to various parties to ensure safe passage and taken their own cut, there wasn't much left to distribute between four of us. But it didn't really matter, perhaps the reward was in the excitement of organising it, the chances taken, the risk of detection. I decided to go straight after this anyway. Vasili and I went to a couple of cinemas the first day, stayed aboard the second day, had dinner ashore the third day, cinema by myself the fourth day, together to the cinema the fifth and sixth days and to the Abdullah club and the Retiro Fun Park on the seventh and final day before sailing.

We had discharged half our cargo in Buenos Aires, the remainder was for Villa Constitucion and not expected to take very long. Villa Constitucion turned out to be a small hot dusty town. The cars looked like Model T Fords, the streets were all but deserted, the roads were potholed and the pavements cracked. There was one presentable street with shops, offices and a solitary bank that seemed to be waiting for Butch Cassidy and the Sundance Kid to happen along. I liked the place, it had atmosphere, but there was nothing to do there.

The 25th March was a Greek annual holiday celebrating independence from Turkey. Two lambs were roasted on a spit which had been set up on the grass near the ship, lots of wine was consumed and general merriment prevailed. Most days were spent ashore, walking around to pass the time though there was nothing much to buy or to see. Regular visits were paid to the small Post Office and one day, upon hearing of my previous connections with the firm, the Postmaster took me on a tour of his office. It seemed better run than some other Post Offices in Argentina, where the counter staff weighed your envelope, took your money, put the stamps on very lightly and removed a pesos worth after you'd left. We continued our games of football on the quayside. Discharging was delayed by rain and we left on the seventh day for Bahia Blanca. A letter arrived from Captain George asking me to go with him on a new ship, but the dates were indefinite and the whole matter so uncertain that it wasn't possible to make plans around it, even had I so wished.

Soon after we arrived at Bahia Blanca I caught the bus for the 20-minute ride into town, being joined on the journey by a very presentable young Greek Chief Officer from another vessel in port. He was on his way to meet his girlfriend and spoke excellent English, having lived in England for three years. It was four years since I was in Bahia Blanca and little had changed; at the Post Office the same counter clerk was sitting on the same stool as he had four years ago. Vasili had been studying me, pronouncing me above average intelligence but stupid because I put it to no good use. In return I taught him some Shakespearean oaths and swearwords which he seemed pleased to have, promising that whenever he used them he would think of me.

Our stowaway had disappeared; this was always on the cards but we were powerless to do much about it, short of incarcerating him in the chain locker. The ship would be fined if he was not on board when we sailed, because Argentina didn't want stowaways any more than we did. The Captain was already blaming Vasili and demanding he pay any fine out of his own salary, which seemed unfair. The Captain and Vasili went on board a nearby Greek ship and our Captain says to the other Captain, 'Why not stop your dynamo every night like we do and save money'. This other ship was henceforth plunged into cold and darkness every night, their crew vowing to lynch our Captain if he set foot aboard their ship again.

One morning I was lying in my bunk before breakfast watching a baby cockroach climbing the bulkhead, marvelling at its minuteness and wondering how such a tiny creature could possess co-ordination of all those legs, an instinctive reaction to danger and the ability to reproduce more little specks of life, identical in every detail, and so on till the end of time. Atomic bombs and space rockets seemed like children's building blocks compared to the omnipotence able to create and breathe life into a baby cockroach.

We were all fed up but needed the trip to extend so that the money would keep coming in, yet this hanging around was tedious in the extreme. It was cold and miserable at night when the generator was switched off, and cutting down on the food was the last straw. Breakfast, in my cabin, was toast and honey with lemon tea; the butter in its jar at the foot of the bunk was frozen solid most mornings when I woke up. There were lengthy conversations with Vasili and arguments with the Captain, but basically I was just tired, fed up and needed a holiday. Vasili and I were similar in many ways, but whereas he was interested in people, my rapport tended more towards animals and nature. A practising Christian, he had regard for the philosophies of Gibral, and quotes from The Prophet often cropped up in our conversation. One day, whilst he was ashore seeking out the remnants of a Russian Orthodox Church community, I was observing ants on the quayside. There were two colonies 100 yards apart and a continuous stream of tiny bodies, six across, moved between the two colonies. Their route took them across a footpath, through some short grass, onto a railway line for 50 yards and so to the other colony, situated between two sets of railway lines. There must have been an awful lot of reconstruction of fallen ceilings after the trains had rumbled past. They seemed to be transporting leaf-mould from one colony to another and were achieving more than I was at the time.

A venture to the British ship next door failed to improve my mood. The R/O was a foppish young Glaswegian with an affected Oxford accent, full of gin and all togged up for a dance at the Mission to Seamen. He failed in his efforts to drag me along with him, even a large neat gin out of a dirty glass failed to elicit any response, other than a desire to help him on his way. There was a Latvian 3rd Officer on board who lived in Bradford and was soon to become naturalised; he knew the Kalev well and we talked about her and the people on board. The Captain of the ship was from Linnaeus Street in Hull but had adopted Wales as his home. The young assistant steward was a gangly youth of the Elvis variety. He was also dressed up for The Dance, his pimply face set off by a black Edwardian suit with drainpipe trousers, black shoes, black shirt with buttoned collar, a string tie, a shock haircut, and thought he was the bee's knees. I wondered if the girls ashore would think so too; I felt sorry for them, mostly they were so lovely and attractively dressed, with a maturity way ahead of the boys, yet what did they get lumbered with but gauche pimply youths full of their own importance and scarce a brain in their heads. Someone encapsulated the enigma in the couplet:

'Little girls grow up to be women,
Little boys have a job for life.'

Naturally there are exceptions, like me, but they are rare and to be greatly prized.

It was the Greek Easter Day and plates were laid out in the saloon for the midnight breaking of the fast and the red eggs ritual. Having been through this many times before I opted out and went to bed complete with ear plugs. Just as the celebrations on board petered out in the early hours and there was a danger of my getting some sleep, floating along the night air from the quayside came the familiar bawdy shouting and singing of the British next door, returning from their bacchanalian pursuits. Next morning Vasili showed signs of being fed up with his countrymen after the previous day's festivities and said to me, 'These people have absolutely no knowledge of the tradition or meaning of the Easter celebration and even though they have been going to church for years they have no idea why they are going'. Apparently he had read some relevant passages from the Bible to them on Easter Day but no interest or understanding had been evinced; all anyone was interested in was the grub.

Our loading commenced with enthusiasm but soon ran out of steam. The ship was loaded with 4,000 of the required 10,000 tons of grain in one short burst and then everything shut down for the weekend. If it had been an all-bulk cargo we could have been away the next day, but 1,500 tons of it was bagged grain, and as there are 16 bags to the ton that meant 24,000 bags to be manhandled and stowed and that seemed likely to take some time. Over the weekend Vasili and I walked around the sunlit tree-lined avenues and squares of Bahia Blanca, refuelling ourselves with milk shakes and steak sandwiches. We were sitting on a bench in the main plaza reading the Buenos Aires Herald, watching the fountain and the passing parade, when a young girl and her mother heard us talking and asked if we had any stamps, so we arranged for them to come to the ship later in the week. On our walk back to the *Manhattan* we were followed by a pack of friendly dogs; out of luck if they expected any tit-bits because they probably had more food to share than we did.

Two things had occurred when we got back on board. Firstly, there had been a letter from the owners, saying that if they were not able to secure a cargo for us during our voyage home, then we should be laid up somewhere in Europe. Secondly, the workers were loading cargo quite rapidly and it seemed we should be leaving sooner than expected. The stamp collectors arrived just before we sailed but were not allowed on board, so we all sat in the police box at the dock gates and exchanged stamps there. In the evening an invitation came from the R/O of the British Queensbury to have supper with them, meat sandwiches, Dundee cake and tea, quite a feast, because we could starve to death on the *Manhattan* after teatime, unless we managed to pinch some bread and cheese from the pantry. Eileen told me that the nurses were so poorly fed at one of her training hospitals they had to buy food to live on, and it wasn't far off this state of affairs on the *Manhattan*.

We called at Montevideo for bunkers at the start of the journey home. The Captain had broken the news to the crew that their overtime rate had been reduced from 2/6d to 2/- an hour. He had received these instructions at the beginning of the voyage but had let them work during the outward trip believing they were on the higher rate. The crew, unsurprisingly, refused to work any more overtime from then on. We were short of potatoes and the trip had only just begun. Worse still, we were short of water, or so the Chief said, and that too was being rationed, the Mess Boy having to pump water up from the tank and carry it amidships in a bucket. Food portions at mealtimes had become greatly reduced and that did nothing to raise morale.

At sea once more, I was writing a letter ready for posting at Dakar, amongst other things describing civilisation as people rushing about like ants getting nowhere, railing against becoming part of it, yet having no alternative of my own to offer. Maybe Vasili was right after all. Dakar was a milestone, the last letters to send and receive, for which neither of us would be sorry. We ran into force 8 gales shortly after leaving and were down to six knots, encountering heavy seas all the way to the Channel, adding a couple of days to the trip. Our orders were to discharge part-cargo in London and the balance in Newcastle, after which it looked like laying-up time somewhere. This was the last time to experience that strange sensation known as 'the Channels', a mixture of anticipation and excitement that you feel on entering the English Channel, homeward bound after a lengthy trip away. We picked up the Pilot off Dungeness at 0130 but had to wait for the tide until 1030, passing Southend at noon and then Tilbury Docks, with the *Iberia* and *Strathmore* berthed alongside. We entered Victoria Dock, London, at teatime and found ourselves in good company with *Port Townsville, Port Sydney, Durban Castle, New Zealand Star, Uganda, Ceramic* and *Carthage* also alongside, a truly wonderful array of ships.

47: FATE LENDS A HAND

From Victoria Dock I walked to Plaistow, caught the tube to King's Cross, telephoned Eileen, then wandered around the station taking in the smell of smoke, oil, steam and the welcome sight of the engines, ate a careworn sandwich in the buffet and read the evening paper until my train was due. Having had less than an hour's sleep the previous night coming through the Channel, I was tired and pretty much working on adrenaline. The midnight train took me as far as Doncaster and, afraid of falling asleep, missing the connection to Hull and being carried on to Newcastle, a good deal of the time was spent walking the corridors. Eileen was waiting on the cold deserted station at five in the morning and suddenly it was all over, the heartache and separation were ended. We walked home through the quiet streets hand in hand, hardly believing that this time it really was the last voyage and that we weren't going to be parted again.

The bed-sit was our first proper home, one spacious room that seemed the most wonderful place in the world to us. We stayed in the next day, eating, sleeping, talking, playing records, until conscience made us get up after tea and walk to see my parents. The following day was Whit Monday, we had breakfast at noon, walked to Rose Street to collect Raffe, taking him with us to the Circle where Hull CC were playing Rotherham in a Yorkshire Council match. We enjoyed the game, which Hull won, and Raffe also enjoyed himself pulling the cushion seats about and having to be restrained whenever the ball came near the boundary.

Next day I returned to the ship in London. Having twice previously requested a routine Wireless Safety Inspection without result, my request had finally borne fruit just as we were about to be laid up, and was scheduled for the following morning. The Certificate was duly issued and as the discharging was proceeding rapidly there was no point in going home again. I hitched a lift in a lorry from the dockside to Canning Town station and took the tube to Leicester Square. It was raining so I browsed amongst the books in Foyle's, then had tea at the Regent restaurant in Wardour Street and saw Peter Sellers in Up the Creek at the Leicester Square Theatre in the evening.

The following morning I caught the ferry to Woolwich and spent a couple of hours wandering around the shops until discharging was completed. We cleared the lock gates into the Thames at nine that night, passed the *Iberia,* changed our River Pilot at Gravesend for a Sea Pilot and dropped him at four in the morning at the Pilot Vessel. It was calm but hazy and the radar was in use for most of the trip north, passing Flamborough Head close in at ten that night and reaching Tynemouth at six in the morning, where it was still very misty. The Pilot came aboard, but we had to anchor until the afternoon to await high water in order to move up river, the time being utilised by the crew taking down the topmasts and aerials to enable us to pass under the Tyne bridges.

We docked at the CWS mill at Dunston and no time was wasted in catching a train from Newcastle, reaching home just before midnight. The next day Eileen and I had breakfast at two in the afternoon, the following day we had breakfast at eleven in the morning and felt that we were making progress towards normality. Over the next few days we visited both sets of parents regularly, took Raffe out often and ate at some strange hours, including finishing a meal at two-thirty in the morning then taking the car to the coast, walking along the beach hand in hand as dawn was breaking. On the Sunday we went to Trafalgar Street church in the morning, the afternoon train taking me to Newcastle ready for sailing the next day.

Discharging was going slower than expected however and it was early in the morning of Tuesday before the tugs came hooting alongside, ready to take us down river. This was to be the old girl's last trip, maybe for some time, maybe forever, orders having been received to take her to Zeebrugge for laying up. The *Golden Eagle* was already laid up in Piraeus needing an expensive boiler repair, so no surprise there then. Word came via the Captain that the owners wanted me to join the *Grecian Emblem* in early July and that my wages would be over the going rate. I asked the Captain to convey my thanks but to decline the offer. There were 300 wireless operators without jobs in Greece alone, so I should have been grateful for the offer and indeed was, but enough was enough; being separated from Eileen for the past couple of years had been emotionally draining and my mind was made up.

Misfortune dogged us to the last. We picked the Pilot up at noon off Zeebrugge and entered the canal locks. A man on the deck of the stern tug was killed as our rope parted and practically cut him in half. We were delayed in the locks for some hours before passing along the canal to join a group of other Goulandris ships, the *Fulmar, Ranger, Falcon* and *Caspiana* were tied up alongside each other and the *Plover* followed us in. It was a sad sight. There was over a score of ships along the canal bank near to us, and more than fifty ships between Zeebrugge and Bruges. Vasili and I went for a last walk along the canal bank, past the dead ships. The wireless accounts were completed the next day, farewells were said and a taxi ordered to take me to the terminus of the Essex Ferry, the British Rail train ferry leaving at six that evening for Harwich. It was June 1958 and the end of a chapter.

The Customs came aboard the ferry at Harwich gone midnight, after which everybody returned to their bunks until the watchman's call at five, ready for the six o'clock train to London. After some strong coffee in the station buffet I went to see the owners, spending time with each of the Directors and consuming lots more coffee. Mr John Goulandris wished me luck, confirming to get in touch if I changed my mind. Eileen met me at Paragon Station that afternoon, we were still talking at midnight and hardly slept all night. Over the next few days we cycled to Beverley Westwood for picnics and took Raffe for so many walks that his legs nearly gave way. It was a good summer for cycling and Raffe-walking and the days passed quickly into weeks. George and Geoff came across the Wawne ferry with me, continuing our quest to visit East Riding country pubs, and tennis battles took place at West Park with Eileen, David, Kathleen and Ken. Eileen and I looked at bungalows for sale at Melton but our hearts weren't really in it. Stamps accumulated over a lengthy period were put into albums. Eileen's leave from the Victoria Nursing Home came to an end and she was off to work in the mornings at eight o'clock on her cycle, coming home at six thirty and was the breadwinner. Our overseas money had been transferred to a local bank and didn't total nearly enough. But does it ever?

Eileen's brother David was home on leave from the RAF in Cyprus and the three of us went across the road to the swimming baths. Raffe, I'm sure, would love to have joined us but had to be content with the beach and the seaside. Eileen performed wonders with the limited cooking facilities at the flat; occasionally we bought fish and chips at the only shop still standing in bomb-damaged Osborne Street. All this was nice and cosy, but the time and the money were slipping away. Reg. was still at the ROU and what he told me about jobs ashore for R/Os only confirmed what I already knew, and was depressing. There was a job at sea just for picking up the phone, but I didn't want to go down that road. There were days at Tunstall on the sands with Raffe, and at Bridlington, where we walked him from the North Pier to White City and back again, having to lift him into the car at the end. He was still game for anything, but wasn't getting any younger. Geoff was at home and came with us for a day out at Scarborough. George had taken over his father's business in Scale Lane and Geoff and I met up at lunch times in his office before repairing to the Black Boy, often joined there by Jimmy Cutting of Burton Pidsea days. Dan and Bunty had moved to the States, where Dan was working as an engineering trouble-shooter for a large packing firm, his job taking him all over the world.

Eileen packed the car and we set out on a camping holiday, letting the route unfold as we went along. The canvas tent we used was the same one-man tent used at Burton Pidsea and on later expeditions. We headed south, stopping at Stratford, exploring Cheddar Gorge and going to Wells cathedral on our way to the north coast of Devon. Somewhere on the way we gave a lift to a couple of German hitchhikers, youngsters on their first visit to England, initiating them in fine style by driving them onto a roundabout in the middle of a main road. The tyres on the Prefect were not in good shape and a slow puncture saw us losing steering as we approached the junction. We wanted to go left, but the car had other ideas, carried straight on and ended up in the middle of a very muddy roundabout. A lorry had seen us mount the roundabout and towed us off in minutes. We were a bit shaken but not overly concerned and the lorry driver thought it all a good joke. What the Germans thought to it remained a mystery, but they took it all in their stride and were very cheerful, and possibly very relieved, when we eventually dropped them off at their destination.

We camped by streams on Exmoor and wended our way along the coast to Penzance and Lands End, stopping to talk to cows and share our food with stray dogs. The weather deteriorated as we neared Penzance and we sought out a B&B, enjoying hot baths and a luxurious double bed. Eileen worked wonders on the Primus and one evening we got back to camp, famished and ready for supper, when disaster struck as the pressure cooker full of stew spilled out over the grass, but we ate it anyway. After Marazion we visited St. Michaels Mount and stopped at Mullion Cove to sunbathe on the beach, later putting on our last set of dry clothes for a walk around the harbour. We had just reached the end of the sea wall when a wave crashed over the wall and drenched us. We both found this very funny, but nothing would have phased us on that holiday, it was wonderful just to be together, to fulfil the dream; the memory of discontented days at sea fading away in the sunshine.

Trevillian, Mevagissy, Polperro and many other places reminded us of the fishing villages along the Yorkshire coast, Staithes, Robin Hoods Bay and Runswick Bay. Some of the country lanes were very narrow, the overgrown hedges touched the car and there was little opportunity to pass other vehicles. On one narrow winding road, we were stuck for mile after mile behind an RAF vehicle, transporting an aircraft fuselage at 10mph. When a reasonably straight stretch of empty road opened up I decided to overtake, pressed the accelerator down as far as it would go, and after a couple of minutes was pushing 40mph. We were halfway along the length of the fuselage when a car appeared on the road ahead and we had to drop back, not bothering to try again. Shopping in Totnes, we found a purse on the pavement, handing it in at the police station but declining to leave any name and address in case someone asked to see my Driving License.

Weymouth brought back my memories of 1944 with Landing Craft jostling in the harbour and streets packed with British and American servicemen. Camping one night on the edge of the New Forest we awoke to find the tent surrounded by wild ponies. After visiting the cathedral at Winchester to see the Round Table we made towards Oxford, spending the afternoon there before camping near Ashby de la Zouch close by some bramble bushes, which supplied us with enough fruit to see us home. The next night we stayed with Les and Mabel near Derby, looking at family photographs and reminiscing, reaching home the following day after 22 nights away.

To celebrate my 33rd birthday we took Raffe to Filey, sitting in deckchairs whilst he tore up and down the sands. Visits to the cinema included a nostalgic trip to see the *Restive* once more. Everybody's favourite clergyman came on a short visit to Transfiguration Church; he was still full of life and enthusiasm but his wartime experiences were visibly taking their toll. Apart from Eileen and close friends, hardly anyone spoke the same language, most people's outlook seeming resolutely parochial. There was a great big world out there waiting to be discovered and I wanted to get back to it, but how and where? Those were the questions to which there seemed no answers. I talked to Raffe about it but he didn't know either.

Just when the night seemed at its darkest, light appeared in the form of a letter that George had received from a wartime friend. The letter contained a proposition which, because of the responsibilities of the family business, George couldn't take up, but he told me about it over the phone and we met in the Black Boy the following lunchtime to discuss it further. The letter was from Tom Hepworth, who had converted a Brixham trawler, sailed her to the South Pacific, was trading between the islands and wanted to know if George and his wife would join him.

George asked me if we wanted to go in their place. It only took me ten seconds to say, 'Yes'. I rang Eileen and asked her if she would like to go to the South Pacific. She said, 'When?' and I replied, 'In a couple of weeks.'

It took the Travel Agent nearly a fortnight to organise the trip from pages and pages of Airline Timetables; cables had to be despatched all over the globe to book seats and hotels, and sometimes wait days for confirmation. The flat was packed up, storage space rented, and Eileen left work the day before we departed. Air-travel was expensive, and practically all the money we had saved went into a one-way trip to the other side of the world. Geoff said he'd never seen anybody get out of town so fast. Everyone else thought we were mad. Unanswered questions abounded. Would it work out? What did the future hold? Would we ever come back? Were we really mad?

There was only one way to be sure. We got on the plane and went to find out.

RESCUE TUGS

ALLEGIANCE	Greenock 10-6-1943	Gibraltar 14-7-43
SALVONIA	Gibraltar 14-7-43	Plymouth 10-11-43
EMINENT	Glasgow 20-12-43	London 9-9-44
ENTICER	Spithead 27-9-44	Plymouth 7-11-44
SUPERMAN (Relieving)	Milford Haven 21-12-44	M Haven 31-12-44
St. MELLONS	Tilbury 7-1-45	Portsmouth 3-10-45
BUSTLER	Greenock 20-11-45	Falmouth 15-2-46
ENVOY (Relieving)	Leith 17-2-46	Rosyth 26-2-46
RESTIVE	Glasgow 8.3.46	Bermuda 5-9-46

MERCHANT SHIPS

	Flag	Signed on	Signed off
St. STEPHEN (Trawler)	British	Hull 28-11-47	Hull 3-4-48
GRAINTON (Cargo)	British	Hull 4-5-48	Hull 14-8-48
KALEV (Cargo)	British	Hull 26-8-48	Blyth 9-1-50
THOMAS *TOMPION* (Trawler)	British	Grimsby 17-8-50	Grimsby 23-4-52
FIDO (Cargo)	Norwegian	Grimsby 26-8-52	Grimsby 25-10-52
LEONARDIA (Cargo)	Swedish	Immingham 19-11-52	Gavle 17-1-53
MILLY (Cargo)	Liberian	W Hartlepool 11-2-53	Granton 20-3-53
FANA (Cargo)	Norwegian	New York 21-5-53	Rochester 5-8-53
GANNET (Cargo)	Liberian	Rouen 14-12-53	Rotterdam 13-10-55
GOLDEN *EAGLE* (Oil Tanker)	Liberian	Kobe 24-2-56	Rotterdam 26-8-57
MANHATTAN (Cargo)	Liberian	Kiel 30-9-57	Zeebrugge 14-6-58